Immigration Controls, the Family
and the Welfare State

Immigration controls, the family and the welfare state

A handbook of law, theory, politics
and practice for local authority, voluntary sector
and welfare state workers and legal advisors

Steve Cohen

Jessica Kingsley Publishers
London and Philadelphia

The right of Steve Cohen to be identified as author of this work has been asserted by him in accordance with the Copyright, Designs and Patents Act 1988.

First published in the United Kingdom in 2001 by
Jessica Kingsley Publishers Ltd
116 Pentonville Road
London N1 9JB, England
and
325 Chestnut Street
Philadelphia, PA 19106, USA

www.jkp.com

Library of Congress Cataloging in Publication Data
A CIP catalog record for this book is available from the Library of Congress

British Library Cataloguing in Publication Data
A CIP catalogue record for this book is available from the British Library

ISBN 1 85302 723 5

Printed and Bound in Great Britain by
Athenaeum Press, Gateshead, Tyne and Wear

Contents

Abbreviations   8
Acknowledgements   10

Preface   11

PART ONE: ISSUES OF LAW, THEORY, POLITICS AND PRACTICE

1   The basic issues   17

2   A brief political history   32

3   An outline of current immigration control   44

4   Basic good practice for welfare professionals
    and legal advisors   54

PART TWO: IMMIGRATION CONTROL AND THE FAMILY

5   Dividing families: spouses   73

6   Dividing families: children, parents
    and other relatives   86

7   Beyond the family: the gay, lesbian, unmarried,
    celibate, promiscuous and single   105

8   Asylum: age, gender and sexuality   116

9   Deportation and removal: tactics and report writing   135

10 Deportation and removal: a critique of the concept
    of compassionate grounds   153

11 Immigration law versus child protection law   165

PART THREE: THE WELFARE STATE

12 Benefits and immigration status 181

13 Housing services and immigration status 204

14 Education services and immigration status 229

15 Social services, community care and immigration
   status 242

16 Medical services and immigration status 249

17 Further health issues for medical workers
   and others 262

18 Probation and immigration status:
   double punishment 275

PART FOUR: RESOLVING THE POLITICAL AND PRACTICE ISSUES

19 Professional practice and campaigning 291

20 Good practice, welfare agencies and non-compliance 302

21 Conclusion: fair controls or no controls? 313

Appendix: Useful addresses 330
Subject Index 341
Author Index 365

For Tomas, Rachel and Fintan

Lotta continua!

Abbreviations

ACOP	Association of Chief Officers of Probation
ALG	Association of London Government
All ER	All England Law Reports
BAAF	British Agencies for Adoption and Fostering
B&B	Bed and breakfast
BASW	British Association of Social Workers
BMA	British Medical Association
CESC	Council of Europe Social Chapter
CPC	Central Point of Contact Unit
CRE	Commission for Racial Equality
Cr.LR	Criminal Law Review
CTB	Council tax benefit
DES	Department of Education and Science
DETR	Department of Environment, Transport and the Regions
DfEE	Department for Education and Employment
DHSS	Department of Health and Social Security
DLA	Disability living allowance
ECHR	European Court of Human Rights
ECO	Entry Clearance Officer
ECSMA	European Convention on Social and Medical Assistance
EEA	European Economic Area
EIN	Electronic Immigration Network
ELR	Exceptional leave to remain
ESC	European Social Charter
EU	European Union
FAIR	Family Immigration Rights
FCR	Family Court Reporter
FEFC	Further Education Funding Council
FLR	Family Law Reports
FPS	Family Practitioner Services
GMIAU	Greater Manchester Immigration Aid Unit
GP	General Practitioner
HB	Housing Benefit
HLR	Housing Law Reports

HMO	House in Multiple Occupation
IAS	Immigration Advisory Service
ILPA	Immigration Law Practitioners' Association
Imm AR	Immigration Appeals Reports
IND	Immigration and Nationality Directorate
INEB	Immigration and Nationality Enquiry Bureau
INLP	Immigration and Nationality Law and Practice
INLR	Immigration and Nationality Law Reports
ISU	Immigration Service Union
JCWI	The Joint Council for the Welfare of Immigrants
LAC	Local authority circular
LAG	Legal Action Group
LEA	Local education authority
LGA	Local Government Association
MP	Member of Parliament
NACRO	National Association for the Care and Rehabilitation of Offenders
NAPO	National Association of Probation Officers
NASS	National Asylum Support Service
NHS	National Health Service
NI	National Insurance
POPs	Partners of Prisoners Support Group
RWLG	Refugee Women's Legal Group
SAL	Standard Acknowledgement Letter
SBC	Supplementary Benefits Commission
SEF	Statement of Evidence From
SSD	Social Services Department
SSI	Social Services Inspectorate
UKCOSA	United Kingdom Council for Overseas Student Affairs
UNHCR	United Nations High Commission for Refugees
WLR	Weekly law reports

Acknowledgements

Thanking those who have helped me in writing this book is not a literary formality. I am very conscious of all those over the years who have helped me formulate my views. In particular I have been inspired and educated by all those individuals and families, adults and children, who have publicly resisted immigration controls, not least Nasira Begum, Manda Kunda, George Roucou, Rahila Siddiqui, Florence, Awele and Anwule Okolo, Rosmina, Shabana, Malka and Azize Rahman, Andy and Farida Anderson, and all the women in the Manchester Wives and Fiancées Campaign. Perhaps more than anyone else, the person who taught me the nobility of openly challenging controls was and is Anwar Ditta. However, I have also learned from literally hundreds of others who have confronted controls anonymously and in private and have achieved their own secret victories. I am constantly in awe of their stamina, which is also a form of resistance. These public and private struggles demand that there be serious discussion on the fundamental question as to what possible justification remains for immigration controls – 'fair' or otherwise.

I am also conscious of learning from professional colleagues at South Manchester Law Centre and Greater Manchester Immigration Aid Unit. In writing this book I am only too aware of not just pestering colleagues for their views but actually receiving them. I would like to thank Pamela Fitzpatrick and Sue Lukes for commenting on Chapters 12 and 13 respectively and Luke Clements and Dianne Keetch for their comments on Chapter 15. For a debt that includes not only help on commenting on the entirety of the present study but also help over the years, I would like to thank Sue Shutter. Naturally assistance from whatever source implies neither agreement with all the views expressed here nor responsibility for any legal or factual errors. The publishers have taken responsibility for the index. Thanks to the editors, Helen Parry and Della Gray, who have made it possible for much material to be inserted at a very late stage, thereby making the book as up-to-date as possible. Finally I want to thank my friend Harriet for nursing me and the book when there were times I thought neither were going to reach the publisher's deadline.

Preface

This is the best and the worst of times to be writing about immigration controls. The best because the latest draconian legislation, the 1999 Immigration and Asylum Act, renders obsolete much previous writings and requires an up-to-date analysis. The worst because the new Act and regulations made under it are becoming operative in stages, with these stages having all the hallmarks of being unplanned. A lot of the time in writing this book has felt akin to sending dispatches from the front.

However, this book is not about the new legislation as such. Rather it is about a process which this legislation simply takes forward but takes forward with a leap, namely the alignment between immigration controls and welfare entitlements. The book is written from the perspective of welfare professionals who have become agents of immigration control through being obliged to enforce internal welfare controls.

The study is both limited and ambitious in its aims. It is limited in that it does not attempt an analysis of the entirety of UK immigration law and its parallel construct, European Union (EU) law. It restricts itself to those areas of controls which relate to welfare and the concept of the family. However, within this sphere it attempts several tasks for a wide readership. First, it offers a theoretical under-standing of controls as seen through their historical development. Second, it shows how immigration controls impinge on the professional lives of a very broad range of workers within the welfare state, local government and the voluntary sector. Third, it attempts to reassure these workers by providing them with good practice guidance while not denying how difficult and contradictory their roles are as both dispensers of welfare and agents of immigration law enforcement. Fourth, it does not purport to be a textbook on immigration law, yet it is hoped that it will be useful to both lawyers and non-lawyers as a work of reference on those areas where issues of the family, welfare entitlement and immi-gration controls intersect, particularly following the 1999 legislation. Fifth, it openly fosters political debate while itself taking a position of opposition to controls. Sixth, it seeks to encourage academic workers to teach and research immigration law and practice, in particular in the fields of family law, child welfare, social work and social policy.

The majority of cases quoted in this book are drawn directly from my own experiences as an immigration lawyer at South Manchester Law Centre and then as co-ordinator of Greater Manchester Immigration Aid Unit. This experience, stretching over a quarter of a century, has taught me various lessons. First, immi-gration controls are destructive. They can destroy the lives of those subject to them. Second, controls are inherently racist. There cannot be 'fair' or 'non-racist' controls. This unfortunately represents a minority view and one rarely articulated. Occasionally it is argued there should be no 'racist immigration controls'. This demand contains a central ambiguity, namely whether all controls are racist or just the existing ones. Of course some people support controls precisely because they are racist. Neither this book nor any other literary study will be sufficient to dissuade such people of their views. However the book, particularly in its concluding chapter, attempts to engage with arguments held by those who sincerely consider there can be fair controls. It is hoped that such engagement will provoke a debate on the issues.

A debate is needed because the political focus in respect to controls has shifted. At the time of the first post-war legislation, the 1962 Commonwealth Immigrants Act, there was a battle for ideas that was open and simple. There were just two ideological positions – for or against controls. However, today the ideological battle is more hidden and far more complicated. There are rival positions among those voicing opposition to controls. The dividing line is precisely between those who favour 'fair' controls and those who favour no controls. One aim of this book is at least to bring this polemic out into the open.

In addition the motives of some of those who argue for 'fair' controls are themselves problematic and open to scrutiny. This is because on a governmental level the concept of 'fair' controls is often used to justify more and tighter controls. For instance the Labour government's 1998 White Paper on controls is aptly titled *Fairer, Faster and Firmer*. Therefore a sub-debate is necessary on whether 'firmer' can ever mean 'fairer' in this context.

These arguments and debates are relevant to welfare and social work practice. Immigration controls pervade the welfare system. Welfare professionals are no longer peripheral to controls. The third lesson I have learned from my experiences as an immigration lawyer is that combining theory and practice is not a luxury. It is a necessity. Good practice, which is a central feature of this book, is achievable only when based on a sound understanding of the political issues behind the legal constructs. The Home Office and its immigration service have achieved this unity of theory and practice albeit in the most reactionary way. Conversely, within limits, welfare workers can do the same but in an enlightened way and in opposition to the ethos of controls.

The wide scope of the nexus between immigration status and welfare entitlement can be seen simply by the topics treated in Part 3 of this study, namely welfare benefits, housing, education, social services, community care, medical treatment and probation. On the one hand this imposes on immigration advisors an obligation to understand major areas of law other than just immigration. On the other hand it means that the debate over the possibility or otherwise of 'fair' controls extends into the realms of welfare.

I have also been taught a fourth lesson. This is that political issues merit a political response. In the context of immigration controls that has meant first and foremost campaigns against deportation and for family unity. These campaigns, led by black people and refugees, with women often in the forefront, have been a conspicuous feature of the 1980s and 1990s. It has been this activity which has in many ways been responsible for producing the ideas supported in this study and in polarising the debate between fair controls and no controls.

The book is structured in such a way as to try to incorporate all these lessons and the aims described at the start of this Preface. It is written in four parts in order to take the reader logically through the issues to the point where he or she feels comfortable in dealing with them. Part 1 lays out the issues of theory, politics and practice within an historical and legal context. It asks the basic questions. It also introduces basic good practice guides in order to establish right at the start the need to develop such practice and to show that the construction of good practice is not a luxury that can be postponed. Part 2 examines how these matters relate to the family and, just as important, to those who live outside the conventional family construct. It shows how immigration controls defend the nuclear family through undermining all other familial and non-familial relationships. Part 3 looks at the major areas of welfare now dependent upon immigration status. It explains how welfare provision throughout the twentieth century was national-istic and tied to immigration status. Part 4 sees how all the issues raised can be resolved politically and, at least in part, in practice. The sheer power of immigra-tion controls means that the practice issues can never be totally resolved except with the negation of controls through their abolition.

Each chapter itself contains a similar, if not always identical, structure. First, there is presented a practical casework problem, which the reader should keep in mind while reading the chapter. Second, there is outlined a real case story. Third, there is a brief description of the scope of the chapter. Fourth, there is a list of further reading resources where they exist. This list is usually included near the start of the chapter in order to reassure welfare professionals that their workplace concerns about immigration controls are not of their own imagination but are very real and there now exists a layer of material, admittedly quite thin, which addresses these concerns. Other reading material is also mentioned in the body of the chapter where appropriate. Fifth is an examination of the particular historical and political issues pertinent to the subject matter of each chapter. The historical material is stressed in order to show that the concerns of welfare professionals have not sprung from nowhere and did not begin with modern controls against black people and refugees. They reflect a trend throughout the twentieth century. Sixth is an outline of the relevant law. Seventh and usually comprising half the chapter is a look at relevant good practice. There is one issue of good practice which continually emerges and which is charted in several chapters, namely good practice in writing professional reports in immigration cases. Finally there are comments on the casework problem presented at the start of the chapter. Usually this discussion is based on the legal and tactical material within the chapter. However, very occasionally the opportunity is used to introduce new points which can best be understood through looking at the practical solution of a casework problem.

Throughout the book I refer to various organisations, their telephone lines and websites. These, along with their addresses, are found in the Appendix at the end of the book. A list explaining the abbreviations used in the book is on p.8.

Names have been attached to cases only where these are already in the public domain through campaigns, newspaper publicity or court reports.

Though the law and Home Office practice is moving rapidly I hope that I have managed to encapsulate both as of 1 September 2000. I have also been able to incorporate some subsequent material and in particular to attempt a brief summary of relevant changes contained in the immigration rules that came into force on 2 October 2000. These alterations were a consequence of the 1999 Act and also brought some (but only some) existing concessions into the rules.

PART ONE

Issues of Law, Theory, Politics and Practice

CHAPTER I

The basic issues

W left her husband due to incompatibility. She took her daughter X, who attended a local authority school. W sought help from X's teacher, who advised she should claim income support. She lodged a claim. W was black. The benefits officer asked her to produce her passport. She did so. The official asked her to return the following week – when she was met by an immigration officer. The Benefits Agency had reported W to the Home Office. W had been allowed entry with X as the wife of a man settled in the UK with permission to stay for twelve months. She should subsequently have asked the Home Office for permanent stay with proof she was living with her husband. She had not done this and became an 'overstayer'. The immigration officer told W that she and X were liable to expulsion.

In subsequent discussions one teacher said that immigration matters were not part of her job. Another said she would be too worried about getting involved professionally because of the consequences of a mistake. A third said she did consider involvement as legitimate but thought it bad practice for teachers to check the immigration status of parents or children.

A FICTIONAL CASE WHERE THE IMMIGRATION ISSUE WAS ADDRESSED

Y and her daughter Z were in a similar situation. The teachers at Z's school had training on immigration issues. The school operated a policy of inviting parents to give their and their children's immigration status. It was explained that there was no obligation to provide this information. If given it would be kept confidential and was being requested to help parents or children who might have unforeseen immigration problems. As a result Y approached the school for help. They warned that she was not entitled to benefits and claiming them was dangerous. The school contacted a social worker, who obtained financial support for Y and Z through the local authority under the 1989 Children Act. The school contacted a trustworthy advisor experienced in immigration matters. Together with the advisor, the social worker, the school, Y and Z, a strategy was planned to help the family to remain. The teachers worked with Y and Z in building a campaign to remain.

THE LESSON OF THESE CASES

These two fictional cases show why professionals do not have the luxury of simply ignoring the issue of controls. Controls appear everywhere, particularly in areas of life concerned with welfare. Immigration control is almost synonymous with welfare control. Controls are far-reaching and no longer the preserve of lawyers. Everyone having professional contact with children or families or the provision of welfare will probably be confronted with immigration control issues. These cases also raise the critical and controversial question of whether it is right or wrong to ask someone their immigration status in order to advise them properly.

IMMIGRATION CONTROL, WELFARE AND THE FAMILY

Immigration controls present many questions. One core question is posed for anyone concerned professionally with issues of welfare. Why have the two waves of control, at the turn of the twentieth century and post–1945, so closely paralleled the rise of state welfare provision?

The first controls, the 1905 Aliens Act, became operative 1 January 1906. This was the date there came into power the Liberal government that created the framework of modern welfare provision through the 1908 Old Age Pensions Act and the 1911 National Insurance Act. Post-war controls began in 1962 with the Commonwealth Immigrants Act. This coincided with what arguably was the flowering of the welfare state.

The question to be addressed is the relationship between immigration control and welfare. It appears paradoxical that controls were developed in periods of welfare expansion. Immigration controls are necessarily repressive. They are about restricting entry and stay. They are literally about control. On the other hand welfare is supposedly about different values, values which are humanistic, universal and caring. So why do they coincide? What does this say about immigration controls? What does it say about perceptions of welfare? Ultimately it poses the question of welfare for whom?

There is an irony at the heart of the nexus between immigration law and welfare. This revolves around the family. Family unity is a central aim of welfare provision. However, a consequence of immigration control is the division of families on a global scale. Every government claims to uphold 'family values'. Yet immigration laws separate families against their will. This raises the question as to whose families are affected by controls? Why are these families under such threat? What interests are being served by the destruction of these families? How does this destruction deepen our understanding of the ideological construction of the family in general – a construction of which this book is not uncritical? How do immigration controls affect those living outside conventional family situations – lesbians, gay men, unmarried partners and single people?

The injury caused to family life by controls has at its axis women and children. When it comes to expulsions it seems that Home Office policy is to follow that essential standard of English gallantry – women and children first. This poses questions as to the relevance of gender, sexuality and age to immigration controls.

WELFARE PRACTITIONERS

This book attempts to answer these questions empirically, by examining immigration controls in operation, and theoretically, by looking at the ideology, history and politics of controls. The empirical investigation is made from the perspective of welfare practitioners. This encompasses a wide range of professionals working within the local state, voluntary agencies and the national state. These include such a diverse range as social workers, care managers, community workers, teachers, other education officers, health workers, probation officers, women refuge workers, welfare rights advisors, benefit agency workers, youth workers, local authority housing workers, personnel officers within local authorities and welfare agencies, workers with refugees and interpreters.

There are four features uniting this apparently disparate group, a group which in this book is referred to generically as welfare (or family) practitioners or professionals.

First, these workers are in close contact with families and individuals under threat of immigration controls. This contact may be coincidental. A child attending a particular school, or a patient attending a particular hospital, or a woman in a particular women's refuge, could coincidentally be under threat.

Second, the close contact can relate directly or indirectly to the immigration threat itself. A family may be homeless and destitute because of immigration status and be seeking social work or housing assistance. A prisoner may be liable to deportation following conviction and requesting help from a probation officer. Someone may have AIDS and be asking a doctor, a hospital social worker or an HIV/AIDS agency to help obtain entry of an overseas partner or carer.

Third, welfare practitioners do not simply have contact with people under threat of controls. They can help in preventing expulsion or in gaining entry. An aim of this book is to illustrate how positive assistance can be given and to provide good practice guidelines. It is also to show such assistance can be legitimately regarded as part of the enabling role of family professionals.

INTERNAL CONTROLS

There is a fourth feature uniting many practitioners. This is a repressive characteristic central to the relationship between immigration restrictions and welfare provision. Controls are not and never have been simply about who can come and who can remain. They are about control from within the state. The issue is internal control. It is the linking of immigration status with entitlement to welfare provision. The apparent paradox of immigration controls appearing in periods of welfare expansion is no paradox at all. Those subject to control are answerable for the use of welfare and ultimately excluded from it.

Core benefits and services are dependent for their availability on the applicant's immigration position. This nexus between entitlements and immigration status poses questions not just about the relationship between welfare and immigration control. It raises questions about the demise of welfare, how this works differentially and how it disproportionately hits those subject to controls. The nexus places in a collusive position workers responsible for providing welfare. These workers are expected to withhold the very provisions for which their jobs exist. They are transformed into agents of immigration control.

THE WELFARE STATE AS AN ARM OF THE HOME OFFICE

The origins of this transformation predate the post-war welfare state (see Chapter 2). Under the welfare state it has accelerated since the 1970s. This trend became recognised in the literature and campaigns of the 1980s. In 1981 South Manchester Law Centre published *The Thin End of the White Wedge: Second Class Citizenship and the Welfare State* by Steve Cohen. This examined the 1981 British Nationality Act within the context of the links between status and welfare entitlement. In 1981 there was also launched *No Pass Laws Here!*, a journal against these developments. In 1982 South Manchester Law Centre published *From Ill-Treatment to No Treatment* by Steve Cohen. This examined the relationship between health service entitlement and immigration status. In 1983 the National Association of Citizens' Advice Bureaux published *Immigrants and the Welfare State* by Wendy Collins and Hugo Storey. In 1985 there was established the Committee for Non-Racist Benefits and that year saw the literature peak. The Child Poverty Action Group and the Runnymede Trust jointly published *Passports to Benefits? Racism in Social Security* by Paul Gordon and Anne Newnham. The Joint Council for the Welfare of Immigrants (JCWI) published *No Passports to Services: A Report on Local Government and Immigration and Nationality Issues* by Geoff Wilkins. Pluto Press published *Policing Immigration: Britain's Internal Controls* by Paul Gordon. *Critical Social Policy* contained an article, 'Immigration controls, anti-Semitism and the welfare state' by Cohen.

It is no coincidence that the literature developed throughout the first half of the 1980s. This was not just a response to the merging of immigration control and welfare. It was also borne out of the energy that saw anti-deportation campaigns develop and peak in this period (see Chapter 19). Much of the literature consisted of samizdat, underground publications produced by advice and campaigning organisations. The decline in the literature post–1985 can be accounted for in part by the absorption into individual casework by law centres and other similar agencies. Also the link between benefits and status grew more slowly than anticipated with the next major developments awaiting the 1993 and 1996 asylum legislation.

THE 'EFFICIENCY SCRUTINY'

The linking of entitlements and immigration status initially proceeded in an ad-hoc manner. It is now consciously driven by the Home Office seeking to universalise the process.

In a press release of 13 October 1993 Michael Howard, then Home Secretary, announced the establishment of a 'study of inter-agency co-operation on illegal immigration'. This so-called Efficiency Scrutiny would 'examine the efficiency of existing arrangements for co-operation between the Home Office's Immigration and Nationality Division and other key central and local government bodies'. These bodies were to include 'agencies of the Department of Social Security, the Employment Service, the Health Service and local government bodies'.

In a written parliamentary answer of 18 July 1995 Howard emphasised that the Scrutiny had two aims. First, 'to ensure that staff responsible for providing benefits and services are given the necessary guidance and training to identify claimants who are ineligible because of their immigration status'. Second, 'to strengthen the arrangements for staff responsible for providing benefits and services to pass information about immigration offenders to the immigration authorities'. Howard said a range of ministries, namely Social Security, Education, Health and Environment, were considering tightening the law 'to align eligibility for benefits and services with immigration status'.

In a written parliamentary answer of 24 October 1996, Ann Widdecombe MP declared that many of the Scrutiny's proposals had been implemented following the 1996 Asylum and Immigration Act which extended the range of benefits and services linked to immigration status.

HOME OFFICE GUIDELINES

In February 1997 the Immigration and Nationality Directorate (IND) of the Home Office published *A Guide to Immigration Awareness*. This was designed for national and local government agencies and purported to offer 'answers to questions which may arise in the administration of benefits and services where eligibility depends on the customer's status under our immigration laws'. It offered the following reassurance – 'Assessing immigration status may not be as difficult as you think'. In fact assessment of status can be extremely complex and should never be undertaken without proper training and experience. The guide made the rhetorical statement: 'But I'm not an immigration officer, I have my own job to do!' and delivered the equally rhetorical response: 'Exactly. We all have our own jobs to do but immigration status is relevant to the work of many people outside the IND.'

'CONTACTING THE IND'

The Home Office *Guide to Immigration Awareness* had an annex on 'Contacting the IND'. It asks that 'Notification of suspected immigration offenders should... include, where available: subject's full name, date of birth, nationality and Home Office reference number'. The Home Office have also compiled a document called 'How to contact the Immigration and Nationality Directorate of the Home Office'. It appears to be standard for this to be annexed or referred to in all circulars explaining the links between status and services administered through local government. Examples are the homelessness legislation, housing benefit regulations, 1948 National Assistance Act and 1989 Children Act.

LOCAL AUTHORITIES

There is one sector which has a central importance in the administration of controls. This is local government. An understanding of controls requires examining the relationship between the local state and the national state within the context of the welfare state. As huge service providers, local authorities are constantly confronted with matters relating to controls. The delivery of services to those subject to controls reveals the contradiction between a repressive and an enabling role. Entitlement to much local authority provision requires investigation of immigration status. On the other hand authorities have resources to help people threatened by controls.

LOCAL STATE AND NATIONAL STATE

The contradictory role of the local state is reflected in its contradictory relationship with the national state. This was particularly vivid from 1979 until 1997 when the national government was Conservative but most major local authorities were Labour.

Throughout the 1980s until the late 1990s some Labour councils took the initiative in voicing degrees of opposition to controls. Manchester is an example. Between 1985 and 1989 the council undertook the following. It sponsored a major demonstration against deportations. It helped organise a conference against controls. It sent two advisors to Pakistan to collect evidence for pending immigration marriage appeal cases. It published a pamphlet, 'What would you do if your fiancée lived on the moon', based on this visit. It published a book, *The Same Old Story*, comparing the experiences of controls by Jewish and black workers in Manchester. It established, along with the old Greater Manchester Council, a trust fund of £100,000 to provide financial help to residents threatened with deportation. It financed an Immigration Aid Unit. A June 1986 report submitted by the Town Clerk to the council's Race Sub-Committee shows there existed an Anti-Deportations Working Party. The report acknowledged that many immigration cases 'have a greater chance of success outside the formal appeals system than inside', that this depends upon political agitation and that 'assistance from the council is crucial to the success of campaigning activities organised by those experiencing immigration problems'. It stressed that council support 'has ranged from the printing of leaflets and petitions to attendance at rallies and demonstrations and…at the hearing of appeals'. This assistance is described as 'crucial to the Council's anti-racist policies'. The report expressed concern at developing internal controls, stating 'the main area of [council] activity is an examination of the question of post-entry controls, i.e. where immigration status is used to determine eligibility for welfare benefits'.

CAMPAIGNS AND LOCAL AUTHORITIES

This reflects another era, that of 'local authority socialism'. Manchester's politics were also the product of another factor. They reflected the number and vigour of local campaigns against deportations and for reunion of families. In 1987 the steering group establishing an immigration aid unit produced a pamphlet, 'Help us set up an Immigration Aid Unit in Manchester'. This itemised thirty-six campaigns established between 1978 and 1987 within Greater Manchester. Twenty-six were formed between 1985 and 1987. These campaigns and others elsewhere forced the issue of controls on to the agenda of local authorities. They created partial conflicts between the local and national state.

HOME OFFICE CIRCULAR TO LOCAL AUTHORITIES

These conflicts have been reduced for three reasons. First, Conservative legislation removed important local authority powers. Second, Labour in national government is strengthening controls through its 1999 Immigration and Asylum Act. This has negated or weakened local government opposition. For instance Manchester councillors have adopted government rhetoric against asylum-seekers. A local Manchester paper, the *Advertiser* of 6 April 2000, reported the arrest of some Kosovan asylum-seekers climbing out of a lorry. Before the Home Office had even considered the case, the council's deputy leader proclaimed: 'What we don't need is people abusing the system'. Ironically the Kosovans were discovered in an area, Crumpsall, where the *Bolton Evening News* of 11 February 2000 had reported two other Kosovans being hospitalised after being attacked with bottles and bricks on Manchester's Metrolink flagship transport system.

Third, the Home Office has ensured through its so-called Efficiency Scrutiny that local authorities and the IND are far more closely aligned. In October 1996 the IND issued its guidelines: *Home Office Circular to Local Authorities in Great Britain. Exchange of Information with the Immigration and Nationality Directorate (IND) of the Home Office.*[1] The circular's purpose is:

- to invite local authorities to use facilities offered by the IND in identifying claimants who may be ineligible for a benefit or service by virtue of their immigration status; and

- to encourage local authorities to pass information to the IND about suspected immigration offenders.

The circular pinpoints relevant departments as those administering:

- the allocation of social housing and homelessness legislation

- Housing Benefit and Council Tax Benefit

- student awards.

The circular has an annex 'How to pass information to the IND about suspected immigration offenders encountered in the normal course of duties'. This mentions two IND contact points with which local authorities or their individual departments can register. One is the Immigration Status Enquiry Unit, now known as the Evidence and Enquiry Unit of the Immigration and Nationality Enquiry Bureau (INEB) and which deals with general status enquiries. The other is the Asylum Screening Unit, whose surveillance function is now handled by the Central Point of Contact Unit (CPC) and which deals with enquiries about known asylum-seekers. The circular suggests that the reporting of suspect immigration offenders be made to the INEB. A letter of 29 February 2000 from Barbara Roche MP at the Home Office to Ivan Lewis MP said in respect of local authorities and their departments that by the end of 1999 INEB had 806 registered contacts and the CPC had 524. Records of enquiries from local authorities were first compiled in 1996. By the end of 1999 INEB had received 8664 enquiries or notification of alleged offenders and CPC 35,661.

The majority of inquiries to the CPC are by local authority social service departments who have been or are still supporting asylum-seekers (see Chapter 12) in order to determine the stage of the asylum application. In 1999 The IND published a 'Guidance to local authority social services departments on contacting the Immigration and Nationality Directorate to establish the status of asylum seekers'. This was issued as Annex B to an IND Local Authority Letter (99)1. This Guidance makes it clear that transfer of information between local authorities and the IND is expected to be two-way when it comes to tracking down refugees for removal. Paragraph 9 states:

> Once an asylum seeker's claim has been finally determined they are usually liable for removal from the United Kingdom. It is common practice for asylum seekers to instruct solicitors or other representatives to assist them in their asylum claim and the Home Office does not, therefore, necessarily hold a home address for the person concerned. It would be of assistance therefore, after final determination of an asylum claim has been notified to the social services department for the home address to be supplied to the Home Office...

THE 1999 IMMIGRATION AND ASYLUM ACT, WELFARE AND LOCAL AUTHORITIES

The 1999 Act represents a watershed. Part VI of the Act, 'support for asylum seekers', constitutes a qualitative leap in the link between welfare and immigration status. It accomplishes this by reducing assistance to asylum-seekers to a form of Poor Law. It attempts to establish a closed system of welfare provision incapable of legal challenge, where the only possible means of support for asylum-seekers are contained within the Act itself. Whether it achieves this is another question.

The 1999 Act is of direct relevance to local authorities. It attempts to relieve authorities from assisting asylum-seekers under the 1948 National Assistance Act and 1989 Children Act. Instead it substitutes a national voucher scheme and requires authorities to enter into voluntary or compulsory contracts with the Home Office for provision of accommodation.

Local authorities have adopted a schizophrenic position towards this legislation which highlights the contradiction between their enabling role as welfare providers and repressive role as immigration control enforcers. This is seen in the written submissions of the Local Government Association (LGA) and Association of London Government (ALG) to the House of Commons Special Standing Committee on the Immigration and Asylum Bill and reproduced in the committee's proceedings of 18 March 1999. Both make numerous principled criticisms of the legislation, such as the stigmatisation caused by the voucher scheme and the danger of asylum-seekers being subject to racism if forced to live in inappropriate localities. However, the LGA submission emphasises that it 'supports the Government's stated aim: to...minimise incentives to economic migration'. The ALG 'welcomes the new framework for the provision of services to asylum seekers'. The ALG states that the 'primary purpose of social services is the provision of children's services and social care to adults and not the support and maintenance of destitute asylum-seekers' and welcomes the fact that the 'government's proposals have the potential to place responsibility for all services to asylum seekers with a single government department'. All else being equal, there can be no objection for asylum-seekers' needs being met through a national government department such as the newly established National Asylum Support Service (NASS) within the IND. However, all is not equal. Asylum-seekers' needs are not being met. Asylum-seekers within the Home Office scheme have no choice where to live. Dispersal is compulsory. They have little or no choice of the conditions under which they are expected to live. They also have no choice about their length of stay and can be evicted without a court order on the refusal of an asylum claim. They have no security of tenure. They are subject to constant surveillance and monitoring by both the Home Office, through NASS, and by the provider of accommodation. Instead of receiving benefits they are subject to a humiliating voucher scheme which is worth only seventy per cent of even income support level (see Chapters 12 and 13). To argue in this context that it is not a social services responsibility to aid asylum-seekers is to condone social exclusion.

The choice for local authorities is whether they co-operate with the Home Office in operating the new legislation, or whether they refuse co-operation as the legislation represents a massive attack on proper welfare provision. There is a danger that authorities may be misled by the Home Office's projection of the new scheme as being progressive. The job description for the initial posts within NASS describes these as providing 'an exciting opportunity to work in a dynamic, team based environment in a high profile organisation'.[2] The reality is that local authorities are opting for co-operation. The policy issues raised by this are examined in Chapter 20.

THE 1999 ACT, WELFARE AND THE VOLUNTARY SECTOR

The Home Office is attempting to draw the voluntary sector into internal immigration controls following the 1999 legislation. Again this is under the guise of allegedly helping asylum-seekers. In March 1999 the Home Office issued a document on *Asylum Seekers Support*. This itemised functions that could be fulfilled by the voluntary sector, such as providing advice on the support scheme established by the Act and offering emergency accommodation to failed asylum-seekers left outside the statutory scheme.

The provision of these services appears benevolent but is highly problematic. It reduces the voluntary sector to junior partners in the operation of repressive legislation. Parts of the sector have adopted this role. This raises major policy questions (see Chapter 20).

VULNERABILITY OF WELFARE PRACTITIONERS

Welfare workers do not simply have a contradictory role as providers of services and enforcers of internal controls. They themselves may be vulnerable to immigration controls. The *Independent* of 27 June 1995 reported that African employees of Hackney Council were being targeted by the Home Office to discover their immigration status. The *Guardian* of 13 March 1996 reported on the personnel department of University College London Hospital Trust writing a letter to domestic and portering staff, the two groups with the largest number of black employees, warning them they were liable to dismissal if working without Home Office permission.

THE POLITICS OF IMMIGRATION CONTROL

Immigration controls are transparently political. They are the result of ever-increasing political pressure constantly narrowing the definition of who is lawfully able to come to or remain in the UK. Yesterday's legal entrant can be tomorrow's outlaw. There is nothing god-given or natural in immigration law as to who and what is legal or illegal.

Politicians, the Home Office and government-sponsored bodies sometimes acknowledge the political and discriminatory nature of controls. Lord Bassam in introducing the 1999 Race Relations (Amendment) Bill in the House of Lords on 14 December justified limiting the impact of the Bill on controls by stating the 'operation of an immigration policy necessarily and legitimately entails discrimination between individuals on the basis of their nationality'. In 1985 the Commission for Racial Equality (CRE) produced a report on *Immigration Control Procedures*. In discussing post-war restrictions it states (p.125):

> However the development of the controls over this period was not concerned with a need to slow or prevent the growth of the population as a whole through immigration. It was concerned primarily with a perceived need to slow or prevent the further growth through immigration of particular ethnic minority communities within the population, and took place as it did precisely because many of those who had taken advantage of the opportunities available – often directly or indirectly in response to explicit encouragement or recruitment by United Kingdom employers – had been black, from the New Commonwealth.

THE POLITICS OF THIS BOOK

This book is explicit in its political position. It concurs with the stance of the Commission for Racial Equality but goes beyond it. Though the thrust of post-war controls has been directed at black people, yet the racism of controls is not necessarily confined to black people. Pre-war restrictions were based on racism (anti-Semitism) towards Jewish refugees from Russia and Eastern Europe. With the collapse of the Soviet bloc in the 1990s controls have again been resurrected against refugees from this area. Racist stereotyping of East Europeans, of Roma and Poles as well as Jews, has been long present in Western culture. In 1991 the *Daily Mail* ran a series of articles on 'The Invasion of Europe' in which it stated: 'Not surprisingly the Germans detest the tens of thousands of gypsies who are now swarming into their country' (7–10 October 1991). In summer 1999 this racism against Roma exploded and took the form of physical attacks on asylum-seeking Roma in the port of Dover.

Racism against East Europeans is documented in the 1993 Greater Manchester Immigration Aid Unit (GMIAU) pamphlet *Immigration controls are out of control.*

The Commission's report considers that there can be such a creature as 'fair and decent' immigration controls. The position of this book is that controls are institutionally and inherently racist. This is a critical issue for welfare practitioners. It means that constructs of welfare, the welfare state and the relations of welfare, are themselves intrinsically racist – precisely because they have been historically premised on the need for immigration controls. It means that the dilemma for welfare practitioners as unwilling enforcers of controls cannot be resolved through their reform but only through their abolition (see Chapter 21).

IN AND AGAINST THE STATE

The purpose of this book is not to present an overview of immigration controls from the outside. Rather, what gives it any claim to originality is that it examines controls from the perspective of those who work within various sectors of the state machinery. It looks at the contradiction for those who work within the system but whose anti-racist and pro-welfare perspectives are antagonistic to the system they are expected to administer. *In and Against the State* is the title of a seminal book written by the London Edinburgh Weekend Return Group of the Conference of Socialist Economics, first published in 1979 and republished in 1980 by Pluto Press. It looked at the dilemmas of welfare workers opposed to the system they operate. In spite of this perspective it made no mention of immigration and internal controls.

Policy and practice issues

FURTHER READING RESOURCES

Immigration controls pose issues of policy and good practice for welfare practitioners. However, practitioners receive little guidance. There is generally an absence of discourse on controls within professional literature, even that which otherwise addresses questions of racism. An exception is *Anti-Racist Social Work* (Macmillan 1988) by Lena Dominelli in conjunction with and presumably with the support of the British Association of Social Workers (BASW). This argues that anti-racist practice requires the 'ending of the theoretical separation between social work and...the Home Office and the Immigration Service' (p.162). However, Dominelli exhibits a common confusion in calling for 'the elimination of the racism inherent in the immigration laws' (p.154). If the racism is really inherent, which is the position of the present study, then it cannot be eliminated and what requires elimination are controls themselves.

GMIAU has started to redress the vacuum in the literature by producing three annotated resource packs, on children, health issues and prisoners, which examine immigration and welfare practice issues.

The 1985 JCWI publication *No Passports to Services: A Report on Local Government and Immigration and Nationality Issues* contains excellent good practice proposals. The Electronic Immigration Network (EIN) is a voluntary-sector website with its own information and direct access to other relevant sites.

THE IMMIGRANT, MIGRANT AND RESIDENT

There is a tendency, due to over fifteen years of anti-refugee rhetoric, to conceive immigration and welfare controls as being directed only against asylum-seekers. It is wrongly assumed that controls and welfare entitlements are no longer an issue for others wishing to come to the UK, for instance to join family members. In fact immigration and internal controls extend well beyond asylum-seekers and affect all immigrants and migrants. Moreover, the linking of immigration status and entitlement is not an issue only for those denied welfare. It is an issue for all those challenged as to their status by agents of welfare. The linkage exposes long-resident black people and others of assumed foreign origin to questioning about their stay in the UK. It renders them accountable for their presence. It is important that codes of good practice embrace all those subject to controls including those settled in the UK, that is those resident with no time limits or other conditions on their stay.

DESKILLING

One unique 1998 study on *The Child Welfare Implications of UK Immigration and Asylum Policy* by Adele Jones at Manchester Metropolitan University refers to the deskilling of social workers in respect to immigration matters.[3] This is relevant to all professionals working with children or families. It states:

The study found that social workers seemed largely to disregard or be disinterested in supporting children with immigration difficulties. Where interest and concern was expressed, often there was a lack of knowledge about the issues, a lack of clarity about the role of the social worker and feelings of being deskilled because they knew little about the field. Factors which practitioners identified as having contributed to this included:

- lack of comprehensive child care policy

- lack of interest and direction from senior managers

- failings of child care legislation and regulations

- issues not addressed within social work education and training

- influence of negative media

- shifts within social work from prevention and support to crisis intervention and resource-led responses

- immigration not regarded as an important social work issue: responses largely reactive, for example in dealing with young asylum-seekers and specialisation of services leading to immigration cases 'falling between stools'

- a marginalising of issues which affect black and minority ethnic families

- social work not geared up to the needs of a multi-racial society.

WELFARE PRACTITIONERS AND POLITICS

It is not surprising that social workers and other welfare practitioners feel ill-equipped to deal with immigration issues affecting clients. It is unusual for professionals to have to grapple with such clear and potent political issues. Welfare in its daily practice usually presents itself as politically neutral. Paradoxically there are attempts by politicians and sometimes by senior managers to present immigration controls as somehow natural and inevitable and therefore non-political and unchallengeable. This is the problem. It is not possible to develop good practice in this field without an understanding of the political implications and the underlying issues. This itself requires historical investigation and ideological reconstruction – which is why this book attempts to combine theory and practice and to do so within an historical and political context.

THE BASIC POLICY AND PRACTICE ISSUES

On the basis of the above it is possible to start to pose some policy and practice issues affecting welfare practitioners in their contradictory position as advocates for those subject to controls and agents of the Home Office:

- Can there be good anti-racist practice in the face of inherently racist laws?

- Is it a legitimate part of a welfare professional's work to help resolve someone's immigration status?

- Should any professional intervention be 'neutral' or should it take the form of positive advocacy on behalf of those threatened by controls?

- Does a welfare professional have a responsibility to carry out a client's wishes on the immigration issue?

- Does a professional have a responsibility to help on the immigration issue where there is no prior professional relationship and no other matter presents itself?

- Should issues of control be included in codes of anti-racist practice and of good practice generally?

- If such issues are to be included then what levels of understanding and knowledge should be achieved? What degree of intervention should be expected by a welfare professional?

- Is it possible to comply without being in breach of anti-racist practice with a job description which requires investigating someone's immigration status for the purpose of welfare entitlement?

- What would non-compliance mean in practice and what consequences could it have for the worker or client?

- Is it good or bad anti-racist practice to investigate a client's immigration status to help avoid expulsion as opposed to facilitating expulsion or deprivation of welfare?

- Should a welfare professional report, or be party to reporting, someone to the Home Office where the job or line manager requires this? Does this match good anti-racist practice?

- Should support be given to someone under threat of expulsion following their violence or other abuse to women or children?

- Can controls ever be used for progressive purposes – such as denying entry to rapists?

- Should a local authority enter into housing contracts with the Home Office to implement the 1999 Immigration and Asylum Act? Have such contracts a facilitating or repressive role?

- Should the voluntary sector enter into contracts providing advice, support and accommodation under the 1999 legislation?

- Does management have responsibility to provide training on the above issues?

Notes

1   IMG/96 1176/1193/23
2   C/99/0638/018
3   See pp.132–3. Available from Department of Applied Community Studies at Manchester Metropolitan University.

CHAPTER 2

A brief political history

The history of controls is not a matter of academic concern for welfare practitioners. This history is a gateway to understanding the relationship between controls, welfare and the family and therefore to understanding the policy issues behind the formulation of good practice.

FURTHER READING RESOURCES

The Alien Invasion (Heinemann 1972) by Bernard Gainer explains the agitation leading to the 1905 Aliens Act. There are several studies showing controls blocking refugees from Nazism. The latest is *Whitehall and the Jews, 1933–1948: British Immigration Policy and the Holocaust* (Cambridge University Press 1999) by Louise London. *From the Jews to the Tamils* (South Manchester Law Centre 1987) by Steve Cohen develops the story of refugee exclusion. *What's Love Got To Do With It?* (GMIAU 1997) by Steve Cohen traces the historic relationship between gender, sexuality and racism within controls. *Slamming the Door* (Martin Robertson 1975) by Robert Moore and Tina Wallace is an early study of the post–1945 legislation. *British Immigration Policy since 1939* by Ian Spencer (Routledge 1997) provides an excellent overview based on internal cabinet papers.

THE MODERNITY OF CONTROLS

Immigration controls may appear timeless. They seem always to have existed and to be part of the natural order of things. This is due to the almost universal ideological acceptance of the need for controls. However, controls are thoroughly modern. Significant agitation began only after 1882. This was the start of notable Jewish immigration from Russia and Eastern Europe following the so-called Czarist 'May Laws' which unleashed pogroms against Jews following the assassination of Alexander II. It took until 1905 for immigration controls to become law. The history of controls is the history of the twentieth century. Much of this early history has been hidden, either unresearched or unpopularised. This apparent lack of history has strengthened the myth of timelessness.

It is no coincidence that controls are a twentieth-century phenomenon. This was the century of mechanised transport allowing for rapid international movement. It was also the century of imperialism and world markets which demand the availability of cheap labour. Immigration laws are not there necessarily to prevent the movement of this labour. They are there literally to control and regulate it (see Chapter 21).

The twentieth century can be divided into three. The first half consisted of restrictions against Jewish refugees. The second half witnessed controls against black people. The 1990s, and its bequest to the twenty-first century, saw controls against anyone fleeing war, disaster or economic mayhem. This was the decade where the European Union came into its own, imposing pan-European controls, justifying them on economic grounds and demonising as 'bogus' all those who sought entry into the EU.

Today opposition to the totality of controls is a position on the political fringes. Just over a century ago the reverse was the case. It required major agitation to implement the 1905 Aliens Act. It was the struggle for this legislation which legitimised the ideology of controls.

In recent years there has been such a plethora of immigration legislation that it has become difficult to conceptualise a reality without controls. Prior to 1945 there were only three major pieces of legislation. The 1905 Aliens Act was strengthened by the 1914 Aliens Restriction Act, passed in one day on the declaration of war. This itself was replaced in 1919 by the Aliens Restriction (Amendment) Act which was subsequently used to restrict the entry of refugees fleeing Nazism. There was no further substantial primary legislation until the 1962 Commonwealth Immigrants Act controlling the entry of black Commonwealth citizens. This was followed by the 1968 Commonwealth Immigrants Act, which excluded and betrayed thousands of East African Asians who had been given the option of retaining United Kingdom citizenship on the independence of Kenya and Uganda. Then there was the 1971 Immigration Act, which remains the cornerstone of immigration law. After the Tory election victory of 1979 immigration controls became out of control. The 1981 British Nationality Act made it more difficult to acquire citizenship. The 1987 Immigration (Carriers' Liability) Act transformed airlines into agents of control by penalising them for carrying passengers without correct immigration documentation. The 1988 Immigration Act contained among other measures restrictions on appeal rights against deportation. The 1993 Asylum and Immigration Appeals Act made it more difficult for asylum-seekers to acquire refugee status and reduced appeal rights for non-refugees. The 1996 Asylum and Immigration Act further limited the rights of asylum-seekers and penalised employers for hiring workers without the correct immigration documentation. The Labour government's 1999 Immigration and Asylum Act represents the most significant tightening of controls since their inception.

CONSEQUENCES FOR WELFARE WORKERS OF THIS HISTORY

The contradiction between the actual modernity and apparent timelessness of controls can wrongly immobilise welfare practitioners in their professional role. It can be used by managers to justify inaction when what is required is a proactive response to help clients threatened by controls. On the one hand management can present controls as a contemporary phenomenon which is manifestly political and too dangerous for professional involvement. On the other hand it can depict controls as timeless, politically neutral and therefore beyond the need for professional engagement or challenge. It is essential managers have appropriate training on immigration control.

WELFARE JUSTIFICATIONS FOR CONTROL

Post–1945 arguments for controls against black people are almost identical to those employed against Jewish refugees. This repetition has given them unwarranted authority. Justifications for controls ultimately relate to issues of welfare and in particular family welfare. There has developed a construct of welfare defined by nationalism. Immigration controls limit access to welfare by determining who enters the UK and with what status. Welfare legislation then defines and excludes eligibility in terms of this given status.

Central to the welfare justification in the pre–1905 agitation was the housing question. For instance Major Evans-Gordon MP claimed in parliament: 'Not a day passes but English families are ruthlessly turned out to make way for foreign invaders... The rates are burdened with the education of thousands of children of foreign parents' (29 January 1902).

The post–1945 agitation coincided with the construction of the welfare state. In 1961 Cyril Osborne MP, a fanatical agitator for the 1962 Commonwealth Immigrants Act, quoted with approval in parliament an editorial in the *Observer* claiming that British workers were concerned about 'competing with immigrants for houses, hospital beds and social services' (16 November 1961). In introducing the 1968 Commonwealth Immigrants Act, James Callaghan MP, then Home Secretary, spoke of the 'pressures on the social services which arise from the differences in language and cultural background' (27 February 1968). His colleague Renee Short justified the legislation 'to prevent the overburdening of health services'.

THE EMPLOYMENT JUSTIFICATION

Closely allied to the welfare issue is the question of employment. Control legislation has been justified as protecting the job market. An editorial in the *Manchester City News* of 12 May 1888 claimed: 'these immigrants have flooded the labour market with cheap labour to such an extent to reduce thousands of native workers to the verge of destitution ... Surely our own people have the first claim upon us'. In 1938 the *Daily Express* argued: 'Certainly there is no room for the Jews in Britain, where we have 1,800,000 of our own people out of work... There are plenty of uninhabited parts of the world where, given a touch of Christian spirit, they may yet find happy homes' (23 August 1938). An editorial in the *Manchester Evening News* of 17 November 1961 stated: 'Unrestricted entry has already hit heavily the housing authorities. Soon it could severely affect employment prospects.'

The early history prefigures the modern justifications for controls in another particular way, namely the whole world has supposedly heard of the UK's benefit system and job opportunities. The Labour government's 1998 White Paper, *Fairer, Faster and Firmer*, stated:

> People living in countries with weaker economies receive daily images of the potential economic and other social benefits available in richer countries across the globe. The knowledge of such opportunities, as it has always done, provides an incentive to economic migration.[1]

The paper included 'welfare facilities' as an economic benefit. This argument echoes that of Arthur Fell MP, who in 1908 was probably the first parliamentarian to have voiced it. In the parliamentary debate on the Pensions Bill he argued that pensions be confined to British-born subjects, otherwise 'It might be that crowds of foreigners of the age of forty-five or fifty might come over here in the hope that having resided in this country for the required time, they might get a pension' (6 July 1908).

THE POPULATION AND EUGENICIST JUSTIFICATION

There are two other relations of welfare that have been historically forged through the agitation for controls (see Chapter 21). The first is Malthusism – based on the nineteenth-century writings of Thomas Malthus. This is the relationship between welfare and population size with overpopulation being held responsible for diminution of living standards and employment. The other powerful component of welfare which entered popular ideology through agitation for immigration controls was eugenics. Eugenics is a pseudo-science premised on the biologically meaningless concept of 'race'. Within this pseudo-world, reality is perceived as the struggle between races in which only the strongest will succeed.

RACISM

Whatever attempts are made to proffer rationalisations for controls, these only conceal an even more fundamental racism. On 22 October 1919, in arguing for the 1919 Aliens Restriction Act, Herbert Nield MP said in parliament:

> These immigrants, in so far as they belong to the Jewish faith, do not assimilate or harmonise with the native race but remain a solid and distinct community whose existence in great numbers in certain areas gravely interferes with the observance of the Christian position.

The language of post-war legislative debates was similar. In arguing in parliament for the 1962 Commonwealth Immigrants Act, Harold Gurden MP referred to 'coloured immigrants' as being responsible for 'murder, rape, bloodshed, theft, dope peddling, sex crimes and so on' (16 November 1961).

ROLE OF THE LABOUR MOVEMENT IN AGITATING FOR CONTROLS

Given the modernity of controls there is posed the question as to why they are so widely and deeply accepted. This profound, popular acceptance is a result of the active campaigning for controls by mass popular organisations and in particular the trade union and labour movement. Alongside this has been agitation by extreme right-wing organisations. These are examined in Chapter 21.

ROLE OF LOCAL AUTHORITIES IN AGITATING FOR CONTROLS

Local authority politicians and officers played a partial but important role in agitating for the 1905 Act and in conflating issues of welfare and immigration control, such as holding Jewish refugees responsible for overcrowding. This is seen in the evidence to the 1903 Royal Commission on Alien Immigration which preceded the legislation.[2] Two of the witnesses advocating controls were A. T. Williams, a member of the Housing Committee of London County Council, and Alderman James Silver of Stepney Council. These were well-known restrictionists. Lesser-known figures such as Councillor Walter Belcher of Stepney also gave evidence in favour of controls. Some medical officers of health gave evidence linking controls with public health issues. Dr Joseph Loane, responsible for Whitechapel and Stepney, advocated the dispersal of aliens. The Royal Commission recommended dispersal and the prohibition of aliens living in designated areas. This was not part of the Aliens Act but is central to the 1999 Immigration and Asylum Act (see Chapter 13).

A HISTORY OF WELFARE LEGISLATION

Migrants, immigrants and refugees are today scissored between immigration controls and laws relating to provision of benefits and services. Eligibility for many benefits and services is dependent upon immigration status. On the other hand recourse to 'public funds' jeopardises immigration status. The 1905 Aliens Act similarly declared that 'undesirable immigrants' be refused entry. This included anyone who 'cannot show that he has in his possession or is in a position to obtain the means of decently supporting himself and his dependants' or 'owing to any disease or infirmity appears likely to become a charge on the rates or otherwise a detriment to the public'. An alien could be deported following a court recommendation after criminal conviction or if 'in receipt of any such parochial relief as disqualifies a person from the parliamentary franchise or has been found wandering without ostensible means of subsistence or been living under insanitary conditions due to overcrowding'.

Early welfare law linked entitlement to immigration status in the fields of pensions, national insurance benefits, educational scholarships and council housing. These and other welfare restrictions are examined in Part 3.

REGULATION OF LABOUR

Regulation of labour is another early example of internal immigration controls. The 1909 Labour Exchanges Act established labour exchanges to direct unemployed people into work. In 1930 the Minister of Labour, Margaret Bondfield, announced in parliament that where 'the applicant is to be found to be an alien who has resided in the United Kingdom for less than six months, he is not to be submitted for any vacancy if suitable British subjects are on the register' (25 June 1930).

THE FAMILY – WHOSE FAMILY?

There is another relationship shared by welfare and immigration controls which can be charted historically. This is the relationship to family. Support for the family is the central concern of social work practice in its widest sense. Issues of the family are also central to immigration control. However, they are pivotal within controls for the most destructive of reasons. Immigration laws weaken and destroy immigrant, migrant and refugee families. Politicians in speaking of respect for family values omit the questions of whose family and welfare for whom.

THE ENGLISH NUCLEAR FAMILY

In *Empire and Efficiency* (London 1901), Arnold White wrote:

> The unit of strong nations is the family. All legislation, habits, ideals, policy or ambitions that increase the welfare and multiply the number of happy families are good for the nation. Things that belittle or ridicule family life are bad for the nation. This is a commonplace but bedrock truth. Turkey is what it is mainly because the harem replaces family life.

This only expresses in an exaggerated way the ideals of modern politicians. It echoes Margaret Thatcher's phrase about there being no such thing as society, only families. At the same time governments have created devastation among black families through controls. Arnold White himself agitated for the 1905 Aliens Act.

None of this is contradictory. This is because the family supported by Arnold White and Margaret Thatcher is the white, British, nuclear and heterosexual family. Other kinds of family relationships, for instance the extended family relationships of migrants, immigrants and refugees, are perceived as alien and un-British. These relationships then become the sacrificial lambs of immigration control with controls themselves becoming an ideological defence of the one true family – the nuclear family as defined by the British state. Those partnerships perceived as ideologically outside all acceptable family norms, in particular same sex relationships, can then be destroyed by UK immigration law (see Chapter 7).

THE DESTRUCTION OF THE JEWISH FAMILY

The primary source of information on the Aliens Act was the *Jewish Chronicle* newspaper. This described the working of the 1905 legislation against Jews in language equally applicable to the modern attack on black family life. The edition for 11 October 1907 stated: 'We have already seen how a girl has been separated from her fiancé. Fathers and mothers have been torn from son, brother has been torn from brother and child from parents. The Act, in a word, has sown misery and tears and bitter anguish.'

Here is an example from the same paper of 25 October 1907:

[An] aged widow named Tratelman last May had come to England to join her only son. The poor woman lost her husband a year ago and found herself without relatives or friends. By undergoing many hardships she had managed to gain a livelihood as a dressmaker but now on account of her advanced age she could no longer work at her trade and so she journeyed to her son in England... But no! This lonely, friendless, wretched old woman was torn from her son and sent back.

THE DIVIDING OF BLACK FAMILIES AND GENDER ISSUES

Central to the undermining of the black family has been the keeping apart of spouses and pivotal to this division has been the global separation of partners of arranged marriages. This has been based on the most regressive assumptions about gender. Within this paradigm men are socially constructed as threats to the indigenous labour market and to be excluded. Women are seen as camp-followers of men, as irrelevant domestic labour and no threat. The detailed history of this has been documented in the excellent *Women's Movement: Women under Immigration, Nationality and Refugee Law* (Trentham Books 1994) by Jacqueline Bhabha and Sue Shutter. The rules relating to marriage go to the cutting edge of defining what relationships are deemed legitimate under immigration control. They are almost a laboratory experiment in what the British state considers as the essential constituents of marriage.

In a debate on the temporary relaxation of the rules in the mid-1970s Ivor Stanbrook MP proclaimed (5 July 1976):

It is part of the British way of life for the father to provide a home for the family and it is the same in India. The husband is expected to provide a home for the wife. There is no rational argument in favour of saying that a wife in another country should be in a position to provide a home for her husband and children. It is contrary to all common sense, human nature and the way of life of both Britain and the subcontinent.

In a debate on 4–5 December 1979 leading to tightening of the marriage rules, Timothy Raison, the Home Office immigration minister, stated: 'the young man seeking to come to the United Kingdom for the purpose of marriage is economically motivated. The reason why women come here is not primarily economic but so they can build a family.' This polemic reached bizarre levels with the intervention in the same debate of Keith Hampson MP. He argued that Asian women

posed as large an employment threat as Asian men because 'These women go to
the highly populated and industrialised centres and produce children, many of
whom are males, who enter the labour force'.

PRIMARY PURPOSE RULE

The attack on arranged marriages peaked with the notorious primary purpose
rule. This was introduced in 1980 and eventually removed in 1997. It was
removed only after campaigning by women's organisations such as the Immigration Wives and Fiancées Campaign in Manchester and the Immigration Widows
Campaign in London. The rule was nominally intended to prevent so-called
'marriages of convenience'. In practice it caused endless inconvenience and
misery to partners in arranged marriages. A spouse or fiancé(e) wishing to come to
or remain in the UK had to show that 'the marriage was not entered into primarily
to obtain admission to the United Kingdom'. The denial of this negative was
extraordinarily difficult. Immigration officials made it more difficult by offering
totally contradictory reasons for refusing applications. Though now repealed, the
rule's cynical deviousness provides a stark illustration of the mind-set of UK
immigration control and explains why in practice arranged marriages continue to
be attacked through other rules (see Chapter 5).

'What would you do if your fiancée went to the moon', a pamphlet published
by Manchester Council in 1986 and written by Steve Cohen and Nadia Siddiqui,
examined refusals by the British High Commission in Islamabad of entry certificates for primary purpose reasons. The pamphlet recorded the following:

> In one case the couple were closely related and therefore it was assumed that the
> families had connived in a marriage of convenience. In another case the families
> were not related and this was used to support refusal on the grounds that it is
> customary to marry within the family. In a further case there was a refusal
> partially based on the fact that the fiancé had not yet arranged a job in the UK –
> this being used to prove he did not take his marriage seriously. Yet in another case
> (that of Arfana Amin and Ijaz Ul Arfeen) there was a refusal based on the fact that
> the fiancé regarded it as important for married life to earn an income through a
> job. In other words you will be refused if you are on the dole or have a job! It is
> interesting to look at the actual questions and answers in this third case:
>
> Q. Would you marry your fiancée if she had lived in Pakistan?
> A. Yes, I may have gone to her house or she may have come to mine.
>   We would have discussed it.
> Q. What would have happened if she had lived in Karachi, whereas you
>   live in Lahore, and she had wanted you to join her in Karachi?
> A. I would have gone to Karachi as my firm has an office there.
> Q. What would have happened if she had wanted you to join her in
>   Mirpur?
> A. I would have gone to join her if she had wanted and found a job.

Q. What would have happened if she had wanted you to join her in Pindi?

A. I would have gone as my company has an office there as well.

Q. Who would have joined who if your fiancée had been in the USA or Canada?

A. If necessary I would have joined her and found a job.

Q. Would you be prepared to follow your fiancée anywhere?

A. Yes, provided work was available.

Q. How do you propose to support your fiancée in the UK?

A. I would do any sort of work.

The ECO in this case concluded from this segment of the interview that the fiancé was only interested in marrying in order to find work! It was patently absurd.

THE BOTTOMLESS PIT THEORY OF THE BLACK FAMILY

A long-term project of immigration controls is to break the links that black people have between the UK and their land of origin. These links are located in the extended family and their retention is viewed as disloyal. This explains the continually expressed concern that the extended family network will result in perpetual immigration and a bottomless pit of migrants, immigrants and refugees.

William Whitelaw, then shadow Home Secretary, attacked Asian arranged marriages: 'girls and boys born in this country can seek a fiancé of their own ethnic group from the country from where their parents originally came...a process which could go on forever' (24 May 1976). In the same parliamentary debate Enoch Powell revealed the existence of the Hawley Report, a government document on the entry clearance system in Bangladesh. This report expressed fear of the infinite consequences of allowing entry to spouses and fiancé(e)s as this subsequently 'entitles parents, grandparents and allegedly distressed relatives' of the couple to apply to come here. This paranoia led to the establishment of a Parliamentary Group on the Feasibility and Usefulness of a Register of Dependants to look at the establishment of a register of every overseas family dependant of people settled in the UK. This reported in 1977 and concluded there should be an ongoing register of husbands, wives, children, parents and grandparents. This register would be for 'New Commonwealth countries and citizens of Pakistan'. It suggested that registration should be compulsory and failure to register should disentitle future settlement applications.[3] The First Report of the House of Commons Select Committee on Race Relations and Immigration, published in 1978, made the recommendation that a yearly quota be imposed on the admission of family members from the Indian subcontinent.[4]

ALIEN SEXUALITY

There is a constant ideological theme in the attack on the family life of migrants, immigrants and refugees. Non-British sexuality is seen as perverse, rampant, a threat to the nuclear family and literally alien. W.H. Wilkins, a campaigner for controls, wrote in his book *The Alien Invasion* (London 1892) 'Many of the immigrants are young women, Jewesses of considerable personal attraction. Men sharks and female harpies are on the lookout for them as soon as they disembark.' This characterisation of alien women as prostitutes re-emerged in the debates on the 1948 British Nationality Act. This removed the automatic acquisition of citizenship by women marrying British citizens. The change was justified by a supposed invasion of French prostitutes following the post-war closure of Parisian brothels. A.L. Symons MP stated in parliament (7 July 1948):

> There was a further difficulty that at this time the licensed houses were being closed down in France and there was a great deal of fear of an increase in that traffic, which had been known before, of women coming to this country, making a marriage of convenience and acquiring British nationality simply in order to get to this country.

Controls against black people were premised on allegations of sexual deviancy. The racist attacks in Notting Hill and Nottingham in 1958 were directed against black people's sexuality. *The Times* explained the racist violence as based on 'sexual jealousy – the sight of coloured men walking along with white women' (27 August 1958). It reported the fascist Colin Jordan circulating his *Black and White News* with headlines such as 'Blacks seek white women' (3 September 1958).

Policy issues

The inextricable link between controls, welfare and the family raises stark policy issues for welfare practitioners, legal advisors and all concerned with justice within social policy.

THE PROBLEMATIC OF THE FAMILY

It is ultimately counter-productive for opponents of controls and of deportations simply to parallel the Home Office's attack on Third World families by demanding the right to family unity. This is because the construct of the family, whether nuclear or extended, is itself politically and personally problematic. One organisation campaigning for reform of controls is Family Immigration Rights (FAIR). This emphasises the different ways that controls divide families. Its manifesto states: 'the family is the natural and fundamental group unit of society and has the right to be protected by society and the state'. This ignores the work of feminists, both European and non-European, who have shown the family unit to be neither 'natural' nor 'fundamental'. It is (literally) man-made. As far as controls are concerned this lauding of family is not just an ideological matter. It has consequences. An inevitable consequence is that it makes it extremely hard for single people and same-sex couples to come to or stay in the UK.

Another consequence is that contradictory arguments are used in campaigns against controls involving women's relationship with men. Opposition to immigration rules preventing husbands joining wives here is frequently articulated in terms of family unity. However, the partially successful opposition to immigration rules constraining women to remain in violent relations in order to retain immigration status (see Chapter 9) is articulated in terms often critical of the family. What is really at stake here is respect for the wishes of the individual to be able to live where and with whom they want. For women this means autonomy and freedom of choice, free of men and free of the state as represented by immigration controls.

GENDER: THE PROBLEMATIC OF EQUAL OPPORTUNITIES IMMIGRATION CONTROLS

There cannot be equal opportunities immigration control. Controls, because of their relationship to family, manifestly discriminate against women on the grounds of gender. They also discriminate against lesbians and gay men on grounds of sexuality. However, any critique of controls which concentrates simply on matters of sexuality and gender is inadequate. Not only does it omit the fundamental racism of controls, but also it ignores the relationship between racism, gender and sexuality. Immigration controls are where racism and sexism coincide and unite into national chauvinism. They represent the unity of patriotism and patriarchy and their transformation into the most virulent nationalism.

There have arisen two specific demands for equality within immigration controls based solely on gender or sexuality. Both resulted in the lowering of rights for everyone and the constructing of equality based on the lowest common denominator. This in part was a result of the complete absence of considerations of racism in the search for equality.

The issue of gender equality was central to the hearing before the European Court of Human Rights (ECHR) of three women, Nargis Abdulaziz, Sohair Balkandali and Arcely Cabales, the so-called ABC case which was finally completed in 1985. All three lived in the UK and wanted entry for their overseas spouses. They argued that the then existing marriage rules were discriminatory against women. The basis of the discrimination was that the rules applied only to women wanting to be joined by male partners and not men wishing to be joined by female partners. The case focused on the then requirement that a woman applying to bring in a partner had to be a British citizen born in the UK. Though the ECHR considers only the situation in a signatory country, yet it is still hard to see how rules making it harder for men than women to gain entry can be classified as discrimination just against women. None the less the court found that Britain was violating the European Convention on Human Rights. The fact that the marriage rules applied only to men seeking to enter was held to be sex discrimination against their partners. However, the government was found not in breach of the race discrimination article of the Convention.

The government dealt with this decision not by abolishing the marriage rules. Instead it extended the rules to the entry of women. It equalised the law on the lowest common denominator of racism. This was achieved through rule changes in 1985 and 1988. These changes established that partners, male or female, who wish to join a person settled in the UK were subject to all the marriage rules, including the primary purpose rule. In other words women overseas were positively harmed by the finding of sexual discrimination against women in the UK.

LESBIAN AND GAY SEXUALITY

The issue of 'equality' with similar perverse consequences is mirrored in the demand by lesbians and gay men for the right to live in the UK with partners from overseas. The separation of same-sex couples can be justified only by the most reactionary homophobia. However, the problem is the context in which the demand has been raised, a context which omits all reference to racism and nationalism and which views immigration laws as being based simply on sexual inequality. It is a context in which the demand is for same-sex relationships to be treated equally along with heterosexual relations, at the same time as heterosexual relationships are being continually undermined by controls. Posing the demand in this way has again resulted not primarily in the increase in rights of lesbians and gay men. It has achieved equality through the diminution of rights for unmarried heterosexual couples (see Chapter 7).

Notes

1   July 1998, Cm 4018
2   Vol. 2, Cd 1742
3   Cmnd 6698
4   303–1

CHAPTER 3

An outline of current immigration control

A CASEWORK PROBLEM

You are a social worker. W, a client, consults you. She has British citizenship and has recently married X, an overseas visitor. He has overstayed his leave. They have a child, Y, born in Britain. She asks if the marriage will automatically confer British citizenship on X or whether he should ask the Home Office to regularise his stay. She wants to know whether Y can be deported and if the family could live in France.

A REAL CASE STORY

A Pakistani heart patient (Mohammed Yaqoob) has died after immigration officials blocked his trip to Britain for a bypass operation in case he overstayed his visa, even though his family had raised the funds for his treatment... A Foreign Office spokesperson stated...the job of entry clearance officers abroad was to act in accordance with the rules, which had happened in this case. The family 'could not be expected to appreciate that' he added. (*Guardian* 2 October 1996)

SCOPE OF THIS CHAPTER

Immigration law can sometimes appear so complicated as to be impenetrable. One reason for this is that every time the government perceives there is a gap allowing migrants, immigrants or refugees to come to or remain in the UK, it rushes to put its finger in the dyke through the creation of new legislation. The plethora of immigration Acts passed since 1962 was explained in Chapter 2. Moreover since the 1971 Immigration Act none of the separate pieces of legislation has ever been consolidated under one Act. This means immigration advisors sometimes have to trawl through several major pieces of legislation in order to advise a client. This book is not primarily intended as a textbook on immigration law and practice. However, it is intended to put into the possession of welfare workers a clear and coherent understanding of the appropriate law. There are two main needs for this understanding. First, it will enable a welfare professional to become alert to any dangers faced by clients. Second, it will help professionals to work better as a team with immigration advisors.

FURTHER READING RESOURCES

There are authoritative texts. One is *Immigration Law and Practice in the United Kingdom* (4th edn, Butterworths 1995) by I. A. Macdonald and N. Blake. A second is *Butterworth's Immigration Law Service*, which provides a comprehensive and regular updating of the law. Third and less legalistic is *Immigration, Nationality and Refugee Law Handbook*, published and updated yearly by the JCWI, which also produces a regular bulletin.

ONE COUNTRY, TWO SYSTEMS

Two parallel systems became operative on 1 January 1973. One was discriminatory and excluded black Commonwealth citizens. This was the 1971 Immigration Act. The other provided an open door to millions of mainly white people. This was the Treaty of Rome whereby Britain joined the Common Market – now the European Union – and became governed by community law.

The 1993 European Economic Area Act created the European Economic Area (EEA), which extends freedom of movement to nationals of former European Free Trade Association countries. At present the EEA comprises Austria, Belgium, Denmark, Finland, France, Germany, Greece, Iceland, Ireland, Italy, Liechtenstein, Luxembourg, the Netherlands, Norway, Portugal, Spain, Sweden and the UK.

FORTRESS EUROPE

The law mainly impacting on immigrants, migrants and refugees is British immigration control. However, the European dimension continually increases in importance.

First, EEA citizens are exempt from UK controls.

Second, freedom of movement extends to a wide number of people compared to domestic law. EEA workers, those seeking work, or those providing or receiving services, have freedom of movement.

Third, rights to family unity for EEA nationals are huge compared to British controls. The following can join an EEA citizen: spouses, children under 21 or dependent on their parents, dependent grandchildren, or in the case of workers non-dependent grandchildren under 21 and finally dependent relatives in the ascending line – parents, grandparents, etc. Family members need not be EEA citizens.

Fourth, for many black people it is fortress, not open, Europe. Freedom of movement is available only to citizens (and their family) of EEA states. A large number of black people and refugees throughout the EEA do not have such citizenship.

Finally, EU law does not necessarily give rights to EEA nationals entering their own country. There has to exist an element of transnational movement within the EEA. This results in absurdities. A husband may be prevented from joining an EEA wife resident in the UK. However, if she goes to work in another

EEA state he can join her there. A decision of the European Court of Justice in the case of Surinder Singh shows that the couple may then return to the UK provided the wife is coming to the UK to work. In this situation the wife enters not just as a British citizen but as an EEA citizen exercising rights as a worker.

RIGHT OF ABODE

The parallel system to EU law is British immigration law. The 1971 Immigration Act amended by the 1981 British Nationality Act gives certain groups the right of abode. They are not subject to controls.

There are three categories of such people. The first two are dying out. These are Commonwealth citizens born before 1983 with a parent born in the UK (most born after this date will be British citizens through descent) and Commonwealth citizen women married before 1983 to a man born, adopted, registered or naturalised in the UK or who is a Commonwealth citizen with a parent born in the UK. An important group of these women are Bangladeshi.

British citizenship

The main group with right of abode are British citizens. Citizenship guarantees more than entry. Citizens cannot be expelled. They can pass on citizenship to children born in the UK and, within limits, overseas. They have the right to travel throughout the EEA. They can stay abroad for more than two years without jeopardising status.

Citizenship is regulated by the 1981 British Nationality Act which became operative 1 January 1983. For most white people citizenship is not problematic. For many black people it is extremely problematic. The absolute right of abode is anything but absolute.

Britain's imperial history means there are six groups with British passports. Only British citizens have the right of abode. The other categories are historical remnants or cosmetic exercises giving no immigration rights. They are

- British subjects – people from the Indian subcontinent who failed to gain Indian or Pakistani citizenship on independence

- British protected persons – people with a connection to former protectorates

- British Dependent Territories citizens – citizens of the remaining colonies

- British nationals (overseas) – people from Hong Kong who acquired no other citizenship on the colony's return to China

- British overseas citizens – mainly East African Asians whose right to come to Britain was withdrawn by the 1968 Commonwealth Immigrants Act.

Many people wrongly think they are British. They unknowingly acquired citizenship of their country of origin on independence. An example is someone who came to Britain from Jamaica prior to immigration controls. Such a person would have travelled on the old-style United Kingdom and Colonies passport but on Jamaican independence would have become Jamaican.

The 1981 British Nationality Act creates obstacles in acquiring citizenship. Previously citizenship was acquired by birth in the UK. People born in the UK after the Act became operative are British only if one parent has permanent stay or British citizenship. 'Parent' means married parent, though the marriage can take place after birth and citizenship can be transmitted via a lone mother.

Citizenship is one thing, proving it another. There are children in Bangladesh who are British by descent after being born to British fathers. Under the 1988 Immigration Act, British citizens and others with a right of abode are denied entry if they cannot produce a British passport or a 'certificate of entitlement'. In the absence of a system of birth certification, immigration officials overseas refuse to accept they are 'genuine' descendants and withhold passports and certificates. Evidential problems will develop for people born in the UK. Any person born after 1 January 1983 requiring a British passport has to prove their parents' British citizenship or settled, and perhaps marital, status.

THE IMMIGRATION RULES

Everyone not an EEA citizen or having the right of abode is subject to constantly changing immigration rules. The rules are concerned with these situations.

- *Pre-entry control.* This is undertaken overseas by entry clearance officers at British posts. Certain applicants, such as those permanently joining family here, require entry clearance certificates irrespective of nationality. Other applicants require a visa because of nationality. Visa control is imposed on citizens of most former black colonies and on refugee-producing countries. The entry clearance system erects a fence around the UK thousands of miles away.

- *On-entry control.* This is undertaken by immigration officers who have the power to refuse or impose conditions on entry even where there has been prior entry clearance.

- The distinction between pre-entry and on-entry control has to some extent broken down following the 1999 Immigration and Asylum Act and the Immigration (Leave to Enter and Remain) Order 2000. Under certain circumstances entry clearance granted overseas can be treated as leave to enter the UK. However, port immigration officers still retain power to refuse entry.

- *After-entry control.* Anyone wishing to prolong or alter the basis of stay has their case determined by civil servants in the Immigration and Nationality Directorate (IND) at Croydon. Another aspect of after-entry control is enforcement – removing those allegedly in the UK without permission.

Who the rules cover

The rules are designed to keep or send people out of the UK. Wishing to come or remain is insufficient. Applicants have to fit within the rules. Otherwise it is necessary to argue 'compassionate' grounds (see Chapter 9).

The rules cover people wanting to come to the UK for temporary reasons, such as a visit, and people wanting settlement. Settlement is lawful permanent residence without conditions of stay. It is the goal in cases contesting expulsion. It does not carry the same rights as citizenship. It gives no entitlement to movement within the EEA. It is no guarantee against future expulsion if obtained by deception nor does it offer protection against a court recommendation for deportation following conviction or a Home Office order on conducive to public good grounds (see Chapter 18).

Wide powers and narrow rules

A feature of the rules is the wide powers given to immigration officials. These powers are often subjective with the appearance of being based on whims. For instance under the rules a spouse can be refused entry unless it is shown 'each of the parties intends to live permanently with the other', the assessment of which is clearly a subjective judgement.

The discretionary powers of immigration officials are so wide because immigration rules are so narrow. One aspect is central to controls. Throughout the rules there occurs the formulation whereby leave to enter or remain 'is to be refused if the Immigration Officer (or Secretary of State) is not satisfied' that the rules' requirements are met. This switches on to applicants the burden of proving they come within the rules, a harsher onus of proof than in criminal cases.

Every rule category is narrowly constructed. This is seen in the visitors' rules. These do not just affect tourists. They relate to family, as visits are often the only way family members can come here. Applicants have to prove availability of maintenance and accommodation, they can afford return travel, will not take employment and intend to leave on completion of the visit. If all obstacles are overcome the stay permitted is six months.

Appeals against refusal of family visits to the UK

This book is mainly about people who want settlement in the UK for whatever reason. However denial of the right to visit the UK is also political. All rights to appeal against refusal of permission to come as a visitor were abolished by the 1993 Asylum and Immigration Appeals Act. As a result of pressure these rights were partially restored by the 1999 Immigration and Asylum Act and the Immigration Appeals (Family Visitor)(No.2) Regulations 2000 which came into force 2 October 2000. The regulations allow appeals for people who apply for prior entry clearance as 'family visitors' only. However family visitor' is defined quite widely and includes, for instance, an unmarried partner (which presumably includes a same-sex partner) in a relationship where the couple have lived together for at least two of the previous three years. It would seem that the family member in the UK need not be living here permanently.

PUBLIC FUNDS AND CONSTRUCTS OF WELFARE

Applicants wishing to come to or stay in the UK must usually show they 'will be maintained and accommodated adequately without recourse to public funds'. The requirement as to accommodation prejudices extended families. The requirement as to maintenance jeopardises the poor. The requirement as to no recourse to public funds transforms welfare from being supportive into being harmful.

Public funds for this purpose were defined in 1985. The list is regularly increased. Benefits or services not within the rules are not public funds. The present rules (as of October 2000) on public funds are slightly out of date and do not reflect changes in the benefit system or how this links to immigration status. It is anticipated that new rules will be issued and these will presumably replicate the benefits/services listed in the 1999 Immigration and Asylum Act as dependent on immigration status – housing under the homelessness legislation, allocation of social (council) housing, income-based jobseeker's allowance, income support, a social fund payment, child benefit, working families' tax credit (previously family credit), housing benefit, council tax benefit, attendance allowance, severe disablement allowance, invalid care allowance, disability living allowance and disabled person's tax credit (previously disability working allowance).

Definitions of maintenance and accommodation

Adequate accommodation has been interpreted as compliance with the over-crowding standards of the housing legislation. The Immigration Appeal Tribunal has held that adequate maintenance should be 'somewhat higher' than income support level.[1] This is because income support is a gateway to housing benefit, council tax benefit and free services such as prescriptions.

Support from third parties, such as the sponsor's parents in a marriage case, is sometimes acceptable but only for a limited period. There will have to be proof that the couple will be self-supporting thereafter. The best advice is not to rely on third party support.

CONSEQUENCES OF CLAIMING PUBLIC FUNDS

Most people without settlement are not entitled under benefit regulations to public funds benefits (see Chapter 12). Attempting to claim public funds can jeopardise status. It can be interpreted as proof of inadequate maintenance or accommodation. The consequences of claiming are as follows:

- The Home Office could curtail existing stay. This is rare.

- An application to vary leave could be refused.

- In a settlement application the Home Office may give limited leave to assess adequacy of maintenance.

- Future entry could be refused.

- The 1996 legislation tightened relationships of welfare. It declared that no recourse to public funds can be made a condition of entry, breach of which may lead to prosecution and expulsion. This criminalisation is redolent of Poor Law values.

POLICIES AND CONCESSIONS AND DISCRETIONS

Knowledge of the immigration Acts and rules is insufficient to advise clients properly. There is a whole series of policies and concessions operated by the Home Office. These used to become known through leaks. The government is now more open about their existence. Some can be found on the IND's website along with the rules and instructions to immigration officials. A few have been incorporated in the October 2000 rule change. Also the IND policy section can be approached directly for clarification on policies and on the Home Office's views on the law.

CARRIERS' LIABILITY AND EMPLOYER SANCTIONS

Controls have been privatised through the imposition of sanctions. The 1987 Immigration (Carriers Liability) Act turned transportation companies into agents of control by penalising them for carrying passengers without the correct documents. The law is now found in the 1999 legislation which extends liability to include carrying clandestine passengers.

Employer sanctions bring controls on to the shopfloor by penalising employers for hiring unauthorised labour. Sanctions were first contained in the 1996 Asylum and Immigration Act. Involving employers in enforcing controls is the flip-side of workplace raids by the immigration service. After a series of raids in 1980 the *Guardian* reported a statement by the Transport and General Workers' Union and the General and Municipal Workers' Union saying black workers now 'have to carry at all times their papers proving their right to live and work here. This is a situation more reminiscent of the apartheid system' (7 July 1980).

EUROPEAN CONVENTION OF HUMAN RIGHTS

The European Convention of Human Rights should be distinguished from community law. The number of signatories is greater than membership of the EU. The court hearing disputes is the European Court of Human Rights. Until November 1998 there used to be a preliminary hearing before the European Commission on Human Rights. The comparable EU court is the European Court of Justice. Individuals as well as states can petition the Court of Human Rights. The Court and Commission have declared unlawful various British and non-British immigration decisions. Relevant provisions are Article 3 (no one to be subjected to torture or inhuman or degrading treatment), Article 8 (right to private and family life), Article 13 (right to an effective remedy) and Article 14 (right not to suffer discrimination).

Prior to the 1998 Human Rights Act (operative from 2 October 2000), the Convention was not part of British domestic law. The incorporation of the Convention presents another line of challenge to Home Office, local authority, welfare agency and court decisions. However, there will be limits to the challenges. First, European Court jurisprudence holds that effective immigration control is legitimate state policy. Second, recent decisions of the European Court are restrictive. Third, it will be the same judges in the UK interpreting the Convention who often support the Home Office in immigration cases.

RACE RELATIONS (AMENDMENT) BILL

Most immigration and internal control would appear to breach the 1976 Race Relations Act. However, there is an exception for anything done under statutory authority. Occasionally in the absence of authority there have been successful actions in respect to welfare. Meru Maher, a 60-year-old Indian man, applied to the then Department of Health and Social Security (DHSS) for an allowance for his wife. The DHSS demanded that he produce his passport. A judge found this to breach the Race Relations Act (*Guardian* 11 February 1984).

The Race Relations (Amendment) Bill presently before parliament offers the opportunity to contest controls by outlawing racial discrimination by, for instance, immigration officers and local authorities. However, there will again be limits to these challenges. The Bill exempts challenges on the grounds of 'nationality or ethnic or national origin in carrying out immigration and nationality functions' where these have been authorised by the Home Secretary or the 1971, 1988, 1993, 1996 and 1999 Immigration Acts, the 1981 British Nationality Act and some other pieces of immigration legislation including European Community law. Lord Bassam, in introducing the first version of the Bill on 14 December 1999, said the exemption allowed 'necessary acts of discrimination to maintain the Government's immigration and nationality policies'. Even the limited possibility of challenging decisions based on 'race' discrimination is going to produce a whole new irrationality into legal discourse on immigration controls. The concept of 'race', however much used in popular discourse, is the product of Victorian pseudo-science and pseudo-biology and ultimately is both scientifically and biologically meaningless. It is based on the same irrational eugenicist ideas that were first used to justify controls themselves (see Chapter 21).

THE 1999 IMMIGRATION AND ASYLUM ACT: APPEAL RIGHTS AGAINST DEPORTATION AND REMOVAL

The 1999 Act undermines procedural protection against arbitrary and rapid expulsion by abolishing most appeal rights against deportation. The legislation is so draconian it makes the deportation processes which it abolishes appear almost benevolent. In the absence of appeal rights the Home Office can invoke the far more rapid 'removal' procedures. The only remaining situation with a deportation appeal is where a person's presence is deemed not 'conducive to the public good', which affects persons guilty of a criminal offence (see Chapter 18). In this book the legal terminology of 'deportation' and 'removal' is often replaced by the generic, non-legalistic description of 'expulsion'.

Prior to the 1999 Act becoming operative, anyone entering the UK lawfully could be expelled only through deportation procedures, which involved a two-tier appeal system. If an application for extension of leave or for settlement was made within existing leave then any refusal could usually be challenged by appeal. If this was lost, or if there was no appeal because leave had expired, then expulsion for overstaying leave or breaching any other condition of entry, such as working without permission, could be effected only after a deportation appeal. The 1988 Immigration Act curtailed the right to argue compassionate grounds in deportation appeals for appellants in the UK less than seven years. However, there was preserved the procedural right of appeal which could gain an appellant time and result in an adjudicator recommending the appellant be allowed to remain. This can be contrasted with persons subject to removal who had no appeal rights in the UK. Removal applied to those the Home Office alleged entered the UK illegally.

The 1999 Act abolishes a separate appeal right against deportation. It substitutes a 'one-stop' appeal against refusal to vary leave which, if available at all, will consider all grounds for remaining in the UK. If this appeal is lost, the Home Office can go immediately to the removal stage. There will not even be a one-stop appeal where someone has overstayed leave or breached other entry conditions. These changes will have significant effects on good practice in resisting expulsion (see Chapter 9). The changes became operative on 2nd October 2000 by virtue of The Immigration and Asylum Appeals (One-Stop Procedure) Regulations 2000.

THE 1999 IMMIGRATION AND ASYLUM ACT: ARE YOU OR HAVE YOU EVER BEEN A BOGUS ASYLUM-SEEKER?

The 1999 legislation takes internal controls nearer to its logical conclusion of transforming the entire state machine into partners of the immigration service. It obliges existing policing agencies to pass on immigration control information to the Home Office. Section 20 provides for information to be supplied 'for immigration purposes' to the Home Secretary by the police, the National Criminal Intelligence Service, the National Crime Squad and HM Customs and Excise.

Section 20 also allows the Home Secretary to make an order obliging a 'specified person' to pass on information for 'immigration purposes'. The danger is that such specified persons may be anyone working within welfare. The provisions in the Act relating to housing for asylum-seekers (see Chapter 13) are a snooper's charter. Section 100 obliges local authorities to disclose to the Home Secretary whatever information about housing accommodation is requested. Section 126 obliges the owner or manager of property accommodating asylum-seekers under the Act to supply information about the occupants. Section

127 obliges the postal service to provide information about any request from an asylum-seeker for the redirection of post.

LOYALTY TESTS

Immigration controls are based on a loyalty test. They demand that anyone settled in the UK make a complete break with the country of origin. Examples are built juridically into the immigration rules. Anyone who obtains the holy grail of settlement but then leaves for more than two years can have settlement rescinded under the 'returning residents' rule. A child adopted overseas and applying to come to the UK must show s/he has 'lost or broken its ties with his family of origin' (Chapter 6). The undermining of Asian arranged marriages through controls is premised on a paranoia of an endless queue of spouses coming from the Indian subcontinent (see Chapter 2). Loyalty testing was explicit in the 1980 White Paper on Nationality Law which preceded the 1981 British Nationality Act.[2] This said that citizenship should be given only to those who 'demonstrate a real intention to throw in their lot with this country' and should not be given to those having 'no sense of loyalty'. Entitlement to welfare is also premised on loyalty testing as evidenced by benefit denial to those not 'habitually resident' (see Chapter 12).

Comments on casework problem at start of chapter

Marriage to a British citizen does not confer automatic citizenship. This can be obtained only through naturalisation when the applicant has permanent stay in the UK. X would not fall within the rules allowing leave to remain after marriage as he has overstayed his leave. Any application would have to be on compassionate grounds in accordance with the Home Office internal instructions relating to the deportation of families and children (see Chapter 9). These instructions require a marriage to have existed for two years prior to enforcement action. Informing the Home Office immediately of any marriage could be a mistake often made by inexperienced advisors. The best advice is to wait for two years following the marriage. The risk of detection is not as great as the risk of removal if the Home Office were to be immediately approached. Y is British because the mother is British and is immune from enforced removal. W could live in France along with Y as an EEA national seeking work. X could join her there although gaining entry to France could itself be bureaucratically difficult. X needs to see an experienced advisor who can accumulate evidence as to why W and Y cannot live in X's country and also whether X has an independent right to remain here such as any asylum claim. Finally, advising someone to remain as an overstayer could be construed by the Home Office as a harbouring offence. Though the risk of this is extremely small and there are no documented instances where this has occurred, advisors should be careful in their use of language.

Notes

1   Azem 7683
2   IMG/97 412/720/4

CHAPTER 4

Basic good practice for welfare professionals and legal advisors

A CASEWORK PROBLEM

You are a social worker. Your client X is threatened with expulsion and is being represented by Y, an unqualified immigration advisor. X has several appeals, to an adjudicator, to the Immigration Appeals Tribunal and to the High Court. All are lost. X tells you that because of losing these appeals he wants a new legal representative who is a qualified lawyer. What do you suggest?

A REAL CASE STORY

The case and successful campaign of the Rahman family against deportation is discussed in Chapters 9 and 19. It is seen how eventually over twenty professional reports along with a comprehensive explanatory letter were submitted by an experienced legal advisor detailing medical and other issues. The Home Office allowed the family to remain on the basis of these reports. Initially the family had gone to a voluntary sector 'race advisor' with no knowledge of either law or tactics. He submitted a half-page begging letter to the Home Office asking that the family be allowed to remain. It was not surprising that the Home Office refused this application – a refusal which led to the family having to spend another three years fighting the case. Best practice would have been for the race advisor to have suggested referring the case on to an immigration expert rather than attempting to deal with it himself. Both could then have worked together as part of a team.

SCOPE OF THIS CHAPTER

In Chapter 1 there was posed the policy question 'Can there be good anti-racist practice in the face of inherently racist laws?' This book argues that it is possible to develop good practice but only within the framework of opposition to controls (see Part 4 of the book).

This chapter examines the most basic good practice points. It does this from two perspectives which inevitably overlap: first, from the perspective of welfare professionals, and second, from the perspective of immigration advisors. It is important that each group understands the perspective of the other so as to enable them to better work as a team.

Basic good practice for welfare professionals

HOME OFFICE IS NOT A BENEVOLENT INSTITUTION

The Home Office is not a benevolent institution and should not be approached as such. It is not uncommon for well-meaning professionals to contact the Home Office to enquire about their client's immigration status – only to discover that this prompts the initiation of expulsion procedures.

The 1985 JCWI pamphlet *No Passport to Services: A Report on Local Government and Immigration and Nationality Issues* illustrated bad practice by a London borough which issued a leaflet on housing benefit and its linking to immigration status. The leaflet advised: 'If you are not certain whether this requirement applies to you, you should look at the immigration rules, which are available from Her Majesty's Stationery Office, or check with the immigration authorities'. This is bad advice. The rules are technical and confusing. The Home Office's job is to administer increasingly harsh immigration laws, not to advise people threatened by them. Good practice is for anyone requiring immigration advice to be directed towards a reputable and expert advisor.

APPROACHING THE HOME OFFICE THROUGH AN ADVISOR

A welfare professional or a client should not approach the Home Office on their own initiative or in response to Home Office enquiries. Contact should be through an advisor who understands immigration law and whose role it is to co-ordinate, or to orchestrate, the case.

THE ROLE OF THE WELFARE PROFESSIONAL

Clarity as to areas of responsibility is vital within a case. The welfare professional's role should not be confused with that of the client's advisor. The client's advisor has the responsibility for the care and conduct of a case. The role of a welfare professional is to work as an equal member of a team with the advisor, the client, other professionals and perhaps campaign members. The strength of a case is often relative to the cohesiveness of this team.

Welfare practitioners have to walk a difficult tight-rope. They rigorously have to avoid usurping the advisor's role. However, it is important that professionals have sufficient knowledge broadly to explain to clients their immigration situation, to warn them if they are in danger, to reassure them if not in danger and to direct them to an immigration expert. Welfare professionals often have regular contact with the client and, following full consultation with the advisor, can have an important role through constantly reinforcing the client's understanding of the case.

Unless the client understands all issues of tactics, strategy, evidence and law, then the chances of a victory will be drastically diminished. A client in a situation of ignorance and confusion will end up defeated. Clients have to become active participants in their own cases and not just passive objects. Welfare practitioners can help clients gain confidence through understanding the issues.

ASKING CLIENTS THEIR IMMIGRATION STATUS, GOOD OR BAD ANTI-RACIST PRACTICE?

How does a welfare practitioner ascertain a client's immigration status and know whether an immigration danger exists? In Chapter 1 there is posed the policy question 'Is it good or bad anti-racist practice to investigate a client's immigration status to help avoid expulsion as opposed to facilitating expulsion or deprivation of welfare?'

This book is opposed to services or benefits being linked to immigration status. It is opposed to national and local state welfare agencies investigating immigration status. However, its reluctant conclusion is that it is good practice to ask clients their immigration status if the purpose of asking is to help them. There is an unbridgeable difference between the Home Office asking someone their status in order to arrest and remove them and a social worker asking the same question to avoid arrest and removal. Good practice requires that:

- all clients are asked this question, not just black clients;

- a proper explanation is given as to why the question is being asked with an absolute assurance as to confidentiality. Management should adopt procedures to ensure that confidentiality is kept and monitored;

- clients must be reassured there is no obligation whatsoever to divulge immigration status. It is their choice.

CLIENTS WHO DO NOT KNOW THEIR STATUS

The cases at the start of this chapter assume that everyone knows their status. However, many people do not know – an example may be a child in care. Another example may be a deserted wife whose husband has retained possession of her passport. Other people may wrongly think that they know their immigration or nationality status. Where there is any doubt about status then the matter needs to be put in the hands of an experienced advisor. An advisor may be able to ascertain status through examining appropriate documents. Since 1996 most immigration applications made within the UK have had to be on special Home Office forms and a client may remember signing such a form. There will be occasions where an advisor has insufficient information. As a last resort, the advisor may conclude that it is necessary to make enquiries to the Home Office with the following provisos:

- It should be explained to the client that contacting the Home Office may reactivate interest in the case to the client's detriment.

- Conversely it should be explained that remaining in the UK without an awareness of immigration status could create future problems.

- The client's address must not be given in any enquiry letter.

HELPING A CLIENT RETAIN DIGNITY

Immigration controls humiliate individuals, families and communities. At every stage of the process an applicant suffers the degradation of having to justify coming to or remaining in the UK. Intervention by welfare professionals should be premised on the need to restore their client's dignity.

Preserving a client's dignity means avoiding moral judgements as to his or her immigration status. This status is a matter of a politically defined law, not of morals. In the eyes of the Home Office 'legal' equals good and 'illegal' equals bad. These definitions constantly change and tighten as a result of legislation and court decisions. Yesterday's lawful entrant can be today's illegal alien. People fall foul of immigration laws through no fault of their own. An example is marital break-up within twelve months of a spouse arriving in the UK. Nothing is neutral in immigration law, including vocabulary. Words such as 'legal', 'illegal', 'bogus', 'abusive' and 'genuine' are all politically value-laden.

HELPING A CLIENT GET PROPER ADVICE

A welfare practitioner's role could include helping a client find an appropriate advisor and warning clients of bogus immigration advisors and of self-proclaimed community leaders who promise everything and deliver nothing, often for a great deal of money. Finding good representation is a problem outside the major cities. Local authorities should keep a register of expert, local immigration advisors. There are guidelines in choosing an advisor:

- Do not trust advisors who claim that everything is easy and they can sort out any problem. Most immigration cases are complex. They require hard work, legal knowledge, tactical skill and careful planning. There can never be a guarantee of success. Even where cases are apparently simple any error could result in long-term and perhaps irredeemable harm.

- Do not trust advisors who promise success if paid lots of money. Paying money will not sort out immigration problems.

- Do not trust advisors who claim they are important community leaders with contacts in the Home Office. The Home Office does not do deals.

- Do not trust advisors who pretend they are miracle workers and can fix everything. Miracles will not get anyone into the UK or keep them in the country.

CHANGING ADVISORS

Clients should exert control in determining their own legal representative. This includes changing representatives. Changing an advisor can be disruptive. Any dissatisfaction or confusion about how a case is handled should initially be discussed with the advisor.

The frightening nature of controls often leads to a situation where a client takes the case to several advisors in turn. This is in the hope of finding someone who has an instant-fix solution. There are no instant fixes. What cases require is stability in their handling and an advisor experienced in immigration laws.

A client may not like the advice given. This does not mean it is incorrect. Often the best advice is the hardest to accept. A good advisor is one who is honest about the situation. It is essential for a client to understand the difficulties of a case before she or he can properly contest it.

LEGAL AID AND LEGAL ADVISORS

There are several agencies which provide free and expert immigration advice and representation. The two leading organisations are GMIAU and JCWI. Many law centres can provide free, quality help. A list of law centres can be obtained from the Law Centres' Federation. Most advice organisations have geographical limits on their operations. Clients should be reassured that just because help is free it is not necessarily inferior – just as expensive help is not necessarily superior.

The Immigration Advisory Service (IAS) and the Refugee Legal Centre also offer expert help, but they concentrate mainly on appeals and being Home Office funded are politically constrained. The IAS has offices in London, Birmingham, Cardiff, Glasgow, Leeds and Manchester.

There exist several excellent firms of private solicitors who undertake immigration cases. There is no reason not to use such firms. Community Legal Services (previously the Legal Aid Board) has attempted some quality control of immigration lawyers by awarding only certain firms and agencies legal aid contracts. It is best to confirm with JCWI or GMIAU the expertise of private lawyers. The major problem even with the best private firms is finance. Legal aid is limited. Free help can be given only where the client is beneath a basic income, usually income support level.

OUTLAWING CROOKED ADVISORS: THE 1999 IMMIGRATION AND ASYLUM ACT

Controls have generated a parasitic advice industry often located physically and politically in the heart of black communities. This has led to a further racism with disreputable sections of the British media exposing these leech advisors while implying that all black people are parasites willing to live off 'their own'.

The 1999 Act attempts to regulate advisors through an Immigration Services Commissioner and an Immigration Services Tribunal. There will be a system to register, suspend or ban advisors. Criminal penalties will be imposed on those providing unauthorised advice.

Professionals working with clients subject to controls need to be aware of this regulatory scheme offering protection against racketeers. However, the scheme is open to criticism on issues of principle, not least the potential it gives for banning politically committed advisors while not doing anything to increase the numbers of good ones (see Chapter 21).

LOCAL AUTHORITY LINK WORKERS

One role for welfare practitioners is, under the guidance of the legal advisor, often one of continually explaining legal processes to the client and of liaising with other appropriate agencies. Community link-workers trained and experienced in immigration procedures can be of enormous help. Local authorities should recruit community-based workers specifically as support for those confronted by immigration controls.

INTERPRETERS

Good practice guidelines for immigration interpreters have been produced by the North West District of the Workers' Education Association.

- Not everyone requires an interpreter. Someone may be more proficient than they imagine in English.

- If there is a danger that language is a barrier to communication then an interpreter must be used. The interpreter should be skilled in the client's mother tongue and correct dialect.

- The interpreter should normally be paid, qualified and/or experienced, acting in a professional capacity and accountable.

- The interpreter must observe confidentiality.

- The client should be able to veto any interpreter. A client may not wish to have an interpreter from the immediate community. A woman may want a female interpreter. In an asylum claim, an interpreter must hold no allegiance to the authorities against whom asylum is sought.

- The role of an interpreter is to interpret – not tell the client what to say or speak for the client. Questions should be addressed, both verbally and through body language, to the client not the interpreter.

- In asylum cases an applicant may have psychological problems and patterns of speech may reflect these problems. The advisor needs to check this with client and interpreter.

- The norm should be that an interpreter is a paid professional. There are exceptions. A client may feel more comfortable with a family member or friend. This could be the case where a child is the client. However, an unaccompanied child seeking asylum may not wish a family member to know all the details. There may be issues of child abuse.

- Some advisors have found it preferable for an adult client's friend or family member to interpret where the client needs help in between seeing the advisor. The client may need to collect documentary evidence or see another professional or insert further information in a statement or attend immigration appeal hearings to become familiar with appeals.

Interpreters at Home Office interviews and appeals

There are particular practice matters at Home Office interviews and appeals:

- The Home Office or the court will provide an interpreter if requested. Formal interpreting can conceal an applicant's or appellant's emotional response to questions. It can be a matter of tactics whether to use an interpreter.

- Advisors should engage an independent interpreter at a Home Office interview or appeal to ensure that everything is translated accurately.

Police station interviews

Police officers in interviewing suspects are governed by the 1984 Police and Criminal Evidence Act. The Act states that Codes of Practice drawn up under it apply to all persons investigating offences. So immigration officers investigating immigration offences must follow the Codes of Practice. Code C is concerned with interpretation. Article 13.3 states:

> The interviewing officer should ensure that the interpreter makes a note of the interview at the time in the language of the person being interviewed... The person shall be given the opportunity to read it or have it read to him.

Article 13.4 refers to written statements and says that the interpreter shall take down the statement in the language in which it is made and the English translation should be made later.

Translation of documents

No foreign language document should be sent to the immigration authorities without being properly translated to ensure that it contains nothing detrimental. The translation can then be sent with the original. Any English statement or report should be translated back into the client's own language before submission.

LEGITIMATE AREA OF PROFESSIONAL WORK

One consequence of the wide-ranging nature of controls is that involvement in immigration issues should be recognised as a legitimate part of professional practice. Refusal to treat immigration status as a matter of professional concern can result in a client's overall situation being misunderstood and best interests jeopardised. To give a blunt example – the fact that a child is under threat of expulsion, or his or her parents are under such a threat, is as much a social work, welfare or educational concern as are cases where children are being subject to other forms of abuse.

MANAGEMENT RESPONSIBILITIES

Issues of policy and practice are matters for which senior management have to take responsibility. It is bad practice to expect individual workers to decide on these issues on a case-by-case basis. At the moment most workers are either ignorant of, or are turning a blind eye to, immigration matters because they have received no management guidelines. Alternatively they are attempting to deal with these issues without the support of management and sometimes behind the back of management. None of this is professionally tenable.

TRAINING

There is a need for training on pre-qualifying professional college courses. Subsequently there is a responsibility for management to provide regular training based on the ever changing and ever more restrictive nature of controls.

One purpose of training is to alert workers to immigration dangers facing some clients so there can be positive and early intervention. Another purpose is to enable workers to reassure other clients who are not under threat from immigration controls. Given fears engendered by controls, this is a significant role. Proper training would also reduce the fear factor for welfare practitioners themselves. Immigration controls need not provoke professional anxiety.

Some agencies have recognised training needs. The Social Services Inspectorate (SSI) has produced a practice guide with a training pack on *Unaccompanied Asylum-Seeking Children*. This contains good advice to social workers such as:

> While you need to be aware of the legal status of the unaccompanied child you are working with and the process of his or her asylum application it is not your responsibility to resolve it. Your role as a worker is to:
>
> - ensure that the application is proceeding
> - help specialist advisors by gathering accurate, relevant information
> - support the child in uncertainty and keep him or her informed of the progress of the application.

GOOD PROFESSIONAL PRACTICE AND GOOD TACTICS

It is the transparent nature of the politics behind immigration law which makes it unique. The fact that controls are political is not an excuse professionally to ignore them. It does require a greater need for training and good practice. The political nature of controls means that many good practice issues pose themselves not as straightforward legal matters but as tactical ones. When is it best for someone who has overstayed their permitted leave to make a settlement application following marriage to a British citizen? Would an immediate application help? Or could it make the situation worse? Should an application to remain on medical grounds be for permanent stay or yearly extensions? Does this case require a psychiatric report? Does that case need a social worker report? Should an application be delayed until after the birth of a British child? These queries and hundreds like them are the regular calculations that have to be made by advisors and need to be understood by other professionals.

Helping someone to come to or remain in the UK frequently requires tactical acumen. Welfare practitioners have to be aware of these tactical implications. They also have to understand that in immigration law it is often inadequate just to follow formal legal processes as these processes often offer no protection. There is no point in relying on law when the law is the problem.

KEEPING UP TO DATE WITH THE LAW

Welfare professionals are not lawyers. This book concentrates on issues of practice and tactics as opposed to technicalities. These issues will remain crucial whatever the technicalities. However, laws do change. The 1999 Immigration and Asylum Act has not yet been fully implemented. There will be many legal challenges to the Act. These developments will require parallel good practice. Ways of keeping abreast of developments are to become members of Greater Manchester Immigration Aid Unit or the Joint Council for the Welfare of Immigrants or the Immigration Law Practitioners' Association (ILPA) or the Electronic Immigration Network.

Basic good practice for immigration advisors

SHOULD APPLICATION BE MADE IN UK OR OVERSEAS?

Asylum applications can only be made once in the UK. Other applications can only be made overseas. A visitor who is a visa national cannot switch to a student. The student application has to be made overseas. Fiancé(e)s must apply overseas. Someone coming to the UK for family unity must have prior entry clearance. However, the rules allow someone who is already lawfully in the UK, for example a student or visitor, to switch to being a spouse, dependent child or dependent (grand)parent.

Applications made within the UK allow the advisor to keep firmer control. Any entry by someone overseas, for instance as a visitor, which conceals settlement as the ultimate purpose could be unlawful. Furthermore any visa application as a visitor which concealed settlement as the aim could be discovered at the visa interview. This will doom to failure the visit application and prejudice any subsequent settlement application. There are particular matters concerning elderly parents (see Chapter 6).

TO CLAIM OR NOT TO CLAIM PUBLIC FUNDS

The immigration rules which came into force 2 October 2000 confirm previous Home Office statements that where a person is dependent on funds provided by a sponsor and the sponsor is reliant on public funds then this is acceptable as long as the sponsor does not thereby become entitled to 'additional' public funds. A typical example considered acceptable by the Home Office is where one married partner is entitled to benefits but the other is not because he or she has not yet acquired permanent settlement in the UK. However, dependency on a sponsor's benefits could raise other problematic issues as to whether there exists 'adequate' maintenance for immigration purposes (see Chapter 3). Best advice therefore is that, if possible, even this should be avoided and the sponsor should not be claiming means-tested benefits at the time of any immigration application or at least should have a credible job offer. There is probably no danger in a sponsor receiving non means-tested public funds such as disability living allowance provided there will be adequate maintenance for the applicant.

The Home Office follows particular practice for two benefits. It accepts that a settled partner can claim child benefit and this will not prejudice the other partner's settlement application. The same applies to family credit – and now presumably working families' tax credit. A letter from the IND of 9 May 2000 also says that the spouse or partner of a British citizen or person settled in the UK can claim working families' tax credit and this will not be considered recourse to public funds.

In any claim for child benefit, the immigration status of the child is irrelevant. What matters is the status of the claimant. A parent, including a lone parent or foster parent settled in the UK, can claim benefit for a child without settled or any status. The only risk is if any unlawful status is brought to the attention of the Home Office.

CORRESPONDENCE TO AND FROM THE HOME OFFICE

Proper case management requires that correspondence to the Home Office should always be sent through the advisor. The Home Office very occasionally may contact a family professional for information. The professional should discuss with the advisor before replying. Replies should be sent through the advisor, who should explain how they fit into the case.

Advisors need to ensure that correspondence to the Home Office is posted by recorded delivery and includes the applicant's reference number where one exists. The number will appear on previous Home Office correspondence and usually on a passport's back inside cover.

REPRESENTATIONS AND PROFESSIONAL REPORTS TO THE HOME OFFICE

A vital part of correspondence to the Home Office consists of 'representations'. This is not a legal term. Representations are the arguments why an applicant should be given his or her desired status.

Representations may include professional reports. Best practice is for reports to be sent as a composite whole accompanied by a detailed explanation of their relevance (see Chapter 9). Other than as a tactic to gain time, they should not be sent in one at a time. This minimises their impact.

BE CAREFUL WITH THE HOME OFFICE

The Home Office keeps a file on everything written to it as well as everything said in interviews in the UK or overseas. Officials are trained in detecting inconsistencies. Advisors and clients must think carefully about information provided to the Home Office. If possible proof should be available of all facts.

PROCEED WITH CAUTION

Applications to come to or remain in the UK need to be prepared carefully. Any rejection could trap the applicant in a bureaucratic appeal system or what remains of it.

There is generally no point in making an application that is bound to fail unless the advisor has sufficient evidence to argue that a positive decision be made outside the rules on compassionate grounds. The only time a weak application may be appropriate is where the applicant is in the UK and the time allowed by the appeal system may be of tactical importance in resisting removal (see Chapter 9).

WARNING: THE MARK OF CAIN

Any refused immigration application does not disappear from the official memory. It remains on file like the biblical mark of Cain. This can have adverse future consequences. The refusal of an application for settlement will usually prevent the applicant being allowed entry even in a temporary capacity such as a visitor. Advisors and other professionals should be aware of this risk in lodging an application. Conversely once a settlement application is lodged any refusal should be contested. There is no point in withdrawing a case to 'appease' the Home Office.

GOOD PRACTICE AND FORM FILLING

It is the advisor's responsibility to complete immigration forms. A welfare practitioner may need to complete forms where the time limits are very tight. Practitioners need to understand immigration documents so they can explain their significance to clients.

APPLICATIONS FROM WITHIN THE UK

Most applications made within the UK must be on Home Office forms otherwise they are invalid. Exceptions are applications to remain for asylum, to remain under European Union law or for an extension of stay for work permit or training or work experience permit holders. However, asylum-seekers will usually, after making an application, be obliged to detail their case on a Statement of Evidence (SEF) form.

Otherwise there are presently seven application forms:

- FLR(M) – for one year's leave following marriage
- FLR(S) – for leave or further leave to remain as a student or student nurse
- FLR(O) – for further leave to remain for other reasons
- SET(M) – for permanent stay following marriage after one year's leave
- SET(F) – for settlement for family members other than spouses
- SET(O) – for settlement for any other reason
- ELR – for an extension or permanent stay for someone granted exceptional leave to remain after an asylum refusal.

Copies can be obtained from the IND's Application Form Unit or the IND website. Where someone possesses leave to remain, the forms must be sent before leave expires, otherwise appeal rights will be lost on any refusal

The introduction of compulsory forms in 1996 represented an increasing bureaucratisation of controls. The forms strengthen internal controls. They state:

> Information you give us will be treated in confidence but may be disclosed to other Government Departments and agencies and local authorities to carry out their functions.

OVERSEAS APPLICATION FORMS

Applications for entry clearance are made to British posts overseas. There is a standard form IM2A accompanied by form IM2B for settlement applications. Usually these are completed by the applicant overseas. They can be completed by someone in the UK, signed by the overseas applicant and sent to the appropriate overseas post. The Migration and Visa Division of the Foreign and Commonwealth Office was previously responsible for managing the overseas entry clearance operation. Since June 2000 this role has been undertaken by the Joint Entry Clearance Unit (JECU) established as a partnership between the Home Office and the Foreign and Commonwealth Office. This partnership is based on a 'Memorandum of Understanding' as to the financial, resource and management framework within which the single integrated structure will operate. Forms can be obtained from JECU or its website.

THE IMPORTANCE TO BE GIVEN TO APPLICATION FORMS

Because the initial application either in the UK or overseas is made through standard application forms, there is a tendency by some applicants to consider applications a routine, formal and easy matter – with the immigration officials simply processing cases in a neutral or even helpful manner. This is absolutely incorrect. For instance the standard forms used in the UK need to be filled in carefully and all issues discussed with the applicant. It is bad practice simply to hand over a form to an applicant and tell him or her to fill it in and send it to the

Home Office. The issues need to be addressed and the form double-checked before sending.

- The form must be carefully completed and all documents requested sent with the form. Otherwise the IND considers the forms to be incorrectly completed and will return them.

- The IND treats returned applications as though they had never been made. An applicant may then overstay an existing leave to remain. Forms should be sent four weeks before the expiry of any existing leave in case they have to be resubmitted.

- Submitting the wrong form will invalidate an application. It is not always clear which form is appropriate. The IND has established a telephone inquiry line advising on forms. A note should be retained of any such advice. If in doubt more than one form can be submitted.

ONE-STOP APPEAL STATEMENTS: THE 1999 IMMIGRATION AND ASYLUM ACT

Where appeal rights exist, designated forms need to be completed. Under the one-stop procedures introduced by the 1999 legislation, there is a parallel obligation to submit a statement of all additional grounds that the appellant would like considered for remaining in the UK. It would appear (although the Home Office may decide to challenge this) to be sufficient to submit grounds in a brief, generalised format, namely

the applicant has a right to remain under the rules and/or on compassionate grounds and/or as a refugee under the UN Convention and/or under the Human Rights Act and/or under the Race Relations (Amendment) Act.

The Home Office if it wishes can seek further particulars later. Failure to submit additional grounds may prevent these being relied on at an appeal.

The explanatory notes accompanying the Act make it clear that the Home Secretary will consider these additional grounds before an appeal is heard. Advisors may in some cases think it tactically worthwhile elaborating on these additional grounds to secure a positive resolution of the case without an appeal hearing.

NATURALISATION FORMS FOR BRITISH CITIZENSHIP

Naturalisation can be obtained only by someone with indefinite leave to remain. Some people with limited leave think they can obtain citizenship through naturalisation – whereas submitting a naturalisation form can jeopardise their existing status by suggesting an intent to remain permanently (see case of Paul Ho., Chapter 4).

Some non-British people wrongly think that submitting a passport form will give citizenship.

Naturalisation is expensive. It is usually not worthwhile for people who do not wish to travel in the EEA or who are not going to have children overseas or who are going abroad for less than two years.

GIVING PROPER ADVICE ABOUT SPONSORSHIP FORMS

Sponsorship forms are informal documents showing that a sponsor can maintain and accommodate an overseas dependant or visitor. Some agencies compose their own forms. Many sponsors wrongly consider this form to be the most important aspect of bringing a relative to the UK. The most important aspect is the entry clearance interview where required. Sponsors do not need a form. They can send proof of earnings and of accommodation with a letter offering to maintain and house the applicant. Even if a form is used, evidence should be sent of everything stated on the form. Solicitors should never be paid for signing or endorsing sponsorship forms as this is unnecessary.

ADVISING ON UNDERTAKINGS: THE 1999 IMMIGRATION AND ASYLUM ACT

Sponsorship imposes no obligation on the sponsor. The rules also allow for formal 'undertakings' to maintain and accommodate which do impose obligations. Undertakings are requested in the case of (grand)parents wanting settlement. Sometimes undertakings are requested on behalf of children between 16 and 18. They are not requested in the case of spouses or other children as the sponsor is under a legal obligation to maintain these dependants.

The consequences of signing are great. The 1980 Social Security Act imposes a lifelong obligation on the sponsor. Under the 1992 Social Security Contributions and Benefits Act income support obtained by the sponsored person can be reclaimed from the sponsor. Government policy is to enforce this only where the sponsor can repay. Under the 1999 legislation the sponsor becomes criminally liable if there is a failure without reasonable excuse to maintain or accommodate someone who becomes an asylum-seeker relying on the Act's support scheme, as described in Chapter 12. Signing an undertaking can also prevent the 'sponsored immigrant' claiming means-tested benefits (see Chapter 12). An advisor should explain the consequences of signing an undertaking. An informal sponsorship form which implies that the sponsor is giving legal undertakings should never be signed.

CASE PREPARATION AND EVIDENCE

The best way to prepare a case is for welfare professionals involved to work as a team with the advisor and the client. Some practitioners may be able to help a client obtain documentary and other evidence. Evidential issues can pose enormous problems. The evidence can be thousands of miles away. Welfare professionals can help physically locate evidence, particularly within the UK.

PREPARING FOR APPEALS

The appellant must be prepared for appeals. The responsibility lies with the advisor though other professionals have a role. GMIAU has produced a leaflet in several languages for appellants on appeal preparation.

- Where the appeal is against refusal of entry clearance then the appellant will be overseas and unable to appear. Only witnesses in the UK can be prepared.

- The best preparation is for the appellant, if present, and witnesses to attend other appeal hearings. Hearings are open to the public unless one party requests that it be heard in private and the adjudicator (judge) agrees. Listening to several appeals will familiarise participants with the way hearings are conducted and the types of questioning. It also may allow adjudicators to become aware of the appellant or witnesses and that they are treating their case seriously.

- One role for welfare practitioners is to accompany appellants or witnesses to hearings and to discuss what has been learned.

- It is pointless appellants or witnesses attending their own appeal unless the case is sufficiently prepared. This means everyone fully understanding not just what questions will be asked but why they will be asked. Family professionals, after themselves being briefed by the advisor, can help in this.

- Appeals can be lodged without expectation of winning but to gain time against removal (see Chapter 9). The client must be made aware of this.

PREPARING FOR INTERVIEWS

Immigration interviews can take place in the UK or overseas at British posts.

- Advisors must treat all immigration applications as important. There is a tendency for some applications, such as visitor applications, to be given less priority than, for example, settlement applications.

- Interviews need to be prepared as though they were appeals. There is no point in starting an interview unless the desired result is achievable. Where the applicant is overseas, preparation will have to take place via a family member in the UK.

- An advisor should never allow a client to attend an interview, in the UK or overseas, without first determining its purpose and without also preparing a written statement on behalf of the client and submitting it in advance. Provided the client is fully aware of the contents of the statement and has agreed it as correct then its prior submission should make the interview far more manageable.

- The advisor should attend all Home Office interviews. It can never be predicted what issues might arise. Even 'screening' interviews where asylum-seekers give proof of identity can develop in unexpected ways. Clients should never be left on their own to face these difficulties. However, Community Legal Services is reluctant to grant monies for advisors to attend screening interviews.

MAKING USE OF MPS

There is a belief that Members of Parliament have the power to persuade the Home Office to reverse decisions. This is normally a fallacy borne as much out of despair as hope. Some MPs wrongly think they have the ability to conduct immigration cases. MPs consulted on immigration issues should recommend constituents to see a reputable advisor. ·

MPs can operate as an effective mailbox to the Home Office on behalf of an advisor. This could prompt a more reasoned reply and, if desired, a speeding up of the case. In an emergency an MP's intervention may be able to delay expulsion. It is useful to have an MP's support in any campaign. It is the parliamentary or constituency assistants of MPs who do most work. Advisors should keep contact addresses for relevant assistants.

The Home Office issues guidelines, 'Information for Members of Parliament about immigration and nationality enquiries', last updated January 2000. MPs should ensure they have a copy of this. The guidelines emphasise:

- The appropriate MP is the constituency MP of the person facing removal. In practice this can mean the sponsor's MP.

- MPs are encouraged not to contact ministers but to write to the port chief immigration officer (in cases of refusals of entry) or the IND (in deportation cases). However, the quality of replies improves if the minister is contacted.

- Ministers will not normally intervene to take an initial decision on a case or where a case is being appealed.

- It is pointless contacting the minister unless there is 'new and compelling information'. Sending a minister old and well-known information is futile.

- Where the issue is one of refusal of entry clearance, including visas, by British officials overseas then MPs should contact the Joint Entry Clearance Unit. If this proves unsatisfactory then the best advice is to contact the Foreign Secretary.

Advisors must fully brief MPs in cases where intervention is sought. Bad practice is to expect MPs to compose their own letters to ministers. Good practice is for the advisor to write such a letter and ask the MP to endorse it and send it on. At this point it might be worthwhile for the client to see the MP in case more active political help is sought in future. Good MPs will in any event want to meet their constituents. This is because such MPs will want to check that their constituents have not fallen into the clutches of crooked advisors who may have charged money for contacting the MP.

Comments on casework problem at start of chapter

The best advice to give X is that she should sit down and discuss with her advisor, Y, why she is losing confidence in him. The fact that appeals have been lost does not mean that Y is incompetent or failing to pursue the best tactics. Likewise the fact that Y is not a qualified lawyer does not mean he is not highly experienced. It may be that Y has explained on several occasions the difficulties of the case and outlined a strategy to win outside the appeal system – but X out of anxiety has not properly understood this. Often the problem is not one of incompetence but one of communication. This is also why it is good practice for other professionals, such as a client's social worker, to help in this communication process from the start of a case.

PART TWO

Immigration Control and the Family

CHAPTER 5

Dividing families

Spouses

You are a hospital welfare rights worker. You are seen by a patient, X, who has multiple sclerosis and is unable to work. She is claiming income support, housing benefit and disability living allowance (DLA). She is a divorcee and last year went to India and married Z. Z is himself slightly disabled but can undertake light work. He has applied for entry clearance to join her. He is being interviewed in two weeks' time. X wants to know if her husband will be entitled to income support and DLA. Neither she nor Z have any idea what will be asked at the interview. She has never taken advice on these matters. What do you suggest?

I am one of the many women victims who are caught up in the British racist and sexist immigration machinery... It is quite humiliating and very embarrassing for women like myself who are usually reserved and shy to have to stand here and tell everyone about our personal lives...but it is the only way open to us if we are to successfully inform the public and educate them... The Home Office has taken advantage of the image of the typical 'Asian woman' who is supposed to be shy and reserved, who never speaks out in public. The Home Office has used these stereotypical qualities to its advantage, knowing that Asian women will not stand up in public and demand from the Home Office that it allows their husbands to stay in the UK with them and their children. But now we have to stand up in public. Because this is the only way we can make the Home Office and the public aware that it is not the typical Asian woman who will take the Home Office's blow after blow just lying down, but it is the typical Asian woman who is going to stand up and express her feelings and demand her basic human right to have her husband live with her... It is important that everyone within the community shows their support and solidarity.

This is extracted from a speech given by Rahela Siddique during her campaign for the entry of her husband Khalid. It was given at a conference in September 1986 in Manchester on 'The Right To Be Here' and is reproduced in the conference report. Following similar events nationally the primary purpose rule preventing spouses coming or remaining here was eventually repealed (see Chapter 2).

However, other mechanisms are now used to keep spouses from joining or remaining with partners in the UK.

SCOPE OF THIS CHAPTER

Division of families is central to immigration control. Central to the division of families is the separation of spouses. This chapter briefly develops some historical and political issues seen previously (see Chapter 2) but emphasises modern law and practice.

Applications for family unity can be made from outside or within the UK. For instance a student or visitor here who marries someone settled can apply to switch to being a spouse. The substantive nature of the immigration rules dealing with before or after entry applications is similar. One exception is for fiancé(e)s – who can apply only outside the UK. Where marriage applications made in the UK are refused then expulsion becomes the significant issue (see Chapter 9).

FURTHER READING RESOURCES

Women's Movement: Women under Immigration, Nationality and Refugee Law (Trentham Books 1994) by Jacqueline Bhabha and Sue Shutter is a political analysis of controls from the perspective of women's experiences.

SOCIAL POLICY RESEARCH

The attack on the extended black family through immigration controls combined with ostensible ideological support for 'family values' has resulted in fantastic legal contortions. This is clear in cases based on the old 'primary purpose' rule – where the applicant had to prove that the purpose of the marriage was not avoidance of immigration control. This led courts and tribunals into an exercise of defining what is in fact the purpose of marriage. These cases represent untapped source material for researchers investigating the construction of family and the relationship which is ideologically pivotal to family, namely marriage.

In one case the Immigration Appeal Tribunal considered the refusal on primary purpose grounds to allow Vinod Bhatia to join his fiancée in the UK. This refusal was upheld by two out of three members of the Tribunal. The third member, Professor Jackson, dissented. It is this dissent, actually designed to help someone gain entry, which shows the bizarre analysis to which marriages and Asian marriages in particular are subjected. Professor Jackson said:

> The majority asserts that the basis of any genuine marriage is the intention to live together but the purpose of bringing any particular marriage into existence is another matter and may well have nothing to do with mutual affection but may be dynastic, pecuniary or economic…this seems to confuse the purpose of marriage with the motives of entering into it. The answer to the question 'what is it that induces you to marry this woman?' may be, for example, love, physical attraction or tradition. The answer to the question 'what is your aim in marrying this woman?' in any genuine marriage is surely…to live with her for life.[1]

INTRUSIVENESS

The most personally demoralising consequence of immigration control is not necessarily refusal of entry or even expulsion. What causes constant demoralisation is the way that controls are used to justify investigation into the most personal details of the lives of black people. This investigation takes the form of a microscopic scrutiny of black family life. What permits this are the immigration rules dealing with family unity. One example is the requirement that settlement following marriage is possible only after the completion of a twelve months' probationary year of married life in the UK. The fact that the couple may have been married for several years with one party living oversees while waiting to come to the UK is considered irrelevant. The courts have also decided it is equally irrelevant that the Home Office bureaucracy takes a long time to determine cases. Any break-up within this determination period will doom immigration status even though the couple have lived in the UK for more than twelve months. This probationary rule is equally intrusive for couples marrying in the UK. There would be an uproar if British couples were expected to wait a year or more to see if the relationship lasted before their marriage was considered legitimate.

Sometimes this intrusion takes a physical form which could amount to assault in any other context. The *Guardian* reported that throughout the 1970s black fiancées wanting to enter Britain were sometimes demanded proof of their virginity and asked to sign a standard form which said they 'agree to a gynaecological examination which may be vaginal if necessary' (1 February 1978). An Indian woman who exposed what was happening explained that on arrival at Heathrow she was taken to a medical inspector: 'He was wearing rubber gloves and took some medicine out of a tube and put it on some cotton and inserted it in me. He said there was no need to get shy.' The *Guardian* also revealed that black people, including pregnant women, were routinely being X-rayed as a method of age estimation in family reunion applications especially in Bangladesh (see Chapter 17).

THE BASIC MARRIAGE IMMIGRATION RULES

No person is allowed entry or leave to remain as a spouse if either party is under 16.

A person seeking entry clearance overseas to come to the UK as a spouse must prove:

- they and their spouse intend to live together permanently as husband and wife and the marriage is still subsisting

- they have met the other party to the marriage

- they will be able to maintain and accommodate themselves adequately together with any dependants, in accommodation they own or occupy exclusively without recourse to public funds.

Someone seeking entry clearance as a fiancé(e) has to fulfil similar requirements.

A person granted entry clearance as a spouse will be given twelve months' leave to remain on entering the UK. They will be able to take employment within this period but will not be eligible for public funds. Before the end of the twelve months they must apply for settlement on the form SET(M) with proof they are living with their partner and there is maintenance and accommodation. A person granted entry clearance as a fiancé(e) will be initially given six months' leave. They will not be permitted to take employment during this period. Before the expiry of the six months and after marrying they must apply for a further twelve months' leave to remain on the grounds of marriage on form FLR(M) and before the expiry of that twelve months must apply for settlement on form SET(M).

A person who marries and seeks settlement while in the UK in some other temporary capacity, such as a student, must fulfil the same requirements as an applicant seeking entry clearance overseas. In addition they must show they are not in breach of any immigration law, such as overstaying their leave, and that their marriage has not taken place after a Home Office decision to remove or a recommendation of deportation by a criminal court. An application is made on form FLR(M). A successful application will result in an initial twelve months' leave.

THE RULES IN PRACTICE: THE NEED TO HAVE MET

This rule is discriminatory. It places an obstacle in the way of a small minority of arranged marriages where the couple do not on religious grounds meet before the wedding or where the wedding takes place by proxy. It is most likely to be an impediment in cases of fiancé(e) applications from abroad where the intention is for the couple to meet for the first time in the UK either prior to or at an arranged marriage.

NO RECOURSE TO PUBLIC FUNDS AND JOB OFFERS

The requirement for adequate maintenance and accommodation without re-course to public funds has become more significant in marriage cases with the repeal of the primary purpose rule. It provides another reason to refuse entry or settlement. The best practice is for neither partner to rely on public funds at time of application (see Chapter 3).

It is possible in marriage cases to argue that the person coming to the UK or applying for settlement has an offer of a job. However, immigration officials will want convincing proof of this. For instance a hand-written letter from a factory owner in the UK offering a job to someone in Pakistan will probably be rejected. The entry clearance officer (ECO) will want to know why this particular job is being offered to this particular person – a person whom the prospective employer may probably never have met. Also the ECO will want to know how long the job will be left open. If the settled partner is a woman who is presently not working but intends to work on her spouse's arrival then, if there are children, it is useful to show what childcare arrangements are intended. These issues are probably best dealt with by an explanatory letter from the sponsor's advisor. The overseas applicant should be given a copy of this letter as questions may be asked at the interview about its contents.

It is important not to inflate artificially the wages offered in a job. Either this will not be believed or it could provoke an ECO into thinking the reason the applicant wishes to come to the UK is to work without an intention to live with the sponsor.

POLYGAMOUS MARRIAGES

English law has always had a problem with polygamous marriages – not out of any concern for women's rights but out of an ideological defence of the nuclear family. In a decision well over a century ago on the status of polygamy Lord Penzance held that the only marital relationship recognised by English law was 'marriage as it is understood in Christendom'.[2]

Subsequently there has been partial recognition of such marriages contracted overseas, for instance to govern property rights on the breakdown of marriage. This recognition has extended into immigration law in that the spouse of a polygamous marriage may be allowed entry to join a partner. However under Section 2 of the 1988 Immigration Act a man can be joined only by one wife of such a marriage.

Douglas Hurd, the Home Secretary responsible for the Act, admitted to parliament: 'The number of polygamous wives coming here is quite small: we estimate that perhaps 25 or so polygamous households are set up here every year' (16 November 1987). Section 2 of the 1988 Immigration Act has ten sub-clauses. That is one clause for every 2.5 wives. This rate of exclusion must amount to a legislative record. The question is why is there such a massive juridical emphasis on an issue that even the law-makers consider virtually non-existent? Douglas Hurd's answer was: 'Polygamy is not an acceptable social custom in this country.' This shows that immigration control is ultimately not about numbers. It is about constructing English identity through the definition of marriage and family to the exclusion of all other identities.

INTENTION TO LIVE TOGETHER AND REPEAL OF PRIMARY PURPOSE RULE

It was hoped that with the repeal in June 1997 of the primary purpose rule, marriages would become immune from intrusive investigation. However, there remains the requirement for a couple to prove they intend to live together and that the marriage is still 'subsisting'. This allows for the re-emergence of the primary purpose rule in another guise. In a letter from the IND to GMIAU of November 1997 it was said:

> We do not accept, either under EC law or the UK immigration rules, that once a married couple are shown to be living together there can be no question of it being a marriage of convenience. They would in addition need to be in a genuine relationship which was not contracted solely to avoid immigration control. It is

not uncommon for people involved in marriages of convenience to be temporarily living under the same roof, for the purpose of convincing the immigration
authorities in the event of an unannounced home visit that they are in a genuine
relationship.[3]

This letter made one concession. The rule as to intention to live together 'does not
require the need for sexual relations, which is considered to be a private matter'.

TWELVE MONTHS' PROBATIONARY RULE

Marriages break down for many reasons. Within immigration control it can be
fatal if there is a breakdown within the twelve months' probationary period. This
can have particular consequences where there has been domestic violence and
there is now a government 'concession' allowing a party to remain where there is
proof of violence (see Chapter 9). There is another concession incorporated in the
immigration rules since 2 October 2000 allowing the overseas partner to remain
where the settled partner dies within the twelve-month period.

EEA NATIONALS

A marriage between a European Economic Area national and a non-EEA national
will enable the non-EEA spouse to remain in the UK irrespective of the immigration rules on the same terms as the EEA spouse – which in practice usually means
indefinitely as long as the EEA citizen is involved in any kind of economic
activity. Irish citizens are also EEA citizens and so marriage to an Irish citizen
living in the UK will normally allow a non-EEA citizen to remain. Paradoxically
British citizens are not regarded as EEA citizens for this purpose as the European
Union is premised on freedom of movement to work or study and most British
citizens have not moved to live in the UK.

The IND letter referred to above acknowledges: 'Neither the regulation on
free movement of workers (Regulation 1612/68) nor the directives on the rights
of residence make explicit reference to marriages of convenience'. The letter then
says 'but all Member States take action against them'. Case-law confirms that
marriages between EEA and non-EEA nationals can be categorised by the Home
Office as ones of convenience and these marriages do not confer rights of
residence. In practice such marriages are not usually investigated.

INTRUDING INTO THE MARITAL HOME

Intrusiveness by the Home Office extends into raiding the marital home to see
whether a marriage is one of convenience. This includes marriages by EEA
nationals to non-EEA nationals. The IND in a letter to the Immigration Law Practitioners' Association on 27 August 1997 states:

At present, where our staff suspect that a marriage may be one of convenience
entered into solely to enable the non-EEA national to benefit from rights of
residence under community law, consideration is given to inviting the couple to
attend an interview at the Public Enquiry Office. Such interviews are sometimes

followed by an unannounced home visit on the couple...unannounced home visits may be conducted without a preceding interview with the couple concerned.

A parliamentary written answer by Mike O'Brien MP, the minister responsible for immigration, on 26 April 1999 states that unannounced visits will be made where 'there are strong grounds to suspect that the couple are not living together or that the marriage is otherwise not genuine'. There is no clarification as to what is meant by 'otherwise not genuine' but it suggests the reintroduction of a test which looks at the initial purpose of the marriage. In a written parliamentary answer of 4 May 1999, Mike O'Brien refused to publish the guidelines given to immigration officers concerning marriage raids.

MARRIAGE REGISTRARS AND INTRUSIVENESS

For many years there has existed a system whereby registrars have reported suspected marriages of convenience to the Registrar-General, who has passed on information to the Home Office. In a written parliamentary answer of 22 July 1996, Angela Knight MP announced:

> During 1994 and 1995, superintendent registrars reported 470 and 555 cases to the Registrar-General where they suspected that a proposed marriage had been arranged for the sole purpose of evading statutory immigration controls. Of this number, information in respect of 404 and 467 respectively was passed to the Home Office. During the first six months of 1996, 309 reports have been received, of which 232 have been referred to the Home Office.

Accompanying this answer there is a league table of marriage registration districts where marriages have been reported to the Registrar-General during the period January 1994 until June 1996. Lewisham tops the list with 329 marriages reported compared to Manchester with 3 reported. The abolition of the primary purpose rule did not affect reporting of marriages. In a letter of 26 February 1999 from the Office for National Statistics to GMIAU it was stated that in 1997 and 1998 the number of marriages reported to the Home Office was 354 and 450 respectively.

THE 1999 IMMIGRATION AND ASYLUM ACT AND MARRIAGE REGISTRARS

The 1999 Immigration and Asylum Act imposes a duty (becoming operative on 1 January 2001) on marriage registrars to report directly to the Home Office where 'before, during or immediately after solemnisation of the marriage' the registrar has reasonable grounds for suspecting a marriage is a 'sham'. Under the Act:

> 'Sham' marriage means a marriage (whether or not void)
>
> (a) entered into between a person ('A') who is not an EEA national and a person who is an EEA national; and

(b) entered into by A for the purpose of avoiding the effect of one or more provisions of immigration law.

The concept of 'the purpose of avoiding' controls reincarnates the primary purpose rule. The Act empowers a registrar to demand evidence of one or both partners' nationality. This raises the question as to whether a suspect marriage involving a non-EEA national is reported to the authorities of the EEA national's country. A letter of 16 August 1999 from Lord Bassam at the Home Office to Ivan Lewis MP states: 'In line with existing practice [registrar] reports may be provided to the immigration authorities of other EEA Member States should they make enquiry'.

THE 1999 LEGISLATION AND THE ANGLICAN CHURCH

The Act changes marriage procedures. Both parties will now have to appear before the registrar in the registration district in which they live to give notice of the marriage. This is based on an assumption that couples of whom one is from overseas shop around to find the least intrusive registrars.

Jack Straw as Home Secretary said in parliament on 22 February 1999:

> changes in marriage law...are aimed at the abuse of civil marriage for immigration purposes. They will not in any way affect those who marry in the Church of England or the Church of Wales after banns. They will affect civil preliminaries for other religious marriages.

There exists a difference between other religious marriage ceremonies and those in the Church of England or Wales. Other ceremonies must follow civil preliminaries. This dates from the 1836 Marriage Act when the registration of non-Anglican marriages was first put on a statutory basis. In the Explanatory Notes accompanying the Immigration and Asylum Act it is said: 'There is no evidence to suggest that religious marriages after (Anglican) ecclesiastic preliminaries are abused for immigration advantage'. The construction of marriage is now seen within immigration laws not just as Christian but specifically as Anglican. This whole part of the 1999 legislation would appear to be in breach of Article 14 of the European Convention on Human Rights which outlaws discrimination on religious grounds.

DRAFT GUIDANCE TO MARRIAGE REGISTRARS

The Office for National Statistics is responsible for registrars. It has now produced (October 1999) draft guidelines on the new 1999 Act. These draft guidelines reveal how intrusive the new procedures are likely to be. In particular:

- The guidelines list factors to be obtained 'by direct observation or questioning of the parties' in determining whether to report a marriage. These are:

  ◦ parties giving the impression of knowing very little about each other

- ○ parties referring to notes to answer questions about the other partner
  - ○ reluctance to provide evidence of name, age, marital status or nationality
  - ○ unable to converse in the same language
  - ○ considerable age difference
  - ○ one of the couple may have exceeded their period of permitted stay in the UK
  - ○ one of the couple is seen to receive payment for the marriage.

- Registrars may ask for documents as proof of evidence of name and surname. Suggested documents in the draft guidelines include current valid full passport, a Home Office Travel Document, Standard Acknowledgement Letter issued by the Home Office in acknowledgement of an application for asylum or a national identity card.

- Other documents 'of less evidential value' may be produced such as a driving licence or a rent book.

- In a letter of 22 September 2000 from the General Register Office of the Office for National Statistics it is said that the October 1999 draft guidance are now being incorporated into the Handbook for Registration Officers 'whish is a technical instruction manual for registration officers and as such is not made avaliable to members of the public'.

Good practice

BETTER SAFE THAN SORRY!

It was seen previously that advisors should prepare cases cautiously and thoroughly in order to avoid clients being caught up in what remains of the immigration appeal system (see Chapter 3). Sometimes sponsors are anxious that an application is quickly resolved and, in the case of an overseas application, an entry clearance interview is held as soon as possible. Where there are complications then the sponsor has to be advised that a quick interview without having first sorted out the complications will result in a negative decision.

OVERSEAS MARRIAGE INTERVIEWS

This matter of proper preparation is posed acutely for applications made overseas. In this situation the applicant not only has to submit an application form, but also will be interviewed. This interview is critical. In marriage cases, the primary purpose rule has been abolished yet significant questions will be asked about intention to live together and the availability of adequate maintenance and accommodation. ECOs continue to doubt some cases based on dubious cultural assumptions. Marriages are being doubted where it is considered that there is a large age gap between the couple, especially if the woman is older.

It is essential that the applicant is prepared in advance for these questions. The preparation by necessity is made at a distance of thousands of miles. The advisor in the UK is consulted by the sponsor not by the applicant. Therefore quality time needs to be spent with the sponsor to enable him or her properly to communicate the relevant information and issues to the applicant.

Where the marriage is to take place overseas then the UK partner will have the opportunity to explain these matters in person to the overseas partner and also attend the interview. Partners will be interviewed separately. It is essential they provide the same account of the history of the relationship and do not contradict each other.

In any event in potentially problematic cases, it is often advisable for the client in the UK to attend the overseas interview – but only after being thoroughly prepared in advance and only after themselves thoroughly preparing the overseas partner.

REMEMBERING WHAT WAS SAID AT ANY PREVIOUS INTERVIEW

In settlement applications made from within the UK, the legal advisor should check what was said previously overseas at any entry clearance or visa application. It is essential that there is no contradiction between what was said overseas and what is being said in the UK. If a man at a visitor's visa interview said he would be returning home in three months to marry his fiancée then it could lead to problems if he married someone within the UK and thereafter applied for settlement. If there are any apparent contradictions then these need to be explained. They should not be ignored. Exactly the same applies to someone who came to the UK without requiring a visa (for instance a visitor from Jamaica) but was fully interviewed on arrival. However, it is unlikely that a brief couple of questions asked on entering through immigration control would be recorded.

PUBLIC FUNDS AND DISABILITY ISSUES

The no recourse to public funds and adequate maintenance rules produce constantly recurring disability issues particularly within marriage cases. This is the case if either the settled sponsor or non-settled applicant is disabled. Recourse to public funds by the former may result in a finding of inadequate maintenance for the latter. Concern about the latter having recourse to public funds on settlement may result in a refusal of application. The following is typical:

One case concerned a young woman who was a permanent resident in the UK whose husband had been refused permission to join her. The woman was caring for her year-old child. Prior to the birth of the baby the woman worked and sustained herself and her household, however afterwards she developed a debilitating illness and was unable to continue working. Although [it was] accepted that the relationship was genuine, her illness was the basis of grounds for refusing the application on the belief that it was 'likely that the family would have recourse to public funds'. The family was unable to attain financial independence without the husband being allowed to enter the UK so that he could work and support the family, however [permission was refused] because the woman was not financially independent.

This case is quoted in *The Child Welfare Implications of UK Immigration and Asylum Policy* by Adele Jones (pp.22–3).

This raises one specific issue of good practice – namely the need for appropriate disability organisations to be involved in the preparation of a case. Unless the husband in this case can secure a credible offer of employment then entry will be constantly denied. In such a situation an application will have to be made outside the rules on compassionate grounds. Another scenario is where an elderly man on a pension and too ill to return to his country of origin wants to bring in his wife to look after him. Pressure will have to be brought in order to secure entry. All effort should be made to enlist the support of disability groups to bring such pressure. This is a particular example of campaigning (see Chapter 19). A letter of 14 March 2000 to the Immigration Advisory Service from the Immigration and Nationality Policy Directorate says that 'a review is being undertaken of the policy with regard to disabled sponsors and their ability to meet the maintenance and accommodation requirements'.

MARRIAGE REGISTRARS

Marriage registrars are statutory postholders. Their posts are created by the Registration Acts. As such they do not have an employer in the usual sense. They are answerable to the Registrar-General. However, local authorities provide the local registrar with office accommodation and pay the salaries of officers. Only the Registrar-General can dismiss these statutory postholders. Local authorities have the responsibility to recruit them. They are represented by UNISON, the local authority union. For most practical purposes therefore they are equivalent to local authority workers and it should be a matter of concern to these authorities that registrars are now expected to police immigration control.

Registrars are confronted by two interlinked issues. They have the power to check on whether a marriage is one of convenience. They have a statutory duty to report such marriages to the Home Office. Any basic good anti-racist practice guidelines would include the following:

- Marriage is an entitlement irrespective of immigration status.

- The assumption should be that a marriage is a matter of private concern between the couple involved.

- In the absence of overwhelming contrary evidence it is misconceived to 'suspect' that a marriage is one of convenience.

- A couple are not under the burden of proving and a registrar is not under the burden of actively investigating that a marriage is or is not one of convenience. In any one case a registrar is entitled to conclude that irrespective of any subjective opinion there are (to quote draft guidelines) no 'reasonable grounds for suspecting that the proposed marriage will be (or is) a sham marriage'. In particular draft guidelines specifically warn registrars to 'ensure that a sham marriage is not confused with a marriage arranged by members of the family of the couple without any intent of avoiding the provisions of immigration law'.

LEGAL ADVISORS AND MARRIAGE CEREMONIES

Of the grounds suggested in the Office for National Statistics guidelines as showing a sham marriage, the most critical is that of either of the couple exceeding their leave to remain in the UK. It is important in these situations to avoid giving registrars documentary evidence that shows this. This may be difficult where, for instance, the only evidence as to age and nationality is a passport. In some cases it may be possible to obtain other sorts of proof from the country of origin – such as a birth certificate where birth in the country confers automatic citizenship.

In circumstances where it is thought the registrar may consider a prospective marriage to be one of convenience then it may now be good practice for a legal advisor to accompany a client who is giving notice of marriage.

In theory a marriage cannot be prevented from taking place solely because it is suspected of being a marriage of convenience. This was confirmed in the letter of 26 February 1999 from the Office for National Statistics to GMIAU. However, the same result can be achieved by refusing the marriage on the grounds that a legal impediment exists – for instance doubts as to the identity of the applicant. Where a marriage is refused then an appeal can be made in writing to the Registrar-General. Legal advisors need to consider this because winning such an appeal may also help in the immigration matter if the registrar reports the marriage application to the Home Office.

The only way of avoiding these internal controls appears to be, where this is acceptable to the couple, for an Anglian wedding to be undertaken, though the priest would also have to agree. Even this presents difficulties. According to 'Guidance of The Clergy with Reference To The Marriage and Registration Acts' issued in 1982 by the Registrar General, the Legal Board of the Church Assembly of the Church of England recommends that all marriages to which a 'foreigner' is a party should be by licence and not after banns – and it is only a marriage following banns that is apparently, according to Jack Straw's above comments of 22 February 1999, exempt from the provisions of the 1999 legislation. The reason given in 'Guidance of the Clergy' for this different treatment for 'foreigners' is 'in order that the Diocesan authorities may ensure that the legal requirement of the foreigner's country are observed' – which seems to place on clergy rather a heavy burden of knowledge of international marriage law. A letter of 21 September 2000 from the Registrar at the Faculty Office of the Archbishop of Canterbury does say that where a foreign national is 'resident' in this country then the priest can decide by which process a marriage takes place. Residency, though, is not defined. Under immigration law 'residency' can exist even where a person's stay in the UK is time-limited, if this is the country where they are normally living for the time being (see Chapter 14).

Comments on casework problem at start of chapter

The basic advice is that X needs to see a specialist immigration representative as soon as possible. You can familiarise her with the problems. Z will have many difficult issues to deal with at his entry clearance interview. His interview is in two weeks' time, which is probably far too short a period for information to be communicated to him about the issues. Z's representative will need to ask the entry clearance officer to postpone the interview, which is usually possible. The next piece of advice is that entry clearance officers in India and Pakistan often assert that there is a cultural bias against men marrying divorced women and therefore may allege that this is a marriage of convenience, with Z having no intention to live together with X. It will be necessary for Z at the interview to show that there is no such cultural norm. It will probably be necessary for Z to give details of how he and X met and how their relationship developed. In this respect it could be useful to produce letters between the couple after X returned to the UK showing devotion between them. This is the sort of evidence that was expected in the old primary purpose cases and is again becoming necessary in order to show intent to live together. It could also be asserted by the entry clearance officer that there is insufficient maintenance available without recourse to additional public funds (see Chapter 3). X's benefits are not sufficient for two people. In any event in law Z will not be entitled to income support or disability living allowance until he has gained settlement; even trying to claim this would be interpreted as recourse to public funds (see Chapters 3 and 12). It is vital that Z gets a job offer which is viable and credible. Moreover this job will have to pay enough money to at least compensate for the fact that X, as a married woman dependant, will lose her entitlement to income support and housing benefit – though she will keep her DLA as it is not means tested. The couple will be able to claim working families' tax credit if they have children (see Chapter 3). X should be advised that it may be best that, if possible, she also went to the interview. It would provide her with an opportunity of directly communicating on the issues with Z. It will allow her at the interview to corroborate what Z says. If she did go to the interview she would be seen separately from Z.

Notes

1   1985 Immigration Appeals Reports (Imm AR) p.39
2   *Hyde* v. *Hyde* 1866
3   Published in *Immigration and Nationality Law and Practice* (*INLP*) vol. 12, no.2, 1998, p.65

CHAPTER 6

Dividing families

Children, parents and other relatives

You work in a day centre for elderly people used by X. He came to the UK in 1972 from Bangladesh, leaving his wife and two children there. Child A was born in 1970 and child B in 1971. X visited Bangladesh in 1979 when another child, C, was conceived. X then returned to the UK. In 1982 Mrs X applied to the British High Commission for herself and her children to join X. The children were refused. Bangladesh had no birth registration system and parentage could not be proved. The family appealed and lost. In 1985 X became a British citizen. In 1989 he visited Bangladesh for the marriages of A and B. Another child, D, was subsequently born. In 1992 Mrs X died. In 1993 X lost his job and is now unemployed. In 1994 A's wife died, leaving him to raise two children. X would like his unmarried child, C, to care for him. He would like D to live with him and B to visit him. A would like to come to the UK with his children to live near his father. X asks your advice.

Why am I going to these meetings? Why am I getting people to help me? Because they are my children. Do you think it is easy to campaign? Do you think that it is easy going out in all weathers to campaign? Do you think it is easy doing all these things? It's really ridiculous, making black people suffer and destroying their families. What kind of law is this? God knows what hell we are going through.

These are Anwar Ditta's words in the 1980 Anwar Ditta Defence Campaign's pamphlet 'Bring Anwar's children home, stop the forced separation of black families'. Anwar was born in the UK but went to Pakistan after her parents separated. She married Shuja Ud Din. They had three children – Kamran, Imran and Saima. Anwar returned to the UK with Shuja and in 1976 applied for the children to join them. The entry clearance officer in Islamabad said that the children were not related as claimed and therefore not 'genuine'. The Home Office made the bizarre speculation that 'there might be two Anwar Sultana Dittas, i.e. one who married Shuja Ud Din in Pakistan and the other whom Shuja Ud Din married in the United Kingdom in 1975'.[1] A massive campaign was built. Granada Television sent a film crew to Pakistan where newly developed blood tests proved parentage. The children were allowed entry.

SCOPE OF THIS CHAPTER

The aim of this chapter is to extend the discussion on the separation of spouses into an examination of how immigration controls generally divide families on a global basis. The very existence of controls makes this division inevitable.

FURTHER READING RESOURCES

Immigration and Adoption by Claudia Mortimore was published in 1994 by Trentham Books. GMIAU has produced a resource pack of annotated documents, *Children, the Family and Immigration Controls,* last updated in 1997. There are two old pamphlets illustrating how entry clearance procedures keep family members out of the UK: 'Where do you keep your string beds?', a study of entrance clearance in Pakistan (Runnymede Trust 1974) by Mohammed Akram and Sarah Leigh and 'But my cows aren't going to England' (South Manchester Law Centre 1983) by Amrit Wilson and Sushma Lal.

INTRUSIVENESS

Controls physically humiliate children. In one case a 'medical report', commissioned by the High Commission in Dacca, Bangladesh, to assess the age of a girl applying to join her father, stated with clinical coldness:

> Pubic hairs appear at 12 and are present, axilla hairs appear at 12/13 and are present, menstruation in girls starts at 12/13 and has already started. External genitals are developed at 13 and had already developed.

This is quoted in 'But my cows aren't going to England'.

SOME HISTORY

Family separation is intrinsic to controls (see Chapter 2). On 11 October 1907 the *Jewish Chronicle* reported: 'the Grimsby Board refused a man named Crystal to visit his son…in London… Another elderly immigrant, who was incapable of work, was rejected although his son was willing and able to take care of him.' On 1 November 1907 the paper reported Meyer Basovski being refused entry to join his brother. A member of the Appeal Board denounced the brother, saying: 'You have been in England three years and yet you know no English. You ought to be ashamed of yourself.'

Children

THE BASIC IMMIGRATION RULES

In addition to the maintenance, accommodation and no recourse to public funds requirements the rules specify:

- 'both parents are present and settled in the United Kingdom…or one parent is present and settled in the United Kingdom and the other is being admitted on the same occasion for settlement.' Children accompanying their mother to join a father receive twelve months' probationary leave and are liable to expulsion if the marriage collapses.

- 'or one parent is present and settled in the UK…and the other parent is dead or one parent is…settled in the United Kingdom…and has the sole responsibility for the child's upbringing'

- 'or one parent or relative is…settled in the United Kingdom…and there are…compelling family or other considerations which make exclusion of the child undesirable…'

- The child must be under 18 and 'is not leading an independent life, is unmarried and has not formed an independent family unit'.

THE 'NON-GENUINE' CHILD: CRITIQUE OF DNA TESTING

There is another hurdle – proving identity. The issue of the 'non-genuine, not related as claimed' child did not disappear with the invention in the 1980s of DNA blood-testing proving parentage. Instead the system becomes a maze as opposed to a dead-end. A critique of DNA testing includes the following:

- It is premised on the superiority of family relationships over other forms of relationship and of the superiority of the nuclear family over other familial relationships. Most children found not 'genuine' are related to the sponsor and partner and raised as members of an extended family.

- It is bodily intrusive. It is literally giving blood to enter the UK.

- It is expensive at approximately £150 per person tested. For parents with five children this would be over £1000. In 1991 the immigration authorities agreed to offer free tests to first-time child applicants but not for children previously refused. It may be possible to obtain legal aid if the sponsor qualifies financially.

- It is not always suitable to prove relationships. This is particularly the case where both parents are dead.

- Parentage may be proven yet most children have become too old for entry, having spent years trying to gain admittance to the UK. 18 is the cut-off age. Douglas Hurd, then Home Secretary, said in parliament on 14 June 1989 that over-age children could be given entry where they are unmarried, dependent on the sponsor and there exist strong compassionate circumstances. Few such children have been admitted and there are no plans to remedy this injustice.

- It can further divide families, for instance where some children are aged under 18 and others over.

- It places mothers in potentially violent situations where tests show the child is the mother's but not the father's. A letter from the IND to GMIAU of 5 May 1999 states 'Where it appears that an illegitimate child has been brought up as the child of the family, it will normally be appropriate to admit the child'. This does not resolve the possibility of violence or rejection of the child if the sponsor sees the test results.

LONE PARENTS

The rules allow settlement to join a single parent where the other is dead. Otherwise there is discrimination against lone parents. The rules demand that a lone parent retain 'sole responsibility for the child's upbringing'. Sole responsibility has been interpreted to mean 'main' responsibility. This rule initially was directed at all male Pakistani households where boys from Pakistan came to join a father. In practice it was used against Caribbean and West African women who came to work while leaving children with grandparents intending to bring them later. More recently the rule has been used against Filipino women who came as exploited labour leaving children with relatives. After long battles the women won settlement but found that they had no right to be reunited with their children.

A misogynistic moralism permeates legal decisions on 'sole responsibility'. It harks back to judgemental attitudes about 'illegitimate' children, with illegitimacy now being transferred to immigration status. The moralism castigates mothers for 'abandoning' children. In one case an adjudicator opined: 'no reasonable person would agree that the mother and child ought to be reunited' where the child had been left in another's care for five years.'

Continued financial and decision-making involvement is necessary to prove sole responsibility. Under pressure the Home Office introduced a 'concession' in 1975 which since 1976 has applied to children under 12. Such children can join lone parents provided there is maintenance available and 'if the parent is the father, there is a female relative resident in the household who is willing to look after the child and is capable of doing so'.

EXCLUSION UNDESIRABLE

There is provision for a child to join a lone parent or any relative where there are compelling family or other considerations making exclusion undesirable and there are suitable care arrangements. It is extremely hard to fit within this rule. The JCWI *Immigration, Nationality and Refugee Law Handbook* (1999 edn, p.60) describes one case where an overseas father had sexually assaulted his daughter but 'only' beaten his sons. The girl's appeal to join her mother was allowed but her brother's was dismissed.

ADOPTION

Adoption poses three questions: whether and how a child adopted overseas can join adoptive parents in the UK; whether and how a child can be brought to the UK for adoption; whether and how an overseas child already here in some temporary capacity can be adopted. This last scenario is discussed in examining whether family court orders can prevent expulsions (see Chapter 11).

The rules deal with the situation of a child adopted overseas coming for settlement. Children coming for adoption were not only included in the rules in October 2000 but there was and is published policy which allows for entry. Both scenarios are explained in the IND leaflet 'Inter-country adoption'.[3] The Department of Health published in May 1997 *A Guide to Intercountry Adoption Practice and Procedures*. These documents will require updating when the 1999 Adoption (Intercountry Aspects) Act comes into force.

NON-FAMILY AND INTER-FAMILY ADOPTIONS

Adoptions of overseas children occur for two reasons. Well publicised are adoptions by non-relatives. These rest on problematic assumptions about the superiority of Western lifestyles. They consist of childless British couples flying to poverty-stricken countries essentially to buy and return with a child – often contravening the requirement for prior entry clearance, confident that the immigration authorities will not object. As long ago as 7 March 1985 the *Guardian* published an article 'Airports turn blind eye on adoption smuggling'. Some adoptions consist of apparent angels of mercy descending on orphanages, as in Romania following the overthrow of the Ceauçescu regime, and bringing back children for adoption. This was criticised in parliament on 23 April 1999 by Ann Coffey MP:

> The British Agencies for Adoption and Fostering say in one of their leaflets that although adoption may be the answer for one individual, it will never be the solution for meeting the needs of millions of children in families in situations of extreme deprivation.

The other reason for adoption is inter-family adoption between relatives and is most common among people from the Indian subcontinent. Inter-family adoptions allow an opportunity for a child to retain contact with the original family. They are usually ignored in official literature. The Department of Health local authority circular on 'Adoption – achieving the right balance' does not mention inter-family adoptions.[4] Likewise the consultation document on Adoption produced in July 2000 by the Performance and Innovation Unit at the Prime Minister's request fails to mention inter-family adoptions.

SEEKING SETTLEMENT AS AN ADOPTED CHILD

The rules for settlement in the UK of children adopted overseas state:

- The adoption must be 'in accordance with a decision taken by the competent administrative authority or court in [the child's] country of origin or the country in which he is resident'. This should be read alongside the Adoption (Designation of Overseas Adoptions) Order 1973 which provides a list of countries whose adoptions are recognised in the UK. Most are Commonwealth or European Union countries and are listed in the IND leaflet. Adoptions are recognised which take place in countries with which the UK has a bilateral agreement – presently only Romania. Adoptions are also recognised in countries which have ratified the 1965 Hague Convention on Jurisdiction, Applicable Law and Recognition of Decrees relating to Adoptions. This is essentially defunct. Only three countries have ratified it: Switzerland, Austria and the UK. It has been replaced by the 1993 Hague Convention discussed below.

- The adoption must have taken place 'due to the inability of the original parent(s) or current carer(s) to care for him and there has been a genuine transfer of parental responsibility to the adoptive parent'. The requirement to prove inability to care is stricter than domestic cases where the issue is the child's best interests.

- The child must have 'lost or broken its ties with his family of origin'. This offends modern adoption practice. It makes inter-family adoptions extremely difficult.

- The adoption must not be 'one of convenience arranged to facilitate his admission to or remaining in the United Kingdom'. This is a cynical example of familial relationships being classified as 'bogus' by immigration laws. A recent case held that advantages resulting from a changed immigration status do not necessarily render an adoption one of 'convenience' (see Chapter 11).

- An adopted child will be given permanent settlement on entry.

INFORMAL (DE FACTO) ADOPTIONS

The rule requiring the decision of an administrative authority or court is designed to overturn judicial decisions holding that informal de facto adoptions are recognised for immigration purposes. This non-recognition of de facto adoptions is directed against inter-family adoptions in Muslim countries such as Pakistan and Bangladesh (unlike India) where there exist no formal procedures. However, according to the IND leaflet there remains government policy allowing entry where the child is so 'integrated in the family that he can be considered to be an adopted child' and the adoptive parent(s) have been resident abroad for 'a substantial period of time'. An IND letter to the GMIAU of 5 May 1999 defines this as 'usually in excess of 12 months'.

A letter of 28 April 2000 from the IND Policy Directorate to the author says

The de facto adoption concession operates to reflect a process where adoptive parents are not restricted to parents who have adopted a child through a process that was legally recognised under United Kingdom law. It is neither intended to, nor does, confer any 'advantage' over other reasons for admittance to the UK as a prospective adoptee.[5]

However, unlike a prospective adoptee, a de facto adopted child will, if allowed entry, normally be given immediate settlement. Moreover formal adoption procedures within the UK are not compulsory for the de facto adopted child to remain in the UK, though in practice such procedures should be initiated to provide the child with a clear legal status.

THE 1993 HAGUE CONVENTION

Inter-family adoptions are subject to bureaucratic delays. This has never been subject to public criticism. However, there was an outcry by English parents in search of Romanian children in 1988–9. This resulted in a section on 'Adopting from overseas' in the 1993 Department of Health White Paper on *Adoption – The Future*.[6] This document essentially ignored inter-family adoptions. It emphasised the implementation of the 1993 Hague Convention on the Protection of Children and Co-operation in Respect of Inter-Country Adoptions. This envisages an international system of mutual recognition of adoptions. The Convention excludes countries, in particular Muslim states, without formal adoption procedures.

THE 1999 ADOPTION (INTERCOUNTRY ASPECTS) ACT

The Adoption (Intercountry Aspects) Act was passed in 1999. It will probably become fully operative by 2001. Under the Adoption (Intercountry Aspects) Act 1999 Commencement Order that part entered into force 31 January 2000 which confirms that in inter-country cases a home study assessment report must be prepared by or on behalf of an adoption agency. There are parliamentary guides to the Act: the Explanatory Notes accompanying the Bill,[7] and a research paper produced by the Social Policy Section of the House of Commons Library.[8] The Act's main details are:

- It ratifies the 1993 Hague Convention.

- An adoption order made by a UK court will be a 'Convention' adoption if it meets requirements to be specified in Regulations. This will lead to recognition by other contracting states.

- Adoption services provided by local authorities must include all adoptions not just those made in the UK.

- Voluntary adoption agencies approved under the 1976 Adoption Act may be approved to provide an inter-country adoption service.

- A Convention adoption made in a child's state of origin will confer British nationality on the child provided that the adoptive parent (or one of them in a joint adoption) is a British national at the time the adoption order is made and the parent (or both in a joint adoption) is habitually resident in the UK. British children are not subject to controls.

- When the Act becomes fully operative there will be two categories of countries whose adoptions are recognised: first, countries which have ratified or acceded to the Convention, and second, designated countries in Regulations made under the 1999 Act. It is expected that these will consist mainly of European Union countries and countries with which the UK has a bilateral agreement. The 1973 regulations will be repealed

COMING TO THE UK FOR ADOPTION

Consideration needs to be given to bringing a child to the UK for adoption where there are no adoption procedures in the country of origin or no procedures recognised in the UK including an informal (de facto) adoption.

The process was previously outside the immigration rules but is now included in the October 2000 rule changes. The basic requirements are similar to those for children in a recognised adoption overseas – inability of original parents to provide care, transfer of parental responsibility, breaking of ties with family of origin and proposed adoption not being one of convenience. Entry will initially be for twelve months while adoption proceedings are finalised.

PROCEDURES

The Department of Health's May 1997 guide contains a summary of procedures for bringing a child for adoption or bringing a child whose adoption is recognised in the UK:

- Applicants contact their local social services department (SSD).

- SSD completes a home study report in accordance with UK requirements and those of authorities in chosen overseas country. It is for the applicants to provide evidence of such requirements.

- Application is considered by the Adoption Panel and agency decision-maker makes and confirms the decision to approve.

- SSD sends home study, medical reports and police references to the Department of Health under cover of agency decision-maker's letter of recommendation.

- If the Department of Health supports the application, a Department of Health Certificate is issued.

- Where required, the Department of Health co-ordinates notarisation of all papers. If notarisation of home study is not required, the applicants make separate arrangements for other papers.

- The Department of Health forwards all papers to the Foreign and Commonwealth Office for legalisation.

- Papers are returned to the Department of Health.

- Translation requirements must be considered here. May be carried out by an independent translator in the UK, the embassy or consulate (of the child's country) or undertaken in the child's country. The Department of Health will co-ordinate.

- Papers forwarded to the child's country of residence either via the foreign embassy or consulate or, more usually, by the Department of Health.

- Agency in country will consider application.

- If approved, agency in country identifies child and sends information on the child to the UK.

- Prospective adopters travel to meet the child. In married couple cases, both must meet the child before entry clearance is granted.

- Adopters apply for UK entry clearance for the child as soon as his/her details are known.

- Adopters fulfil country's conditions and requirements for adoption hearing or equivalent in that country.

- Following adoption or equivalent in child's country, UK entry clearance procedure is completed.

- Adopters and child travel to the UK.

- Adopters inform SSD (in cases of non-recognised adoptions) of their intention to adopt under UK law.

- Child is treated as privately fostered child pending application to court and Schedule 2 process.

Elderly parents and grandparents

THE BASIC IMMIGRATION RULES

In addition to the no recourse to public funds, adequate maintenance and accommodation requirements it is necessary to show:

- They are widows or widowers aged 65 or over or are travelling together as a couple and one is aged 65 or over.

- If they have married again they are 65 or over and cannot look to the spouse or children of the second marriage for support.

- If they are under 65 they are living alone in the 'most exceptional compassionate circumstances'.

- They are financially wholly or mainly dependent on the children or grandchildren in the UK.

- They have no close relatives in their own country to whom they could turn for financial support.

THE PROBLEMS: PROOF OF AGE

All of these requirements represent impediments to family unity. The age requirement presents practical problems for elderly people from countries with no birth registration system and who do not know their exact date of birth. Passports sometimes show only an approximate date.

FINANCIAL DEPENDENCY

The requirement for financial dependency on children or grandchildren in the UK poses problems of proof. These may be overcome by the sponsor keeping copies of all evidence of finances transferred overseas. The evidence needs to go as far back in time as possible to show that dependency has not been created for immigration purposes. Problems of proof arise when monies are physically taken overseas via friends or relatives. The friend or relative should make a dated note of the monies. The need to retain evidence on the hypothesis that the (grand)parent may one day want to live in the UK is degrading.

EMOTIONAL DEPENDENCY

There are old judicial decisions suggesting that emotional dependency on an adult (grand)child in the UK will fulfil immigration rule requirements. This has now probably become of marginal significance because the present rules explicitly mention the need for financial dependency. By implication little weight will be given to emotional ties.

PARENTS UNDER 65 AND OTHER RELATIVES

There is theoretical provision for (grand)parents under 65 and other relatives to settle in the UK. Other relatives are defined as sons, daughters, brothers, sisters, uncles or aunts over 18. It is necessary to show that the relative is living alone in 'the most exceptional compassionate circumstances', a test which hardly anyone can fulfil. Nephews, nieces, cousins, half-brothers and half-sisters are not mentioned in the rules – although they could all identify as members of the same extended family.

Good practice

The rules concerning family members wanting settlement do not facilitate unity of families. They lead to their global separation. Therefore many of the practice issues relating to spouses re-emerge and should be consulted (see Chapter 5).

REPORT WRITING

The rules for children, parents and other relatives are narrowly defined. There is always the option of making an application for entry clearance or settlement outside the rules on 'compassionate' grounds. This will probably require welfare reports (see Chapter 9).

There are some applications for family unity made within the rules that may also require social enquiry reports including reports from overseas. International Social Services may be able to provide country of origin reports. Sometimes the rules explicitly refer to compassionate grounds as in the case of parents under 65 and other relatives. Another example is the rule relating to the entry or stay of a child on 'compelling' grounds rendering exclusion 'undesirable'.

In cases concerning 'compelling' or 'compassionate' grounds, case law and ministerial statements emphasise that these grounds are applicable to the situation of the applicant overseas rather than the sponsor here.

Good practice in children cases

CHILDREN AS AUTONOMOUS BEINGS

The Children's Rights Development Unit, established in 1992 to encourage the implementation of the UN Convention on the Rights of the Child 1989, produced an action report – *UK Agenda for Children*. This comments (paragraph 5.1.1):

> Historically adoption has tended to be viewed as a service for adults wanting a child rather than one promoting the rights of children… The very language used – 'available for adoption' – implies a commodity for parents rather than a service for children.

Immigration restrictions reduce children to passive objects whose destiny is under the control of immigration officialdom. There are two good practice standards. First, the best interests of the child should be the only concern. Second, the wishes of the children must be ascertained and heeded. Children should be treated as autonomous human beings and it not assumed that their wishes are the same as their parents' or guardians'. If there emerge conflicts between the wishes of the child and those of the parent(s) or guardian(s) then the advisor should not act for both. Where the child is overseas it may be difficult to discover directly his or her wishes. The advisor should probe parent(s) or relative(s) here about the child's desires.

LISTENING TO THE CHILD: UN CONVENTION ON THE RIGHTS OF THE CHILD 1989

The UK signed this Convention with the reservation that none of its provisions extended to Britain's immigration and nationality laws. It is arguable that many standards contained within the Convention have achieved sufficient international acceptance that the reservation may be irrelevant.

The Convention has moral authority and should be quoted by welfare practitioners in immigration reports (see Chapter 9). There are three Articles containing the underlying principles of the Convention which conflict with British immigration control. Article 2 confirms that all rights must apply without discrimination. Article 3 refers to the need to consider the best interests of the child. Article 12 endorses the right of a child to express an opinion and have that opinion taken into account. *UK Agenda for Children* says, in respect to Article 12:

- provision for the views and wishes of affected children to be heard either directly or through representatives should be mandatory in all immigration hearings affecting the child...

- whenever children are interviewed by entry clearance officers, immigration officers, or staff at the Asylum Division of the Home Office, the following should apply: the interviewing officer must be properly trained in interviewing children; the child should be accompanied by a trusted adult or representative; the surroundings should be agreeable to the child and not intimidating; where interpretation is required the interpreter should be skilled in interpreting for children.

INTERVIEWING CHILDREN BY IMMIGRATION OFFICIALS

A letter of 23 June 1999 from the IND to the GMIAU explained the interviewing of children overseas:

Applicants are only interviewed by entry clearance officers if they are over the age of 14 years. Children between the ages of 10 and 14 may be interviewed but only in the presence of a parent, guardian or responsible adult... ECOs should confine their questions to relatively simple matters... All interviews are carried out by fully trained entry clearance officers. Their course consists of extensive role playing exercises in order that they practise and hone their interviewing techniques.

Another letter of 14 June 1999 from IND to GMIAU dealt with interviews of children in the UK. This said:

> Some immigration officers are specially trained to interview asylum-seeking unaccompanied minors. While no specific training is given to immigration officers concerning the interviewing of children who are not seeking asylum, officers who have been trained to interview asylum-seeking children will be used wherever possible in all interviews concerning children.

Asylum interviews are considered later in Chapter 8.

Children aged 14 years are too young to be interviewed alone. Good practice demands that an advisor should attend any interview of a person under 18; in fact advisors should attend all interviews of clients of whatever age (see Chapter 3). The advisor should ask in advance that the interviewing officer be trained in child interviews and also ask about the interview's purpose.

It is helpful if the advisor draws up a statement on behalf of the young person and submits this in advance to the immigration official. Where the interview is overseas it will be far more difficult for the advisor to attend – though in extreme cases this may be advisable. The advisor should insist that no one under 18 be interviewed without a responsible adult such as a relative being present. An overseas child should be prepared for the interview by the advisor in the UK through family already in the UK.

CHILD IMMIGRATION ISSUES AND SOCIAL SERVICE CORPORATE PLANNING

Principles of social inclusion require that social services departments incorporate the needs of children subject to immigration controls within local authority corporate strategy. This rarely happens. A 1995 Manchester Council/National Children's Bureau report on *Championing Children* omits all reference to children threatened by controls. A Manchester Council/Manchester Health Authority report, *Children's Services Plan 1997–2000: A Strategic Framework*, fails to mention immigration issues.

ADOPTION CASES: USEFUL NON-GOVERNMENTAL GUIDES

There are guides to adoptions with an overseas element which clarify the procedures and suggest good practice. These are *Intercountry Adoption* produced by British Agencies for Adoption and Fostering (BAAF) and *Intercountry Adoption: Pre and Post-adoption Practice and Procedures* produced by the Post-Adoption Centre.

THE PROBLEMATIC OF 'FULL' ADOPTIONS

An adopted child should be allowed contact with the birth family. This raises issues for inter-country adoptions. Some countries have processes which retain links with birth parents. These are known as 'simple adoptions'. UK law is based on the concept of 'full adoption', a process which is irrevocable and severs all legal ties with the birth family. This is problematic: it is based on assumptions about nuclearity of families and ownership of a child rather than on the best interests of and responsibilities towards the child. It assumes that a child's background can be obliterated and a new life started without reference to the past. The White Paper, *Adoption: The Future*, proposed a system of 'Inter-Vivos Guardianship' orders as an alternative to full adoptions. This has not been implemented.

LOCAL AUTHORITIES AND ADOPTION

Good practice entails social services departments assuming responsibility for assisting entry of children adopted overseas and entry of children coming for adoption.

Some authorities have been reluctant on principle to assess parents wishing to adopt from overseas. The principle appears to be one of opposition to inter-country adoptions. Such a refusal is problematic. It is a form of blanket immigration control. The Adoption (Intercountry Aspects) Act will impose the following duties on local authorities (or accredited adoption agencies):

(a) collect preserve and exchange information about the situation of the child and the prospective adoptive parents, so far as is necessary to complete the adoption;

(b) facilitate, follow and expedite proceedings with a view to obtaining the adoption;

(c) promote the development of adoption, counselling and post-adoption services.

DEMANDING PAYMENT

The White Paper, *Adoption: the Future*, stated that it was intended to give local authorities power to charge for inter-country adoption services but not for the domestic adoption process. It is often existing practice for those authorities prepared to provide an inter-country adoption service to demand payment. A letter of 11 May 1999 from the Assistant Director, Families and Children, of Manchester Council to GMIAU said that social services charged up to £4500 to prepare reports on Manchester residents wishing to adopt a child from overseas. To charge for inter-country adoption services but not domestic services is discriminatory and may be in breach of race relations legislation.

GOOD PRACTICE IN LOCAL AUTHORITY REPORTS

There are two situations where local social services will be required to prepare reports in inter-country adoptions: first, when requested by authorities in the country of origin for adoption proceedings there, and second, for entry clearance purposes.

Social inquiry reports should follow the guidance in *Adoption: The Future* and should be 'free from any prejudice against the principle of intercountry adoption'. The same criterion of child welfare should be used as in domestic adoption cases. The Post-Adoption Centre guidelines suggest:

- Format – It may be helpful to adapt the usual (domestic) format to incorporate in a systematic way the additional dimensions of intercountry adoptions…

- Content – It is important to bear in mind the perspectives and sensitivities of the relevant state of origin. Implied criticisms of the state will not be favourably received and may prejudice individual applications.

- Length/style – Translation is often necessary and costly. Brevity and simplicity of writing styles are therefore appropriate aims.

REPORTS REQUIRED FOR ENTRY CLEARANCE

In addition to an up-to-date social services home study report, the IND leaflet says there is also required

> a contemporary report from the overseas equivalent of the social services department which details the child's parentage and history, the degree of contact with the original parent(s), the reasons for the adoption, the date, reasons and arrangements for the child's entry into an institution or foster placement and when, how and why the child came to be offered to the adoptive parent(s). Where no legal adoption has taken place, or where a legal adoption has taken place and the adoptive parent(s) were previously related to the child and for this reason the social services department did not complete a report, a full written account which covers these points should be provided by the adoptive or pro-spective adoptive parent(s).

A 'contemporary' report is one done at the time of adoption.

GOOD PRACTICE, ADOPTION AND JUDGE BRACEWELL

In 1999 in the case of Re R (Inter-Country Adoptions), Judge Bracewell suggested a series of practice guides for all agencies involved in inter-country adoptions.[9] Some of these reflect and reproduce the tension between repressive immigration laws and the welfare of the child. For instance the judge recommended speeding up procedures to allow for the speedy expulsion of children where UK courts do not allow an adoption. However, other suggestions are relatively positive. They are unusual as they are particularly directed against white 'angels of mercy' who assume that they have the privilege to circumvent rules and procedures. The suggested guidelines are lengthy and include the following suggestions:

- To local authorities: inter-country adoptions should be dealt with at director level: if authorities are not satisfied about the welfare issues and adoption proceedings have not commenced then proceedings should be commenced under Parts IV (care and supervision) and V (protection of children) of the 1989 Children Act.

- To the court: the case should be transferred immediately to the High Court if there is a failure to comply with the Department of Health guidelines: in this case the Official Solicitor should be invited to act as guardian ad litem. If the natural parents have never given a written consent to the adoption then consideration should be given to summarily dismissing the application and making the child a ward of court.

- To the guardian ad litem: the Official Solicitor should be proactive and seek the court's directions: priority should be given to interviewing the natural parents. Where the local authority has previously rejected the applicants as potential adopters then the Official Solicitor should inquire as to all the information on the authority's file.

Good practice in the case of parents, grandparents and other relatives

THE AUTONOMY OF ELDERLY PEOPLE

Elderly people should be treated as independent human beings. A common scenario for settlement applications is where a widowed elderly parent is in the UK on a visit and the adult son or son-in-law seeks advice as to how she or he can remain. It is vital to confirm with the parent that she or he wants to remain.

COLLECTING PROPER EVIDENCE

David Jackson, vice-president of the Immigration Appeals Tribunal, has written in his own textbook, *Immigration Law and Practice* (Sweet and Maxwell 1996), that

Dependent relative cases are notorious for the unsatisfactory nature of the evidence on appeal in that (perhaps understandably) there is often lack of any precise evidence as to the circumstances in the home country. This applies to all aspects of the case – in particular financial dependency and the roles played by various members of the family. Quite often the case initially made will have been based on flimsy evidence.

Good practice requires care and effort in the accumulation of evidence. This is evidence of financial support from the sponsor here and evidence of the family situation overseas – which latter can often be best verified by an independent report, perhaps compiled by International Social Services.

WHERE AND WHEN A SETTLEMENT APPLICATION SHOULD BE MADE

It is important to evaluate the advantages and disadvantages of making settlement applications in the country of origin or in the UK (see Chapter 3). This is a crucial issue for elderly (grand)parents visiting the UK. It is probably better to make a settlement application in the UK. The legal advisor will have more control and it may avoid the elderly (grand)parent being interviewed.

However, there are dangers in planning in advance to apply from within the UK. If the purpose of entry was settlement, this can lead to allegations of illegal entry as a visitor. If the (grand)parent is a visa national then he or she may be disbelieved at the visa interview and not be allowed to come as a visitor or subsequently to come for settlement. If an application for settlement made in the UK is refused then it is unlikely the applicant will be allowed back as a visitor.

If it is intended to make a settlement application in the UK it is sometimes best not to do this on the first visit but to accumulate some credibility by having one or two visits where the requirement to return home has been complied with.

REMEMBERING WHAT WAS SAID AT THE VISITOR'S INTERVIEW

In settlement applications made in the UK it is imperative to know what was said at any visitor interview overseas (see Chapter 5). This has particular relevance in elderly person cases. If a visitor to the UK applies for settlement as a (grand)parent then, if she or he is a visa national, the Home Office will check what was said at the visitor interview. For an elderly person to visit the UK it is tactically necessary to show that there is family to return to in the country of origin, otherwise it will be thought the person will want to remain in the UK. However, to remain in the UK as a (grand)parent it is necessary to show the direct opposite – namely that there are no close relatives in the country of origin to turn to for financial support. It is imperative for the advisor to question the applicant about the visitor interview and also which family members were recorded on the visitor's application form. If it was said at the visitor's interview that there were family members in the country of origin to provide for the (grand)parent then very good evidence will have to be produced showing that there has been a change in circumstances.

Unless there is an outstanding appeal, it is usually impossible to obtain access to the notes made by an entry clearance officer at a visitor interview. However, attempts should always be made by the legal advisor to obtain such notes, perhaps through an MP.

OVER 65 CONCESSION

A parliamentary reply of 29 May 1998 from Mike O'Brien, the immigration minister, revealed that it is general Home Office policy not to deport people over 65. The timing and pace of settlement applications should, if possible, be geared round achieving this age. The IND letter of 5 May 1999 to GMIAU put limits on the concession:

Deportation of people over 65... It is not normal policy to proceed with enforcement action in such cases although an exception would be made if blatant deception had been used to gain admission/leave to remain. It might also be appropriate to proceed if the person was over 65 on arrival and remained in good health.

Comments on casework problem at start of chapter

With DNA testing it is possible to show that the children A, B, C and D are related as claimed. Normally DNA samples are taken from the children and both parents. As Mrs X is dead, it will be necessary to take a sample from one of her brothers or sisters or for Mrs X to be exhumed. It is unlikely that X will obtain payment for DNA tests under the legal aid and assistance scheme for A, B and C as they are over the age of 18 and it will be considered that their cases are without 'merit'. However, payment for DNA tests for D should be available because D's case is that he is British by descent, being born after his father became British, and therefore has the right to enter irrespective of age.

Once D is accepted as 'related as claimed' then he will need a British passport or certificate of entitlement obtainable from the High Commission.

X is unemployed and cannot show that he can maintain his children. This could prevent B coming on a visit and A and C coming permanently. Financial support from a third party may be accepted as sufficient in the case of B (see Chapter 3). B's visitor application will have to be prepared carefully as there have been previous settlement refusals. It would help the visitor application if B's wife and children remained in Bangladesh because this can show an intention to return. Families in this situation play the role of hostages. Under the 1999 Immigration and Asylum Act it will, when this scheme becomes operative, be possible for a sponsor to put up a bond guaranteeing the return of a visitor. However, X will not be able to afford this. The 1999 legislation will, when this part becomes operative, also allow an appeal against refusal of family visits

A and C are over 18. Under Home Office policy they have to show 'compassionate' grounds to gain entry clearance for settlement. These grounds must relate to the situation in Bangladesh. A could perhaps start to make out a case if it can be shown that he is without support in rearing the children but it is highly unlikely that this will be sufficient to gain entry. C could attempt to obtain entry clearance outside the rules as a carer (see Chapter 17).

X should also be advised that if he decided to return to Bangladesh and join his children then he will be able to get any state pension transferred there.

Notes

1   J. Leighton, 'How Britain helps to create broken homes', *New Statesman* 9 May 1980
2   McGillvray, 1972 Imm AR p.63
3   Previously referenced as RON 117
4   LAC 98 20
5   IMG/99 20/552/6
6   Cm 2288
7   52/2
8   99/45
9   1999 *Immigration and Nationality Law Reports (INLR)*

CHAPTER 7

Beyond the family

The gay, lesbian, unmarried, celibate, promiscuous and single

A CASEWORK PROBLEM

You are a residential social worker. A young man, W, and two young women, V
and Y, are in your care. All three are British and ask for your suggestions. W is 15
years old and V and Y are aged 16. W is gay and is having a relationship with X,
who is 18. They want to live together in the UK. X is an overseas student whose
country has outlawed homosexual relations with a sentence of severe corporal
punishment. Y is having a heterosexual relationship with Z, another foreign
student, and is pregnant. They also want to live together in the UK with their baby.
V has a penpal, T, in Nigeria. T is an orphan with no extended family. V and T
regard each other as sisters. T would like to come to the UK and share a house
with V.

A REAL CASE STORY

A gay Romanian refugee fighting deportation has won his battle to stay in
Britain. The Home Office has given Sorin Mihai, 28, the right to remain
indefinitely in Britain, revealed his spokesman Tarlochan Gata-Aura of
solicitors Harrison Bundey in Chapletown Road, Leeds. Mr Mihai had
claimed he would be put at risk of being put in prison or a mental institution if
he was sent home... He says he received death threats, malicious calls and
hate mail because he was gay and was arrested and assaulted by police.
(*Yorkshire Evening Post* 9 September 1998)

ANOTHER REAL CASE STORY

The humiliating steps that a gay person will sometimes take to remain in the UK
are revealed by the *Guardian* (22 August 1992):

a man pretended to be a woman for a registry office wedding so his male
lover could stay in Britain, a court heard yesterday... They were each given
nine-month prison sentences suspended for two years... Judge Pyke said
the pair had engaged in calculated deception and the courts would protect
the institution of marriage and the immigration requirements from abuse.

SCOPE OF THIS CHAPTER

There is a terrible symmetry at the heart of immigration laws. Controls represent a direct attack on the extended black family. However, advisors put tremendous energy into defining as family members applicants who want settlement in the UK. This is because the context of family usually presents itself as the only one appropriate for settlement.

This emphasis on family by the Home Office and advisors has negative consequences for those people who by choice or necessity live outside what are popularly perceived as the paradigms of the conventional heterosexual family – whether this be nuclear or extended. This chapter poses the question as to why family should be the holy grail for entry and settlement. Why cannot those outside the family construct have rights of entry? Indeed, why cannot those living outside any relationship, or any monogamous relationship, enter and remain in the UK?

There is an ongoing tension within immigration control on the level of sexuality. On the one hand there is the perceived political need to assert the primacy of heterosexual over same-sex relationships. On the other hand there is the desire to assert the primacy of the institution of marriage over common-law heterosexual relationships. Within this tension there exists a romantic concept of marriage which devalues and destroys arranged marriages at the expense of nuclear, 'love' matches. All this has led to a constant merry-go-round of policy changes within immigration control.

FURTHER READING RESOURCES

In 1999 Butterworths published *Advising Gay and Lesbian Clients* by Anne Barlow and others. This contains a chapter on immigration issues. Stonewall Immigration Group produces a magazine and periodic pamphlets.

THE WIDER ISSUE OF SEXUALITY

A constant justification for controls is the need to suppress alien sexuality (see Chapter 2). In 1979 the *Guardian* carried a headline 'Abnormal sexuality used to ban immigrants' (see Chapter 17). In the committee stage of the 1981 British Nationality Act the minister itemised the criteria used to establish 'good character' for the purpose of naturalisation. He said (19 March 1981):

> Sexual morality, however, is not normally taken into account, nor are, for instance, homosexual activities within the law. Scandalous sexual behaviour might, however, when combined with other personal characteristics be a factor.

SOME HISTORY

There has never been any provision in law for the entry or stay of same-sex partners. None the less there is a politically significant history of same-sex relationships and immigration control. Much of this remains hidden.

Until the partial decriminalisation of male homosexuality in the 1967 Sexual Offences Act, the main issue of freedom of movement for British gay men was probably not the right of partners to join them here. The issue was the other way. It was the ability to flee quickly from the UK in response to homophobic repression. Richard Ellmann in his biography of Oscar Wilde writes that on the night of Wilde's arrest 600 men crossed from Dover to Calais.[1]

In addition to gay British men seeking sanctuary outside the UK, there is probably another side to the story. This is the deportation of non-British gay men following convictions for homosexual offences. It is unlikely that a conviction today would result in deportation. Before 1967 deportation would have been more probable.

HOMOPHOBIA, SEXISM AND RACISM

There is historically an ideological connection between homophobia, sexism, racism and immigration control. This first occurred with the agitation for controls in the nineteenth century. The combination of sexism and racism results in the virulent nationalism behind immigration restrictions (see Chapter 2). Homophobia can be thrown into this mixture. On 11 February 1893 Henry Labouchere MP spoke in favour of controls and helped force an unsuccessful vote on the issue. This was the same Henry Labouchere who personally had criminalised male homosexuality by introducing an amendment to the Criminal Law Bill on 6 August 1885. Labouchere's intervention in the 1893 debate was in support of a resolution for immigration controls by James Lowther MP. It was James Lowther who, as speaker of the House of Commons, on 27 January 1913 blocked a vote on women's suffrage on the grounds that 'in all franchise Acts, the word "person" has always hitherto been held to mean "male person"'.

MODERN JUDICIAL HOMOPHOBIA

Homophobia evidences itself in many modern judicial determinations concerning the rights of lesbians and gay men to come and settle in the UK. One recurrent theme is that gay men should revert to sexual abstinence to prevent persecution in their country of origin. The High Court in the case of Zia Mehmet Binbasi, from the Turkish Republic of Northern Cyprus, declared: 'the risk of prosecution would be avoided by self-restraint'.

HISTORY OF NON-MARITAL HETEROSEXUAL RELATIONSHIPS

Following the 1962 Commonwealth Immigrants Act the rules allowed a man to be joined by a common-law woman partner. The 1973 rules, echoing the colonial white man's imperial prerogative to claim a black lover of choice, required examination of 'any local custom or tradition tending to establish the permanence of the association'.

This discrimination, as racist as it was sexist, was removed by the 1985 rule changes. This was achieved not by raising the rights of women to be joined by a common-law partner but by abolishing the rights of men to be joined by such partners.

While removing rights in law to be joined by unmarried partners the Home Office issued instructions to officials saying that such partners, male or female, may be admitted to the UK on a discretionary basis. These instructions, 'Applications from common-law husbands and wives/mistresses', were leaked in the October 1986 issue of the journal *Immigration Law and Practice*.

In February 1996 Neil Gerrard MP proposed a parliamentary motion to include same-sex relationships within immigration law. He argued by analogy with the recognition of non-marital relationships. The minister responsible for immigration, Timothy Kirkhope, responded by abolishing the policy for unmarried heterosexual relationships. Kirkhope argued on 22 February 1996: 'The only objective test for the strength of a relationship in an immigration context is marriage.'

CURRENT POLICY AND IMMIGRATION RULES

In October 1997 the Home Office announced a 'concession' for same-sex and unmarried heterosexual partners seeking settlement. This was the consequence of campaigning by the Stonewall Immigration Group plus others. The immigration rules of October 2000 incorporated the concession into the rules. The new rules allow for entry or stay providing the following requirements are met:

- If the partner is overseas, prior entry clearance is required. If the partner is already in the UK, for instance as a student, she or he must not have overstayed any limited leave.

- Any previous marriage or similar relationship by either partner must have permanently broken down.

- The partners must be legally unable to marry under UK law (other than on grounds of age or blood relationship).

- The couple must have lived together in a relationship akin to marriage for two or more years. Prior to June 1999 the period was four years. The alteration was announced by Mike O'Brian MP in a written parliamentary answer of 16 June 1999.

- They must intend living permanently together.

- There is adequate maintenance and accommodation without recourse to public funds.

The rule is not specific on the age issue. Presumably, immigration officials will attempt to exclude the overseas partner where either partner is under the age of consent – 16 in hetrosexual relationships and 18 in gay male relationships.

If the requirements are fulfilled then the overseas partner will be given stay for an initial probationary two years to see if the relationship subsists. Prior to June 1999 the probationary period was twelve months.

In another written answer of 16 June 1999 Mike O'Brien stated that where the settled partner dies or where the overseas partner is the victim of domestic violence during the probationary period then this partner will be allowed to remain as in heterosexual marriages. The concession as to bereavement is now incorporated in the rules but that as to domestic violence still remains outside the rules (see Chapter 9).

THE TWO YEAR COHABITATION REQUIREMENT PRIOR TO APPLICATION

The requirement of two years' cohabitation prior to any application is particularly harsh on same-sex couples whose chances of cohabitation are restricted by UK immigration laws and usually the immigration laws of the overseas partner's country.

IND instructions to immigration officers says that short breaks from cohabitation 'would be acceptable for good reasons, such as work commitments, or looking after a relative which takes one partner away for a period of up to 6 months'.

CRITIQUE OF THE CONCESSION/RULE

The requirement of two years' pre-existing cohabitation is discriminatory compared to the rules for heterosexual married couples which do not demand cohabitation pre-existing the marriage.

The requirement of a two year probationary period is discriminatory. For heterosexual marriage the period is twelve months and there is a longstanding campaign to abolish even this one year period.

The requirement to show the breakdown of all previous relationships is judgemental. It seems aimed against a caricatured image of gay men as promiscuous.

The demand for proof of cohabitation outside marriage is hypocritically at odds with the still dominant morality which asserts cohabitation should take place only within marriage. This hypocrisy is borne out of the ideological need to give some recognition to heterosexual if unmarried relationships.

The requirement that the couple must be legally unable to marry is automatically fulfilled by gay or lesbian couples. It can force heterosexual couples into involuntary marriages. There are many reasons why a couple may not want to marry including ideological objections. The fact that one partner is already married presents a bar to remarriage. However, the instructions say that immigration officers 'should not ask applicants the reasons why they are not seeking a divorce'. This is important for people who have a religious objection to divorce.

THE PROBLEMATIC OF EQUALITY UNDER IMMIGRATION CONTROLS

The concession is not progressive. It discriminates against same-sex and non-marital relationships. It is not a victory. In many ways it is a defeat. It leaves unmarried heterosexual partnerships in a worse position than under the previous concession. It renders it harder for single people who are neither sexually active nor emotionally attached to argue for the right to come to or remain in the UK. It is intrusive into the lives of gay men and lesbians. Paradoxically it is a defeat partially caused by the demand for gay and lesbian sexual equality under immigration controls. The justification given by Neil Gerrard MP in proposing that same-sex relationships be included in the rules was that such a change 'would provide only equality with heterosexual relationships: that is all that is required'. The problematic of equal opportunities immigration controls was considered in Chapter 2. It is perverse to be demanding equality with heterosexual partnerships when the daily experience of, for example, heterosexual couples from the Indian subcontinent is that they are divided and their relationships often destroyed by the immigration marriage rules.

What is lacking from this demand for 'equality' based on sexual orientation and what makes the demand highly problematic is any recognition of the racism and nationalism central to controls. It is as though there are two different worlds. On the one hand black people have for years been fighting the immigration marriage rules. On the other hand lesbian and gay activists are fighting to be included in these rules.

It is important to learn from the black experience. One lesson is that the immigration rules allow government officials to intrude directly into the most intimate details of the lives of black people – to 'prove' the 'genuineness' of relationships. However, this is precisely what is proposed by the advocates of 'equality'. Neil Gerrard said in the parliamentary debate: 'I would expect partners to be able to produce evidence to back up their claims that they were in a relationship that they intended to be long-standing and permanent.' This is unacceptable as a way forward. It legitimises immigration control as another form of sexual intrusion. It is doubly unfortunate that these views were expressed by Neil Gerrard as his is one of the few voices of opposition within the parliamentary Labour Party to the government's tightening of controls. For instance he voted against the 1999 Immigration and Asylum Act.

Good practice

Good practice issues are as important for non-marital heterosexual relations as for same-sex relationships. However, there are issues specific to same-sex partnerships.

LEGAL AID UNDER THE ADVICE AND ASSISTANCE SCHEME

Same-sex partners are not considered 'spouses' for the purposes of legal aid and assistance. If the settled partner is working but the applicant is not working then the incomes are not aggregated and the applicant partner may be eligible for free advice and assistance. Unmarried heterosexual partners are considered as spouses.

SUPPORT FOR SAME-SEX COUPLES

Gay and lesbian groups should be trained to offer support and basic advice on immigration issues. The same is true for local authorities who employ workers to tackle gay and lesbian issues. The Stonewall Immigration Group offers immigration help to same-sex couples.

HELPING CLIENTS TO 'COME OUT'

Advisors will not necessarily know whether a client is gay or lesbian. Clients may not necessarily know that it is potentially possible to claim settlement based on a same-sex relationship. Advisors should make their offices 'user-friendly' to gay and lesbian clients.

- Stonewall Immigration Group and GMIAU have produced an advice leaflet for gay men and lesbians. This has been translated into Spanish. The leaflet should be prominent and available.

- It may be helpful if surgeries were run at particular and advertised times for clients whose sexuality is a relevant issue.

- Interpreters should be vetted to ensure that they are not homophobic.

- Immigration advice outreach surgeries should be held in gay and lesbian venues.

MAKING THE APPLICATION

If an application is made in the UK or overseas then it is necessary to complete the correct forms: FLR(O) for internal applications and IM2A and IM2B for overseas applications (see Chapter 3). These forms are not specifically designed for same-sex or unmarried heterosexual relationships. In addition to the forms it is useful to submit a detailed chronology of the relationship showing periods of cohabitation and the continuance of contact during any period the couple were not physically together.

EVIDENCE OF COHABITATION

Any couple contemplating an application based on the concession should retain evidence of their commitment and cohabitation. The Home Office instructions suggest that it is useful to submit the following:

- joint commitments (such as joint bank accounts, investments, rent agreements, mortgage, death benefit, etc.)
- if there are children of the relationship, a record of their birth entry
- correspondence which links them to the same address
- any official records of their address (e.g. doctors' records, DSS records, national insurance records, etc.).

It would be useful to keep any date-stamped envelopes of correspondence to the couple. It is worthwhile submitting dated photographs of the couple, plus letters, faxes, emails or itemised telephone statements showing continuity of the relationship when the couple were apart. It would also be helpful to obtain letters from friends or family which confirm the relationship and submitted chronology.

ACCUMULATING TWO YEARS' PRIOR COHABITATION

The problem confronting unmarried heterosexual and same-sex couples will be the accumulation of two years' cohabitation prior to any application. This will be particularly difficult where the leave of the overseas partner is about to expire. Good practice for advisors is to try to slow down the case after the initial application to stretch out the cohabitation to two years before a decision is made. The length of time required to accumulate the necessary evidence may achieve this.

The instructions to immigration officers say that an overseas partner can use the 'visitor' category to accumulate the required two years. This suggests that it may be possible to obtain a multiple entry visitor's visa for the explicit purpose of building up two years through six months' visits with short breaks between each visit. This possibility of accumulating two years through transnational visits discriminates in favour of the wealthy.

SHOULD AN APPLICATION BE MADE IN ANY EVENT?

Should an application be made where it is not possible to accumulate two years? There is no definitive answer. The closer to the two year requirement then the better the chances – provided, in the case of applications made in the UK, the applicant has not overstayed leave to remain. It may take several months for the Home Office to make a decision and several more months for an appeal to be heard if this is a negative decision, by which time the two year requirement may be met.

If the applicant has overstayed then the matter becomes one of potential expulsion. As yet the Home Office has not published detailed removal guidelines where someone is in a same-sex or non-marital heterosexual relationship. It is a matter of tactical discussion with an advisor whether to approach the Home Office during an existing leave with a short period of cohabitation or whether to run the risk of overstaying leave and waiting before making a settlement application.

COMPASSIONATE GROUNDS: HIV/AIDS

Advisors need to be alert to other avenues if the concession is inadequate. One possibility is an application on compassionate grounds outside the rules. Charles Wardle, then immigration minister, said in parliament with reference to same-sex couples (16 May 1994):

> Factors which may be taken into account in assessing whether compelling circumstances are present in such an application are the health of a settled partner and the length and stability of the relationship.

Presumably health grounds is a reference to either partner having HIV/AIDS (see Chapter 17).

COMPASSIONATE GROUNDS AND FAMILY APPROVAL

The concept of 'compassionate' grounds can lead to the presentation by advisors of problematic arguments (see Chapter 10). An example occurs with same-sex relationships. Often such relationships are perceived as legitimate within compassionate arguments only if they are accepted by the settled partner's heterosexual family. It is as though same-sex partnerships are viewed as valid only after assimilation into the heterosexual norm. This was the approach of the adjudicator and the Immigration Appeal Tribunal in 1987 in one of the first deportation appeals, that of John Webb, concerning a same-sex partner. At the adjudicator hearing the brother of the appellant's partner gave evidence that he was 'almost one of their family'. The appeal was successful.[2]

EUROPEAN CONVENTION ON HUMAN RIGHTS

The issue is whether a gay or lesbian partner can rely on Article 8 of the Convention, which says:

> Everyone has the right to respect for his family and private life, his home and his correspondence... There shall be no interference by a public authority with the exercise of this right except such as in accordance with the law and is necessary in a democratic society.

In cases heard in Europe it has been held that same-sex relationships do not amount to 'family life'. In *Yusoff and Lowther* v. *UK* decided in 1983, a Malaysian citizen was served a deportation notice in spite of his relationship with a British citizen. The Commission held:

> Despite the modern evolution of attitudes towards homosexuality, the Commission finds that the applicants' relationship does not fall within the scope of the respect for family life ensured by Article 8.

In the case of *WJ and DP* v. *UK* concerning a British and New Zealander couple decided in 1986, the Commission confirmed:

the family (to which the relationship of heterosexual unmarried couples living together as husband and wife can be assimilated) merits special protection in society... the difference in treatment between the applicant and somebody in the same position whose partner must be of the opposite sex can be objectively and reasonably justified.

These cases are relatively old. With the incorporation of the Convention into UK law there is an opportunity again to mount challenges under Article 8, particularly as to whether using controls to prevent same-sex couples cohabiting is an interference with private, as opposed to family, life.

EUROPEAN UNION LAW

There is no case-law as to whether a same-sex partner is a 'member of the family' for EU law purposes. According to the Stonewall Immigration Group document 'United Kingdom immigration law and rules as they affect same-sex couples', there are five EEA countries which have provision for a foreign national to remain because of a long-term same-sex relationship with a resident. The countries are Denmark, the Netherlands, Norway, Spain and Sweden. A British citizen who has acquired residence in one of these countries can be joined by a non-EEA gay or lesbian partner. This leaves unresolved the question as to whether the couple could then use European Union law to return to live in the UK together – as is possible for a married heterosexual couple (see Chapter 3).

POLITICAL ASYLUM AND SEXUAL IDENTITY

The case of Sorin Mihai at the start of this chapter shows that the granting of asylum, based on persecution for sexual orientation, is another possible way for a gay man or lesbian to remain in the UK. This raises important and controversial issues on the relationship between the personal and the political within asylum law. These are examined in Chapter 8.

Comments on casework problem at start of chapter

X could in theory be open to criminal prosecution if his gay relationship with his underage partner, W, were brought to the Home Office's attention. He needs advice in deciding whether to postpone any application until W reaches 18. Also two years' cohabitation is presently not possible as W is in residential care. If W leaves care when he is 16, the Home Office may try to disregard cohabitation prior to the gay age of consent of 18, though this should be challenged. X should try to retain his immigration status as a student as long as possible. Given the threat of corporal punishment in his country of origin, X should consider an asylum application (see Chapter 8).

The situation of Z, whose girlfriend Y is pregnant, is different. The best advice is to get married and apply for settlement during any current leave to remain. Z must show that he can fulfil the maintenance and accommodation rules. If this is not possible, he should continue to renew his student leave until such time as Y has suitable work or he has a credible offer of employment. For a marriage application to succeed, Y must leave the care home and the couple must live together. An advisor needs to confirm with Y that marriage is what she wants and that she is not feeling pressurised.

T as a single person with no family has no status under the immigration rules to come to or stay in the UK permanently. Platonic friendships provide no such status. Any application would have to be made outside the rules on compassionate grounds. Alternatively T could consider coming to the UK on a visit or as a student but then she must not say that she would like to stay in the UK permanently.

Notes

1   Richard Ellmann, *Oscar Wilde*, Penguin 1988, p.430
2   *Immigration Law and Practice* January 1988

CHAPTER 8

Asylum

Age, gender and sexuality

A CASEWORK PROBLEM

You are a psychotherapist treating asylum-seekers. A was tortured following political activities in his country. B was caught up in a civil war. C, a conscientious objector, was conscripted into the army. D, a young boy, was forced to join an army at war. E was subjected to domestic violence in her country. F was threatened with imprisonment for his gay sexuality. They ask about their chances of asylum.

A REAL CASE STORY

Ms J is a 27-year-old woman from Pakistan. When she was 20 years old she was raped by the man who is now her estranged husband. She knew she could not return to her family as she would have been punished severely, publicly castigated and treated like a social outcast for having dishonoured her family and brought shame to her community. Moreover, she knew it was impossible to prove rape... The couple were arrested under *Hudood* laws and accused of *Zina* (sex outside marriage). So she had no choice but to marry the man who had raped her, who later sponsored her to come to the UK as a visitor. As soon as Ms J entered the country, her husband took away her passport and all other documents. He subsequently subjected her to intense abuse and she lived in constant fear of him. In the end he reported her to the Home Office who then treated her as an illegal entrant. In Pakistan, Ms J will either face death by stoning or up to ten years' imprisonment and thirty lashes for *Zina*. Her claim for asylum must therefore be seen in the context of Pakistan's discriminatory treatment of women.

After a campaign Ms J was allowed to remain. (Case taken from Heaven Crawley, *Women as Asylum Seekers: A Legal Handbook*, Refugee Women's Legal Group 1997, p.54)

SCOPE OF THIS CHAPTER

Apart from itemising some important general issues, this chapter is not about the entirety of asylum law. Rather it spotlights three categories of claims. These are applications by unaccompanied children, applications based on gender and applications based on sexuality. These claims contradict the image of the typical asylum-seeker as an adult male involved in public political activity. Child-based asylum claims illustrate the autonomy of children. Claims relating to gender or sexuality incorporate the personal into the asylum concept by showing the personal may have a political dimension. They challenge, albeit in a problematic manner, the right of immigration control to define and construct the experiences of heterosexual women, lesbians and gay men.

THE FALSIFICATION OF HISTORY

There exists a myth that the UK has always welcomed refugees. This is used to justify laws against so-called 'bogus' asylum-seekers. The Labour government White Paper *Fairer, Faster and Firmer* asserts: 'The UK government has a long-standing tradition of giving shelter to those fleeing persecution' and then proposes further restrictions (para.8.1). This pattern is traced back to 1905 in *From the Jews to the Tamils.*[1]

Free entry is a fiction. The 1905 Aliens Act was designed to exclude refugees. The Act theoretically exempted anyone fleeing 'persecution or punishment on religious or political grounds'. However, the *Jewish Chronicle* regularly revealed exclusions. On 25 October 1907 it reported:

> Aaron Hecht Millore, who had come from the town of Sokorow, was also rejected. His narrative formed a tragic tale. One of his children, he said, had been killed in a pogrom. His family had then fled in a state of panic and frenzy, and in the confusion he had become separated from, and, for the time being, lost to them. Yet the immigrant was rejected on the grounds of want of means.

In May 1938 visa controls were imposed on German and Austrian nationals, effectively excluding Jews fleeing Nazism (see Chapter 2).

THE POLITICS OF ASYLUM

Issues of asylum do not exist independent of immigration controls. Without controls, asylum laws would be unnecessary. Refugees share a communality of interest with immigrants and migrants. Each group is confronted by restrictive laws. To justify controls a distinction is made between 'genuine refugees' and 'economic migrants'. This fails to explain why 'economic migrants' should be excluded. The line between political and economic refugees is itself blurred. Were the Jews who escaped from Germany when there was a state-imposed boycott on Jewish shops and Jewish labour political refugees or economic migrants?

Ambalavaner Sivanandan, director of the Institute of Race Relations, has recently argued that with the economic impoverishment and political mayhem caused by the global market the distinction between economic migrant and political refugee has in any event collapsed (*Guardian* 8 August 2000)

INTERNATIONAL FRAMEWORK OF MODERN ASYLUM LAW

Asylum law is international law. It rests on the 1951 United Nations Convention relating to the Status of Refugees as amended by the 1967 Protocol. The Convention defines a refugee as:

> a person who has a well-founded fear of persecution for reasons of race, religion, nationality, membership of a particular social group or political opinion and who is outside his country of nationality.

Because asylum law is based on the UN Convention, UN guidelines can be used to interpret it. The most important is the *Handbook on Procedures and Criteria for Determining Refugee Status* by the United Nations High Commission for Refugees (UNHCR).

BASIC LEGAL ISSUES

Each country decides how to implement the UN Convention. Before 1993 there was no UK asylum legislation. Following European-wide anti-refugee agitation there now exists the 1993 Asylum and Immigration Appeals Act, the 1996 Asylum and Immigration Act and the 1999 Immigration and Asylum Act.

If the Home Office decides that a person's case fails Convention standards it can grant 'exceptional leave to remain' (ELR) where applicants would be in danger if returned to their country. Though often sufficient, this is inferior to asylum. Applicants granted asylum can be joined by their immediate family. Those granted ELR have to wait four years.

The UNHCR *Handbook* confirms that 'persecution' is not confined to activity by state authorities but extends to activities 'knowingly tolerated by the authorities or if the authorities refuse, or prove unable, to offer effective protection'. This allows the possibility of persecution claims within the 'private' domestic sphere where state protection is denied.

STEREOTYPING NON-WESTERN COUNTRIES

Most asylum applicants in the UK are Third World or East European nationals. This suggests that the UK is the last remnant of civilisation. In fact countries hosting most refugees are non-Western. There exist regional accords which are wider than the UN Convention. An example is the 1969 Organisation of African Unity Convention Relating to the Specific Aspects of Refugee Problems in Africa. This recognises as refugees those fleeing 'external aggression, foreign domination, or events seriously disturbing public order'. The UN Convention does not include those escaping war or civil war.

There is an incorrect assumption that asylum claims are inappropriate against Western states. In 1997 the Canadian courts granted asylum to a British child victim of incest whom social services had failed to protect.[2]

One way of understanding rejected asylum claims based on age, sexuality or gender is to analyse their rejection as premised on the same violation of human rights in the UK as forms the basis of the asylum claim itself.

Unaccompanied children

FURTHER READING RESOURCES

There are two essential guides: *Representing Unaccompanied Children in the Asylum Process* (Children's Legal Centre 1994) by Vicky Guedalla and *Supporting Unaccompanied Children in the Asylum Process* (Save the Children 1998) by Wendy Ayotte. Save the Children also publishes *Seeking Asylum in the UK* for adults supporting children. The Social Services Inspectorate has published a practice guide, *Unaccompanied Asylum-Seeking Children*, with a training pack (see Chapter 4). Amnesty International in 1999 published *Most Vulnerable of All – The Treatment of Unaccompanied Refugee Children in the UK* by Simon Russell. This includes useful recommendations and guidelines. In July 2000 the child charity Barnardos produced *Children First and Foremost – Meeting the Needs of Unaccompanied, Asylum-seeking Children*. As well as containing important suggested guidelines for local authorities this also contains empirical evidence on support presently provided to unaccompanied asylum-seeking children by such authorities. Following the 1999 Act some of the law in these publications is outdated. However, the practice issues remain.

The Immigration and Refugee Board of Canada has issued its own *Guidelines on Child Refugee Claimants*.

THE IMMIGRATION RULES

The Immigration Rules define an asylum-seeking child as 'a person who is under the age of 18 years or who, in the absence of documentary evidence, appears to be under that age'. The 1997 UNHCR *Guidelines on Policies and Procedures in Dealing with Unaccompanied Children Seeking Asylum* define an unaccompanied child as 'separated from both parents and is not being cared for by an adult who by law or custom has responsibility to do so'.

The rules deal with issues for unaccompanied children:

- 'Close attention is to be given to the welfare of the child at all times.'

- 'More weight should be given to objective indications of risk than to the child's state of mind and understanding of the situation.'

- 'A child will not be interviewed about the substance of his claim' where information can be obtained elsewhere. Where 'an interview is necessary it should be conducted in the presence of a parent, guardian, representative or other adult'. A letter of 14 June 1999 from IND to GMIAU stated: 'There is no formal age below which children will not be interviewed.' This contradicts practice in other immigration interviews from which children under 10 are excluded (see Chapter 6). The letter says:

All unaccompanied children (within reason) are spoken to on the desk to establish basic details. These desk interviews are in the presence of a British Airways 'nanny' who presents the child to the immigration officer.

- It is bad practice for interviews to be conducted without an adult whose primary concern is the child. An airline 'nanny' hardly fulfils this role.

THE UNHCR *Handbook*

The UNHCR *Handbook* suggests that a child accompanied by a family member should be given any asylum status that is conferred on the adult. An unaccompanied child should 'if appropriate have a guardian appointed whose task it would be to promote a decision that will be in the minor's best interests'. A child may not possess 'a sufficient degree of maturity to make it possible to establish a well-founded fear' and 'it will generally be necessary to enrol the services of experts conversant with child mentality'. Any application by an unaccompanied child 'may call for a liberal application of the benefit of the doubt'.

UNHCR *Guidelines*

The 1997 UNHCR *Guidelines on Policies and Procedures* confirm that children can claim asylum independent of any adult. Examples are:

the recruitment of children for regular or irregular armies, their subjection to forced labour, the trafficking of children for prostitution and sexual exploitation and the practice of female genital mutilation.

THE 1990 UN CONVENTION ON THE RIGHTS OF THE CHILD

Article 22 of the 1990 Convention states that asylum-seeking children should be given special protection. Article 37 confirms that no child should be subjected to torture or other cruel, inhuman or degrading treatment. The UK signed this convention with a reservation that it will not affect immigration law (see Chapter 6). This should not negate obligations concerning asylum-seeking children. These are so widely accepted as to constitute international law.

PANEL OF ADVISORS FOR REFUGEE CHILDREN

The UNHCR *Handbook* recommendation that an unaccompanied child should have a guardian appointed remains unimplemented. In 1994 the Home Office funded a Panel of Advisors for Refugee Children run by the Refugee Council. Advisors are sessional workers with a variety of languages and knowledge of childcare and asylum issues. A Memorandum of Understanding between the Home Office and the Refugee Council defines the panel's role. It has responsibility to ensure that health care, education and accommodation are provided. Referrals to the panel are made by voluntary and statutory organisations. The Immigration Service at ports of entry (for port asylum applications) and the Immigration and Nationality Directorate (for in-country applications) are instructed to notify the panel of unaccompanied child asylum-seekers. In 1995 the National Institute for Social Work published a report, *He Said He Would Help and He Did*, on the panel.

HOME OFFICE *GUIDANCE NOTES* AND LOCAL AUTHORITY SOCIAL SERVICES

In 1996 the Unaccompanied Children's Module of the Home Office published *Guidance Notes for Those Working with Unaccompanied Children Claiming Asylum in the UK*. These were designed for social services departments and contain the following Home Office undertakings:

- Any unaccompanied child who claims asylum at a sea or airport is immediately referred to the local Social Services Department by the Immigration Service Ports Directorate.

- Even when an application from an unaccompanied child is refused removal action will not be pursued unless we can be satisfied that there will be adequate reception and care arrangements.

- If it is decided that refugee status is not appropriate our view is that it would normally be in the child's best interests to be reunited with its family.

- If it proves impossible to trace a child's family, consideration will be given to whether or not there are other appropriate care facilities available in his or her country of origin.

It is arguable that family unity should be achieved within the UK rather than by removing the child. Unity is not always appropriate, for instance where there has been sexual abuse.

FINGERPRINTING AND DETENTION

Asylum-seeking children are vulnerable to the repressive apparatus of control. The Home Office can pressurise children into leaving. The 1996 *Guidance Notes* state:

> The Home Office's view is that once a child has exhausted his appeal rights and has no further basis of stay in the United Kingdom it is better for him to return home voluntarily... The child should be made aware of the implications of

having removal action taken against him/her. The adverse effect on later study and career prospects of being unable to visit the United Kingdom could prove significant.

The White Paper *Fairer, Faster and Firmer* declared: 'Unaccompanied minors should never be detained other than in the most exceptional circumstances and then only overnight with appropriate care' (para.12.6). This misses the point. Minors are detained because the Immigration Service claim that they are adults.

The 1993 Asylum and Immigration Appeals Act allows fingerprinting of asylum-seekers. A High Court decision held that this applies to children.[3] This case revealed Home Office policy whereby 'Children under the age of 16 who apply for asylum in their own right or as dependants, are fingerprinted only if there is doubt as to their identity'.

Gender persecution of women

GENDER BLINDNESS

Women are as likely as men to be persecuted for UN Convention grounds. Until recently there has been no acknowledgement in the asylum process of gender-linked persecution within the 'personal' sphere – for example domestic violence.

FURTHER READING RESOURCES

The UNHCR issued *Guidelines on the Protection of Refugee Women* (1991) and *Sexual Violence against Refugees, Guidelines on Prevention and Response* (1995). The Canadian Immigration and Refugee Board published in 1993 *Guidelines on Women Refugee Claimants Fearing Gender-Related Persecution* (updated in 1996). The Australian Department of Immigration and Multicultural Affairs published *Refugee and Humanitarian Visa Applicants: Guidelines on Gender Issues for Decision Makers* (1996). There are no official UK guidelines. The Refugee Women's Legal Group (RWLG) published *Gender Guidelines for the Determination of Asylum Claims in the UK* (1998). Numerous individuals and organisations, including the Law Society, sponsored these. The RWLG has produced the definitive text, *Women as Asylum Seekers: A Legal Handbook* (1997), by Heaven Crawley from which was taken the case of Ms J above.

DEFINITIONS AND CLARIFICATIONS

The RWLG *Guidelines* make the definitional point:

'Gender' is not the same as 'sex' which is biologically defined. The term 'gender' refers to the social construction of power relations between men and women, and the implications of these relations for women's (and men's) identity, status, roles and responsibilities. (para.1.8)

These *Guidelines* make other clarifications (para.1.14). A woman 'may be persecuted *as* a woman (e.g. raped) for reasons unrelated to gender (e.g. activity in a political party)'. This raises the question as to what gender-specific harm amounts to 'persecution'. A woman 'may not be persecuted as a woman but still *because* of gender (e.g. flogged for refusing to wear a veil)'. This raises the question as to the appropriate Convention ground for gender related persecution. A woman 'may be persecuted *as and because* she is a woman (e.g. female genital mutilation)'.

PERSECUTION AND SERIOUS HARM

The commonly accepted definition of 'persecution' is serious harm plus absence of state protection. The 1995 UNHCR *Guidelines* stress that human rights standards, found in international instruments, provide criteria for defining unacceptable harm (para.4.2). Some instruments specifically relate to women:

- The 1979 United Nations Convention on the Elimination of All Forms of Discrimination Against Women.

- The 1993 UN Declaration on the Elimination of Violence Against Women includes, but does not limit, violence to

physical, sexual and psychological violence occurring in the family, including battering, sexual abuse of female children in the household, dowry-related violence, marital rape, female genital mutilation and other traditional practices harmful to women, non-spousal violence and violence related to exploitation.

- The 1995 UN Platform for Action extends this to include 'sexual slavery and forced pregnancy' and 'coercive/forced use of contraceptives, female infanticide and prenatal sex selection'.

UK CASE-LAW AND 'SERIOUS HARM'

Crawley (p.59) quotes adjudicator decisions where rape by state officials was held to be a human rights violation. This contrasts with the High Court decision in *Okonkwo*.[4] The appellant was raped by an army officer whom the police refused to arrest. The appellant claimed that rape was torture. Judge Dyson upheld the adjudicator's determination treating rape as a personal foible peculiar to the perpetrator. The adjudicator said: 'I see no distinction between rape and any other offence of serious violence' and equated it to an act of robbery.

Baroness Blatch, the Home Office minister in the House of Lords, said on 20 June 1996:

Rape, or serious sexual assault imposed by agents of the state, or in circumstances where the state is unwilling or unable to afford protection, is likely to constitute grounds for asylum.

FAILURE OF STATE PROTECTION

The RWLG *Guidelines* emphasise:

> State responsibility includes those instances where social mores dictate gen-der-related abuse as an acceptable practice and where there are no effective means of legal recourse to prevent, investigate or punish such acts.

The state can promote gender-related persecution for private conduct through the operation of law such as sanctioning of violence for adultery.

THE CONVENTION GROUND

The UN Convention does not grant refugee status just because of persecution. Persecution must be linked to one of the grounds – race, nationality, religion, political opinion or membership of a social group.

A recent House of Lords decision was a victory for the women concerned. This was the joint case of *Shah and Islam*. Both involved Pakistani women married to violent men and falsely accused of adultery. They fled to the UK. It was accepted that if they returned home they would suffer physical abuse by their husbands and could, under Sharia law, be stoned to death. It was successfully argued that women, or a subgroup of women such as women in Pakistan, could be categorised as a 'social group'.

Crawley, writing before this decision, argues that a more productive approach is to shift the ground for gender-related persecution to political (or religious) opinion. This is opinion that can be imputed or attributed to a woman by dint of her conduct or alleged conduct. The reasons this is seen as more productive are twofold. The first is strategic, given problems associated with defining 'social group'. The second is that women's resistance to social mores, though often taking place in the sphere of the private, is inherently political. It cannot simply be conceptualised as an issue of personal motivation.

This approach was adopted by the Immigration Appeals Tribunal in the 1996 case of Mashid Ahmady quoted in Crawley (p.138). The appellant offended Iran's dress code by wearing make-up and refusing to wear a veil. She was arrested, fined and rendered unemployable. The Tribunal held: 'the perception will be that she is making a political statement and therefore the persecution will be for a Convention reason on that basis'.

This decision could expose those Western countries who refuse to allow Muslim women to wear the veil (such as France's prohibition on Muslim school-girls) to an asylum claim.

COMMENTARY

It is manifestly wrong that women suffering gender-related harm be denied sanctuary. Progress in respect to 'social group' or 'imputed political opinion' grounds is welcome.

However, neither ground can always accurately reflect women's experiences. To define women as a 'social group' ignores the fact that, as Crawley says, 'in reality "women" are not a cohesive group; even within individual countries women fall into their own sub-groups – economically, socially and culturally'(p.144).

To define women's behaviour within the private sphere as being an inevitable expression of political activity or opinion (albeit imputed) strains language. The RWLG *Guidelines* give as an example of imputed opinion 'the characterisation of a raped woman as adulterous'(para.4.18). It would seem more correct to impute any political opinion, of the most profoundly reactionary nature, to the rapist.

The political problematic is the relationship between the 'personal' and the 'political'. This recurs in respect to issues of sexuality grounding an asylum claim (see below) and 'compassionate grounds' contesting deportation (see Chapter 10) However, these two spheres are not necessarily identical. What matters is their relationship to each other. The tendency to see them as identical leads to a strained interpretation of the Convention. One answer is to campaign to add 'gender' (and 'sexuality') to the Convention as a specific ground. The underlying problem is immigration controls. Without controls there would be no need for the Convention.

Persecution of gay men and lesbians

The irresolvable contradictions on the level of gender of asylum claims are reproduced in analogous claims on the level of sexuality by gay men and lesbians.

There has been one Immigration Appeal Tribunal case (heard in 1994) concerning a Romanian, Ioan Vraciu, which went against previous decisions and held that gay men can be a 'social group' for asylum purposes. In many ways this decision was progressive. It emphasised that the UN Convention was based on 'the underlying theme of basic human rights'. It rejected the argument that homosexuals should practise sexual abstinence to avoid persecution, stating that a gay sexual orientation is a 'basic human right the exercise of which a person should not be expected to forgo'.

Subsequently Lord Steyn in *Shah and Islam* commented: 'I regard it as established that depending on the evidence homosexuals may in some countries qualify as members of a particular social group'. As a result of *Shah and Islam* the IND wrote to Amnesty International on 20 May 1999 saying:

we can no longer argue that homosexuals (or other persons defined by sexual orientation) are not capable of being a social group. Discrimination against homosexuals in a society may be such as to single them out as a social group depending on the factual circumstances in the country concerned.

COMMENTARY

The refusal to allow entry to gay men or lesbians, irrespective of the persecution issue, can be justified only by homophobia. However, the defining of gay men or lesbians (or both together?) as members of a social group again leads to a political impasse.

There is a particular problematic central to sexual orientation cases which does not strongly figure in gender-defined cases. The decision in Ioan Vraciu's case becomes ideologically dubious in defining membership of a sexually defined social group as being based on an 'immutable characteristic'. It is questionable whether sexual orientation is 'immutable' in the sense apparently meant here: namely it is genetically determined, a conclusion which presupposes the scientifically unproven notion of the 'gay gene'. Inasmuch as sexual orientation is socially determined then its degree of immutability will depend on the individual.

There was a highly political twist to Vraciu's case. Eventually the case was heard again by an adjudicator to determine whether Ioan would suffer persecution in Romania. To a large extent this turned on the question as to whether prosecution can amount to persecution and if so what degree of prosecution is required. This issue remains unresolved with conflicting Tribunal decisions. The unexpected point in the adjudicator's determination is that he did not accept Ioan was gay because he 'does not belong to any homosexual group or club. There has been no authentication of his alleged status.' This shows that the raising of sexual orientation by an applicant exposes him or her to intrusive inquiries of the most intimate nature. This is another example in immigration law of how attempts to liberalise the law can result in further intrusion and indignity.

Good practice

Good practice in all asylum cases requires accumulating evidence of persecution both specifically in respect of the asylum-seeker and generally in respect of the country of origin. Country of origin reports are now available from various sources: Amnesty International, UN Commission on Human Rights Reports, UNHCR, Refugee Legal Centre Documentation Centre, Refugee Studies Programme Documentation Centre and US Department of State Country Reports.

Good practice: children

LEGAL REPRESENTATIVES: ETHICS

Although a client is a child, he or she is also a client and is entitled to be so treated. The Immigration Law Practitioners' Association, the Law Society and the Refugee Legal Group have jointly produced a *Best Practice Guide to Asylum Appeals* written for advisors by Mark Henderson. This emphasises:

It is not acceptable for a child to be switched between representatives whether or not they are from the same firm. You should endeavour to be present at every hearing or interview with your client. If it is impossible for you to be present you must ensure that your client is accompanied by someone she knows and trusts. It is not acceptable to send a clerk who does not know your client or her case. If you wish to use another advocate at any hearing, you must ensure that the advocate is introduced to your client well before the date of the hearing.

This reflects the undertaking solicitors give in becoming members of the Children's Panel of the Law Society.

OTHER PRACTICE ISSUES FOR LEGAL REPRESENTATIVES

Advisors should:

- clarify they are not Home Office officials

- clarify the law and legal procedures

- keep appointments. It is good practice to give the client a phone card. This shows that the advisor is accessible. There should be regular, planned, client contact

- ensure children are referred to the Panel of Advisors and local social services

- ask the child if she or he wishes another adult, such as a social worker, member of the panel or someone from their community, to be present at an interview

- consider obtaining an expert assessment of the child's mental development. This accords with the emphasis in the UNHCR *Handbook* that a child may not have sufficient maturity to possess a 'well-founded fear'. In 1995 the Children's Legal Centre and the Refugee Council compiled a list of expert assessors in London

- consider asking a member of the Panel of Advisors to adopt the role of being a guardian ad litem as the child's age may prevent full or any instructions being taken.

ADJUDICATOR GUIDELINES IN APPEALS

Guidelines have been issued to adjudicators for appeals involving child asylum-seekers. These appear in the case of *Orman*.[5] They comprise this checklist:

1. What was the age of the child at the date of the application for asylum?

2. Should the hearing be held in camera or should it be open to the public? Has the representative requested the public be excluded

pursuant to rule 32(3)(a) of the Immigration Appeals (Procedure) Rules?

3. Should the venue of the hearing be shifted to accommodate a more child-friendly surrounding?

4. Have immigration rules 350–352 and the UNHCR guidelines concerning children's evidence been considered? Is it possible for a child to give evidence by video?

Note: A pre-hearing review will be held for all applicants who, at the date of the application for asylum, are under the age of 18.

The guidelines referred to in point 4 include those already mentioned plus others such as the UNHCR 1994 publication *Refugee Children: Guidelines on Protection and Care*. The immigration rules referred to are those presently in use.[6]

WELFARE ISSUES, LOCAL AUTHORITIES AND THE CHILDREN ACT

Welfare issues for unaccompanied children cannot be separated from the asylum process. Unless welfare issues are addressed a child cannot properly contribute to the case. Under the 1989 Children Act local authorities have a responsibility to promote the welfare of children in need under 18. The Social Services Inspectorate guide states that unaccompanied asylum-seeking children are 'by definition children in need'(para.3.1).

In January 1991 the SSI sent a circular 'Unaccompanied refugee and asylum-seeking children' to directors of social services saying:

the local authority for the area in which an abandoned child…is physically present when his or her 'unaccompanied' situation comes to the attention of social services has a duty to receive the child into its care if this is necessary in the interests of the welfare of the child.[7]

Local authorities have a Children Act duty under Section 24 to inform a recipient authority when a young person they have been advising and befriending moves there. The SSI guide emphasises that it is impermissible 'for one SSD to define itself out of responsibility before first negotiating and gaining agreement of another to take over responsibility' (para.2.21).

Article 39 of the UN Convention on the Rights of the Child obliges states to ensure that child victims of armed conflicts, torture, neglect, maltreatment or exploitation receive appropriate treatment for recovery and social integration. This requires local authority, education and community health services to be resourced for meeting the mental and physical needs of refugee children.

'CHILDREN FIRST AND FOREMOST'

This excellent pamphlet from Barnardos is mainly concerned with accommodation issues for young asylum seekers (see chapter 13). It also quotes two government documents on good practice within child care and suggests that local authorities should follow this practice in their treatment of asylum-seekers. The documents are:

- *Framework for the Assessment of Children in Need and their Families* published in 2000 by the Department of Health. This has specific reference to 'children separated from their country of origin'. It also refers with approval to a December 1999 document *Separated Children in Europe Programme – Statement of Good Practice* published in 1999 by UNHCR and the International Save the Children Alliance in Europe.

- *The Quality Protects Programme.* This is part of the government's programme to transform children's services following the 1998 Department of Health's publication *Modernising Social Services* and instituted in September 1998. It lays out 8 National Objectives which local authorities must prove they will meet in order to obtain ring-fenced monies. Though these Objectives do not specifically refer to asylum-seeking children yet most of the indicators are directly relevant to such children. Examples are to ensure a) children are securely attached to carers capable of providing safe and effective care, b) children are protected from emotional, physical, sexual abuse and neglect, c) children in need gain maximum life chance benefits from education opportunities, health care and social care, d) young people leaving care, as they enter adulthood, are not isolated and participate socially and economically as citizens, e) children with specific social needs arising out of disability or a health condition are living in families or other appropriate settings in the community where their assessed needs are adequately met and reviewed.

LEGAL REPRESENTATION, LOCAL AUTHORITIES AND THE ASYLUM DETERMINATION PROCESS

The SSI guide states:

> It is important to ensure that the child's asylum claim is lodged and pursued…and any implications this legal status might have for future rights to benefits, education entitlements etc. Local authorities should be proactive in ensuring that the process of establishing the child's immigration status does not drift. (para.2.41)

This obliges the responsible social worker to ensure that a legal representative is appointed.

PARTICULAR SOCIAL WORK PRACTICE ISSUES IN THE ASYLUM DETERMINATION PROCESS

Any child not already referred to the Panel of Advisors should be referred.

The immigration rules say that children should not normally be interviewed by immigration officials as to the substance of the claim if information can be obtained elsewhere. Children applying for asylum on entry are often required to attend a 'pro forma' interview supposedly confined to basic details of identity and method of entry. In practice substantive asylum issues are often addressed. It is important that a legal representative or a panel advisor accompany a child to any pro forma interview. An interview may be scheduled very soon after the social work referral when there is no legal representative or panel advisor available. The social worker should argue that the interview be postponed but this may be refused, in which case the social worker should attend. If a social worker does attend a pro forma asylum interview with a child, then full notes of what was said should be taken. These notes are the child's property and should be given to the child or the legal representative when appointed.

If the Home Office opts for a full substantive interview, it is essential that a legal representative is present. A social worker should never be the sole adult supporter of a child at such an interview.

Asylum applicants are normally given a Statement of Evidence (SEF) form to complete. This was previously known as a Political Asylum Questionnaire. Some children apply for asylum only after entry. In these cases a child is normally given a Political Asylum Questionnaire (PAQ). Only legal representatives should complete this. The Children's Legal Centre's guide warns: 'If inexperienced adults take on this task, they are jeopardising the child's future safety and well-being.'

Social services may be contacted by the immigration authorities to look after an unaccompanied child. Other than this, a social worker should never contact the Home Office.

It is the unaccompanied child and not the social services department who is the client of the legal representative. The child and the representative are in a confidential relationship and the local authority has no automatic entitlement to information disclosed by the child.

DRAFT GUIDELINES ON THE EXAMINATION AND DETERMINATION OF ASYLUM CLAIMS BY UNACCOMPANIED REFUGEE CHILDREN

The Amnesty pamphlet *Most vulnerable of all* contains a list of guidelines mainly aimed at immigration officials concerned in the asylum determination process for unaccompanied children. These guidelines can be equally well followed by representatives. Examples are:

- '…the protection of the child shall take priority over all other matters'
- 'Children have the right to participate in decisions about their future'
- 'Where an interview is required, scheduling should take into account the child's needs, such as school-times'

- 'Consideration (in an interview) should be given to child-friendly or novel techniques such as typing the statement directly onto a screen which the child can see. Confirmation of evidence should be taken every step of the way and not at the end of a page or interview'

- 'The term "persecution" should be construed to take into account the fact that certain acts that may not amount to persecution of an adult will amount to persecution of a child'

- 'Refugee children should never be held in detention... Where refugees are held...pending referral to social services, it should be for the shortest possible period of time and every effort should be made to assure the child of this fact'.

PRACTICE ISSUES FOR SCHOOLS

Children sometimes enter the UK on documents giving the wrong age. This causes problems if children are then placed in an inappropriate age group at school.

A school may be unaware that a child is applying for asylum. The Save the Children guidelines on unaccompanied children suggest that there should be school procedures identifying unaccompanied refugee children in order to provide pastoral support. If a child is in local authority care, this should not be a problem. However, a child may be in an informal fostering situation. The only non-discriminatory way a school could identify such an asylum-seeking child is if all parents/carers were asked about the child's immigration status (Chapters 1 and 4).

If the school is aware of an asylum application, teachers should verify that the case has been referred to the Panel of Advisors. They should check that the child has a suitable and expert legal representative.

Good practice: gender

ENGENDERING THE ASYLUM PROCESS

The central practice issue is for all professionals working with women constantly to raise issues of gender within the asylum process. This is not easy. Crawley states:

a gendered approach...will also meet with either passive resistance, because it shakes the routine and the comfortable assumption of stereotypes, or active opposition, because it ultimately challenges traditional gender roles. (p.5)

The case of *Shah and Islam* will make it easier to raise gender issues. Advisors should, where it is appropriate to claim gender-based asylum, argue both 'social group' and 'imputed political opinion' grounds.

It may often be more appropriate in many instances to argue cases of gender or (see below) sexual persecution under Article 3 of the European Convention on Human Rights (right not to be subjected to torture or inhuman or degrading treatment) as this does not require showing any of the UN Convention grounds.

GENDER AND PROCEDURAL ISSUES

The following points apply equally to both advisors and Home Office officials:

- Women arriving with family members should be informed of their right to make an independent asylum claim. It is bad practice for advisors to assume that a woman's claim is dependent upon that of a male relative.

- Women should be informed in private about their right to make an independent claim. Women may be reluctant to discuss issues of a personal nature in the presence of family members.

- Women should be given the opportunity to be interviewed apart from the rest of the family.

- Women should be given the choice of a woman advisor and interpreter.

- Advisors should insist that the Immigration Service provide women interviewers and interpreters. A letter of 27 March 2000 from the Asylum and Appeals Policy Directorate of the IND to ILPA says: 'If it is not practical to provide an interviewer or interpreter of the same sex as the applicant, consideration will be given to deferring the interview'.

ASKING THE RIGHT QUESTIONS

Typical questions asked by advisors presuppose that the refugee client is a male involved in conventional politics. In advising women it is important to avoid language with ambivalent meaning. For instance many women may not associate some harm (such as genital mutilation) as 'torture'. The RWLG *Guidelines* suggest 'Non-confrontational open and/or indirect questions should be asked in order to establish a woman's reasons for fleeing' (para.5.26). The following open questions are proposed by the *Guidelines*:

- Why did you leave your country?
- Did you have any problems?
- Were you treated badly?
- Was anyone you know treated badly?
- Why did you think this happened?
- Who was responsible?

- How did you feel?
- What difficulties did these experiences cause you?
- Did you complain to the authorities and if not why not?
- What would happen to you if you were to return to your country?

OTHER GENDER-SENSITIVE TECHNIQUES

The UNHCR *Guidelines on the Protection of Refugee Women* offer gender-sensitive techniques in interviewing women (para.72). These are also applicable to the Immigration Service and advisors should use them to evaluate the propriety of Immigration Service interviews. Examples are:

Be patient with female applicants to overcome inhibitions, particularly regarding sexual abuse. Questions may need to be asked in a number of different ways before victims of rape and other abuses feel able to tell their stories.

Recognise that women who have been sexually assaulted exhibit a pattern of symptoms that are described as Rape Trauma Syndrome. These symptoms include persistent fear, a loss of self-confidence and self-esteem, difficulty in concentration, an attitude of self-blame, a pervasive feeling of loss of control, and memory loss or distortion. These symptoms will influence how a woman applicant responds during the interview. If misunderstood they may wrongly be seen as discrediting her testimony.

DOCUMENTARY EVIDENCE

Advisors need to familiarise themselves with the experiences of women in refugee producing countries. The RWLG *Guidelines* suggest the following relevant information (para.5.43):

- the position of women before the law
- the political rights of women
- the social and economic rights of women, the consequences for women who refuse to abide by social, religious or cultural norms
- the incidence and forms of violence against women
- the efficacy of protection available to women
- the consequences that may befall a woman on her return.

ADJUDICATOR HEARINGS

Advisors should be prepared to argue:

- The hearing should be held in camera pursuant to the Immigration Appeals (Procedure) Rules.

- The adjudicator should be a woman. The Procedure Rules allow for cases to be transferred to another adjudicator where 'expedient'.
- Evidence should be given by video.

Good practice: sexuality

Most significant good practice issues regarding gay men and lesbians coming to or remaining in the UK are dealt with in Chapter 7.

ACCUMULATING EVIDENCE

There are specific sources of information about the persecution of gay men and lesbians in the country concerned. The International Gay and Lesbian Human Rights Commission Asylum Project, based in San Francisco, produces bundles of documents on a country by country basis for a relatively small fee.

Comments on casework problem at start of chapter

A has an asylum case under the UN Convention if he can provide proof of political activity and persecution through torture. B, who was endangered in a civil war, and C, conscripted into the army, have difficulties. Neither of these situations is ground for asylum. They will have to try to show that they were singled out because of their politics or religion or other Convention grounds. D has a claim. The 1997 UNHCR *Guidelines on Policies and Procedures* state that child conscripts can claim asylum – presumably as members of a social group. E and F should have a social group claim. F has the problem of showing that imprisonment in itself equals persecution. As their psychotherapist you should check that they all have advisors whom they trust and if not you should refer them to suitable advisors.

Notes

1   Steve Cohen, *From the Jews to the Tamils*, South Manchester Law Centre 1987
2   In the Matter of T.C.V. quoted in J. Bhabha and Young, 'Through a child's eyes', *Interpreter Releases*, vol. 75, no. 21, June 1988, p.757, n.55
3   Ahmed Tabed, 1994 Imm AR
4   *INLP*, vol. 12, No. 4, p.142
5   1988 Imm AR
6   HC 395
7   reference C1–91–2

CHAPTER 9

Deportation and removal
Tactics and report writing

A CASEWORK PROBLEM

You are a community worker. Immigration officers raided a local factory. A, who has lived in the UK for fifteen years, was detained as an alleged illegal entrant. The Immigration Service claim that he was brought to the UK on a false passport when aged 2. B was detained for similar reasons. He has lived in the UK for nine years. Their families ask your advice.

A REAL CASE STORY

My name is Manda Kunda. I am under threat of deportation and the reason the Home Office wants to deport me is that, according to the immigration laws, I am guilty because I have left my husband. Even though my visa is valid for another one and a half years they want to withdraw it and send me away. I'd say that immigration laws are sexist in the sense they don't waste time in issuing deportation orders or deportation threats when it comes to women. These immigration laws are forcing women to put up with violence. I have managed to escape from a web of violence in which I have been entangled for many years... I refuse to be pushed back to the misery that I was kept in. You cannot understand the feelings and misery that swell up inside you. The Home Office doesn't realise what it puts us through, as women we are just labelled as creatures of our husbands... Now is the time to put my foot down and refuse to let anybody intimidate me.

ANOTHER REAL CASE STORY

Azize and Rosmina Rahman and their daughters are from Djibouti. While visiting the UK, Rosmina was diagnosed as having cancer, and one daughter, Shabana, as having a genetic disease, Fragile X Syndrome. A family settlement application was rejected. After a huge campaign and the submission of reports, the Home Office relented.

AND ANOTHER ONE

Anwar Haq overstayed his leave as a visitor. He married Ruby, a British citizen. They had a child, Shariq. The Home Office refused Anwar's settlement application. Ruby had to choose between having the family split or uprooting herself. Under strain, Anwar was hospitalised for psychiatric care. After the submission of medical reports he was allowed to remain.

SCOPE OF THIS CHAPTER

This chapter goes to the core of immigration control enforcement, namely the Home Office's powers of expulsion. It examines the different scenarios in the expulsion process affecting families.

It examines the main points of good practice in helping someone remain here. In particular it looks at both the creative use of time and the compilation of welfare reports in resisting removal.

FURTHER READING RESOURCES

Right To Be Here: A Campaigning Guide to the Immigration Laws was published in 1985 by the former Greater London Council Anti-Deportation Working Group. It included the case of Manda Kunda. Though the law is outdated, the issues remain.

THE ROUTES TO EXPULSION

People can be expelled for

- entering the UK illegally

- obtaining leave to remain by deception

- overstaying permitted leave

- breaching a condition of entry by working or failing, when required, to register with the police or having recourse to public funds

- engaging in conduct unconducive to the public good

- following a court recommendation

- as a family member (a non-British spouse or child under 18) of someone being expelled.

It has been seen in Chapter 3 that there are two methods of expulsion - deportation and removal. Deportation has certain procedural safeguards, in particular a right of appeal. The 1999 Immigration and Asylum Act abolished most deportation procedures and replaced them with removal. Of the routes to expulsion the only ones retaining deportation safeguards are expulsion on grounds of behaviour not conducive to the public good, a court recommendation following a court recommendation and expulsion of a family member of someone being deported.

HISTORY AND POLITICS OF EXPULSION

The 1905 Aliens Act sanctioned deportation following a court recommendation after criminal conviction or proof that an alien received parochial relief (see Chapter 2). The 1919 Aliens (Restrictions) Amendment Act and the 1920 Aliens Order allowed deportation by the Home Office on conducive to public good grounds. Though painful to the individual, the significance of expulsions is not just about individuals. It is about the demoralisation of black and asylum-seeking communities vulnerable to controls.

The above cases were argued on 'compassionate grounds'. There is nothing in the rules allowing settlement on grounds of illness, violence, child vulnerability, division of families or uprooting of entire families. The categories of compassionate grounds are infinite. However, the above scenarios continually reproduce themselves. They show intrusion into black people's lives, the denial of their autonomy to live with or apart from whom they wish and the invasion of physical privacy.

There is another reason why these scenarios recur. The presentation of compassionate grounds arises as a challenge to Home Office practice but often results in being a mirror-image of this practice. Advisors, unable to contest expulsion in principle, create or emphasise scenarios which accord with ideologically acceptable and sympathy producing constructs. (see Chapter 10).

COMPASSIONATE GROUNDS AND THE IMMIGRATION RULES

The concept of compassionate grounds is in the immigration rules:

> the public interest will be balanced against any compassionate circumstances…Deportation will normally be the proper course where a person…has contravened a condition or has remained without authority… the Secretary of State will take into account all relevant factors…including:

(i)   age

(ii)   length of residence in the United Kingdom

(iii)   strength of connections with the United Kingdom

(iv)   personal history, including character, conduct and employment record

(v)   domestic circumstances

(vi)   previous criminal record and the nature of any offence of which the person has been convicted

(vii)   compassionate circumstances

(viii)   any representations made on the person's behalf.

The new October 2000 immigration rules extend this definition of compassionate grounds to removal cases.

EXPULSION OF FAMILY MEMBERS OF PEOPLE SETTLED HERE

Home Office policy on expelling family members of those settled here is contained in instructions to immigration officers – documents DP 3/96 (marriage policy), DP 4/96 (children) and DP 5/96 (children with long residence). The instructions explain when removal should not happen. Where the criteria cannot be met, expulsion is not automatic but advisors need to explain why it should not occur.

EXPULSION OF CHILDREN IN THE UK WITHOUT PARENTS

Instructions DP 4/96 state: 'There is no bar to taking deportation/illegal entry action against children of any age.'

Children could be in the UK without parents. Overseas students on returning to their country of origin may leave children with relatives in the UK to continue their education. Such informal fostering gives no protective status.

Instructions DP 4/96 impose limits on expelling people under 16:

> If there is any evidence that the care arrangements are seriously below the standard normally provided in the country concerned or that they are so inadequate that the child would face a serious risk of harm if returned, consideration should be given to abandoning enforcement action.

Similar instructions prevented the removal of Sujon Miah, aged 11, to Bangladesh. A case report states:

> he had been violently treated in Bangladesh by his mother and father who had beaten him with sticks and told him to go. The Social Welfare Department of Dhaka stated that it had no child protection role and that there was no monitoring of child abuse. There were no children's homes; orphanages were for younger children and were full. A child rejected by its family would usually live on the streets. The International Social Services of the United Kingdom expressed concern about the applicant's future.[1]

CONSTRUCTIVE EXPULSION

British citizens theoretically immune from removal can be forced to leave. This is constructive expulsion. A typical scenario is where one parent and children are British but the other parent is threatened with expulsion. Accompanying this partner effectively exiles the British family members.

PRESENCE OF CHILDREN

The presence of children is tactically often the main weapon in resisting adults' expulsion. This is ideologically problematic (see Chapter 10). Instructions DP

5/96 describe relevant factors such as 'whether return to the parent's country of origin would cause extreme hardship for the children or put their health seriously at risk'. In a press release of 1 March 1999 the Home Office announced: 'A child who has spent a substantial, formative part of his life in the UK should not be uprooted without strong reasons' and young children in the UK for seven (previously ten) years should be recognised as 'established in their community' and their family should remain.

PARENT WITH ACCESS RIGHTS

In 1994 a rule was created attempting compliance with the European Convention of Human Rights through facilitating contact by a parent, including an expelled parent or one threatened with expulsion, with a child here. The provision was extremely narrow. It was modelled on the visitors rule and was confined to married partners now divorced or separated. The October 2000 rule alterations liberalised the provision to some extent. It now applies to a parent (married, single, divorced or separated) who:

- wishes to enter the country for a period initially of up to twelve months. Prior entry clearance is required. Proof must be given of an intention 'to continue to take an active role in the child's upbringing' and evidence produced of a residence or contact order from a court or a 'certificate issued by a district judge confirming the applicant's intention to maintain contact with the child'. There is no prohibition on employment.

- is already in the country and wishes to remain, initially, for up to a further twelve months. The rules are similar to an entry application except that if there is no court order then evidence will be required from the parent settled here (or, if contact is supervised, from the supervisor) of maintenance of contact. The rule is limited in two important ways. First the applicant's existing leave to be in the UK must be as the partner, married or unmarried, of the other parent. The rule does not apply, for instance, to someone here as a visitor or student. Second the rule does not apply where the applicant's presence in the UK is in breach of the immigration law. In either of these cases the Home Office will expect the applicant to leave the UK and apply from overseas to exercise access rights. However the best advice is to try and fight the case whilst still in the UK. This is to avoid the inconvenience of leaving the country and also, where the couple are on good terms, to avoid the need for a court order or certificate as opposed to a statement from the parent settled here.

- wishes permanent settlement following an initial twelve month stay as a parent exercising rights of access.

CHILDREN BORN IN THE UK

Since 1983, children born in the UK are not automatically British (see Chapter 3). Non-British children born in the UK are in limbo. There is no obligation to obtain leave to remain. They are not illegal entrants or overstayers and cannot be expelled as such. Leave should be sought if the child is to travel overseas and will need readmission. Under the rules a child will be given the same leave as parents. If the parents have different leave the child will be given the longer. Children born and living in the UK for ten years can automatically register as British citizens.

EXPULSION OF ENTIRE FAMILIES AND OF FAMILY MEMBERS OF SOMEONE BEING EXPELLED

The Rahman family case illustrates how entire families can be threatened with expulsion where none has settlement.

There is an extraordinary provision within the 1971 Immigration Act and 1999 Immigration and Asylum Act which permits expulsion of family members, with settled status, of someone being expelled. This in practice is the only way of removing non-British children born in the UK. If the parents leave voluntarily, such children become immune from expulsion but also become prisoners within the UK as they would have no right to readmittance if they left the country.

According to the immigration rules there are limitations in practice on the expulsion of family members. A settled spouse of someone being deported or removed will not normally be expelled as well if he or she has settlement in his or her own right or if the couple are living apart. A child of someone being expelled will normally be allowed to remain if he or she is living apart from the expellee with the other parent, or is nearing the age of 18, or has left home and is living independently or is married.

The immigration rules also mention some specific compassionate circumstances to be considered where someone is being expelled (by deportation or removal) as a family member of someone else being expelled (by deportation or removal). These are:

- in the case of a spouse, the ability to maintain himself or herself and any children in the absence of the other partner

- in the case of a child of school age, the effect of expulsion on his or her education

- the practicality of any plans for a child's care and maintenance in this country if one or both parents are expelled.

These circumstances should logically be considered in every case of deportation or removal not just that of family members of someone being expelled.

EXPULSION OF PARTNERS

The rules allowing settlement after marriage do not apply to someone marrying after overstaying leave or entering unlawfully. Instructions DP 3/96 provide guidance on when expulsion should not take place:

- Expulsion should not normally be initiated where the couple have lived together after marriage for two years before enforcement action. Enforcement is defined as a Home Office warning a person should leave the country or service of a notice of deportation or illegal entry papers or a court recommendation for deportation. And:

- It must be unreasonable for the settled partner to move overseas. Examples are she or he has close family ties in the UK; or has been settled and living in the UK for at least the preceding ten years; or medical evidence shows her/his life would be significantly impaired overseas.

EXPULSION FOLLOWING DOMESTIC VIOLENCE

The 1981 case of Nasreen Achtar shows a demeaning attitude towards black women. Nasreen came from Pakistan after undertaking a proxy marriage by telephone. She left the relationship after domestic violence. The Home Office claimed that the marriage was invalid and tried to deport her. The adjudicator said:

> She could not possibly have considered herself married as she let her husband beat her up and throw her out while pregnant…having discovered (not surprisingly) that the alliance was a disaster she is resolved to live here on social security… she has brought her troubles upon herself.

A further appeal held that the marriage was valid. The case is quoted in *Women's Movement.*[2]

GOVERNMENT POLICY CHANGES

During the 1980s and 1990s black women highlighted domestic violence within the twelve months' 'probationary' period after marriage – presenting women from overseas with the choice of staying in a violent relationship or being expelled. The Southall Black Sisters produced the pamphlet 'A stark choice, domestic violence or deportation? Abolish the one year rule!' Mike O'Brien MP in a parliamentary written answer of 16 June 1999 announced a concession outside the rules. Women subject to violence would be allowed settlement on proof of 'an injunction, non-molestation or other protection order (other than an ex parte or interim order) or a relevant court conviction, and full details of a relevant police caution'. The concession extends to violence within the two year probationary period of an unmarried relationship.

CRITIQUE OF THE CONCESSION

This concession will help some women. However, it can be criticised for further legitimising Home Office intrusion into black women's lives. The concession assists only women who came to the UK intending settlement. There is another scenario concerning women who did not come for settlement but require settlement following violence. An example is a wife such as Manda Kunda accompanying an overseas student and subjected to violence.

THE BEREAVEMENT CONCESSION AND RULE

At the same time as announcing the domestic violence policy, Mike O'Brien also introduced a further concession. This permitted permanent stay where the settled partner died during the 12 month probationary period or, in the case of an unmarried or same-sex relationship, the two year probationary period. The immigration rule changes of 2 October 2000 incorporated this concession into the rules.

ILL-HEALTH AND EXPULSION

Settlement can be obtained for health reasons only on compassionate grounds. Mukesh Patel is Indian with severe spinal defects. His family lived in the UK. He was refused entry, being over the age permitting children joining parents. The *Guardian* (2 November 1981) quoted an immigration official stating: 'One of the considerations with a disabled person is that they should be able to stand on their own two feet'. Mukesh was eventually allowed settlement (*The Times*, 7 June 1982).

Good practice

MAKING TIME

No communication should be made to the Home Office without understanding timing implications. Use of time is a tactical issue in contesting expulsion. How to delay or accelerate a case is a constant issue for both the Home Office and advisors. Time in immigration cases is a battlefield.

BAD TIMING

Bad timing destroys cases. Someone overstaying leave may marry a person settled in the UK. If the Home Office is immediately notified, then a settlement application may be refused as being based on a suspected marriage of convenience. Home Office policy is that expulsion is the norm unless a marriage existed for two years before enforcement. A rule of thumb for someone overstaying leave is that the longer a relationship lasts before approaching the Home Office, the better.

GOOD TIMING

Any settlement application should preferably be made within the period of existing leave. This will preserve one-stop appeal rights. Advisors should be aware that the risk of any failed application and appeal will be a refusal to allow re-entry for any purpose. This is the mark of Cain (see Chapter 1).

PLAYING FOR TIME: LONG STAY CONCESSIONS

Advisors may need to slow down cases so that time limits are reached – such as a child being in the UK for seven years. It is Home Office policy to consider granting settlement to someone lawfully in the UK for ten years or unlawfully for fourteen years before enforcement. The periods do not include time waiting for an unsuccessful immigration appeal nor time spent overseas other than short absences.

TIMING OF FRESH REPRESENTATIONS

If the Home Office rejects representations it may be counter-productive to ask immediately for a reconsideration. It is pointless re-sending old information. The Home Office does not respond well to repetition. Information has to be new, used to illustrate a new angle or confirm previous arguments.

TACTICS, TIME AND THE 1999 IMMIGRATION AND ASYLUM ACT

Before the 1999 Act advisors had devised strategies using the two-tier appeal procedure and the deportation process as a shield against enforcement just as the Home Office had strategies to accelerate matters. This allowed time to develop legal tactics and for clients to develop roots. The timetable of expulsion has been severely curtailed with the abolition of deportation appeals, the creation of one-stop appeals and the generalisation of rapid removal procedures (see Chapter 3).

The Home Office issued a *Consultation Paper on Review of Appeals* in July 1998. This justified abolishing deportation appeals as

> appellants with hopeless cases can nevertheless achieve their objectives not by winning their appeal but by spinning out the process so... [it] may even become impractical to remove them.

This categorisation of 'hopeless cases' is self-fulfilling. It is constant tightening of the law and abolition of appeal rights which renders cases 'hopeless'. Advisors now have to explore new tactics.

CLIENT CONTACT WITH THE HOME OFFICE

Abolishing deportation appeals will have consequences. There will be increases in judicial review. People subject to removal will change address and break Home

Office contact. This will be through fear or attempted consolidation of roots before applying to regularise status. Advisors have a professional responsibility to explain the consequences of ceasing contact – the main one being probable detention if uncovered. Any resumed Home Office contact should be through an advisor without disclosing the applicant's address.

HOW MUCH TIME TO CONTEST EXPULSION?

This fundamental question raises issues as to what legal processes and tactical planning are available and realistic. A one-stop appeal can act as a protective shield for several months. Without an appeal the Home Office could go rapidly to the removal stage. The only way to prevent this is the submission of new representations, the taking of the case to judicial review or the submission of an asylum claim or a claim under the 1998 Human Rights Act or the Race Relations (Amendment) Bill now before parliament.

REGAINING APPEAL RIGHTS

The 1999 legislation grants an adjudicator appeal against breach of the European Convention and preserves appeal rights against asylum refusal. These appeals can be used as partial substitutes for the abolished deportation appeals. They can be joined to any existing one-stop appeals in which case they must be explicitly included in the statement of 'additional' grounds for remaining here, although failure to include them is not necessarily fatal. Alternatively they can constitute a separate free-standing right of appeal where there is no one-stop appeal. In this case other grounds, such as compassionate grounds, can be attached to the appeal through a statement of additional grounds.

The 1999 legislation is designed to prevent repetitive applications and appeals. Advisors must be careful when and how applications are presented. A refused asylum claim will not attract an appeal if lodged after the Home Office has made removal directions. In some circumstances the Home Secretary can guillotine a human rights or asylum appeal by certifying that the claim was submitted to delay removal with no other 'legitimate purpose'.

The Race Relations (Amendment) Bill presently going through parliament also allows an immigration appeal in cases of alleged discrimination.

STAYING WHILE CONTESTING A CASE

No one should leave the country during their expulsion case. Re-entry will be refused. It is usually bad practice to return to the country of origin and make a fresh application there: it will probably be refused automatically because of the previous immigration record. Best advice is to stay and fight.

GIVING UP THE FIGHT?

Contesting expulsion is dispiriting. There will be occasions when clients consider giving up. This is particularly the case if there is detention with little prospect of release. The longer a case is fought, the longer this may prolong detention. An advisor can provide an honest assessment of the chance of securing settlement and emphasise, except in cases of detention, that there is nothing to lose by continuing the challenge.

INFORMING OTHER PROFESSIONALS IN GOOD TIME

Advisors need a long-term tactical perspective on each case. They need to determine quickly whether professional reports are needed and to involve other professionals rapidly so they feel part of a team. Reports need to be commissioned at an early stage. It takes time for a report writer to win the client's trust, become acquainted with the issues and prepare a draft and final report.

REPORT WRITING

The cases starting this chapter relate to constructs of the family, its break-up and issues of ill-health. These are scenarios where compassionate grounds have to be argued and not merely asserted. They have to be objectively proven. This is why at the heart of good practice is the provision of written reports. The next chapter develops a critique of compassionate grounds and the danger of stereotyping black people.

General issues

- It is the advisor's responsibility to provide the report writer with instructions as to the issues to be addressed, with relevant documents, including appropriate legal material, and with an explanation of their relevance.

- Any case continuing over a lengthy period may require updating reports.

- The report writer should provide oral evidence at any appeal. This confirms the report's significance.

- Reports should start with the writer's qualifications and experience.

- Notifying the Home Office that reports are being prepared could stall any precipitate enforcement action.

- There is no obligation to submit unhelpful reports. It is often best not to be specific with the Home Office about why a report is being commissioned. This will create suspicion if the report is not submitted.

- As a matter of anti-racist practice no charge should be made for reports. If charges are demanded then legal aid may be available.

- No report should be used without the client having read it (in translation if necessary) and agreed to it.

Multiple reports

More than one report may be necessary. In the Rahman case there were, exceptionally, twenty-four reports.

Where more than one report is submitted they should fit together like a jigsaw. There is no point in reports simply echoing each other. Each must have its purpose. It is a core responsibility of the advisor to define what is optimally required from each report so they tie together as a whole. It is good practice for the advisor to make this definition with the active participation of the proposed report writers. It will clarify matters if writers are aware of the nature of other proposed reports.

Advocacy

A report writer should discuss the report in draft with the advisor. The writer should be prepared to make reasonable alterations consistent with his or her opinion. This is normal legal practice with expert reports.

Family workers need not feel alarmed in assuming an advocacy role through reports. The problem in immigration cases is not the compromising of professional integrity. It is convincing the immigration authorities of harm caused by expulsion.

Social work reports

Social work reports are often central to a case. Where there are several reports there should be a 'lead' report which places in context all other reports which can then be attached as appendices. The social work report can undertake this role. The contextualising and cross-referencing of other reports illustrates their interlocking relationship.

Manchester guidelines

Manchester Council has created a post of Social Services Immigration Liaison Officer through which are routed requests for reports from advisors. The council has issued a 'Protocol for commissioning social circumstances report from Manchester social services department'.

The service is not advertised and the protocol limits it to two categories of cases. This is not good practice. One category is where a 'key carer for an adult disabled person is under threat of deportation' (see Chapter 17). The other is where

> there are children under the age of 18 years who are themselves at risk of deportation or whose parents/carers are at risk. Children in these circumstances may then be deemed to be children in need under the Children Act.

The 1989 Children Act

A letter of December 1998 from Manchester Social Services Immigration Liaison Officer to GMIAU explains that the power to provide reports for children or parents threatened by controls comes from Section 17 of the 1989 Children Act. Section 17(1) declares: 'It shall be the duty of every local authority...to safeguard and promote the welfare of children within their area who are in need'. Section 17(10)(a) defines a child as in need if 'he is unlikely to achieve or maintain...a reasonable standard of health or development without the provision for him of services by a local authority'. Section 17(11) defines development as meaning 'physical, intellectual, emotional, social or behavioural development' and health as 'physical or mental health'.

Social work report contents

A social work report should address the compassionate grounds listed within the rules and deal with matters contained within Home Office instructions to immigration officials. In cases concerning children, relevant Articles within the European Convention and the UN Convention on the Rights of the Child (see Chapter 5) should be addressed along with every point within Section 1(3), the 'welfare checklist', of the Children Act. The latter includes:

(a) the ascertainable wishes and feelings of the child concerned (considered in the light of his age and understanding);

(b) his physical, emotional and educational needs;

(c) the likely effect on him of any changes in his circumstances;

(d) his age, sex, background and any characteristics of his which the court considers relevant;

(e) any harm which he has suffered or is at risk of suffering;

(f) how capable each of his parents, and any other person in relation to whom the court considers the question to be relevant, is of meeting his needs.

Section 1 declares: 'the child's welfare shall be the court's paramount consideration'. The High Court has held in immigration cases that child welfare is not necessarily paramount (see Chapter 10). None the less it is one consideration that the Home Office should examine.

Reports dealing with domestic violence

No further report is needed if there exists the legal evidence required by the concession. If this evidence does not exist then best practice is for reports to be provided by a refuge worker, by any witness to the violence, by any medical worker who can vouch to the medical condition and by the woman herself. Advisors should argue that evidence of violence is sufficient to ground settlement even if not the type required by the concession. What matters is the violence not the type of evidence.

Violence to women in the UK in a temporary capacity

The concession does not cover cases of women in the UK in a temporary capacity, for instance with student husbands, wanting to stay permanently following the break-up of a relationship through violence.

A dependent partner admitted temporarily has a problem contesting expulsion. On relationship breakdown she cannot contend that her original intention was settlement. The Home Office argues that expulsion is therefore not detrimental. Reports have to deal with this issue:

- It is necessary to show that the situation has radically altered since arrival and like is no longer being compared with like. Initial entry was as a married woman. Removal will be as a separated partner devoid of previous material resources, including her family home, and perhaps with sole childcare responsibility.

- There may be a danger of the violence being reproduced overseas or of the male partner kidnapping any children.

- The welfare of children will be served by their remaining here and not being uprooted from school and community.

These points reproduce problematic issues of stereotyping and the fact that without children it is extremely hard for an abused partner to defy removal. It is children, as much as the abuse, that are often the key to a woman remaining.

Other issues of marriage breakdown

The problematic nature of compassionate grounds is seen in the fact that marriage breakdown without violence or children is not usually sufficient to prevent expulsion of a male or female partner. A welfare report needs to address the following:

- The wife will in some cultures be subject to shame if she returns alone. She may be threatened with family violence grounding an asylum claim (see Chapter 7).

- Where there are children accompanying the overseas partner they might effectively be cut off from one parent.

- Where there are children remaining in the UK it may be possible to argue on behalf of the partner threatened with removal that he or she fits within the rule concerning parents with access right or else, if removed, may be able to return under the rule.

- Other than in exceptional circumstances it is irrelevant that the break-up was not the responsibility of the overseas partner. The Home Office stresses it does not operate as a matrimonial court.

Medical reports

- In cases involving health issues, specific reports must be prepared. It is insufficient simply to inform the Home Office of the medical condition.

- A report from more than one health worker may be required. Where an applicant is receiving hospital treatment there should be obtained, in addition to any social services report, a hospital social worker report emphasising the adverse effect on personal or family life of removal given the pre-existing medical condition.

- Reports from doctors should be at consultant level as these are considered more authoritative.

- Reports will be read by immigration officials without medical training. Technical medical language should be explained.

- Reports are taken more seriously where the applicant is a pre-existing patient rather than being especially commissioned. Therefore a consultant should be seen for treatment as soon as possible.

- Doctors do not like being told by advisors what should be included in reports. The two professionals should work as a team developing a dialogue between themselves.

Contents of the medical report

Reports should be sufficiently detailed to prevent Home Office challenges and should contain the following:

- a diagnosis of the illness including a history of any prior treatment in the UK or overseas

- an account of the treatment being given and/or being planned in the UK

- a prognosis as to possible future development of the illness based on two scenarios – where treatment is to continue and where it is stopped or reduced following expulsion

- an explanation as to why treatment has to take place in the UK and not overseas. This may be because family support exists only in the UK or because of lack of medical facilities elsewhere.

Length of stay requested

The advisor and doctor need to address the length of stay being requested. Should permanent settlement be requested or an extension of stay year by year? This question has medical, legal and tactical implications. The client may wish to stay only for a short period, receive any necessary treatment and then return home. Otherwise best practice is usually to argue for settlement. This is for the following reasons:

- Where settlement is wanted it is pointless to try to 'impress' the Home Office by offering to pay for treatment and/or asking for short-term stay.

- Where settlement is medically required it is distressing regularly to have to justify further stay. It prevents future planning.

- It is tactically best to ask for the maximum. If the Home Office grants less, this can then be contested.

- Where permanent stay is requested, this must be justified. Details have to be provided as to the anticipated length of treatment. If treatment is going to be indefinite or of an extremely prolonged nature this has to be explained. Any need for prolonged after-care or continual observation, assessment and monitoring has to be clarified.

- A settlement application allows for free hospital treatment (see Chapter 16).

- In weaker cases it may be inappropriate to request settlement and this must be discussed with the advisor.

Gravity of illness

The Home Office requires proof of illness or incapacity of a high order to grant settlement. This must be reflected in medical reports. This also applies to mental health. One way of resisting expulsion is showing the adverse mental health consequences of proposed enforcement action. What the Home Office requires is evidence the applicant has reached a genuinely suicidal stage and is capable of harming him or herself.

Home Office rejections of medical reports

In some cases medical reports are rejected by officials without obtaining any independent report themselves. The courts have held:

> It is not appropriate for a civil servant without medical expertise to reach a conclusion contrary to that reached by a psychiatrist simply by drawing on his own native wit.[3]

Advisors should ask when reports are rejected whether the Home Office sought medical advice.

Educational reports

- The basic issue for educational reports is the disruption caused to education by expulsion. The Home Office asserts that children often change schools without detriment when their parents move home. Reports should emphasise the qualitative difference between a planned change of school and one forced upon children globally separating them from friends.

- Reports should show that a child being uprooted from his or her friendship network can have harmful welfare and social consequences.

- It should be emphasised that there are stages within education where disruption is particularly harmful, such as a child making, or about to make, the switch from primary to secondary school.

- Reports should show how other children may be adversely affected through the involuntary removal of a friend and member of the school community.

- It is necessary to distinguish educational reports from letters of support. An educational report should normally be prepared in the name of the headteacher. It should deal with all issues itemised above plus others relevant to the particular child. Teachers, governors, pupils and parents should write letters of support to the Home Office. Schools have sometimes initiated campaigns against removal (see Chapter 19).

Community worker reports

Community workers are another source of reports. The use of such reports is sanctioned by the Labour government's White Paper, *Fairer, Faster and Firmer*. In discussing the backlog of unresolved asylum claims the paper says that consideration will be given to settlement where the applicant shows 'a continuing record of voluntary or other work by the applicant in the local community'.

Specialist country of origin reports

The presentation of compassionate circumstances often presupposes that necessary services, such as hospitals or schools, are unavailable or inadequate overseas. It is insufficient to make assertions about lack of facilities. It is necessary to provide proof. The best proof is often through a report. There are problematic issues of stereotyping concerning the content of overseas reports (see Chapter 10).

There is often difficulty in discovering an expert in the UK or overseas who is able to provide an authoritative report. It is good practice for social services to compile a list of individuals or agencies able to prepare overseas reports. ILPA has produced a *Directory of Experts on Conditions in Countries of Origin and Transit*.

International Social Services may be able to provide a report. This is a social work agency specialising in migration issues. It charges for reports – presently

£350 per case, which may be recoverable under the legal aid scheme. The ISS have produced a referral guide for immigration cases. This states: 'ISS obtains reports from our overseas colleagues on the understanding that a full report will be made available to the Immigration Adjudicator/Home Office whatever its contents', though this is not strictly adhered to. Reports are sometimes obtained by ISS from ministries of social welfare and these may not be disposed to be critical of matters relating to their own country.

Sometimes there may be available pre-existing United Nations reports. For instance in May 2000 the UN Interim Administration (Department of Health and Social Welfare) issued a short report on *Treatment possibilities in Kosovo*. This was directed at countries considering the repatriation of Kosovon refugees. It detailed areas where Kosovo's health service could not provide adequate care.

Probation and asylum reports

Other sources of reports are dealt with elsewhere: probation reports are dealt with in Chapter 18 and medical reports in asylum cases in Chapter 17.

Comments on casework problem at start of chapter

Your role is to suggest an expert advisor and explain the issues. A and B as alleged illegal entrants have no appeal against removal. They can challenge removal by judicial review, arguing that they cannot be unknowingly guilty of deception, though case-law suggests they can be so guilty. If A can provide comprehensive proof of being in the UK fourteen years, this should secure settlement under the Home Office concession. Proof will include medical, national insurance, benefit, tenancy and perhaps school records, along with utility bills and any local authority records. B will have to rely on compassionate grounds to remain. Under the 1999 Immigration and Asylum Act there is provision for two automatic bail hearings within the first eight and the first thirty-six days of detention. Until this part of the Act becomes operative (anticipated spring 2001) a bail application needs to be lodged before an adjudicator. As A and B are personally innocent of deception then bail may be granted.

Notes

1   *Legal Action Bulletin*, March 1995
2   Jacqueline Bhabha and Sue Shutter, *Women's Movement: Women under Immigration, Nationality and Refugee Law,* Trentham Books 1994, p.103
3   Khaira, 1988 *INLR* 731

CHAPTER 10

Deportation and removal

A critique of the concept of compassionate grounds

A CASEWORK PROBLEM

You are a lecturer. Two students, X and Y, are Nigerian. They tell you that they have had removal notices served on them. Both came to the UK on a visit within the last three years. Neither applied to switch their status to that of a student – having been correctly advised that under the immigration rules visa nationals cannot switch from visitors to students. Both have overstayed their leave. X is a lone parent. Before her visit she left her husband due to violence. While in the UK she has sought psychiatric help as a result of the violence. She has two children born in Nigeria. Both are with her. One child is disabled and is in a special school. The other is in the local primary school. She has no close family in Nigeria. Y is healthy, childless and not in any relationship in the UK; he has extended family and a job in Nigeria. X and Y want to remain permanently. What is best practice for yourself and a legal advisor?

A REAL CASE STORY

A is gay and has overstayed his leave to remain. His British partner, B, has been diagnosed as HIV-positive. The Home Office and the appellate authorities rejected A's application for settlement. The case did not fit within Home Office policy as to gay relationships (see Chapter 7) or remaining as a carer for someone with AIDS (see Chapter 17). A's advisors were about to lodge papers for a judicial review. B's consultant sent an urgent message that his reports could not be used as B was not HIV-positive. There had been a check and it was discovered that B had substituted someone else's blood. This seemed unbelievable. However, B confirmed that the consultant was correct. An HIV-positive friend took the initial tests posing as B. The explanation given for this was that B had been told by a friend that the only way A could remain was on 'compassionate' grounds as a carer.

ANOTHER REAL CASE STORY

Florence Okolo came to the UK with her children Awele and Anwule to join her husband who was in the UK temporarily as a student. The marriage subsequently broke up. Florence and her children were threatened with deportation. Florence and the children did not come to the UK with any expectation of or desire for settlement. Unlike the case of Manda Kunda (see Chapter 9) there was no domestic violence. In the absence of these typical 'compassionate' grounds it required a major national campaign to fight the deportation successfully.

A QUOTATION

'Some [immigration] lawyers themselves admitted dilemmas in representation where they battled with using whatever means were available to them to obtain a positive outcome and the negative consequences such action might have for children. An example of this was in relation to the use made of distressing personal information. One lawyer was particularly concerned about this and felt she had lost sight of the children's needs and rights in the process of representation. Although an effective and competent lawyer who was often sought out for her skills in representing young people, she believed she had become an unwitting party in the oppression of children and at the same time felt that she was often left with little option. She was disarmingly honest and frank about this and her comments included the statement "if a young person tells me they were raped, I say good! tell me the details, the more sordid the better".' (This quote is from Adele Jones, *The Child Welfare Implications of UK Immigration and Asylum Policy*, Manchester Metropolitan University 1998, p.136)

THE STRANGE WORLD OF COMPASSIONATE GROUNDS

These cases and quotation indicate the Kafka-like universe in which people defend themselves against immigration controls. Within this context undesirable human conditions, such as being HIV-positive or being the victim of child rape or domestic violence, become positive attributes in contesting expulsion.

Within this universe challenging expulsions appears not so much to oppose Home Office practice but to mirror such practice. The humiliation of the threat of expulsion is matched by the humiliation of having to justify presence in the UK.

The issue is the overwhelming strength of control enforcement, to the point where those under threat of controls and their advisors will understandably do or say almost anything, however demeaning, to escape expulsion. This should concern welfare professionals and advisors because it is essential anti-racist practice to try to avoid becoming complicit in the reproduction of reactionary ideas stereotyping clients. It is equally important to help empower clients so they do not feel obliged to stereotype themselves.

SCOPE OF THIS CHAPTER: WHOSE REALITY IS IT ANYWAY?

The purpose of this chapter is to help professional workers stand present reality on its head and so help clients. It is to challenge one of the central orthodoxies of advisors contesting expulsions. It is to redefine as at best problematic and at worst as reactionary something normally viewed as an unproblematic lifeline. It is a matter that normally goes unquestioned in the literature on immigration controls – namely the whole concept of 'compassionate grounds'. Undoubtedly raising these grounds has helped many people remain in the UK. However, the cumulative effect is to patronise, dehumanise and further victimise those under threat of immigration control, while providing a spurious justification of controls on the basis that the Home Office retains sufficient flexibility to find in favour of 'hard cases'.

What this chapter does not do is present any complete resolution to the issues of professional practice discussed here. This is because they admit of no complete resolution. At best they can be only partially resolved. Though they appear in daily life as professional issues they are ultimately highly political. They are inextricably linked to the very existence of immigration controls. They will disappear only with the disappearance of controls.

The arguments developed here are premised on the belief that cases should be contested by all means necessary – including the presentation of compassionate grounds. However, what is being argued is that since the imposition of post-war immigration controls in 1962 and after over three decades of scraping the barrel looking for compassionate grounds, it is time for reflection on professional practice.

COMPASSIONATE GROUNDS AS A TACTICAL DEVICE

It has been seen that there are scenarios continually reproducing themselves in the presentation of compassionate grounds (see Chapter 9). These are:

- domestic violence leading to a break-up of marriage
- the adverse effect on the welfare of any children
- family separation due to the deportation of one member
- the deportation or removal of entire family units
- issues of ill-health.

What needs to be emphasised is that none of these matters is ever raised by the Home Office as a justification for enforcement procedures. No one is under threat of expulsion *because* they have been subjected to violence, or *because* they are a child or *because* they are a spouse or *because* they are ill. They are under threat because of immigration laws which allow for settlement only in certain defined circumstances. This may be a strange way of describing an obvious situation. However, in many cases the compassionate factors are so strong they themselves often assume the appearance of being the reason for expulsion.

Compassionate grounds are simply a device of advisors to help clients. This is not surprising given that there is often no other apparent way forward in a case. They are an artificial, tactical construction and are part of an awful game of cat and mouse. Within this real-life game clients often become pawns. This is clearly the case with respect to children. Child welfare issues are raised not necessarily to keep a child in the UK. Rather they are often raised as a device to keep the rest of the family in the UK.

None of this game is the responsibility of advisors or welfare professionals – whose first, though not only, concern has to be the winning of cases. Responsibility rests on immigration controls. However, professionals do have a responsibility to question the way they play the game and the consequences of their game play.

THOSE LEFT OUTSIDE THE GAME

Experienced advisors have developed to a fine art the presentation of cases involving domestic violence, child welfare, split families and ill-health. Legal representations in these cases often involve a series of medical, educational and welfare reports.

The consequence of this is that healthy, childless, unbattered, single people living outside any family context or other relationships find it almost impossible to construct compassionate grounds to remain. It is ironic that those most vulnerable to immigration controls are the young, childless, fit and healthy.

IDEALISATION OF THE FAMILY

Settlement applications outside the family construct are discriminated against or doomed (see Chapter 7). Likewise one recurring theme in the presentation of compassionate grounds is the need to preserve the unity of the family, preferably a marital, nuclear, heterosexual and child producing family. If anyone under threat of controls cannot fit easily within this model then they have the burden of trying to fit within its nearest approximation. This results in the further idealisation of the family per se, an idealisation which is extremely problematic.

DEHUMANISATION

The quotation at the start of this chapter is appalling. It transforms something barbaric (child rape) into something positive for the purposes of fighting expulsion. However, it is honest. It shows how professional involvement in the legal processes can dehumanise clients. This is seen in cases involving ill-health. Even the most reputable advisors are continually searching for indications of sickness or disability on the part of clients threatened by controls, particularly where there are no issues of family unity. The sickness or disability can then be transformed into arguments for the postponement or permanent lifting of the threat. It is as though there exists some unacknowledged point-scoring system among advisors: one point for influenza briefly postponing an air flight, two points for a surgical operation delaying departure longer...five points for a nervous breakdown caused by fear of expulsion...eight points for risk of suicide...ten points for terminal illness.

It is this constant pathologisation which patronises black people, defines them as sick, gives them the appearance of passive victims of controls and adds, albeit unwittingly, to the sum total of racism around immigration restrictions. Emphasising issues of ill-health and other vulnerabilities and ignoring the political reasons for expulsions actually dehumanises the individual. It replaces their real humanity with an accumulation of perceived weaknesses. It substitutes political explanation with a list of individual pathologies. This is the reality needing to be stood on its head.

STEREOTYPING OF BLACK PEOPLE

Much of what passes for compassionate grounds perpetuates classic myths and stereotypes of black people. An example is the portrayal of black men. The most common representation of black men within the literature of opposition to immigration control appears to be that of batterers of female partners. Male violence is widespread among both black and white men. Patriarchy is not defined by colour. However, because violence by black men can jeopardise a partner's immigration status and because there have been well-publicised cases of this jeopardy, this has reinforced the myth of the black man as savage brute.

This stereotyping has become a source of tension in some campaigns. Najat Chaffee, a Moroccan woman, came to join her husband in the UK but left him following violence. This jeopardised her immigration status. In the book *Women's Movement* the campaign in defence of Najat is described:

> Central to the campaign were two particular features of Najat's situation. One was that the only reason for her being under threat of deportation was because she was treated as the dependant of her deported husband. The other was that Najat had suffered from her husband's violence and would again face that threat if deported. Within the Friends of Najat Chaffee Campaign there was a continuing debate as to whether the opposition to Najat's deportation should focus on the racism and sexism of the laws under which she risked being deported or on the domestic violence she had suffered.[1]

In most campaign cases emphasis is given to the male violence. The irony of this is that men (and women) who are caught by the twelve months' rule and whose relationships break up without violence find it extremely difficult to receive support or win cases. Conversely very difficult practice issues arise where violent men are subject to expulsion following marriage breakdown (see Chapter 21).

STEREOTYPING OF COUNTRIES OF ORIGIN

Pathologisation transcends the individual. It encompasses her or his country of origin to the point where fact and fantasy become indistinguishable. To contest expulsion on health grounds it is regularly and by necessity argued that there are no, or no adequate, medical support systems in the country of origin. In the case of children it is often argued that there is no adequate schooling available in the country of origin. Women are seen as being at risk if deported – at risk of having children kidnapped by former partners, at risk of being assaulted or shunned by entire communities because of alleged marital misconduct in the UK. Sometimes these are real issues. However, cumulatively there is being painted a picture of a world beyond Britain and Western Europe which is an uncivilised welfare and educational desert and in which women and children are defenceless against the state or the individual. In comparison the UK is, if only implicitly, presented as a gilded palace of welfare, educational and cultural enlightenment in which men, women and children are equal citizens and in which patriarchy no longer exists.

It is true that the world outside the industrial heartlands is hugely unresourced relative to the West. This does not mean that these former colonies have lapsed into social barbarism and reverted to a supposedly natural state of primitive savagery. Community and family support is often much stronger in these countries than in the UK. Professional workers, including advisors, have a responsibility to oppose grotesque characterisations. Instead we often end up reinforcing them.

LIVING IN THE WESTERN WORLD

This stereotyping is seen in other ways. It appears in social work reports commissioned by advisors to look at the welfare of children under threat of expulsion. These reports frequently emphasise how 'westernised' children have become in terms of dress, language and culture generally. Implicit within this is the notion of the superiority of Western values.

One way this stereotyping can be understood is by a fantasy. Imagine you are an immigration advisor or a social worker in India. You are consulted by a British citizen who is contesting the Indian government's decision to expel her and her children. It would not take you long to obtain documentary evidence that the UK is a country in which welfare is rapidly disappearing – with huge hospital waiting lists, with rationing of medical treatment, with dilapidated, overcrowded schools and with male violence and child abuse rampant.

EXCEPTIONALISM AND THE COMPETITION OF THE OPPRESSED

Presenting cases on compassionate grounds raises a competition among black people threatened with expulsion. The immigration rules make it clear that expulsion should be the norm or 'proper course' where there has been a breach of any condition of stay. Ultimately the concept of compassionate grounds rests on an insidious form of exceptionalism. It requires a case to be defined and accepted as an exception to the norm of immigration control before the Home Office will recognise it as worthy.

This results in a contest to find the most extreme points to put to the Home Office so as somehow, anyhow, to distinguish cases and show that the present case is 'exceptional'. The consequence is that the stakes rise with each case. This results in a humiliating scramble with everyone under threat seeking to prove they are more ill or vulnerable or abused than the previous one in the expulsion queue. It makes contesting removal seem like a pilgrimage to Lourdes. Reach the holy waters of being an exception and you will be saved.

NEW LABOUR – OLD PROBLEMATIC

The 1998 government White Paper *Fairer, Faster and Firmer* made two recommendations relating to compassionate grounds. First, it proposed that compassionate grounds should be given 'a higher profile at every stage in the case-working process and said that the government was developing 'criteria which would allow due weight to be given to any such factors'. Second, it proposed that women given twelve months' permission to remain on the basis of marriage should be granted settlement if they leave the marriage because of domestic violence within the probationary twelve months.

These proposals were presented as being self-evidently progressive. However, both proposals reproduce the problematic issues raised in this chapter. They raise them in a form which arguably makes the present situation worse. This is because the proposals appear to be an attempt to 'codify' what is meant by compassionate grounds. The project of 'developing criteria' for such grounds will in practice result in those under threat of expulsion embarking on an even more frantic scramble to fit within the criteria. The need for advisors to intrude into the private lives of clients will intensify.

DOMESTIC VIOLENCE

The concession in respect to domestic violence is now operational (see Chapter 9). For some women subject to violence this will be of great benefit. However, for many others the concession is insufficient or intrusive. It is insufficient because many women, anxious to distance themselves from the violence as quickly as possible, may not have any of the required proof, namely an injunction, non-molestation or other protection order (other than an ex parte or interim order) or a relevant court conviction, and full details of a relevant police caution. In any event it is not standard police practice to caution perpetrators of violence.

The concession is intrusive because women subject to violence are now liable to have their privacy doubly invaded. Advisors will now routinely question them as to the issue of violence. Women will be put in the situation of reliving the nightmare of the violence by seeking domestic court orders to safeguard their immigration status. A failure of the court to make an order will not just jeopardise a woman's safety but also imperil her status.

A BATTLE OF IDEAS

The concession ignores those women who wish to leave a marriage where there has not been violence. In practice these women will be penalised precisely because they have not been battered. So once again something undesirable (to be subject to violence) becomes positive in immigration law. Conversely something desirable (to be free of violence) becomes a handicap.

Many of these problems would have been avoided if the government had abolished in its entirety the twelve-month probationary rule. This would also have protected men who wish to leave a relationship within this period.

The situation becomes even more difficult where a marriage breaks up and there has not been violence nor has the woman partner come to the UK for settlement. An example is the case of Florence Okolo and her children described above.

All this raises a fundamental question – why should entry or stay be conditional on relationships or 'compassion'? There is a battle for ideas here. This is because the notion of compassionate grounds presupposes its own converse, namely uncompassionate grounds. The world is divided not as in Victorian days between the deserving and undeserving poor. Instead it is divided between the worthy and unworthy entrant. Every time a case is defined as 'worthy' there is redefined and excluded the 'unworthy'. Every time it is argued that a client is in the camp of the meritorious there is legitimised the whole ideology of immigration control which asserts its own authority on the backs of the 'bogus', the 'non-genuine', the 'unworthy' and the 'non-meritorious'.

Good practice

GOOD ANTI-RACIST PROFESSIONAL PRACTICE

This is yet another instance within immigration control where the challenge is to formulate good practice in the face of bad law. Advisors and other family workers do not have to accept the situation where clients are continually reduced to and stereotyped as victims. All the good practice suggestions detailed here require commitment. Such a commitment may involve appreciable time in the preparation of a case. It will ultimately, however, enormously enhance the presentation of case not simply by the way clients are portrayed but also by facilitating their active, positive involvement.

BALANCE OF FORCES

The balance of forces within immigration control is such that the state is overwhelmingly more powerful than the individual. Within this context it would be idealistic to expect an individual threatened by controls to forgo the opportunity of arguing any grounds, in particular compassionate grounds, which might help repel the threat. This does not mean the issue is irrelevant. It remains important to resist caricaturing black people, refugees and their countries. Moreover it is vital to make a clear distinction between how a case is presented to the Home Office and how it is presented, for example, to the public in the course of a political campaign (see below and Chapter 19). There is no excuse whatsoever for pathologisation to take place in the course of a campaign.

BASIC GOOD PRACTICE POINTS

- The issues of stereotyping must be discussed with the client to appreciate how he or she would like the case to be presented.
- The client's voice must be heeded as well as heard. No assumptions should be made about how a client would want a case presented or a report prepared.
- Representations and advocacy should never be on the basis of begging for mercy but on the basis of demanding rights.
- Advisors have a professional responsibility to go beyond discussion of the law and to suggest appropriate, if any, tactical ways forward including campaigning.

AVOIDING PATHOLOGISATION IN REPORT WRITING

Avoiding stereotyping and pathologising is important in the commissioning of welfare reports. These reports are written by professionals such as social workers, child psychologists or teachers. It should be made clear to report writers that neither client nor country of origin should be pathologised. Where examples of pathologisation occur then the advisor has a responsibility to draw this to the client's attention and, if the client agrees, to request that the report be amended.

Conversely welfare professionals have a responsibility to challenge advisors who ask for reports to be written in ways which lead to the stereotyping of black people or countries of origin.

GOOD PRACTICE AND CHILDREN

Good practice issues clearly exist in respect of children when cases are presented on 'compassionate' grounds. This is because of the relative powerlessness of children. One of the few researchers, Adele Jones, to have addressed this issue has written:

Advocates representing children should be adequately trained in child development and must be able to demonstrate competency in working in this field in which children can be particularly vulnerable and isolated... Standards for representation should include the following:

- young people are treated with dignity and respect
- young people are kept informed about the progress of their case
- stages and processes are explained and clarified in language young people can understand

- where unmet welfare needs are identified by advocates, young people should be referred to other agencies for support
- advocates should ensure that they are aware and fully explain the consequences of action that might be taken in a particular case
- lawyers should be approachable and supportive in their manner.[2]

These points are directed at advisors but are applicable to other child professionals. Few advisors are child-friendly in their practice. Other than in the case of unaccompanied children, it is rare for advisors to see children involved in a case, let alone seek their views and feelings. Cases are conducted through adults, be they parents, guardians or social workers. Quality time needs to be spent to ascertain children's wishes. Where the children involved are too young for direct communication then their views should be discovered not just through parent(s) but through other adults and young people trusted by the children.

Professionals should stop seeing children as just a tactical mechanism for parents to remain in the UK. This mechanism may lead to a positive resolution of a case. However, children must be treated as people with their own integrity, views and emotions. Advisors need to appreciate that children, even when accompanied by adults, are clients in their own right and should be respected as such.

GOOD PRACTICE AND WOMEN

- All women must be given the choice of a female advisor.
- Where interviews are conducted through an interpreter, a woman must be given the choice of a female interpreter (see Chapter 8).
- Where reports are commissioned from other professionals who need to interview the client, then she should be given the choice of a female welfare professional.
- Where a woman raises issues of abuse then both she, and where necessary her children, should be offered support and counselling through appropriate agencies.
- Advisors and other professionals should never encourage a woman to re-enter an abusive relationship to preserve immigration status.

GOOD PRACTICE AS STRENGTHENING A CASE

It is a myth that the portrayal of clients as vulnerable and their countries of origin as barbaric deserts will persuade the immigration authorities necessarily to act with 'compassion'. The opposite may the case. Advisors and other professionals need to avoid victimology. On the other hand an affirmative characterisation, particularly when linked with campaigning, can result in victories. In the case of Florence Okolo and her two children, the adjudicator, in recommending that the family remain after desertion by the husband/father, described Florence as a 'woman of strength and courage who has found herself in a most unfortunate situation (the loss of immigration status) through no fault of her own'.[3]

COUNTRIES OF ORIGIN

Avoiding the stereotyping of countries can be difficult, particularly where expulsion is contested on ill-health grounds. In these cases it is vital to show what facilities exist, or more precisely do not exist, in the country of origin. This inevitably leads to implications about the incapacity of some countries, particularly Third World countries, to develop welfare infrastructures. None of these issues can possibly be resolved in reports. Good practice though demands an awareness of the issues so the language of reports maligns neither countries nor people.

CAMPAIGNS

There is one activity that starts to break the humiliating and degrading circle of compassionate grounds. This activity is campaigning against expulsion. Good professional practice requires a positive attitude towards campaigns as part of legal strategy (see Chapter 19). It means recognising that campaigns provide the context for the presentation of compassionate grounds. They are the context which resituates compassionate grounds as part of a movement for demanding rights as opposed to free-standing pleas for mercy.

This can be understood through a critique of a quotation from the handbook *Right to be Here: A Campaigning Guide to Immigration Law* (see Chapter 9): '"The personal is political"... For anyone to dismiss fighting on compassionate grounds as a non-political compromise is to dismiss the reality of women's (and many men's) lives.'

As a method of justifying the presentation of compassionate grounds this is inadequate. The personal is political only in relation to the context. Begging to remain in the UK on compassionate grounds is in and of itself hardly political but rather leads to the awful political contradictions outlined in this chapter. Begging to remain is not even personal. It is anti-personal, it reduces the person to a victim. However, the quotation is prefaced with another statement which situates the presentation of compassionate grounds within a campaigning context, namely:

> there is no contradiction between embracing the strategy of ending all immigration controls and being determined to win individual cases...it is essential to combine fighting individual cases with opposing all immigration controls because it prevents you sinking into particularities and losing your focus.

It is this combination which allows the personal to become political in a positive sense. It is this combination which neutralises or stands on its head the ideological negative features of the presentation of compassionate grounds.

Comments on casework problem at start of chapter

This problem poses the difference between cases with typical 'compassionate' aspects and those with none. When the appeal sections of the 1999 Immigration and Asylum Act become operative (October 2000) both X and Y will have neither a 'one-stop' appeal, having overstayed leave, nor a deportation appeal (see Chapter 3).

The Home Office concession for domestic violence is inapplicable for X as the violence occurred overseas. However, the danger of repetition of violence following expulsion is a possible compassionate ground. There are other such grounds, mainly relating to child welfare and in particular that of the disabled child, though the policy of allowing children to remain after seven years cannot be complied with (see Chapter 9). The central good practice issue is the avoidance of stereotyping. You could suggest that X consults a female advisor who is experienced in both law and campaigns. You could contact JCWI or GMIAU to find the nearest appropriate advisor. If X wants a campaign then you could offer to come to the first meeting and to raise the case in your union. You could suggest that X speaks to her student union asking them to initiate a campaign.

The advisor should discuss with X and, where appropriate, the children and liaise with any report writers to ensure that neither X nor her children nor Nigerian men nor Nigeria itself are pathologised. This may best be done by collective discussions with all involved. The advisor should discuss with X the possibility of an asylum claim as a member of a social group liable to violence in Nigeria (see Chapter 8).

Y appears to have no compassionate circumstances. As a lecturer you could prepare a report showing he is a good student – but this falls far short of the *exceptionally* compassionate grounds required. You could tell Y that there is probably no point in returning to Nigeria and reapplying to come to the UK as a student. His having overstayed leave will be sufficient justification for a visa refusal. A campaign against expulsion would have to be massive to succeed, though it could lead to the Home Office conceding that Y stays to complete his course. You could suggest to Y and X that they have a joint campaign as this could strengthen both cases. One issue an advisor could explore in investigating compassionate grounds is whether Y has undertaken voluntary work in the community.

Notes

1   Jacqueline Bhabha and Sue Shutter, *Women's Movement: Women under Immigration, Nationality and Refugee Law,* Trentham Books 1994, p.121

2   Adele Jones, *The Child Welfare Implications of UK Immigration and Asylum Policy,* Manchester Metropolitan University 1998, p.144

3   TH/43445/95

CHAPTER 11

Immigration law versus child protection law

A CASEWORK PROBLEM

You are the social worker for X, who came to the UK to join her husband. They have split up. X tells you she has not got settlement and has overstayed her twelve months' probationary leave. She has two children living with her, A who is Pakistani and B who is British. X's husband has threatened to remove the children to Pakistan. Could a child protection order prevent him doing this? Could a court order stop the Home Office expelling X and A?

A REAL CASE STORY

Michelle Ricablanca was born in the Philippines. Her mother subsequently married Brian, a British citizen, who assumed the role of stepfather. Michelle and her mother were granted entry clearance to join Brian in the UK. They were given leave to enter for the usual twelve months' probationary period. The marriage broke up within this period. The mother returned to the Philippines. Michelle wanted to remain with her stepfather and a baby brother, John, born in the UK. She had no independent right to remain. Her stay depended on the continuation of her mother's marriage. The rules allow settlement where one parent is settled in the UK and there are serious or compelling considerations making exclusion undesirable (see Chapter 6). However, Brian is not a 'parent' under the rules as this includes only the stepfather of a child whose father is dead. There was a campaign for Michelle to remain. Brian applied for a residence order under the 1989 Children Act as in law no one in the UK had responsibility for Michelle. It was hoped that a residence order would dissuade the Home Office from any expulsion. The Home Office was informed of the application. It did not intervene in the proceedings and an order was granted. Following the granting of this order and after a short campaign the Home Office allowed Michelle to remain.

SCOPE OF THIS CHAPTER

This chapter has two linked purposes. First, it will show in juridical terms the contradiction on a national level between the promotion of child welfare through child protection laws, and the negation of this welfare through immigration laws.

Second, it will see how, if at all, this contradiction can be used to protect children from immigration laws.

FURTHER READING RESOURCES

Children, Nationality and Immigration (Children's Legal Centre 1985) by Kathryn Cronin discusses in depth many important issues, though some of the law is now out of date. *Children and Immigration* (Cavendish 1997) by J. Rosenblatt and Ian Lewis contains a very brief introduction to some of the issues along with legislative extracts.

LEGAL AND POLITICAL POWER OF IMMIGRATION CONTROL

One feature of controls is not simply their power compared to other branches of British law. It is their power *over* other areas of law. Whenever there is a conflict between other legislation and immigration law then the latter usually dominates. This becomes important for social workers and court welfare officers when the conflict is with child protection law. A letter of 15 June 1998 from the Immigration Service to GMIAU states: 'it is clear that deportation or removal overrides the provisions of the Children Act'.

In some cases judges declare the supremacy of immigration law. Usually, however, they speak of the need for a 'balancing act' between the welfare of the child and the need to uphold controls. This is an unreal exercise. It does not balance like with like. There is no relationship between the repressive needs of immigration controls and the best interests of children.

There is no legal doctrine which necessitates this ascendancy of controls. It is a political decision. This is clear in wardship proceedings. These are designed to place children under the overall protection of the court yet when it comes to children threatened by immigration laws judges have usually abrogated this responsibility. This is a matter of judicial timidity.

The relationship between child protection and immigration law is undeveloped. There remain issues requiring clarification and around which it may be possible to mount legal challenges to prevent expulsions.

POLITICAL AND LEGAL SUPREMACY OF IMMIGRATION CONTROLS

Examples can be given of the ascendancy of immigration law. The first concerns the expulsion of convicted prisoners granted parole. Release on license is governed by statute. The question is whether the expulsion provisions of the Immigration Act can overrule any obligation for probation supervision. This is now of historic interest. Under Section 46 of the 1991 Criminal Justice Act prisoners 'liable to removal' can be released on licence without probation supervision (Chapter 18). Previously it was the view of the Prison Service that 'the deportation order supersedes the parole licence' (letter to GMIAU from N. McLean of HM Prison Service, 30 December 1991).

The second example concerns powers under mental health legislation to detain patients. The question is whether someone ordered to remain in hospital under Mental Health Act powers can be removed to another country under the immigration laws. In the one reported case on this subject, that concerning Dhanniah Hahiru Alghali, a High Court judge held:

> it is in my judgment quite impossible to conclude from the legislative scheme, whether one looks at the Immigration Act 1971 or the Mental Health legislation or both together, that the general powers conferred over immigrants by the 1971 Act are to be regarded as suspended, superseded or otherwise necessarily replaced in all cases where the immigrant is also an in-patient.[1]

A third example of the supremacy of immigration laws is seen in their relationship to equal opportunities legislation. In one case it was argued that immigration rules which allowed the admission of a wife but not a husband of an overseas student breached the 1975 Sex Discrimination Act. The Court of Appeal dismissed this argument, though this rule was subsequently altered, allowing husbands' entry.[2] It remains to be seen whether the proposed Race Relations (Amendment) Act will allow meaningful challenges to controls (see Chapter 3).

A fourth example, and one more directly related to child protection, occurred in the case of Shabana Rahman (see Chapter 9). Shabana was under threat of deportation. She attended a special school in Bolton. Bolton Education Authority had drawn up a Statement of Special Educational Needs required by Shabana. This was under Section 168 of the 1993 Education Act. Section 168 imposes a duty on an education authority which 'shall arrange that the special educational provision specified in the statement is made for the child'. Nonetheless the Home Office was prepared to override this local authority duty by deporting Shabana. The issue was never tested in court as a campaign in defence of Shabana and the rest of the Rahman family was successful outside the legal processes (see Chapter 19).

UNDERMINING CHILD PROTECTION LEGISLATION

The trend is to undermine child protection law when these conflict with Immigration Act powers. This can be seen in a Court of Appeal case concerning Khalid Khan.[3] Khalid was granted twelve months' leave to join his wife. The marriage broke down within the twelve months. The Home Office refused to grant him settlement and he became an overstayer. There was a child, Saira, of the marriage.

Khalid's lawyer contended that the interests of Saira were paramount and the deportation of her father would be a serious loss. Various arguments were used. There was quoted Article 3 of the 1989 United Nations Convention on the Rights of the Child which provides:

> in all actions concerning children, whether undertaken by public or private social welfare institutions, courts of law, administrative authorities or legislative bodies, the best interests of the child shall be the primary consideration.

It was argued that protection of Saira should be afforded by Section 8 of the European Convention on Human Rights declaring everyone has the right to family life. There was reference to Section 1 of the 1989 Children Act stating that a child's welfare should be the court's paramount consideration (see Chapter 9).

The court rejected all these arguments, saying:

> In the field of immigration, particularly decisions relating to deportation, the interests of the child are not, and cannot be, paramount or primary... If it were otherwise it would be difficult ever to make a deportation decision in relation to children.

However, it went on to state:

> the interests of the child are of great importance and must be given separate consideration, including consideration of the child's family ties in this country, and, in the case of an adult in respect of whom a deportation decision is taken, the adult's ties with the child must be taken into account in the balancing exercise.

This recognition of the 'great' importance of the interests of the child, though welcome, is inadequate. It does not meet the standards of child protection legislation which places the child's interests as foremost. Instead it substitutes an almost existential balancing act between the welfare of real children and an abstract 'public interest' in immigration control enforcement. In this balancing act it is almost invariably the child who falls. This happened to Saira as the court held 'on balance' that her contact with her father was insufficient to prevent his deportation.

CAN A CHILD PROTECTION ORDER PREVENT REMOVAL? HOME OFFICE GUIDELINES

The above discussion leaves open the question as to the consequences of an actual child protection order given by a court. Can it overrule Home Office powers of control enforcement? The present Home Office guidelines on the deportation of children, DP 4/96 (see Chapter 9) express annoyance that some court orders may 'frustrate enforcement action' and 'The Family Court will generally attach much more weight to the child's welfare than to irregularities surrounding the immigration status of the child or a parent'. The guidelines list five orders.

Adoption orders

The guidelines confirm that where an adoptive parent, or one of two adoptive parents, is British then a UK court adoption confers British citizenship on the child giving immunity from expulsion. This transmission of citizenship now derives from the 1981 British Nationality Act.

Custodianship

This less final form of adoption was abolished by the 1989 Children Act. The guidelines commit the Home Office not to remove children still under a custodianship order.

Wardship and residence (custody) orders

The guidelines say that children made wards of court or children subject to a residence order should not be removed without the court's consent. Section 13 of the 1989 Children Act declares:

> Where a residence order is in force with respect to a child...no person may remove him from the United Kingdom without either the written consent of every person who has parental responsibility for the child or leave of the court.

As seen below some judges have suggested that children can be removed without the court's consent where the child is warded or subject to a residence order. However, the guidelines are Home Office policy and the Home Office is obliged to follow them.

The guidelines also state that:

> where an order has been made under the Children Act this cannot in itself deprive the Secretary of State of the power conferred by the Immigration Act 1971 to remove or deport any party to the proceedings although it may be something to which he should have regard when deciding whether to exercise his powers under the Act.

This is a Home Office assertion that it is entitled to remove an adult who has obtained a residence order in respect to a child. There is some judicial support for this. The guidelines give no commitment not to expel a parent or guardian carer in those rare cases where a child is made a ward.

Contact (access) order

The guidelines give no commitment to seek permission of the court before ordering the deportation or removal of a child subject to a contact order. In the case of Khalid Khan described above there was already a Children Act court order allowing him contact of four hours every two weeks but the Court of Appeal did not even bother considering whether this limited access could block removal.

HOME OFFICE INTERVENTION TO STOP A COURT ORDER BEING MADE

Guidelines DP 4/96 state that the Home Office will intervene in court hearings to try to prevent orders being made where

> it is clear that the court proceedings are designed purely to enable the child or the parents to evade immigration control... *There must be evidence, not just a suspicion,*

that there has been a serious attempt to circumvent the immigration control. (emphasis in the original)

Intervention operates as follows in wardship, residence and adoption proceedings.

WARDSHIP PROCEEDINGS

Wardship proceedings, whether or not connected to immigration proceedings, will diminish as a consequence of the 1989 Children Act. Section 100 removes the power to commit a ward of court into the care or supervision of a local authority. This will restrict wardship actions being initiated by local authorities. Private wardship actions will decrease because Section 8 gives the court wide powers in all family proceedings.

The one remaining advantage of wardship is its immediacy. As soon as the wardship application form is issued the child becomes a ward and nothing of significance can be done relating to the child without the court's consent until the wardship ceases by court order.

The leading case

The leading case was decided in 1968.[4] A boy arrived from Pakistan. He claimed admission as the son of Hanif, who was resident in the UK. The immigration officer was not satisfied he was the son and refused admission. The father issued an originating summons, to which the Home Secretary was made a respondent, seeking to ward the youth. The court found for the Home Secretary.

Lord Denning used a phrase that has been repeated in all wardship cases since then: 'The wardship process is not to be used to put a clog on the decisions of immigration officers.' Lord Russell's judgment was more extreme. He said: 'any lawful deportation order…would override any existing express order of the judge in the wardship proceedings that the infant was not to depart from the jurisdiction.' Russell noted that the courts could not prevent a ward convicted of a criminal offence being moved from one prison to another or a ward in the army being posted overseas. In his mind there was an analogy between military, penal and immigration law.

Other cases

In most of the cases decided since 1968 the courts have refused to entertain wardship proceedings to prevent deportation or removal. There are some cases where wardship was allowed for a temporary period.

In one case an adult sister sought to persuade Judge Hollis to ward her six brothers and sisters.[5] The parents had brought the children from India and unsuccessfully sought asylum. The father had already been deported. The mother was about to be deported. None of the children had had deportation notices served on them as the Home Office had anticipated that they would accompany their mother. Hollis was prepared to grant wardship 'until such time as the Home Office has obtained a deportation order against the plaintiff [eldest sister] and her time for appealing such an order has expired'. It seems that Hollis envisaged some sort of skittles match with the eldest siblings getting wardship in turn until deported or being allowed to remain on compassionate grounds.

RESIDENCE PROCEEDINGS

The leading Children Act case shows judges forsaking the welfare of children.[6] This concerned an Eritrean adult who unsuccessfully applied for asylum on arrival. His younger siblings had previously been granted leave to remain. He then applied for a residence order over his siblings under the Children Act. This was refused and the refusal appealed to the Court of Appeal. The Home Secretary threatened to remove him before the residence issue was determined. It was argued that this would be contempt of court.

The court found for the Home Office. Lord Justice Hoffman gave the judgment. First, he held that even if a Children Act, or wardship, order was made by the court this could not stop the Home Secretary removing the child 'or any other party to the proceedings'. Second, he held that given the Secretary of State could remove irrespective of whatever the court decided about granting a residence order then it would not be contempt of court to enforce removal before judicial proceedings were completed. Third, it was understandable that the Home Secretary should want to intervene in cases where it was thought proceedings were being used to circumvent controls. However, there was no need for intervention as the Home Secretary could still exercise his powers of removal or deportation.

A glimmer of hope

There is one reported case where a residence order was granted in spite of Home Office intervention.[7] A father came with his young daughter, Fleur, from Zaire. He claimed asylum. The Home Secretary refused the claim and intended removing them both. In the mean time the father abandoned Fleur and it was discovered he had abused her. Social services placed her with an experienced foster-carer. The carer, with the agreement of social services, applied for a residence order. Judge Bracewell said:

> Even in those cases where the motivation of the applicant is promoted by welfare considerations alone, the courts cannot adjudicate by ignoring the immigration law and relying on welfare in isolation... If it were otherwise, the immigration laws would be meaningless because would-be immigrants would invoke welfare per se as the criteria for permission to remain within the jurisdiction and the immigration laws would be circumvented wholly contrary to the wishes of parliament.

This argument assumes too much. It might as well be said, and with more truth, that child protection laws are usually rendered meaningless and circumvented through invoking immigration control.

However, the judge said that in 'extraordinary circumstances' child welfare could prevail over immigration law. In this case he found that such circumstances existed and granted a residence order. Finally, he said that once a residence order was made then under Section 13 of the Children Act the child could not be removed without the court's consent.

ADOPTION PROCEEDINGS

It was seen above that guidelines DP 4/96 confirm that adoption in a British court by a British citizen automatically confers citizenship on the child and therefore immunity from deportation.

The guidelines do not comment on the effect on the status of a child adopted by a non-British adopter who has permanent settlement in the UK. Such an adoption does not confer citizenship. Some commentators have suggested that it automatically confers settlement. The immigration rules do not support this. The best view is that such an adoption does not alter immigration status. None the less it provides a strong and perhaps irresistible basis for an application to remain permanently as a child of parent(s) settled in the UK.

Home Office intervention in adoption cases

The Home Office has the power to intervene in adoption hearings and argue that an 'adoption of convenience' is being sought for immigration purposes.

Section 6 of the 1976 Adoption Act provides that

> In reaching any decision relating to the adoption of a child a court or adoption agency shall have regard to all the circumstances, first consideration being given to the need to safeguard and promote the welfare of the child throughout his childhood.

Case-law shows when faced with a child of limited or no immigration status then welfare has not always been the court's first consideration. The case of *Re H* confirmed the general principles when an adoption application is opposed by the Home Secretary.[8] These principles required a two stage approach by the court. First, there has to be considered the 'motive' for the application. If there is a 'nationality/immigration motive' then the application should be dismissed at this stage. This makes immigration control and not welfare the first consideration. If the applicant gets beyond this stage then the court must 'carry out the balancing exercise between public policy and welfare'. As has been seen, this is unrealistic. This lack of realism is compounded by the court constructing a definition of 'welfare' which excludes any benefit to be obtained by the child in living here. As the judge said:

I do not take into account any benefit to him of being able to continue to live with the applicants in England since that would improperly bring in nationality or immigration considerations.

However, the most recently decided case on immigration and adoption is also the most enlightened.[9] The House of Lords recognised that a change in immigration or nationality status can lead to improvement in the welfare of a child. A visitor child was left with her grandparents after her mother returned home. Both mother and grandparents agreed that a transfer of parental responsibility was in the child's interests. The grandparents applied for adoption. The Home Office intervened. The court sanctioned the adoption. According to the headnote:

a court should not ignore benefits which would result solely from a change in immigration status when determining whether a child's welfare called for adoption... But benefits which would accrue only after the end of childhood were not welfare benefits during childhood to which first consideration had to be given.

This decision presents an opportunity to argue in cases under the Children Act that preserving or regulating immigration status should not be ignored in determining a child's best interests.

Good practice

CHILDREN ACT WELFARE CHECKLIST

The need to treat the welfare of the child as paramount, as demanded by Section 1 of the 1989 Children Act, does not automatically apply in immigration-linked cases. However, there is an obligation on the Home Office to consider the issue of child welfare in deciding whether to expel children or parents. This was explicitly stated by the Court of Appeal in the case of Khalid Khan, which said that the interests of the child are of great importance. This is why child-centred welfare reports addressing all the points within the Children Act checklist should be submitted to the Home Office in deportation and removal cases (see Chapter 9).

MAKING EARLY APPLICATIONS FOR A COURT ORDER

The Home Office does not automatically intervene in child protection proceedings. However, DP 4/96 makes it clear that the Home Office will be suspicious of any application for a child protection order made at a time where the issue of expulsion is a live one. If an application is to be made then this should be done at the earliest possible time and if possible while the child who is to be made subject to the order or the adult applying for the order still has leave to remain.

THE VALUE OF A COURT ORDER

An adoption order made in the UK to a British citizen automatically confers citizenship and the Home Office is left powerless to enforce removal. According to its own guidelines the Home Office will not remove a child subject to a wardship or residency order without the court's consent. There is also an issue as to whether any overseas country would accept a child known to be subject to a UK court order.

Bringing child protection proceedings is a major decision. In many cases it may be unnecessary as there are already sufficient 'compassionate' arguments to put to the Home Office. However, in some cases the obtaining of an order may help to establish the credibility of someone whose motives the Home Office might otherwise question. This was a consideration in Michelle Ricablanca's case. Her advisors were concerned that the Home Office might claim that her entry had been manipulated by her mother and stepfather and even an independently commissioned child welfare report might not dispel this suspicion. An authoritative court decision, based on a court welfare report, granting a residence order would be a lot stronger.

LOCAL AUTHORITY ORDERS

The Home Office guidelines DP 4/96 make no mention of a child subject to a local authority supervision or care order under the 1989 Children Act. Schedule 3 of the Children Act obliges a child under a supervision order to reside at any address directed by the supervisor. Any removal of the child would render this impossible. Section 33(1) of the Act states:

> Where a care order is made with respect to a child it shall be the duty of the local authority designated by the order to receive the child into their care and to keep him in their care while the order remain in force.

The removal of a child in care would prevent a local authority fulfilling the childcare duty imposed on it by the court. Section 33(7) prohibits the removal from the country of a child in care by any person 'without either the written consent of every person who has parental responsibility for the child or the authority of the court'. This leaves open the question as to what would happen if the Home Secretary tried to remove a child in care or under supervision. There is also another question as to the legal position of a local authority which co-operated with the Home Secretary. Schedule 2, paragraph 19(1), declares that a 'local authority may only arrange, or assist in arranging for, any child in their care to live outside England and Wales with the approval of the court'.

There is no authoritative judicial statement about the immigration consequences of care or supervision orders. The Immigration Service letter of June 1998 to the GMIAU acknowledges that in the case of a care order, the Home Office 'would need to obtain the leave of the court to deport or remove…we would take the views of the local authority into account'.

SHOULD THE LOCAL AUTHORITY APPLY FOR AN ORDER?

There is no authoritative decision as to whether a local authority could obtain a care or supervision order simply to stop or hinder expulsion. Section 31(2) of the Children Act says that an order should be made only where a child is likely to suffer 'significant harm' and this harm is attributable to the 'care given to the child, or likely to be given to him if the order was not made, not being what it would be reasonable to expect a parent to give him'. The legal problem is that the potential harm is not being caused by the parents but by the Home Office. In some cases parents under threat of expulsion, in order to force the Home Office to change its mind, have threatened to leave their children alone in the UK. Under these circumstances a care order may be appropriate as a moral block against parental expulsion with the child residing with the parents in the mean time. This raises many questions especially for black families, who have historically been wary of their children being involuntarily taken into care.

REGULARISING THE STAY OF A CHILD IN CARE OR UNDER SUPERVISION

Even if a care or supervision order cannot in itself block expulsion yet local authority social workers and lawyers need to be aware of the immigration issues. They need to be alert to their responsibility of best defending the immigration interests of a child already in their care or under their supervision but who has not got settlement. Unknown to social services a child may have immigration problems.

Local authorities need to be proactive. The immigration situation of children in care cannot be ignored as otherwise some children may be in danger once they have left care. Section 24 of the Children Act imposes a duty on local authorities to 'promote a child's welfare when he ceases to be looked after by them'. The legal departments of most authorities have neither the training nor the experience to undertake immigration cases. Independent legal advice usually needs to be obtained. The authority needs to take advice on how to formulate an application for settlement to the Home Office on compassionate grounds. If there is significant parental contact with a possibility of the parent(s) resuming care then the authority will have to take legal advice as to whether it is tactically better to argue for leave to remain on a year-on-year basis. If parents are overseas then they may need to be traced to ascertain the child's immigration status and their own parental intentions.

It is good anti-racist practice for local authorities to investigate the immigration status of children in care in order to protect them against any possible immigration threat. This requires every child in care, not just black children or children with non-English names, having their status ascertained (see Chapter 4). Depending on their maturity, this ought to be undertaken with the knowledge of the children concerned.

The immigration rules have a specific provision allowing for indefinite leave to be granted where a child born in the UK is not British but 'is a child in respect of whom parental rights and duties are vested solely in the local authority'.

There is a provision in the 1981 British Nationality Act whereby there is a presumption that the qualifying conditions for citizenship through birth in the UK are to be met by a 'new-born infant…found abandoned'. There is no definition of 'new-born'.

Comments on casework problem at start of chapter

An application on compassionate grounds emphasising that child B cannot be expelled could perhaps persuade the Home Office to allow X and child A to remain. X should apply for a residence order to formalise custody of the children. The Home Office should be informed of the proceedings, allowing it the opportunity to intervene if it considered the case was being undertaken purely for immigration reasons. The kidnapping threat by the father, if believed, is arguably a sufficient reason to obtain an order. If X is granted a residence order over A and B then this in itself cannot prevent removal of either mother or child A by the Home Office except in exceptional circumstances. It is arguable that a threatened kidnapping overseas could amount to such circumstances. However, a residence order could strengthen an application on compassionate grounds. If there is immediate danger of the father kidnapping the child, then wardship can be applied for.

There is also specific legislation aimed at preventing a child being abducted overseas. The 1984 Child Abduction Act renders such kidnapping a criminal offence. The 1985 Child Abduction and Custody Act ratifies two international conventions under which legal procedures are agreed with a number of other countries to assist in returning an abducted child. These are the Hague Convention on the Civil Aspects of International Child Abduction and the European Convention on the Recognition and Enforcement of Decisions concerning Custody of Children and on Restoration of Custody of Children. A High Court Practice Direction has instituted a system of prevention where there is an imminent threat of abduction overseas.[10] This is the Port Alert System. It is operated through the police who liaise with officials at all ports of exit. Reunite: International Child Abduction Centre is an agency dedicated to helping parents in these situations.

Notes

1   1986 Imm AR
2   *Kassam v. Immigration Appeal Tribunal* (1980 2 All ER) p.330
3   1998 Imm AR p.106
4   Re A (1968 2 All ER)
5   Re K and S (1992 1 FLR)
6   Re Teame (1994 Imm AR 368)
7   Re Fleur Matondo (1993 Imm AR)

8   Re H (1996 2 FCR)
9   Re B (1999 1 FCR) p.529
10   Practice Direction (1986 1 All ER) p.983

PART THREE

The Welfare State

CHAPTER 12

Benefits and immigration status

A CASEWORK PROBLEM

You are a refugee community worker. X is single, living at a friend's house. He has applied for asylum. He was refused income support because of lack of immigration status. The local authority refused him cash or voucher support for essential living needs as he does not require accommodation. He asks if these refusals are correct.

A REAL CASE STORY

An asylum seeker... was left destitute by social services in ... Kensington and Chelsea and had to sleep rough during the whole winter...unable to cope any longer with the...inhuman conditions under which he had to pursue his claim, he gave up...and signed an agreement to be sent back... Advisors managed to convince him to reconsider his decision. Shortly after a decision on his case recognised he was a refugee. (This is quoted from 'Surviving the asylum process' by Monica Feria-Tinta and Curtis Doebbler).[1]

SCOPE OF THIS CHAPTER

The relationship between benefit entitlement and immigration status represents the paradigm of the relationship between the welfare state and immigration controls. The chapter looks at how this nexus is taken to its logical conclusion through denying all means-tested and contributory benefits from those subject to controls. This is part of a process of removing immigrants, migrants and asylum-seekers from the welfare state. Instead asylum-seekers are having imposed on them a return to the Poor Laws while everyone else subject to controls does not even have this precarious safety net. In this sense asylum-seekers are relatively privileged. They do have a support system of sorts – but this is a privilege of the damned.

Eligibility for benefit is found not in the immigration rules but in benefit regulations. However, benefits dependent on immigration status are now almost identical to the benefits constituting public funds in the rules. This chapter examines both the benefit regulations plus the alternative, inferior system established under the 1999 legislation for asylum-seekers.

FURTHER READING RESOURCES

The Child Poverty Action Group's *Immigration and Social Security Handbook* contains detailed advice on benefits and immigration status. A new edition is due in late 2000. The Refugee Council publishes a regular *Asylum Support Update* on the 1999 legislation. The April 2000 edition of the *Legal Action Group Bulletin* has an article by Nadine Finch on 'Providing support for asylum-seekers' under the 1999 legislation. The London Advice Services Alliance produces a newsletter on benefits and immigration. The JCWI *Immigration, Nationality and Refugee Handbook*, due to be updated in 2000, has a very useful chapter on benefits and other state provisions. In 1999 the Department of Community Studies at Manchester Metropolitan University published *Immigration, Asylum and the Provision of Services in Manchester* by Ed Mynott. 'Immigration control, anti-Semitism and the welfare state' by Steve Cohen in *Critical Social Policy* (vol. 13), reproduced in David Taylor (ed.) *Critical Social Policy: A Reader* (Sage 1996), traces the history throughout the twentieth century of the link between welfare entitlement and immigration status.

THE PRE-HISTORY

The 1999 Immigration and Asylum Act has been understandably criticised for introducing a poor law for asylum-seekers. Paradoxically aliens suffered no discrimination under the original Poor Laws. An 1803 case considered the rights of a German baker and family. Lord Ellenborough said: 'the law of humanity which is superior to all positive laws, obliges us to afford [aliens] relief, to save then from starving'.[2]

HISTORY OF BENEFITS AND IMMIGRATION STATUS PRE-1914

A relationship between welfare entitlement and immigration status has existed since the inception of controls and of the welfare system – which were created simultaneously. The 1905 Aliens Act instituted poverty tests which could deny entry or lead to deportation (see Chapter 2). The Act became operative on the day, 1 January 1906, that a Liberal government came into power initiating major welfare reforms. First, there was the 1908 Old Age Pensions Act, which introduced state financed pensions. Second, was the 1911 National Insurance Act, which provided both for unemployment benefit and for sickness, disablement and maternity benefit based on national insurance.

This legislation linked entitlements to residency and nationality status. The Old Age Pensions Act required twenty years' citizenship and twenty years' residency. The National Insurance Act made entitlement to health benefits dependent on five years' residence, otherwise non-British citizens were eligible only at a reduced rate. Bureaucratic obstacles were erected against acquiring citizenship. The *Jewish Chronicle* (31 July 1925) reported someone applying before 1914 awaiting an answer in 1925.

BENEFITS AND IMMIGRATION STATUS 1919–45

In 1919 the government authorised 'out of work donations' to those unemployed after war-work. The *Jewish Chronicle* (28 March 1919) reported: 'The Ministry of Labour has refused to extend out of work benefit to aliens.' This affected Jewish tailors producing military uniforms. The 1921 Unemployment Insurance No. 2 Act empowered the Minister of Labour to extend unemployment benefit payments beyond sixteen weeks. The Minister, Dr T. Macnamara, stated: 'I have decided that benefit beyond 16 weeks should not be granted to aliens.' (*Jewish Chronicle* 23 June 1922) The 1925 Widows, Orphans and Old Age Contributory Pensions Act established a pension scheme for the widow or orphan of an insured man. No benefit was payable if the insured had been out of the UK for two years prior to the claim.

BENEFITS AND IMMIGRATION POST–1945

The relationship between entitlement and status has developed from being ad hoc to being almost comprehensive. A 1957 tribunal decision on unemployment benefit under the 1946 National Insurance Act shows the post-1945 link. The headnote reads:

> An Italian woman had a permit to stay in this country subject to certain conditions. She did not comply with these conditions, the permit was withdrawn and she was ordered to leave the country by a certain date. She claimed unemployment benefit after that date. Held – that she was not available for employment until she was notified that the deportation order was revoked. She had no right to be here and no right to be employed in the period in question.[3]

This case is important as it concerned a benefit to which the appellant had been making contributions. However, the relationship between status and entitlement became systematic following the 1966 Supplementary Benefit Act in relation to non-contributory benefits. Supplementary benefit later became income support. Benefit officers were governed by a secret document – the 'A Code'. This contained a section on 'Aliens and immigrants'. The code acknowledged that the 1966 Act 'makes no distinction between aliens, immigrants and native-born citizens' but said that benefit should be denied to 'people admitted to this country by the immigration authorities on the specific understanding they will not become a charge on public funds'. This practice was regularised by the 1980 Supplementary Benefit (Aggregation, Requirements and Resources) Amendment Regulations. By 1982 the *Guardian* was running articles headed 'Social security officers refusing benefits to blacks and Asians' (13 August 1982). Housing benefit started to become linked to immigration status with the exclusion of overseas students from benefits by the 1984 Housing Benefit (Amendment) No. 3 Regulations. These exclusions were widened to include others subject to controls and extended to council tax benefit by the 1994 Housing Benefit and Council Tax Benefit (Amendment) Regulations.

FAMILY ALLOWANCES, CHILD BENEFIT, CHILD TAX ALLOWANCE

In 1978 the JCWI produced *Divide and Deprive*, exposing the relationship between family allowances, child benefit and tax allowances and immigration status.

Family allowances were introduced in 1946. They provided cash payment for second and subsequent children. Allowances were linked to residency status – the child had to be present in the UK. This was to discriminate against certain groups depending on migration patterns and the operation of controls excluding children (see Chapter 6). The 1975 Child Benefit Act replaced family allowances with child benefit which again was not payable for children outside the UK.

This discrimination could have been alleviated through child tax allowance which was introduced in 1909. Relief was available for children overseas. The 1980 Finance (No. 2) Act abolished allowances after a long transition period. This Act was delayed by a campaign headed by JCWI. However, the abolition of allowances was prompted by the introduction of child benefit and also by the British High Commission in Bangladesh which issued a document, *The Sylhet Tax Pattern*, claiming tax fraud within the UK by Bangladeshis from Sylhet.

THE INLAND REVENUE

In 1977 the Birmingham Community Development Project published *People in Paper Chains*. This described the effect of immigration controls on the Pakistani community of Saltley in Birmingham. It revealed the Inland Revenue's involvement in internal control. Before the abolition of child tax allowances, revenue officials, like immigration officers overseas, would make unannounced visits to Pakistani households in Saltley demanding proof of the relationship with children in Pakistan.

HABITUAL RESIDENCY

In August 1994 there was introduced another test for means-tested benefits, that of 'habitual residence'. There are exceptions for people granted refugee status or exceptional leave to remain and for EEA nationals exercising community law rights.

Habitual residence is undefined. The hardest hit are black people who return overseas on extended family visits. After the European Court of Justice found against the UK, the Social Security Minister, Angela Eagle, stated in a press release of 14 June 1999 that habitual residence would be satisfied by people

> who were once habitually resident in the UK; then moved to work in another EEA state and became habitually resident there; and then subsequently returned to seek work in the UK where their family lives.

A parliamentary answer of the same date went further and said 'we believe it would be wrong to limit this important principle to people returning from a member state of the EU'.

LIAISON WITH HOME OFFICE

The A Code stated:

> The SBC [Supplementary Benefits Commission] have agreed to notify the Home Office of claims for Supplementary Benefit by people whose admission to this country is subject to a time-limit or some other form of control. It is then for the immigration authorities to decide whether the person's right to remain here is in any way affected.

Local authorities also acted as Home Office agents. In February 1981 Manchester Council's Treasurer wrote to South Manchester Law Centre about a student refused rent rebate – the forerunner of housing benefit. Rebate eligibility was not then dependent on immigration status. The JCWI pamphlet 'No Passport to Services' quotes the Treasurer:

> The rebates section do not notify the Home Office of all foreign students who make an application for rebates or allowances. It is however the intention to do so for those applicants who decide to proceed with their application and who are subsequently granted rebates.

LIAISING WITH THE HOME OFFICE: MODERN LAW AND PRACTICE

Exchange of information between the Benefit Agency and the IND was formalised in an October 1995 'Memorandum of Understanding'. This is contained in an internal June 1996 Benefit Agency book, *A Guide to Persons from Abroad*.

The 1997 Social Security Administration (Fraud) Act allows the supply of information between government departments relating to 'passports, immigration, nationality'. This goes beyond preventing fraud, stating: 'This section does not limit the circumstances in which information may be supplied.'

Local authorities administer housing and council tax benefit. The Department of Social Security guidance HB/CTB A1/96 concerned claims by asylum-seekers. One section was headed 'Obtaining information from the Home Office'.

NATIONAL INSURANCE NUMBERS

In a parliamentary answer on 19 June 1973 on obtaining national insurance (NI) numbers Sir Keith Joseph said:

> I am introducing generally a procedure whereby applicants who hold passports will be asked to produce them...if any irregularities are noticed which give rise

to suspicion of illegal entry or presence the Home Office Immigration Service will be informed.

Under Section 19 of the 1997 Social Security Administration Fraud Act, claimants for most benefits have to produce a national insurance number or enough information to get one. Documents other than passports will suffice but people from overseas may not have such documents.

THE 1996 ASYLUM AND IMMIGRATION ACT

Asylum-seekers and some other groups remained eligible for benefits. All this changed with the 1996 Asylum and Immigration Act combined with the 1996 Social Security (Persons From Abroad) Miscellaneous Amendments Regulations, which linked virtually all non-contributory benefits, including child benefit, to immigration status. Initially regulations were introduced in February 1996 prior to the 1996 Act coming into force but these were held unlawful. Asylum-seekers remained eligible for income support (including income-based jobseeker's allowance), housing benefit and council tax benefit in just two circumstances: first, if the asylum claim was lodged on entering the UK and second, if the Home Secretary declared the country of which the applicant was a national was in a state of upheaval and the asylum claim was lodged within three months of the declaration. Non-asylum-seekers subject to the public fund requirements of the immigration rules were, with some exceptions, totally denied benefits.

THE 1948 NATIONAL ASSISTANCE ACT AND THE 1989 CHILDREN ACT

Following the 1996 Asylum and Immigration Act, advisors turned to local authority administered legislation. Section 17 of the 1989 Children Act (see Chapter 9) was one source of financial and/or accommodation support for unaccompanied children and for families with children. More innovative was the use of Section 21 of the 1948 National Assistance Act to help single adults and childless couples. Section 21 provides 'residential accommodation for persons aged eighteen or over who by reason of age, infirmity or any other circumstances are in need of care and attention which is not otherwise available to them'. Court cases held that Section 21 obliged local authorities to accommodate asylum-seekers and provide financial assistance to those accommodated.[4] Assistance had to be in kind – vouchers or services such as meals on wheels.[5] Voucher assistance was not available unless accommodation was also being provided under the Act.[6]

Support under the 1948 and 1989 Acts was not confined to asylum-seekers. Children Act provision was available to children or families with children unable to access benefits because of immigration status. A High Court case held that an overstayer with AIDS, too ill to travel and without benefits, was entitled to help under the 1948 Act as 'humanity stood above the law'.[7] 'Sponsored immigrants' subject to an undertaking (see Chapter 3) and therefore ineligible for basic benefits were also able to utilise the 1948 Act in cases where, for instance, the sponsor had become unemployed or left the UK.

SOCIAL SERVICES

The 1948 and 1989 legislation is administered through local social services. This placed the latter in contradictory roles.

Many social services saw themselves as helping asylum-seekers. However, they were effectively enforcing internal controls through assessing applicants' immigration status to determine eligibility for local authority support.

The distinction between social services' facilitating and repressive roles became blurred. *The Highbury and Islington Express* of 15 October 1999 reported the manager of Islington's Asylum-Seekers Service advocating the immediate withdrawal of all local authority support from asylum-seekers whose asylum claim was rejected.

SOCIAL SERVICES LIAISON WITH THE HOME OFFICE

The Department of Health through the 1988 Local Government Finance Act partially compensated authorities for expenditure under the 1948 and 1989 legislation. This led to breaches of confidentiality. The department issued yearly local authority circulars explaining how to account for expenditure. These circulars insisted that 'records such as the Home Office Immigration and Nationality Department forms SAL1 or SAL2 and the reference number on these forms…should be maintained and the auditor should have access to such written evidence'. SAL (standard acknowledgement letter) forms are issued as proof of an asylum application and can also be used as proof of identity. Annexed to the local authority circulars was Home Office advice on 'notification of suspected immigration offenders'.

THE 1999 IMMIGRATION AND ASYLUM ACT: EXCLUSION FROM STATE BENEFIT

Section 115 of the legislation removes entitlement to the following non-contributory benefits from 'persons subject to immigration control':

(a) The core means-tested benefits of last resort

- income support
- income-based jobseeker's allowance
- housing benefit
- council tax benefit
- a social fund payment

(b) Family and disability benefits

- child benefit
- working families' tax credit
- attendance allowance
- severe disablement allowance
- invalid care allowance
- disabled person's tax credit
- disability living allowance

A person subject to control is defined as a non-EEA national who

- has no leave to remain in the UK, or
- whose leave is subject to no recourse to public funds, or
- a 'sponsored immigrant' given leave to enter after a maintenance undertaking, or
- who has had leave extended to pursue an immigration appeal.

The most important categories exempt within this definition and remaining eligible for benefits are EEA nationals (and their families), UK nationals (as they require no leave to remain in the UK), those people granted refugee status or exceptional leave to remain (as they are not subject to the no recourse to public funds requirement) and those people granted settlement (as they are also not subject to the public funds requirement) other than sponsored immigrants and those not habitually resident.

EXEMPTIONS UNDER THE SOCIAL SECURITY (IMMIGRATION AND ASYLUM) CONSEQUENTIAL AMENDMENTS REGULATIONS 2000

This removal from benefits became operative on 3 April 2000 under the above regulations. The regulations also include some further exemptions. These differ as to the nature of the benefit claimed.

Means-tested benefits

- Asylum-seekers who claimed asylum on arrival before 3 April 2000. They remain eligible until a decision is made on their asylum claim. There are conflicting Social Security Commissioner decisions as to what is meant by 'on arrival'. Eligibility applies whether or not the benefit claim itself was lodged before or after 3 April 2000 and whether or not there has been any break in entitlement through obtaining employment.

- Asylum-seekers in receipt of benefit before 5 February 1996 until the next decision on their asylum claim.

- Nationals of countries which have ratified (not just signed) the Council of Europe Social Charter – presently EEA countries plus Cyprus, Czech Republic, Hungary, Malta, Poland, Romania, Slovakia, Switzerland and Turkey. Future ratifications can be checked from the council's website. The national has to be 'lawfully present' in the UK. The Department of Social Security tries to define 'lawfully present' very narrowly so as to exclude, for instance, nationals who enter the UK quite lawfully under temporary admission while their status is being determined. This should be resisted. There is a similar exemption under the European Convention on Social and Medical Assistance but presently this does not include any further countries.

- Asylum-seekers from the Democratic Republic of Congo (Zaire) and Sierra Leone who applied for asylum within three months after the Home Secretary declared these countries to be in a state of upheaval.

- Persons who left Montserrat after 1 November 1995 because of volcanic eruption. Most of these have been granted settlement.

- People who are temporarily without funds as remittances from abroad have been disrupted, provided there is a reasonable expectation funds will be restored.

- A 'sponsored immigrant' whose sponsor has died or who has been in the UK for five years or it has been five years since the undertaking was given, whichever is the longer. It is important to distinguish 'sponsorship undertakings' from normal sponsorship forms as the latter do not prevent benefit claims (see Chapter 3).

Family and disability benefits

- 'Member of a family' of an EEA national. This is not defined. It would include a family with a British citizen child.

- A person lawfully working who is a national of a state which has signed an equal treatment in social security treaty with the EEA. These states are presently Algeria, Morocco, Slovenia, Tunisia and Turkey. The European Court of Justice has held that 'lawfully working' includes someone no longer employed because of unemployment, sickness, maternity or retirement. The Department of Social Security has been reluctant to acknowledge that asylum seekers are covered by these agreements and there currently is a case pending before the Commissioners.

- A family member of the above. The family member does not have to be an EEA national.

- A sponsored immigrant.

- Transitional protection for those continuously receiving benefit since before 5 February 1996 (6 October 1996 for child benefit). Protection is lost if the Home Office rejects the asylum claim.

RESTRICTIONS ON 1948 NATIONAL ASSISTANCE ACT AND 1989 CHILDREN ACT

The 1999 Immigration and Asylum Act attempts to disentitle asylum-seekers and others from reliance on Section 21 of the 1948 National Assistance Act and Section 17 of the 1989 Children Act for benefits or accommodation.

Section 21 is no longer available to accommodate 'persons subject to immigration control' where the need 'for care and attention has arisen solely – (a) because he is destitute; or (b) because of the physical effects or anticipated physical effects of his being destitute'.

A person is destitute if

(a) he does not have adequate accommodation or any means of obtaining it (whether or not his other essential needs are met) or (b) he has adequate accommodation of the means of obtaining it, but cannot meet his other essential needs.

It should be noted (as explained above) that support under the 1948 National Assistance Act was available to a much wider group than asylum-seekers and therefore exclusion affects a wider group (see Chapter 13).

Section 17 is not to be available to a dependent child and members of the child's asylum-seeking family where adequate accommodation or essential living needs are being provided, or should be being provided, under the Act's support system. Restrictions are placed on equivalent Scottish and Northern Ireland legislation.

THE NEW 'SUPPORT' SCHEME

There is a new Home Office funded support scheme for destitute asylum-seekers and dependants. It is run by the especially created National Asylum Support Service within the IND. Support can consist of financial support for 'essential living needs' or of accommodation or a package of both. Accommodation issues are examined in Chapter 13. NASS is responsible for determining eligibility and level of support. Some NASS documents are on its website.

The scheme is based on Part VI of the 1999 Act with details contained within the Asylum Support Regulations 2000. The regulations became operative on 3 April 2000 with some asylum-seekers being phased in later.

For the purposes of obtaining support under the new scheme the 1999 legislation includes, for the definition of an asylum-seeker, someone claiming protection under Article 3 of the European Convention on Human Rights (no one to be subjected to torture or inhuman or degrading treatment).

DETAILS OF THE SCHEME: ASYLUM SUPPORT
REGULATIONS 2000

An asylum-seeker's dependant for support purposes is defined as

- a spouse

- a dependent child under 18 of the asylum-seeker or spouse or a close family member of either, living with the asylum-seeker since birth or six of the last twelve months

- a disabled person over 18 who would otherwise fit within the above category

- an unmarried partner living with the asylum-seeker for two of the last three years

- a person receiving Section 17 Children Act support immediately before commencement of interim regulations on 6 December 1999

- a person receiving support under equivalent Scottish or Northern Irish child legislation immediately before 3 April 2000

- anyone else being treated as a dependant by the Home Office.

The regulations go beyond the general description of 'destitution' contained in the 1999 legislation and define it in relation to the adequacy of existing accommodation, essential living needs and availability of income, assets or other support.

Financial support is through vouchers, £10 of which is redeemable in cash, distributed via post offices.

Essential living needs explicitly exclude costs of faxes, computers and computer facilities, photocopying and travel other than initial travel to accommodation provided under the scheme. All this excludes consequential legal expenses for the asylum claim itself.

Also excluded from essential living needs are entertainment and toys. Barbara Roche MP, the minister for immigration, said in parliament on 12 April 2000: 'Those who are in receipt of vouchers can use them to buy toys.' This is cynical as the limited funds given asylum-seekers are calculated to exclude such purchases.

NASS can determine whether applicants have intentionally made themselves destitute to enter the new scheme. This scenario echoes the Victorian concept of the 'feckless' poor. In a letter of 17 April 2000 from Barbara Roche to David Crausby MP it is admitted: 'The Home Office is not specifically aware of any asylum seekers who have deliberately squandered their resources.'

A destitute asylum-seeker includes someone likely to become destitute within a prescribed period of fourteen days.

Support ceases fourteen days after the determination of the asylum claim including the disposal of any immigration appeals.

Under the Act families with children under 18 will continue to receive support even if the asylum claim is rejected.

HARD CASES FUND

Failure to support after the refusal of an asylum claim and exhaustion of appeals will leave many people penniless – such as those applying for judicial review, those too ill to travel or who have no papers to return home or are stateless or are pursuing their case on compassionate grounds. On 20 March 2000 NASS issued an explanatory pamphlet on 'The new asylum support scheme'. This revealed the existence of a 'small budget for hard cases, where asylum seekers are unable to provide any support for themselves and would otherwise be exceptionally vulnerable'. In a letter of 4 April 2000 from the Refugees Integration section at NASS to the Refugees Arrival Project at Heathrow Airport it is said that the criterion for eligibility is whether it is impracticable to travel 'by reason of physical impediment' or 'the circumstances of the case are exceptional'. Hard cases support consists of

> basic full accommodation outside London. The ex-asylum seeker will have no access to other vouchers or cash. The ex-asylum seekers must also subject themselves to regular monthly reviews in which they will be expected to demonstrate the steps they have taken to enable themselves to leave the country. If there is not sufficient evidence that this has happened then hard cases support will be terminated.

APPLICATION FORM AND NOTES

Included within the regulations is a standard twelve page application form to be completed by an asylum-seeker claiming support. The regulations state that an application will be rejected unless made in English.

Accompanying the form are explanatory notes, in English, produced by NASS. The notes suggest that to ensure a more rapid decision the form should be faxed to NASS – though the regulations state that faxes are not an essential living need. The notes contain a so-called 'Statement of confidentiality' which reveals an in-built tension within NASS as to whether it exists to help asylum-seekers or the Home Office. It states: 'We will treat information you give in confidence… We will give the police information, if necessary, so they can…prosecute criminal offences.' Ultimately NASS is another arm of immigration control.

The explanatory notes state that personal jewellery will not be considered as 'assets'. However, it also states that NASS must be told of all jewellery worth more than £1000, including watches, and whether any has been sold for cash.

APPEALING AGAINST SUPPORT REFUSAL

A new appeal system has been established with appeals heard by asylum support adjudicators. These will hear only appeals against refusal or withdrawal of support. There is no appeal against the level of support – which will result in more judicial review cases. No support from NASS is available while appealing refusal of support. Support adjudicators are appointed by the Home Secretary, which hardly gives an appearance of impartiality. Adjudicators are located in Croydon.

According to the Community Legal Services Commission (previously the Legal Aid Board) there is no legal aid for these appeals. It is unclear how appellants can even finance the journey to Croydon if they opt for an oral hearing. Under the Asylum Support Appeals (Procedure) Rules 2000 there are only two days to lodge the appeal and ensure it is received by the support adjudicator.

COST OF TRAVEL TO INTERVIEWS AND APPEALS

It is not clear what costs asylum seekers and dependants can claim from public funds when they have to travel to interviews or appeal hearings. A Home Office letter of 22 June 2000 to the Asylum Processes Stakeholder Group attempts to clarify the situation at least in part:

- 'A claimant receiving support from a Local Authority under the Asylum Support (Interim Provisions) Regulations 1999 may apply to the Local Authority who will provide support to meet travel expenses under regulation 5(3) of the Regulations.

- A claimant receiving support (accommodation and/or vouchers) from the National Asylum Support Service (NASS) can apply to NASS for a ticket to be provided for return travel to the interview or appeal hearing. In particular circumstances accommodation may be provided if an overnight stay is required.' It is not clear whether the appeal hearing referred to includes an appeal against support refusal. As the letter does not specifically exclude this then it should be argued that it is included.

- 'A claimant receiving Income Support from the Department of Social Security is expected to meet the cost of travel from the Income Support provided.'

LIVING WITH FRIENDS/RELATIVES ON BENEFITS

The Department of Social Security has issued a circular to housing benefit (HB) and council tax benefit (CTB) staff on 'Asylum Seekers and Persons from Abroad: New arrangements from April 2000'.[8] This states: 'Asylum seekers supported by NASS will attract a non-dependent deduction if they choose to stay with people who are receiving HB or CTB'. At present this deduction from the friend or relative's benefit is £7.40 for HB and £2.30 for CTB. Under the regulations (for instance Regulation 63 of the Housing Benefit General Regulations) this deduction may apply even if the asylum-seeker is not being supported by NASS and is on nil income. Under Regulation 61 of the Housing Benefit General Regulations, the tenant can argue there should be no deduction as this is an exceptional circumstance. There is another issue. Council tax payers living alone receive a rebate of 25 per cent. If another adult lives with them the rebate is lost. The issue is whether a short stay by an asylum-seeking friend or relative counts towards losing the rebate.

There is an alternative scenario. This is where a supported asylum-seeker is joined by a partner or minor child. The question is how the partner's or child's support rights are affected. According to NASS guidance (in its Bulletin No 11) the following rights apply irrespective of whether the partner or child is claiming asylum in their own right:

- If the asylum-seeker already in the UK is on income support or income-based jobseeker's allowance then the benefit is increased to take account of the new family member

- If the asylum-seeker is being supported under the interim scheme then the new family member is entitled to local authority support.

- If the asylum-seeker is receiving NASS support then the new family member is also entitled to NASS support.

SURVEILLANCE OF SUPPORTED ASYLUM-SEEKERS

NASS is not neutral on the substantive asylum claim but is part of the Home Office machinery. Before the Act was passed NASS requested that local authorities provide the names of asylum-seekers in receipt of National Assistance Act support. NASS checked Home Office records and informed authorities of those applicants whose claim had been refused and advised authorities to cease support. A letter of 30 November 1999 from the director of NASS to directors of social services said: 'this information had been passed to the Immigration Service Enforcement Directorate who may take steps to ensure removal of the individuals concerned'.

A feature of the new scheme akin to the old Poor Law is the right of NASS to obtain constantly updated personal information about supported asylum-seekers. Under the regulations an asylum-seeker must inform NASS immediately and in writing if she or he:

(a) is joined in the United Kingdom by a dependant

(b) receives or gains access to any money

(c) becomes employed

(d) becomes unemployed

(e) changes his name

(f) gets married

(g) starts living with a person as if married to that person

(h) gets divorced

(i) separates from a spouse, or from a person with whom he has been living as if married to that person

(j) becomes pregnant

(k) has a child

(l) leaves school

(m) starts to share his accommodation with another person

(n) moves to a different address...

(o) goes into hospital

(p) goes to prison or is otherwise held in custody

(q) leaves the United Kingdom

(r) dies.

CRITIQUE OF THE SUPPORT SCHEME

In November 1999 NASS issued a 'Consultation document on the main regulations under Part VI of the Immigration and Asylum Act 1999'. As an exercise in consultation this was cosmetic. The final regulations contain the worst features of the proposed scheme.

A voucher-based scheme is intrinsically objectionable. It stigmatises the recipient.

A French firm, Sodexho Pass International, has been contracted to administer the scheme. The vouchers can be used only at designated Sodexho Pass Trading Partners, that is shops who have agreed with Sodexho to join the scheme. Sodexho have issued a document 'Asylum seekers Voucher System – April 2000' to retailers encouraging them to accept the vouchers. One major advantage for retailers is:

> Change should not be given, e.g. if goods to the value of £4.50 are purchased with a £5 voucher the 50p change should not be handed back, but you as a Trading Partner will receive the full £5 value of the voucher.

The *Guardian* of 3 April 2000 reported that 4411 retailers with 10,789 shops had joined the scheme. Sodexho also circulated another document in April 2000, 'Information for Local Authority Organisations'. This emphasised: 'Payment with vouchers can not be accepted for home delivery of goods.' A letter of 16 May 2000 from Sodexho said that this is not intended to exclude delivery of goods from supermarkets once purchased in person but excludes any catalogue orders or any good purchased with credit over the Internet or telephone.

Like the old Poor Law the scheme is petty in its restrictiveness; examples are:

- time tests in the definition of dependants, such as the requirement for unmarried couples to have lived together for two of the last three years

- cessation of support immediately a youngest dependent child turns 18

- the disregarding of personal clothing preferences in determining essential need.

Like the old Poor Law the scheme is punitive. Barbara Roche MP said in parliament on 12 May 2000 that 'NASS is presently in the process of establishing its intelligence and investigation functions'. This apparently is •to prevent supported asylum-seekers selling their vouchers even at face value. The minister said that an asylum-seeker who sold the vouchers for cash could be charged with conspiracy to commit an offence under the 1999 legislation even though she acknowledges: 'There are no specific provisions in the Immigration and Asylum Act 1999 directly covering the sale or purchase of vouchers.'

Other than for children under 16, essential needs of asylum-seekers and dependents will be met only at 70 per cent of income support level. A March 1999 document, 'Asylum Seekers' Support', produced by the Asylum Seekers' Support Project Team (now NASS), justified this on the grounds that support is intended to be short term, utility costs such as heating are included as part of accommodation, and 'it is unlikely that asylum seekers will need to purchase replacement items'. None of this makes it possible to live on 70 per cent of income support particularly as it disregards the fact that most asylum-seekers arrive in the UK with few possessions and little clothing. If an asylum-seeker's application is not determined within six months then a one-off payment of £50 may be given, which will be insufficient to meet the actual needs of the asy-lum-seeker.

The fourteen-day period when support continues after determination of a case is inadequate to arrange income support and rehousing even in a successful asylum claim. The Home Office takes months to give refugees the asylum documents necessary to access benefits, especially after an appeal.

GOVERNMENT FORCED TO AGREE VOUCHERS REVIEW

There is one particular aspect of the new asylum poor-law which has attracted criticism. This is the voucher scheme. The *Guardian* of 28 and 29 September 2000 reported the Transport and General Workers Union (TGWU) condemning the scheme at the Labour Party conference. The TGWU made public at the conference a dossier it had used to lobby ministers for an end to the scheme, including evidence linking the scheme to racial harassment. This followed a resolution at the Trades Union Congress that unanimously opposed the scheme. As a consequence the government has agreed to review the voucher system and in particular to review the iniquitous situation whereby retailers subscribing to the scheme are allowed to keep any change. However, though this review is welcome, the voucher scheme is only the tip of the iceberg of what is wrong with the new Poor Law. What is required is the restoration of full benefits to all claimants irre-spective of immigration status.

INTERIM PROVISION

The original Home Office timetable was for all support provisions to be effective by April 2000. It was always doubtful if this deadline would be met. Interim arrangements were therefore specified in the Asylum Support (Interim Provisions) Regulations 1999 operative from 6 December 1999. Responsibility for the interim scheme rested with local authorities and not NASS. A letter of 19

November 1999 to local authority chief executives from the director of NASS explains the interim provisions. Obligations assumed by local authorities can continue until April 2002. The main elements of the interim scheme are:

- Local authorities continue to support people they are already supporting under the National Assistance or Children Acts. This support is deemed to be under the 1999 Act's support provisions. Local authorities to whom new claims are made by asylum-seekers not yet phased into the NASS scheme are responsible for determining eligibility, level and provision of support. These asylum-seekers will probably continue to be supported by local authorities for the duration of their asylum claim and will not enter the full scheme.

- People claiming asylum on entry before 3 April 2000 remain eligible for basic means tested benefits until their claim is determined. If a negative decision is made after the full scheme became operational on 3 April 2000 then, if an appeal is lodged, they enter the full scheme.

PHASING IN OF FULL SUPPORT SCHEME

Barbara Roche made a parliamentary announcement on 7 March 2000. She said that the full support scheme would be operative from 3 April for

- new port of entry applicants who would therefore have no entitlement to social security and housing benefits

- new in-country applicants claiming asylum in Scotland or Northern Ireland

- new in-country asylum-seekers in England or Wales who are detained at the new Oakington internment centre but are applying for bail.

Under various Directions made by the Home Secretary under the Act, new in-country applicants in England and Wales entered into the full scheme on a phased geographical basis with the support scheme becoming fully national by 25 September 2000.

NEW PROPOSALS

An inevitable result of the inadequate support and voucher scheme has been the appearance of asylum-seekers and children begging on the streets. The *Guardian* of 20 March and 5 April 2000 reported the government responding to this by instituting procedures allowing for the rapid determination of asylum claims and removal of those caught begging, including children. The *Guardian* of 21 March 2000 reported that Eurostar passengers will be checked in France to deter refugees, with a Home Office minister claiming that asylum-seekers have no need to beg as they 'have benefit entitlements' – though the 1999 legislation explicitly abolished most such entitlements.

ZIMBABWEAN FARMERS AND THE INCOME-RELATED BENEFITS AND JOBSEEKER'S ALLOWANCE (AMENDMENT) REGULATIONS 2000

These regulations ensure that people who are deported from another country to the UK (mainly British citizens) are treated far more favourably than migrants and immigrants, most of whom the UK government would wish to deport back to their countries of origin. The regulations ensure that anyone deported to the UK will not be caught by the habitual residence test and therefore will immediately become entitled to benefits. This positive discrimination shows clearly the nationalistic basis of welfare.

It appears to have been enacted to ensure that if white farmers were expelled from Zimbabwe they will be immediately eligible for benefits. This contrasts starkly with the treatment of asylum-seekers.

Good practice

STATE BENEFITS

The 1999 Act's intention is to remove asylum-seekers from state benefit or local authority assistance and force them on to the new support provisions, while removing everyone else subject to controls from any support. The role of immigration advisors is to ensure that this is not achieved through widening the exemptions to the scheme, through utilising loopholes and through looking for alternative legislation.

The novelty of the 1999 legislation means much suggested good practice in respect to circumventing it is inevitably speculative. Because this whole area is extremely technical it is important that immigration advisors work closely with benefit advisors both generally and on a case-by-case basis.

WHAT IS LEFT OF THE 1948 NATIONAL ASSISTANCE ACT AND THE 1989 CHILDREN ACT

The 1948 and 1989 legislation clearly continue to be available in these circumstances:

- An asylum-seeker is defined for the purpose of the support provisions of the 1999 Act as someone not under 18. Therefore unaccompanied asylum-seekers under 18 will still be able to rely on Section 17 of the Children Act. There are provisions whereby young people leaving analogous support under Section 20 of the Act at the age of 18 may remain eligible for local authority help including financial assistance and accommodation. However the Department of Health denies these provisions apply to asylum-seekers (see Chapter 13)

- Immigrant and migrant families with children who are not asylum-seekers but are subject to immigration control and ineligible for benefits can continue to rely on Section 17 of the Children Act.

- Non-asylum seekers, even if their presence in the UK is unlawful, can also in extreme circumstances continue to rely on Section 21 of the National Assistance Act where the reliance does not arise solely due to destitution or its physical effects. This was confirmed in June 2000 in the unreported Court of Appeal cases of *Bhika* v *Leicester City Council*. Lord Justice Simon Brown said Section 21 could offer help where the 'need for care and attention is to any material extent made more acute by some circumstances other than the mere lack of accommodation or funds... If, for example, an immigrant, as well as being destitute, is old, ill or disabled'.

LOOPHOLES: CHALLENGING LOCAL AUTHORITY REFUSALS UNDER THE NATIONAL ASSISTANCE AND CHILDREN ACTS

The inadequacy of the 1999 Act's support provisions means that there will be legal challenges against local authorities in respect of restrictions on the 1948 and 1989 legislation. Overall this legislation offers relatively more 'generous' support than the 1999 Act's support scheme even when the latter is available.

Advisors should try to argue in respect of the National Assistance Act that need is not 'solely' due to destitution or its physical effects. It may be possible to argue that the need for statutory help arises not from destitution but from the necessity to remain in the UK for whatever reason, such as waiting for another country to accept documentation. Explanatory Notes issued alongside the Act say that asylum-seekers 'who need care and attention for more specific reasons (such as a particular physical disability or mental health problem) will retain that entitlement'. Likewise entitlement will be retained where the need for care and attention arose from age or pregnancy or any illness as opposed to destitution. In many cases it will be crucial to stress the adverse or potentially adverse mental health, as opposed to physical health, consequences of deprivation of benefits or services and of destitution.

It is perhaps arguable that if an accompanied child under 18 is an asylum-seeker in her or his own right then both child and family are re-entitled to reliance on Section 17 of the Children Act.

Children (and their asylum-seeking families) will still be able to use all other provisions of the Children Act in cases of special need.

It is arguable that asylum-seeking families can invoke Children Act support where they have been refused support under the 1999 Act as a result of allegedly squandering their own resources or breaching any contract for accommodation.

The Act obliges asylum-seeking families with children to be supported under the support scheme as long as they remain in the UK even if the asylum claim and appeals have been refused. It seems odd describing as 'asylum-seeking' families those refused asylum, or those who have dropped an asylum claim, but are pursuing a claim to remain on other, for instance compassionate, grounds. In these circumstances it may be possible to challenge denial of Section 17 Children Act support.

CHALLENGING THE NEW SUPPORT SCHEME

There will be legal challenges against the Home Office for failure to support or properly support under the new scheme.

Asylum-seekers claiming asylum based on membership of a social group or imputed political opinion, such as lesbians or gay men or women in fear of violence in their country of origin, should be able to avail themselves of the scheme (see Chapter 8).

The inadequacy of the level of support can be challenged by judicial review.

Article 3 of the European Convention of Human Rights refers to 'inhuman or degrading treatment'. Arguably this is designed to protect physical integrity including the need for proper nourishment. In one case food provided under the National Assistance Act by Westminster Council was shown as failing to meet nutritional standards as described in the British government report *Dietary Reference Values for Food Energy and Nutrients for the United Kingdom*. This is quoted in *Surviving the Asylum Process in the UK*. Advisors need to investigate whether support provided under the 1999 Act meets nutritional standards.

Other Articles of the European Convention are available to challenge the new scheme. For instance the removal of sponsored immigrants and others from the National Assistance Act with no access to any benefits may breach the right to life under Article 1. Article 6, the right to a fair trial, is arguably breached both by the two-day time limit for an appeal against refusal of support and by the fact that the Home Secretary will both appoint asylum support adjudicators and also be a party to the proceedings.

There should also be challenges under the UN Convention on the Rights of the Child. For instance the exclusion of assistance for toys breaches Article 31 of the Convention which protects the child's right to play.

Refusal by stores to refund change on under-spent vouchers should be challenged as a straight breach of contract.

Refusal by retailers to accept vouchers for home delivery discriminates in particular against the disabled who cannot carry purchases. A complaint is presently pending before the Disability Rights Commission.

SEARCHING FOR ALTERNATIVE LEGISLATION

The removal of benefits by the 1996 Asylum and Immigration Act led lawyers to investigate using the National Assistance Act and Children Act. The 1999 Act will result in similar investigations. Some community care legislation may be found useful, though much of this is itself restricted by the 1999 Act. The Local Government Association issued December 1999 guidance on the interim arrangements. This suggested that single adults with special needs ineligible for support under the 1999 Act may be entitled to a local authority assessment of needs under Section 47 of the National Health Service and Community Care Act, though the provision of assistance will be subject to locally determined criteria (see Chapter 15).

CHARITY SUPPORT AND THE 1999 ACT

It is wrong that asylum-seekers may have to depend on charity. Moreover there is concern that help from charities in kind will be taken into account in assessing whether an asylum-seeker is 'destitute'. Following a campaign of donation of toys for asylum-seekers' children, the Home Secretary said in the *Guardian* of 3 May 2000 that the value of donated toys would not be taken into account when assessing the need or level of support. However, it is not at all clear if this applies to other non-cash donations such as clothes, food or household implements. Moreover an award of monies, as opposed to a donation in kind, to an asylum-seeker probably could be interpreted as rendering him or her no longer destitute.

LOCAL AUTHORITY CHARITY INITIATIVES

Manchester City Council illustrates how an authority can initiate good practice. In 1985 the council established along with the former Greater Manchester Council an Immigration Needs Trust. Both paid £50,000. The purpose of the trust is 'To provide financial assistance to needy Manchester residents who... are seeking to establish a right to reside in Manchester'.

A June 1997 briefing note 'Asylum seekers and persons from abroad: what help is available in Manchester' produced by the Manchester Advice Services describes the trust as follows:

> The Trustees have said they will try to make one-off small payments of £100 to asylum seekers and persons from abroad refused benefit. Applications can also be made for longer term support.

This provision of money may remove someone from being classified as 'destitute'. The trust like other charities may need to alter its term of reference so as to make provision in kind. However the trust retains a role in helping non-asylum-seekers and also asylum-seekers who are no longer eligible for support under the 1999 Act because their asylum claim has been refused with all appeals exhausted and NASS has declined help under its hard cases fund.

CLAIMING PUBLIC FUNDS

The issue for advisors is not simply whether a client is entitled to benefits outside the 1999 legislation's support scheme. It is also whether the client should claim benefits even if entitled. One danger is that the act of claiming may fall foul of the immigration requirement to show there is adequate maintenance without recourse to public funds (see Chapter 3).

Welfare professionals should be aware of one tactical matter. Some cases present so many difficulties that whether a person claims public funds is not the decisive issue. Someone may be threatened with removal as having entered the UK without permission and may be applying for settlement on compassionate grounds because of illness. In such circumstances reliance on public funds by the applicant could be irrelevant in the determination of the case and without funds the applicant could be starved out of the country.

Finally, it should be noted that recognised refugees are not subject to the public funds requirements of the immigration rules and are entitled to benefits. Asylum-seekers, though not normally eligible for benefits, will not have their asylum claims prejudiced by either applying for or, in rare instances, receiving benefits.

NATIONAL INSURANCE NUMBERS

There are no restrictions on anyone applying for an NI number. However, it is dangerous to apply for a number where there is a prohibition against working. Where someone is allowed to work then a number should be applied for. The most common categories of those allowed to work are

- spouses who are in their probationary year

- asylum-seekers who have applied to the Home Office for permission to work after six months waiting for a decision on their asylum claim

- anyone with settled status or exceptional leave to remain or who has been granted asylum

- work permit holders.

Benefits Agency staff sometimes claim that an NI number can be granted only once someone has found work. This is incorrect. There may be cases of people granted settlement who previously used another person's NI number or a false number to avoid Home Office attention. Once settlement has been granted, it is important to consider applying for a number in the proper name and to ask the Contributions Agency to transfer contributions already made to the new number. People should be warned that though prosecution is unlikely, it is a criminal offence to use someone else's number.

HABITUAL RESIDENCE

Someone refused benefit on habitual residence grounds should appeal and make fresh claims at regular intervals. These claims may eventually succeed. The longer that someone is in the UK the easier it is to prove residence. It may be illegal to refuse benefits on grounds of habitual residence to nationals of state signatories to the 1953 European Convention on Social and Medical Assistance and the 1961 Council of Europe Social Charter.

Comments on casework problem at start of chapter

If X had applied for asylum on entering the UK before 3 April 2000 then he would be eligible for income support and housing benefit until a decision were made. If he applied on entry after 3 April 2000 then he would be eligible for voucher assistance under the NASS administered scheme. It is irrelevant that he does not require accommodation through NASS or the local authority.

If he applied in-country in England or Wales before the NASS support scheme became operational in the locality where he applied then support is the responsibility of the local authority under the interim arrangements. However, unlike in the full scheme, he is not entitled under the interim scheme to voucher assistance unless he also accepts accommodation.

Notes

1   *INLP* vol. 13, no.2, 1999
2   *R* v. *Inhabitants of Eastbourne* 1803 4 East 103
3   R(U) 13/57
4   *R* v. *Hammersmith, Lambeth and Fulham councils, Independent* 16 October 1996 (the decision was upheld on appeal)
5   *R* v. *Secretary of State for Health ex parte Hammersmith and Fulham,* Court of Appeal, 27 July 1998
6   *R* v. *Newham London Borough Council ex parte Gorenkin, The Times* Law Report 9 June 1997
7   *R* v. *Brent LBC ex parte D,* January 1998
8   A18/2000

CHAPTER 13

Housing services and immigration status

A CASEWORK PROBLEM

You are a housing advisor consulted by X, who claimed asylum on entry in May 2000 and is housed in local authority accommodation under the 1999 legislation. The locality is full of racists. The electricity company has disconnected the power because of dangerous wiring. The flat is on the fourth floor without lifts. X is disabled. Her extended family has been rehoused two hundred miles away. What do you suggest?

A REAL CASE STORY

An asylum seeker from Algeria was repeatedly refused assistance…by social services from Hammersmith and had to sleep rough for two months during winter. He also had to walk to the Refugee Council day centre every day to get a hot meal and a food parcel, despite having a seriously injured leg as a result of a bullet wound he had received in Algeria. While sleeping rough by Victoria station he was once attacked by individuals who cut his ear badly. A woman nine months pregnant, whose baby was due at any time, was equally denied assistance by the same authority…many female asylum seekers were forced into prostitution… An asylum seeker from Iran slashed his wrists unable to cope any longer with the lack of adequate assistance by Islington social services. (This quotation is from 'Surviving the asylum process in the United Kingdom'.)[1]

SCOPE OF THIS CHAPTER

Nationalists have always been preoccupied with private ownership and control of land as providing status and the right to be in a country. Placing restrictions on the right to housing is just another example of this. This chapter traces the link between immigration status and housing entitlement and the replacement of remaining entitlements for asylum-seekers with the new support scheme introduced by the 1999 legislation. The issues raised run in parallel with those discussed in Chapter 12 in respect of welfare benefits.

FURTHER READING RESOURCES

An article by Sidney Jacobs, 'Race, empire and the welfare state: council housing and racism' in *Critical Social Policy* (issue 13, 1985) reveals racist discrimination in public housing. It does not deal with immigration controls. However, nationalistic concepts of welfare in relation to housing, also expressed in legal decisions, made it ideologically easier to link housing entitlement to immigration status through statute.

The Commission for Racial Equality (CRE) has produced reports on investigations into the discriminatory housing policies of two London boroughs. In 1984 it published *Race and Council Housing in Hackney* and in 1988 *Homelessness and Discrimination in Tower Hamlets*.

The Local Government Association monitors the housing dispersal scheme under the 1999 legislation. Information is on its website. Sue Lukes has written *Immigration, Asylum and Housing Rights* as part of a training package and has an up-to-date website. 'Governing at a distance: the elaboration of controls in British immigration' by Lydia Morris in *International Migration Review* (December 1998) traces some of the recent history of internal controls particularly in respect of housing and records observations of the assistant director of housing in an inner London borough. 'Housing for the homeless and immigration control' by Simon Rahily in the *Journal of Social Welfare and Family Law* (1998) examines the 1996 Housing Act and 1996 Asylum and Immigration Act.

LOCAL GOVERNMENT HISTORY

In 1925 the London County Council excluded non-British citizens from council housing. A *Jewish Chronicle* editorial of 20 March 1925 said: 'Why the Council should imagine that it is conducive to a well ordered Metropolis for a certain number of its inhabitants to be forced to homelessness…we cannot divine.' A member of the Board of Deputies of British Jews stated:

> This country in its treatment of aliens has been making a descent to Avernus, beginning with its restriction of alien immigration and from that proceeding to impose disabilities on the aliens already here.

Black people post–1945 met with racism in housing allocation. Jacobs gives examples. In 1957 Lambeth's mayor boasted: 'six West Indian families have been rehoused in the worst type of requisitioned property – because no one else would take it'. Throughout the 1950s Lambeth did not enforce the overcrowding provisions of public health legislation, otherwise, as the mayor said: 'any coloured person evicted would have gained priority on the council list'. Newham changed its housing points scheme in 1975, otherwise, as one councillor said: 'we would have been doing nothing but giving homes to Asians'.

In the early 1980s Greater London Council and the boroughs of Kensington and Chelsea and of Barnet refused to accept work permit holders on to housing waiting lists. The CRE in a press release of 16 November 1982 declared this unlawful under race relations legislation.

The *Guardian* of 18 May 1982 reported Dudley, Wolverhampton, Birmingham, Newham and Haringey councils as demanding passports from black housing list applicants.

THE JUDICIARY, HOMELESSNESS LEGISLATION AND IMMIGRATION STATUS

A duty was first placed on local authorities to provide homelessness accommodation by the 1977 Housing (Homeless Persons) Act. The legislation did not link entitlement with immigration status. Local authorities and the judiciary invented the nexus.

The case-law highlights the role of Tower Hamlets in denying housing provision for its Bangladeshi population; the role of one judge, Lord Denning, in making homelessness provision dependent on status; and the attempt to limit rights of EEA citizens, revealing an anti-Europeanism lurking within aspects of control.

Illustrative cases

Two Italians came to work in the UK claiming accommodation from Crawley council under the homelessness provisions of the housing legislation. The Court of Appeal held that by leaving accommodation in Italy they made themselves intentionally homeless and lost all entitlements. Denning said:

> Every day we see signs of the advancing tide. This time it is two young families from Italy. They had heard tell of the European Economic Community. Naturally enough, because it all stemmed from a Treaty made at Rome. They had heard that there was freedom of movement for workers within the Community. They could come to England without let or hindrance. They may have heard, too, that England is a good place for workers. In Italy the word may have got round that in England there are all sorts of benefits to be had whenever you are unemployed. And best of all they will look after you whenever you have nowhere to live... The local council at Crawley are very concerned about these two cases. They have Gatwick Airport within their area... They should be able to do better than King Canute. He bade the rising tide at Southampton to come no further. It took no notice. He got his feet wet. I trust the councillors of Crawley will keep theirs dry – against the new advancing tide.[2]

An Ethiopian asylum-seeker claimed homelessness accommodation from Hillingdon Council. The Court of Appeal said she was entitled. Having no prior connection with the authority was irrelevant. However, Denning said:

> Of course if he is an illegal entrant – if he enters unlawfully without leave – or if he overstays his leave and remains here unlawfully – the housing authority are under no duty whatever to him... As soon as any such illegality appears, the housing authority can turn him down – and report his case to the immigration authorities. This will exclude many foreigners.[3]

The 1993 Tower Hamlets case: housing officers as Home Office agents

The anti-immigrant doctrinal basis of these cases culminated in a 1993 decision in favour of Tower Hamlets. Tower Hamlets brought a case against the Secretary of State for the Environment claiming that the Department of Environment's Code of Guidance on the 1985 Housing Act was wrong in stating 'everyone admitted to this country is entitled to equal treatment'. Tower Hamlets argued that Bangladeshis who claimed they had 'adequate accommodation' for entry clearance purposes and subsequently claimed homelessness accommodation were illegal entrants. The Court of Appeal agreed. Lord Justice Stuart Smith held: first, 'if the immigration authorities have decided that such a person is an illegal entrant...the local authority owe no duty to him or her'; second, a local authority can come to its own conclusion whether a person entered unlawfully; third, telling an entry clearance officer there is adequate accommodation when the family on arrival requires homelessness accommodation constitutes unlawful entry; finally, if

> the housing authority suspect that the applicant is an illegal entrant not only is there nothing to prevent the authority from informing the immigration authorities of their suspicion...but it would be its duty to do so.[4]

THE 1993 AND 1996 IMMIGRATION ACTS AND THE 1996 HOUSING ACT

The 1993 Asylum and Immigration Appeals Act placed asylum-seekers in an inferior position to other homelessness applicants by denying housing to those who had any accommodation 'however temporary'. Under this criterion a church floor would be sufficient.

The 1996 Housing Act (which was shadowed by the 1996 Asylum and Immigration Act) provided a comprehensive link between status and housing entitlement. Section 185 of the Housing Act removed rights to homelessness accommodation from all persons subject to control. Section 161 contained a new area of provision linking eligibility to status. Council house allocation was no longer to be available to those subject to control. Regulations made under the Housing Act contained exemptions. For instance those claiming asylum on entry were exempt from Section 185.

A report on *Immigration and Housing* to the 19 September 1995 Housing Committee of the Association of Metropolitan Authorities (now the Local Government Association) recognised that this legislation not only adversely affected housing applicants but also had 'operational and equalities policy implications for mainstream staff and their management'.

THE 1999 IMMIGRATION AND ASYLUM ACT

The 1999 legislation restructures previous measures by bringing asylum-seekers into the so-called 'support' scheme (see Chapter 12). The legislation leaves unrepealed Sections 161 and 185 of the 1996 Housing Act so non-asylum-seekers subject to controls remain without housing support unless they come within regulations considered below. The 1999 Act specifically states that housing authorities should not grant a tenancy or licence to persons subject to immigration control other than where accommodation is provided under the Act's support provisions or under regulations. The 1999 legislation defines 'persons subject to immigration controls' for housing purposes as those requiring leave to enter or remain. This definition differs from that for benefit purposes (see Chapter 12) but has the same effect.

THE REGULATIONS

Exceptions allowing housing to some people subject to controls are contained in three statutory instruments which became operative 3 April 2000. A letter of 14 March 2000 from the Department of Environment, Transport and the Regions (DETR) to all council chief executives in England provides a more detailed explanation of these instruments. There are different provisions for Scotland, Wales and Northern Ireland.

Persons subject to Immigration Control (Housing Authority Accommodation and Homelessness) Order 2000

This Order, made under the 1999 Immigration and Asylum Act, designates people subject to immigration controls who qualify for local authority housing other than by going on the housing register; however, such housing will not amount to a secure tenancy:

- people granted refugee status

- people granted exceptional leave to enter or remain not subject to a condition of no recourse to public funds

- people with current leave to remain permanently except those not habitually resident (see Chapter 12) in the Common Travel Area (the UK, Ireland, Channel Islands and Isle of Man) and except those who are sponsored immigrants (see Chapters 3 and 12) in the UK less than five years and whose sponsor is alive

- people from Montserrat who left after 1 November 1995 because of volcanic activity

- nationals of states which have ratified the European Convention on Social and Medical Assistance (ECSMA) or the Council of Europe Social Charter (CESC) who are habitually resident in the Common Travel Area and lawfully here (this restriction on habitual residence grounds may be unlawful – see Chapter 12)

- overseas students in otherwise hard-to-let accommodation which has been let directly to themselves or to their education institution

- persons still owed a duty under Section 21 of the National Assistance Act (see Chapter 12)
- children in need or members of the family of a child in need (see Chapter 12)
- people owed a homelessness duty
- asylum-seekers owed a duty under the asylum support interim provisions – see below
- existing secure tenants.

Allocation of Housing (England) Regulations 2000

These regulations, made under the 1996 Housing Act, determine which persons subject to controls qualify to go on the housing authority register waiting list for a council secure tenancy. These comprise the first five groups listed in the above Order. In addition they include nationals of a state which has signed, not necessarily ratified, either ECSMA or CESC and were being housed as homeless under these Conventions prior to 3 April 2000. The regulations specifically exclude persons from the register who are not habitually resident in the Common Travel Area (which may be unlawful in cases of nationals of ECSMA and CESC signatories) except

- EEA workers or other EEA nationals with a right to reside in the UK
- persons who left Montserrat after 1 November 1995 because of volcanic eruption.

Homelessness (England) Regulations 2000

These regulations, made under the 1996 Housing Act, determine those groups subject to control who can be housed under the homelessness legislation. These consist of all the groups in the Allocation of Housing (England) Regulations 2000. In addition there are transitional provisions for certain classes of asylum-seekers and others who were able to claim homelessness accommodation under previous exemptions. These are:

- persons who claimed asylum on entry before 3 April 2000 and whose asylum claim has not been initially decided or abandoned
- persons who claimed asylum in-country within three months of the Home Secretary declaring their country one of upheaval and whose asylum claim has not been initially decided or abandoned
- persons who claimed asylum before 5 February 1996 and were then entitled to housing benefit and whose claim has not been initially decided or abandoned or have had an outstanding appeal pending since 5 February 1996

- persons on income-based jobseeker's allowance or income support except those claiming these benefits because funds from abroad have been disrupted.

The regulations exclude from homelessness entitlement persons not habitually resident in the Common Travel Area except:

- EEA workers or other EEA nationals with a right to reside in the UK

- persons who left Montserrat after 1 November 1995 because of volcanic eruption

- persons on income-based jobseeker's allowance or in receipt of income support.

THE 1999 ACT'S SUPPORT SCHEME: DISPERSAL

Unless asylum-seekers come within the above Order or Regulations then they have to rely on the 1999 Act's support scheme. Central to this is dispersal of asylum-seekers away from London and the South East. A refusal to disperse will be met by a refusal to support. Schedule 14 contains powers to prohibit residence in a particular area. The government portrays the legislation as modernistic. Its 1998 White Paper, *Fairer, Faster and Firmer*, was subtitled 'A Modern Approach to Immigration and Asylum'. However, proposals for dispersal and exclusion from designated areas are nearly a century old. The 1903 Royal Commission on Alien Immigration recommended them (see Chapter 2). According to Professor Robert Moore in a letter to the *Guardian* both the rhetoric and policy of dispersal was adopted by a Labour government in the late 1960s (18 April 2000). This programme, aimed mainly at East African Asians, fuelled a racism which culminated in the growth of the National Front in the 1970s.

DETAILS OF THE NEW SCHEME: THE ASYLUM SUPPORT REGULATIONS 2000

The Act's support provisions for essential needs of destitute asylum-seekers and dependants have been examined (see Chapter 12). Similar issues, including the definitions of dependants and destitution, apply to accommodation support. The National Asylum Support Service will assess the claim and, if entitlement is confirmed, will arrange accommodation. The relevant law is contained generally in the Act and specifically in the Asylum Support Regulations 2000.

1.   Accommodation can be provided, through contracts with NASS, by private landlords, local authorities or registered social landlords in England and Wales or registered housing associations in Scotland or Northern Ireland or the Northern Ireland Housing Executive.

2.   NASS has to determine whether any existing accommodation occupied by an asylum-seeker is 'adequate'. The Act says that in assessing adequacy it is irrelevant if the asylum-seeker has no legal right to

occupy the accommodation, the accommodation is shared or the accommodation is temporary.

3. The support regulations list factors that must be taken into account in assessing adequacy of existing accommodation. These include whether:

- the accommodation can be afforded by the asylum-seeker
- s/he can gain entry to the accommodation
- s/he has permission to live in a mobile home
- the accommodation can also be occupied by the applicant's dependants
- the applicant is subject to domestic violence in the present accommodation
- it would be reasonable for the applicant to live in the accommodation.

In assessing reasonableness account may be taken of the housing situation where the accommodation is located. This suggests if the asylum-seeker is living in an area of bad housing stock then s/he cannot use this to argue the accommodation is inadequate. The explanatory notes to the NASS application form say it would be unreasonable to live in an area of 'violence or threats such as…racial harassment or attacks, physical violence, sexual abuse or harassment and harassment because of…religion'. This criterion was added as a result of political protest.

4. Where existing accommodation is inadequate (or there is no existing accommodation) NASS should arrange for adequate accommodation to be provided under the support scheme.

5. The Act says an asylum-seeker's preferences as to locality of accommodation must be disregarded and the regulations say the same about the nature of the accommodation and of fixtures and fittings.

6. The Act excludes asylum-seekers housed under the scheme from assured and secure tenancy regimes and from protection against eviction under the 1997 Eviction Act.

7. The Act allows for temporary emergency accommodation for asylum-seekers while NASS is assessing the support application. The explanatory notes accompanying the support application form say that emergency accommodation will be provided by a 'voluntary organisation that is funded by the Home Office' for this purpose.

8. Several major refugee organisations have been funded both to provide this accommodation and also to act as 'assistants' advising asylum-seekers generally on the 1999 Act. A critique of this voluntary sector involvement is made in Chapter 20.

LOCAL AUTHORITY CONSORTIA

NASS views local authority accommodation as vital to the scheme. Authorities can provide accommodation outside their own borders and can provide services with non local authority partners. The Home Secretary can designate certain areas as 'reception zones', make special rules for these zones and can requisition property by ordering authorities to provide accommodation.

Concerns about the use of compulsory powers impelled local authorities to establish regional consortia for the purpose of distributing or redistributing asylum-seekers within the consortia areas and between consortia. This allows horse-trading between authorities as to how many asylum-seekers each will accommodate. In November 1998 the Local Government Association wrote to local authorities requesting that they establish regional consortia and in June 1999 the LGA produced a *Tool Kit* for development of consortia. Presently there are eleven regional consortia. These are North West, Yorkshire and Humberside, West Midlands, East Midlands, North East, South West, South Central, Eastern, Wales, Scotland and London. The role of London is not to house but to disperse asylum-seekers away from the South East.

Consortia are intended to be multi-agency organisations which though led by local authorities are designed to include representatives from, for example, private and registered social landlords, the health service, refugee organisations and the advice sector.

An example of one consortium is seen in a Bury Metropolitan Borough Council document of November 1999: 'Implications of the dispersal of asylum seekers for Bury'. This reveals a North West consortium with two subdivisions, East (Lancashire, all authorities within Greater Manchester, Blackburn, Darwin and Blackpool) and West (Liverpool, Cumbria, Cheshire, Merseyside and Knowsley). Liverpool is the lead authority on legal issues and Manchester on financial issues. Bury has assumed responsibility for a business plan. Manchester and Liverpool will be the contracting party with NASS and will have agreements with the other authorities regarding such issues as permanent rehousing for successful asylum applicants and other support services. A major bureaucracy is being established to support the consortium.

CONSORTIA POLITICS

Individual authorities within the consortia play a contradictory role. While often wishing to help asylum-seekers they have become Home Office agents for internal controls and with an agenda which is not always about helping asylum-seekers. The director of Manchester social services presented a report on the North West consortium to the 20 October 1999 meeting of the council's Strategy and Overview Scrutiny Committee. This quite rightly expressed concern about ghettoisation of asylum-seekers. However, its concern was not for refugees but with problems in 'regenerating certain areas of the city' if there were an excess of asylum-seekers.

Similar contradictions appear within the consortia themselves as is evidenced by the North West consortium and its lead authorities Manchester and Liverpool, which are walking a tight-rope in their relationship with government. This is clear from their January 2000 response to the NASS November 1999 'Consultation document on the main regulations under Part VI of the Immigration and Asylum Act 1999'. The lead authorities make an objection to dispersal on human rights grounds while expressing confidence the government will pay regard to human rights in the dispersal scheme. Liverpool council has been unable to live with some contradictions, mainly financial, and has withdrawn from the entire support scheme (see Chapter 20).

The North West consortium has taken some reactionary positions. In a letter of 2 February 2000 to NASS, single adult Kosovan asylum-seekers are stereotyped as being 'manifest in disruptive and criminal behaviour' and NASS is asked not to disperse them out of London. Though this seems to be the position of only one North West authority the consortium in no way disassociates itself from these views. On a national level the consortia collude with NASS and the Home Office. There are monthly national meetings of the asylum-seekers regional consortia. Minutes can be found on the LGA website. NASS representatives attend these meetings. This presence of a Home Office agency clearly puts into question the independence of the consortia. The minutes for 20 March 2000 show a police representative attending. In an important discussion on the safety of asylum-seekers the director of NASS announced: 'information on NASS placements will be made available to local Police Commanders'. It is highly questionable whether asylum-seekers would wish their addresses to be routinely given to the police without their consent or even knowledge.

According to paragraph 52 of an Audit Commission report on the dispersal scheme (see below) the Kent police force has appointed a nominated field intelligence officer who identifies potential offenders within asylum-seeking communities – and the Association of Chief Police Officers is currently preparing a good practice guide for the policing of asylum-seekers and refugee communities drawing upon the Kent experience. It seems the police have a two-fold strategy. One is to prevent undue civil disorder by racists attacking asylum-seekers. The other is to harass asylum-seekers who are deemed to be acting anti-socially, for instance by begging to supplement a voucher scheme which puts them below the poverty level.

CRITIQUE OF THE NEW SCHEME

The scheme is ideologically underpinned by a disparaging stereotyping of asylum-seekers. In August 1999 the Home Office issued a consultation paper, 'proposed interim support arrangements'. This recommended excluding from support asylum-seekers 'damaging the property provided under the support arrangements'. Barbara Roche MP in her letter of 17 April 2000 to David Crausby MP acknowledged: 'The Home Office does not keep statistics of the number of occasions where asylum seekers have damaged accommodation.' The only reported incident of such damage has been in Newcastle where Iranian asy-lum-seekers went on hunger strike after being housed alongside political enemies from Iraq and having their financial support cut. They claimed they were being treated like prisoners (*Newcastle Evening Chronicle* 29.5.2000)

The scheme has little to do with the well-being of asylum-seekers. It has everything to do with the prejudice of those who do not want asylum-seekers near them. The whole project is housing-led and driven by a determination to direct asylum-seekers away from London and the South East.

The only other groups who get compulsorily moved around like asy-lum-seekers are criminals, mental health patients and people in the care system. All these groups have one factor in common: they are effectively regarded as being outside society.

Local authorities are inadequately funded under the scheme. The government has indicated that grant level will be £150 for a single person and £220 for a family unit of two adults and two children. This must cover an asylum-seeker's essential needs and accommodation and local authority administrative costs and obligatory statutory provision such as education.

SURVEILLANCE OF ACCOMMODATED ASYLUM-SEEKERS

Asylum-seekers are to be tied to accommodation as the Victorian poor were tied to the workhouse. The asylum support regulations say that asylum-seekers and dependants cannot be absent for more than seven consecutive days and nights or more than a total of fourteen days and nights in any six-month period without the permission of the Home Office (which presumably means NASS). Breach of this requirement can lead to eviction.

Local authorities and other agencies are legally obliged to pass on to the Home Office information about both accommodation and its asylum-seeking occupants (see Chapter 3).

Conversely the Home Office is obliged to respond to a local authority request for a person's immigration status. This obligation is ostensibly to determine Housing Act eligibility though it appears wide enough to allow authorities to demand information for any reason.

PRIVATE LANDLORDISM AND THE 1999 ACT

The 1999 Act will lead to a market in unregulated private lettings. The November 1999 Bury Council document says the Home Office intends 40 per cent of all accommodation to be provided nationally by local authorities and 60 per cent by private landlords and registered social landlords. It also says that Woodcote Property Management hopes to build two to three hostels in each consortium region with Securicor acting as managing agents. The *Guardian* of 16 December 1999 reports one private landlord bidding for a contract to house over 1000 asy-lum-seekers in spite of allegations of 'physical assaults, racism, over-crowding, inadequate food, mismanagement of the asylum voucher system and children left at risk'. An article in the Shelter journal *Bedsitaction* for August 1999 revealed how private landlords were then treating asylum-seekers. Examples were

- houses in multiple occupation (HMOs) being suddenly transformed into bed and breakfast (B&B) accommodation through the provision of powdered milk for breakfast – the advantage to the landlord of premises classified as B&Bs being the reduction in statutory room sizes compared with bedsit HMOs

- the emergence of annexes to hotels and B&Bs with a resultant confusion as to the address of asylum-seekers

- poor safety standards.

The *Guardian* of 18 December 1999 reported Securicor bidding to house asylum-seekers on two barges on the Mersey. Liverpool City Council's spokesperson on housing said: 'It is unbelievable that a major company could propose this 150 years after we managed to get rid of the Victorian hulks...that we used to house prisoners.' In fact Tamil asylum-seekers had been imprisoned on the Sealink-owned *Earl William* in 1987. They were evacuated after the ship almost sank. This is described in *From the Jews to the Tamils* (South Manchester Law Centre 1988).

An article in the *Manchester Evening News* of 14 September 2000 was headed 'Slum Landlords Exploit Refugees'. The article was based on a report of 4 September 2000 by Manchester's Chief Executive entitled 'North West Consortium for Asylum Seekers'. The newspaper reported 'evidence of terrible conditions, with some asylum seekers placed in boarded-up houses and others crammed several to a room'. The article itemised the following complaints against private landlords who had signed accommodation contracts with NASS:

- landlords classifying unrelated single adults as a family to circumvent the law on multi-occupancy

- landlords buying up cheap property and quickly recouping their outlay

- asylum-seekers left without support or information on local community services.

The *Manchester Evening News* of 29 September 2000 reported that:

Plans to squeeze 230 asylum seekers into a block of flats designed for 50 people have been slammed by council bosses. Housing chiefs are horrified at the move by government-approved Leena Corporation Limited which has a contract with the Home Office to provide accommodation for refugees. It follows concerns over conditions for asylum seekers in north Manchester provided by other private landlords on Home Office contracts.

This dumping and overcrowding of asylum-seekers only serves to reinforce any negative popular image of refugees. The *Manchester Evening News* reported one resident living near the Leena Corporation scheme as complaining 'We are not happy with this. It's already a rundown area. I can't see this making it any better.'

It's only a short step from criticising the accommodation to blaming the occupant.

Shelter is being presently funded by the Gulbenkian Foundation to monitor the use and standards of the private sector to accommodate asylum-seekers and their families.

CRITICISM BY LOCAL AUTHORITIES

Local authorities such as Manchester and Liverpool have made many valid criticisms of the role of private landlords within the new so-called 'support' scheme. However this is yet another example of the contradictory roles they are playing. To put it at its most generous, many local authorities want to help asylum-seekers but have opted for a system which is repressing asylum-seekers. Moreover it is all too late. Local authorities were the main agencies outside of government which argued in favour of the support scheme in the first place. This was to avoid their obligations under the National Assurance and Children Acts. The only rational position, the only position with any integrity, is for authorities to themselves withdraw from the scheme and campaign for the restoration of full entitlements to asylum-seekers.

INTERIM SCHEME

Interim arrangements were made under the following Regulations and Orders until the full scheme became operative:

- Asylum Support (Interim Provisions) Regulations 1999. The regulations are concerned with local authority obligations to assist and accommodate asylum-seekers and were operative from 6 December 1999 (see Chapter 12).

- Homelessness (Asylum-Seekers)(Interim Period)(England) Order 1999. During the interim period asylum-seekers applying for asylum on entry retained the right to homelessness accommodation. On 22 November 1999 the DETR circulated English authorities explaining this order. This shows that the interests of asylum-seekers are not primary and 'Where authorities are considering placing asylum seeker applicants in accommodation in resort areas…they should give careful consideration to…any potential impact on tourism in the area'.

- The Housing Accommodation (Amendment)(England) Order 1999. This removes restrictions contained in the 1996 Asylum and Immigration Act on local authorities granting tenancies or licences to asylum-seekers supported under the interim provisions.

Implementation of the full scheme has been delayed and since 3 April 2000 has been phased in (see Chapter 12).

CHAOS OF DISPERSAL SCHEME AND RESISTANCE OF ASYLUM-SEEKERS

All independent assessments of the dispersal scheme have emphasised its chaotic character in practice. Moreover according to an article in the *Times* and in the *Independent* of 21 September 2000 the Home Office acknowledged that at least a third of all asylum seekers seeking state assistance have declined accommodation under the NASS scheme, preferring to stay with friends or relatives in London or else opting to sleep rough and accepting vouchers only. One way this can be interpreted is as resistance by asylum seekers to forced dispersal. As a consequence, according to the *Times*, the government considered temporarily freezing the scheme – though this was later denied in a letter to the paper of 23 September by Barbara Roche MP. However it is not inconceivable that administrative chaos, withdrawal of some councils from the scheme and asylum seeker resistance will ensure that the scheme will eventually implode in on itself.

Good practice

THE 1999 IMMIGRATION AND ASYLUM ACT

Many practice issues are similar to those rehearsed previously (see Chapter 12). In particular accommodation in some circumstances may still be available under the National Assistance Act or Children Act. What follows are additional issues.

- Whether or not local authorities should as a matter of anti-racist practice enter into voluntary housing arrangements with the Home office is considered in Chapter 20.

- The *Independent* of 7 March 2000 reported some local authorities such as Kent County Council raising their council tax to pay the costs allegedly caused by asylum-seekers. This is a provocation to local racists. Best practice would require local authorities to campaign collectively alongside asylum-seekers for greater funding from central government and, more crucially, for the restoration of benefits and housing rights.

- Section 1 of the 1977 Eviction Act remains unamended and so occupants of accommodation under the 1999 Act are protected from harassment.

- The Home Secretary said in parliament that asylum-seekers who have 'waited a year or two in a particular area' are exempt from dispersal (9 November 1999).

LOCAL CONSORTIA: SECRETIVE OR ACCOUNTABLE?

Good practice determines that all decisions relating to refugees be open and transparent and therefore accountable to those seeking asylum. Unfortunately local consortia act in just the opposite way. In a letter of 20 April 2000 the team leader of the Asylum Seeker's Team in Bury Council said that she had been instructed not to release the minutes of the North West Consortium.

POSITIVE GOVERNMENT STATEMENTS

Preferences of asylum-seekers as to type and locality of accommodation are to be disregarded. However, pressure on the Home Office has forced it into issuing statements to some extent contradicting this by making a strange distinction between 'preferences' and 'circumstances'. In a letter of 24 March 1999 to Andrew Rowe MP, Mike O'Brien MP on behalf of the Home Office said:

> Although in allocating accommodation to an asylum-seeker we will not pay any attention to an asylum-seeker's preferences, we will take into account his circumstances. Thus we will disregard an asylum-seeker's preference to be located in Birmingham, for example, but will take account of the fact that an asylum-seeker has friends or family living there and, if places are available in Birmingham, allocate him one.

Failure to follow this published policy could be judicially reviewable.

This policy statement reflects, expands and makes more positive the Asylum Support Regulations which state that the regulations 'shall not be taken to prevent' an asylum-seeker's 'individual circumstances' being taken into account in the provision of accommodation. The explanatory notes accompanying the application form for support say 'suitable' accommodation will be provided which takes into account 'the size of your family, ethnic, racial and cultural backgrounds and health issues'. Applicants for accommodation are asked to provide details of ethnic group and religion, any health or disability issues and dietary needs.

GOVERNMENT GUIDELINES ON 'CLUSTER' AREAS

The government has issued guidelines to local authorities which have some positive content. On 1 December 1999 NASS offered guidance to chief executives of local authorities regarding transference of responsibility for assessing or providing support to another local authority under the interim scheme. Advisors should argue that NASS ought to take into account these criteria when deciding on dispersal of any asylum-seeker under the full scheme and irrespective of any future transfer between authorities.

The guidance suggests when placing asylum-seekers the receiving authority should consider Home Office criteria for the development of 'cluster' areas. Cluster areas will exist where

- there is likely to be suitable accommodation available

- there exists a multi-ethnic population or infrastructure able to assist asylum seekers
- it would be possible to link with existing communities and access support structures.

The emphasis on dispersal to a pre-existing similar community is positive in that this could offer solidarity and familiarity. However, local authorities and NASS should avoid a ghettoisation that could make the whole community more vulnerable to racism. They should also avoid assuming or imposing any form of collective responsibility on already impoverished communities to provide material assistance to newly arrived refugees. This is the responsibility of local and national government

The guidance recommends that in some cases an asylum-seeker should remain in London or Kent, for instance where there are particular medical needs which can be met only locally (such as access to the Medical Foundation for the Care of Victims of Torture) or close family members live in the area.

LOCAL GOVERNMENT ASSOCIATION GUIDELINES

Another source of guidelines is the Local Government Association. In December 1999 this issued 'Guidance notes to local authorities in England and Wales: interim arrangements for asylum seeker support'. This guidance contains model 'specifications' for local authorities as service providers contracted to NASS as a service purchaser and for asylum-seekers in local authority accommodation. These specifications reflect the contradictions between the facilitating and repressive role of local authorities in respect of controls.

A positive aspect is an emphasis on 'client rights' including the need for regular resident meetings and for each resident to be 'offered appropriate support to gain access to advocacy, legal, health, social and education services'. A negative, intrusive and unnecessary feature is the reporting to the Home Office of 'any dispute with local neighbours or other agencies' or 'the arrest of any client' or 'any violent incident involving a client' or 'a client moving out of the premises'.

THE LONDON CONSORTIUM AND MEETING DISABILITY NEEDS

It was seen above that 'suitability' of accommodation is to be measured against any disability issues. Nadine Finch in her article on 'Providing support for asylum-seekers' has written:

> The London consortium has advised all participating London authorities to make a detailed assessment of the physical and psychological needs of all asylum-seekers presenting themselves for assistance, before referring them to the London Consortium for dispersal. In particular they have advised that any asylum-seeker with a special need should be assessed by a qualified social worker, who should prepare a written report. In practice this does not appear to be

happening… Advisors should, therefore, devise non-discriminatory means of taking instructions about possible special needs.[5]

CHARTERED INSTITUTE OF ENVIRONMENTAL HEALTH

The institute has produced with the LGA 'Asylum seekers' temporary accommodation good practice principles' which basically repeats government policy on cluster areas. The institute has compiled its own 'Good practice principles on asylum seeker accommodation' for the private sector. This is reproduced in *Bedsitaction* for August 1999 and is available on the institute's website. Perhaps the most important principle is that:

All local authorities should set up liaison arrangements between Social Services, Housing and Environmental Health Departments. Social Services/Housing must advise Environmental Health where asylum seekers are being placed, both within and outside the local authority's area. Environmental Health must undertake to confirm conditions within the accommodation and inform Social Services/Housing. Performance targets for a response should be agreed and monitored. Consideration should be given to formalising these arrangements in a service level agreement.

FURTHER ENVIRONMENTAL HEALTH GOOD PRACTICE

Bolton Council's Environment Department has produced a useful legal guide, 'Asylum seekers accommodation: required standards'. This explains Section 604 of the 1985 Housing Act which requires property to be fit for human habitation and also Section 326 which governs the minimum floor area sizes for rooms occupied as bedrooms and stipulates the permitted numbers of persons allowed to use rooms in a house for sleeping purposes. The guide contains information on gas and electrical installation safety.

Under the 1998 Gas Safety (Installation and Use) Regulations, the landlord of rented accommodation has a duty to have the gas installation checked and provide a yearly gas safety certificate.

REPAIRS AND OTHER CONTRACTUAL RESPONSIBILITIES ON HOUSING PROVIDERS AND NASS

Immigration advisors need to work with housing experts to develop legal remedies for unsuitable housing conditions. A letter of 29 February 2000 from the NASS Support Team to the author attempts to clarify the contractual basis of the complicated tripartite scheme involving NASS, the property provider and the occupier. The letter states:

- The accommodation will be provided under contract with providers in the public, private and independent sectors who will subsequently enter into an occupancy agreement with the asylum-seeker. Consequently NASS is not the landlord/licensor, rather those accommodation providers who enter into contract with NASS will be the landlord/licensor.

- The asylum-seeker will enter into an agreement with NASS upon accessing support which sets out the conditions of the support being offered by NASS.

- The asylum-seeker will sign an occupancy agreement with the landlord and this will give an outline of both the landlord's obligations in terms of management and maintenance and the asylum-seeker's obligations in terms of conducting the occupancy.

- Consequently, the accommodation provider may be able to be pursued for disrepair under both the terms of the occupancy agreement and in terms of the contract signed with NASS. Additionally the local Environmental Health Authority could take action against the landlord if the condition of the property causes a 'statutory nuisance' or contravenes the terms of any local schemes that are in operation e.g. Registration Schemes for Houses in Multiple Occupation. There may also be issues in relation to planning requirements.

AGREEMENT BETWEEN HOUSING PROVIDER AND NASS

NASS refuses to make public its accommodation contracts with housing providers. However, in an undated letter of April 2000 from NASS it would appear that under these accommodation contracts 'repairs must be carried out within a reasonable timescale and the premises must be maintained to a high standard throughout the occupancy'.

AGREEMENT BETWEEN LOCAL AUTHORITY HOUSING PROVIDERS

The above-mentioned report of Manchester's Chief Executive of 4 September 2000 clarified another set of legal relationships. It states 'The Principal Contract with NASS can only exist with one authority, acting on behalf of others. In other Regions one authority has taken the lead, and in turn protected itself with regard to liabilities by having a sub contract with each of the Consortium members.' Manchester council agreed to adopt this model with itself acting as the lead authority for contractual purposes with NASS.

AGREEMENT BETWEEN ASYLUM-SEEKER AND LOCAL AUTHORITY

The North West Consortium has adopted a standard licence agreement with asylum-seekers. This is based largely on existing local authority secure tenancy agreements. It commits the local authority to keep in good repair the structure of the property, all fixtures and fittings and also the following services: electric wiring, sockets and light fittings and gas and water pipes, and heating equipment such as fires, radiators and storage heaters and kitchen and bathroom fixtures.

AGREEMENT BETWEEN ASYLUM-SEEKER AND NASS

It is not clear in law whether the submission of a standard application form to NASS amounts to a contract with NASS. However, the explanatory notes to the form (as well as the form itself) are contained within the Asylum Support Regulations 2000. Therefore failure to comply with its obligations specified in these notes, such as the requirement to ensure the property is 'suitable' for the applicant, should be judicially reviewable.

STATUTORY OBLIGATIONS OF HOUSING PROVIDERS

Decisions by providers to house asylum-seekers in unsafe or unhealthy property could be judicially reviewed on the grounds that such accommodation is not 'adequate' as required by the 1999 Act or alternatively the provider could be sued for breach of contract.

It will become important to develop existing statutory repair duties on housing providers. The 1972 Defective Premises Act imposes liability in negligence on lessors for defective repairs made prior to any letting. This liability extends to third parties, such as visitors to the premises. Part 3 of the 1990 Environmental Protection Act establishes liability for statutory nuisance which is prejudicial to health. This includes nuisance to occupiers caused by housing conditions such as dampness or dangerous wiring. Local authority environmental health departments have a responsibility to investigate these conditions. The 1985 Housing Act deals with HMOs. Local authorities can insist that work is done on these properties in order, for instance, to ensure proper fire escape exit points.

GOOD PRACTICE BY MANCHESTER

Manchester is one council that has been prepared to enforce the statutory obligations on private landlords housing asylum-seekers. Its Chief Executive's report of 4 September 2000 said:

> In Manchester the Consortium has been made aware of properties requiring the intervention of Council officers. This has involved officers from the Private Sector Team in Manchester to serve local notices on landlords to carry out repairs on sub-standard properties. The Council has powers to do this under Environmental and Housing Acts.

THE HOUSING CORPORATION REPORT

Local authorities are not intended to be the sole providers of accommodation under the new scheme. Private landlords can tender under the scheme. Registered social landlords (RSLs) can also provide, or be compelled to provide, housing.

RSLs is the new name under the 1996 Housing Act for social landlords that are independent and non-profit making. Most are housing associations, but there are also trusts, co-operatives and companies. Whether RSLs, as voluntary sector organisations, should willingly engage in the scheme again raises policy issues which are discussed in Chapter 20.

The Housing Corporation was established by parliament in 1964. It now supervises RSLs. In November 1999 the Corporation published *Guidelines for registered social landlords on the provision of housing and support services for asylum seekers* by Roger Zetter and Martyn Pearl. This offers numerous examples of possible good practice – but all based on the unquestioned assumption that RSLs should engage in the new scheme. The guidelines stress the need for RSLs

- to work as partners within the consortia
- to collaborate with statutory providers including education, social and health services
- to fund refugee community organisations for translation, counselling support and other services.

The guidelines also quote instances of existing good practice. The example is given of Mosscare which has 'worked proactively with Manchester Social Services Department and Manchester Housing Department. In addition Mosscare have also developed new-build schemes in partnership with the local community groups, including the Somali community. A third strand of partnership is the link with Refugee Housing Association (RHA) through which Mosscare provide office space and 10 units from their general stock and 6 short-life dwellings which RHA manage.'

THE AUDIT COMMISSION REPORT

The Audit Commission was established in 1983 to monitor expenditure of public money. In June 2000 the Commission published an extensive report, *Another Country*, accompanied by a shorter 'Briefing' on the dispersal scheme. The purpose of this work was to help local authorities and other local agencies ensure the consortia function properly not just in respect of housing but in respect of services generally. The Commission was highly critical of how dispersal was operating in practice. The Briefing stated that:

- 'poor information about asylum-seekers' needs often hinders service planning
- language barriers and low staff awareness of asylum-seekers' rights and entitlements are persistent problems
- some schools and GPs are reluctant to accept asylum-seekers...'

The Briefing also stated that: 'Only 12 per cent of social services authorities have a refugee strategy in place.'

The report made various recommendations for regional consortia and local authorities and agencies. This included improved accessibility of services to asylum-seekers through better signposting, staff training, interpretation, translation and advocacy services. It also recommended the development of effective consultation mechanisms to involve asylum seekers and refugees in service planning.

HOUSING OF UNACCOMPANIED ASYLUM-SEEKING CHILDREN

Unaccompanied asylum-seekers under 18 remain eligible for financial and accommodation support by local authorities through Section 17 of the 1989 Children Act (see Chapter 12). Accommodation can also be provided under Section 20 of the same Act. Section 20 places a duty on an authority to 'look after' a child in need if the child appears to need this higher level of support. The Barnardos pamphlet *Children First and Foremost* (see Chapter 12) emphasises that: 'The section of the Act under which a young person is offered (accommodation) services has a huge impact on the level and type of support they receive'. Support under Section 17 need not be linked to a named social worker, need not be based on a proper assessment of care and any accommodation may be in bedsits or in bed and breakfast hotels. On the other hand accommodating a child under Section 20 should usually result in a foster or residential placement along with an allocated social worker and a detailed needs assessment within the LAC (Looked After Children) material. This material refers to the process and documents that local authorities must use in assessing the needs of and planning for children who are looked after. The Children Act regulations provide instructions on the writing of a care plan for a child looked after as well as on the frequency of visits by a named social worker. The Barnardos pamphlet therefore recommends to local authorities that: 'Unaccompanied asylum seeking children should receive a detailed assessment of need and unless the plan states that a young person's needs can be met in other ways should be accommodated under Section 20 of the Children Act 1989'.

HOUSING FOR UNACCOMPANIED ASYLUM-SEEKING CHILDREN AFTER 18TH BIRTHDAY

Section 24 of the Children Act imposes a duty on a local authority to continue to provide a service up to the age of 21 for young people who have been looked after under Section 20 (see Chapter 12). There is presently a Children (Leaving Care) Bill due to be implemented in April 2001. This will extend local authority obligations to those leaving care under Section 20. However according to the pamphlet *Children First and Foremost* the Department of Health has suggested that all asylum-seeking children are presently and will continue automatically to be transferred to the NASS scheme on their 18th birthday and will therefore be liable to dispersal. Further details of this can be found in the June 2000 Refugee Council briefing *Support arrangements – 16 to 17 year old unaccompanied asylum seeking children*. According to this Briefing, NASS has said that the only group leaving care on their 18th birthday and exempted from dispersal would be those in exam years of education (GCSEs and 'A' levels) and those receiving treatment from the Medical Foundation for the Care of Victims of Torture. It may be that this automatic transferal to the NASS scheme is judicially reviewable. It is yet another example of the assumption that immigration laws negate child protection legislation when the two clash (see Chapter 11). As a matter of good, non-discriminatory, practice young people supported under Section 20 who have been granted refugee status (and also those refused it) should be treated for child care purposes like any other care leavers.

Those young people being supported only under Section 17 are not entitled under Section 24 or the proposed Bill to a leaving care service (as they are not being 'looked after'). Asylum-seeking children in this situation can automatically be transferred to the NASS scheme on becoming 18.

ASYLUM SEEKERS WITH POSITIVE HOME OFFICE DECISIONS – MOVING HOME

Asylum seekers granted refugee or exceptional leave status become immediately eligible for welfare benefits. There has been an amendment to paragraph 3070 of the Social Fund Guidance Manual. This now states that where asylum-seekers have been housed through NASS under the new support scheme then if a positive decision is made on their asylum application they become eligible for a community care grant. This is designed to help a person establish a home in the community as part of a planned resettlement programme following a period of an unsettled way of life. Advisors should argue that where an asylum-seeker has been supported either by a local authority or friends then this is equivalent to NASS support and should also lead to a community grant.

ADEQUATE ACCOMMODATION AND ENTRY CLEARANCE

There is one area where local authorities can be of positive assistance irrespective of the 1999 Act. The immigration rules for family reunion demand proof of 'adequate accommodation'.

Local authority housing departments should as a matter of good practice provide 'certificates of accommodation'. These should certify the existence and size of a council or private tenancy or privately owned accommodation in the name of the sponsor and that the accommodation would not become 'overcrowded' under the definition of the Housing Act if family members were admitted from overseas. Many authorities already provide these services.

Where a property would become overcrowded then the local authority should provide larger accommodation. This should be provided prior to any application to come to or remain in the UK – otherwise it could be interpreted as recourse to additional public funds. Councils could consider referral to housing associations as one means of providing accommodation in these circumstances.

FREE AND WELL-PUBLICISED LOCAL AUTHORITY SUPPORT

Some authorities, such as Manchester, provide housing reports for entry clearance purposes but make charges. Charging is bad practice. It discriminates against residents or their dependants subject to immigration control. Good anti-racist practice should be based on the provision of free mainline support services for all residents at the point where they are affected by controls. This would recognise the disproportionate hardships endured in confronting controls.

Local authority support on immigration issues should be publicised. Keeping it secret defeats the object. In a letter of 11 March 1999 to GMIAU the senior environmental health officer of Trafford Council confirmed that the authority could provide a house inspection (albeit at a fee of £70 plus VAT). However, it acknowledged that 'the service is not publicised'. This explains why the writer stated: 'I am not aware of ever being asked to inspect a Council-owned property to ensure that it won't become overcrowded when an immigrant begins to occupy it.'

It would perhaps be more appropriate if the assessment of adequacy of accommodation was made by a council's housing aid and advice service with a commitment by the council that the service should be free.

THE NEED TO MONITOR CONTENT OF CERTIFICATES OF ACCOMMODATION

Management should monitor certificates of accommodation. Oldham local authority provides certificates. In one case in 1998 a housing officer confirmed that accommodation was not overcrowded. However, he gratuitously informed the entry clearance officer that the accommodation was on a private tenancy, there was no guarantee the tenant would remain in the property and the tenant and the dependant coming from Pakistan might in future 'call upon council resources'.

LIMITING THE TOWER HAMLETS DECISION

A problem for town hall workers is the 1993 Tower Hamlets case which declared there was a duty by housing authorities to notify the Home Office if a service user was suspected of illegal entry.

It is not clear whether there is such a 'duty' and if so how far it extends. The term 'illegal entrant' does not include someone who entered lawfully but has overstayed leave. The *Code of Guidance on Parts V1 and V11 of the Housing Act 1996 (Allocation of Housing Accommodation and Homelessness)* issued by the Department of the Environment is less draconian than the Tower Hamlets decision. The Code simply 'recommends' contacting the Home Office where the authority is 'not certain' that a person may be an unlawful entrant. The Code says that an authority has a 'duty' only where it is 'satisfied' that a person is in the UK illegally. A housing authority and its workers will hardly ever have sufficient factual information or knowledge of the law's complexities to be properly 'satisfied'. If there is a duty to inform, it is not clear what are the legal consequences of a failure to inform.

Comments on casework problem at start of chapter

As X claimed asylum on entry after 3 April 2000, her case is determined by the Asylum Support Regulations 2000. These say that local authorities can, but need not, disregard any preference a supported person has as to locality or nature of accommodation and nature of fixtures and fittings. The Home Office letter to Andrew Rowe MP says preferences *will* be taken into account. To house a disabled person on the fourth floor without a lift suggests that X's personal circumstances have been positively disregarded. Likewise the notes attached to the NASS application form says it could be unreasonable to be housed in an area of racist attacks. It would seem there is a possibility of a judicial review of the local authority's decision to house X in this accommodation. The dangerous wiring places the authority in breach of its contractual repair obligations and its statutory obligations under the Environmental Health Act.

NASS may itself be able to bring an action for breach of contract against the local authority if it breaches the terms and conditions of its agreement with NASS.

It is less clear whether X can bring an action against NASS. One possible action for judicial review is that X has a legitimate expectation that NASS would, if possible, not disperse her away from her family. This commitment was given in the letter to Andrew Rowe. Also the notes attached to the NASS application form say NASS will consider health issues and 'any factors that affect your well-being when we decide what accommodation to give you'. The responsibility of NASS for the allocation of any particular property is unclear but NASS here seems to be accepting some responsibility for which it may be judicially reviewable.

There is also the possibility of challenging under Article 8 of the European Convention on Human Rights (the right to family life) the decision of NASS to divide X's family by dispersing X two hundred miles away.

NASS and the local authority may be singularly and collectively liable, through judicial review, for the provision of 'inadequate' accommodation.

It is not totally clear whether X can appeal to an asylum support adjudicator (see Chapter 12). It has been seen that there is only an appeal against refusal, not level, of support. However, the accommodation in this case is so inadequate as to perhaps amount to a refusal.

The best option, rather than litigation which might take longer than the determination of the asylum claim, is to persuade the local authority to rehouse X. However, this would still leave her with the problem of being distant from her family.

Notes

1   *INLP*, vol. 13, no. 2, 1999
2   *De Falco* v. *Crawley BC*, 1980 2WLR p.664

3   *R* v. *London Borough of Hillingdon ex parte Streeting*, 1980 WLR p.1425   •

4   *London Borough of Tower Hamlets* v. *The Secretary of State for the Environment*, 1993 25 HLR p.524

5   *Legal Action Group Bulletin*, April 2000

Education services
and immigration status

A CASEWORK PROBLEM

> You are a headteacher of a maintained school. X is aged 6. X's mother wants to enrol him. You agree. You receive an anonymous letter saying that X entered illegally because X's mother had said he would attend a private school. The letter says that you commit an offence by enrolling X. What should you do?

A REAL CASE STORY

> Paul Ho was a Hong Kong student. He yearly renewed his leave to remain. Then the Home Office threatened deportation. Paul had been incompetently advised that instead of yearly applications he should become a British citizen. Paul applied for naturalisation. He had no right to naturalise as this requires having permanent settlement. The rules require an overseas student to show intention to leave the UK on completing studies. Applying for naturalisation suggests a wish to remain permanently. After a campaign Paul was allowed to finish his studies. Because of length of stay in the UK he was eventually granted settlement.

SCOPE OF THIS CHAPTER

This chapter looks at both school and post-school education. The link between education provision and immigration status, particularly in terms of student fees and grants in further and higher education, has existed throughout most of the post–1945 expansion in education. Perhaps more than in any other area of provision this link has grown to seem 'natural'. Student protests against the removal of grants and imposition of tuition fees in 1998 and 1999 simply ignored the fact that overseas students had been long discriminated against in terms of eligibility for grants and the payment of fees. Far from being natural the situation of overseas students is highly political. Britain exhibits a vanity in imposing huge fees and other conditions on overseas students. In one case Lord Denning said:

> For many years parents in countries overseas have sent their…sons and daughters to our public schools and to our universities. On finishing here, they have returned to their own countries, often to exercise much influence there, for good.

The most distinguished being Jawaharlal Nehru of Harrow and Trinity College Cambridge. Many have been called to the English Bar and gone back to be prime ministers and judges. Even revolutionaries, such as Mahatma Gandhi. Some have come to Sandhurst and gone back to become generals and heads of military governments.[1]

FURTHER READING RESOURCES

Much of the law and practice explained in this chapter was predicted in the *Thin End of the White Wedge* published in 1981 by South Manchester Law Centre. There are no comprehensive modern studies.

HISTORY

Student education and teacher employment have historic links with status. The *Jewish Chronicle* of 4 April 1919 reported Middlesex County Council agreeing that 'children of aliens' should be refused scholarships. On 25 July 1919 it reported London County Council coming to the same decision even for natural-ised British pupils. Opponents of restrictions were not necessarily radical. The *Jewish Chronicle* of 20 March 1925 reported Stuart Samuel MP saying:

> To refuse a scholarship to a bright child is to cause it to grow up under a sense of injustice and of dissatisfaction of the state and this policy would drive them into the ranks of revolutionaries.

The *Jewish Chronicle* of 16 July 1920 reported the London County Council voting against 'the employment of aliens, even naturalised aliens, in the Council's service'. This was aimed against teachers.

In 1938 the League of Nations formulated the Geneva Convention on Refugees Coming from Germany. The UK ratified this with reservations – refugees should not enjoy equal educational facilities. Details are in *British Policy and the Refugees 1933–1940* by Yvonne Kapp and Margaret Mynett, written in 1941 but first published by Cass in 1997.

POST–1945

The 1944 Education Act excluded from educational grants students not 'ordi-narily resident'. Differential fees for overseas students were introduced in 1967 through administrative guidance. Details are in *Overseas Students Fees and Grants* (Runnymede Trust 1984) by J. Beale and A. Parker. The Housing Benefits Amendments No. 3 Regulations 1984 denied housing benefit to overseas students.

ADMISSION TO SCHOOLS

The *Guardian* of 24 April 1980 reported Sheffield's Education Director instructing schools to demand passports where a child's immigration status was unclear. On 31 October 1981 the *Guardian* revealed Newham Council being reported to the Commission for Racial Equality. Earlham Primary School told an Asian mother to produce her children's passports. Newham's Education Director had incorrectly informed schools that the 1971 Immigration Act removed obligations to admit children not resident in the UK.

Various circulars have stressed school admission cannot be denied because of immigration status. Annex B to DES Circular 11/88 'Admission of pupils to county and voluntary schools' confirms this.

LIAISON WITH HOME OFFICE

Co-operation with the Home Office is implicit in the *Code of Practice: School Admissions* drawn up under the 1998 Schools Standards and Framework Act. The Immigration and Nationality Directorate's address and telephone number is given so schools and education authorities can obtain 'general advice about immigration rules'. It is unclear why the advice is needed. The inclusion of IND contact details encourages reporting of pupils.

The Code requires schools or education authorities to investigate matters in which they have no competence. It warns that pupils who have come to the UK to study are expected (as explained below) to attend a private school and 'LEAs and governing bodies will wish to bear this in mind when considering a request for a transfer in respect of a child from overseas who has been previously attending a fee-paying school'. The Code says that schools may receive an application from parents overseas for a child not physically in the UK. It recommends that

consideration should be given to the likelihood of the family in question... being granted leave to enter the country for a period which would make it practicable for the child to attend school.

PREVIOUS CIRCULARS

The Code does not explicitly require school liaison with the Home Office. However, other circulars have developed this culture. DES Circular 11/88 suggested that where 'doubt exists exploratory approaches should be referred to the Immigration Department at the Home Office'. In October 1993 the government launched its Efficiency Scrutiny on 'inter-agency co-operation on illegal immigration' (see Chapter 1). In a written parliamentary answer of 18 July 1995 the Home Secretary said that this included consultation with the Department for Education and Employment (DfEE). In June 1996 the DfEE circulated draft guidance on admission to maintained schools of overseas pupils. This invited notifying the Home Office where 'during the course of normal admissions procedures, reasonable suspicion is aroused that an applicant may be in the UK without permission'. This draft was never formalised but indicates the pressure on schools.

PUBLIC FUNDS AND PRIVATE EDUCATION

School education is not a 'public fund' within the immigration rules. No child can have status prejudiced under the public funds requirements by attending a maintained school.

However, there are other rules which can prejudice status. This is because under the immigration rules someone wanting to come or stay as a pupil must attend 'an independent fee paying school outside the maintained sector'. Some observations can be made about this rule:

- It does not prevent a maintained school admitting an overseas pupil but this could undermine the child's status.

- It applies only to pupils coming to or staying in the UK in that capacity. It does not prevent children in the UK in another capacity attending maintained schools – such as dependent children of visitors or of college students.

- There is no provision for dependent children remaining at a maintained school if their parents leave the UK. This creates problems at vital stages of education – such as taking examinations. By using the appeal system and making further representations it may be possible to gain enough time to take examinations.

- There was previously a Home Office concession allowing a parent to come or remain here temporarily on the basis of a child attending a private school. This concession, with some changes, has now been incorporated into the immigration rules that came into force on 2 October 2000. The provision only applies where the child is under 12 years of age. The period of permitted stay is 12 months. It is unclear from the rules whether repeat applications can be made but logically this should be possible until the child reaches the age of 12. Evidence must be produced of funds for a second home here and the parent must meet the requirements of the visitor rules. A letter of 28 May 1999 circulated by ILPA from the IND confirmed that the previous concession applied to an unmarried or divorced parent and it would seem the new rule operates in the same way. The new rule would also seem to apply to the entry or stay of both parents – whereas the previous concession was limited to one parent.

- Commonwealth citizens between 17 and 27 can come to the UK on a working holiday but not where a child will become 5 during the visit. This is designed to prevent such children attending school in the UK.

- Rules allowing children to study at independent schools do not mention care arrangements. This is a local authority matter.

DUTIES TO ATTEND SCHOOL AND OBLIGATIONS TO ADMIT TO SCHOOL

Parents have duties under the 1998 Schools Standards and Framework Act to ensure school attendance of children between 5 and 16. Local authorities have obligations to provide education. It is unclear when parents temporarily in the UK become obliged to send a child to school or the school becomes obliged to accept a child. The code of practice says:

> Families not entitled to remain permanently may be in the country for a stay of several months or for a short holiday. It may be reasonable for an application for a school place to be rejected if the stay is so short that it would not be practicable to admit the child to school.

Under the 1948 Education (Miscellaneous Provisions) Act, schools generally have no obligation to admit children except at the start of a term.

EUROPEAN NATIONALS

Department of Education Circular 5/81 refers to education authority duties to educate children of European Community migrant workers under a European Council directive of July 1977. The directive obliges authorities to provide both English language and mother-tongue teaching.

SCHOOL LEAGUE TABLES

According to a Refugee Council Briefing of August 2000, the DfEE announced in July 2000 that newly arrived children from overseas whose first language is not English will not have their examination results included in school league table results for the first two years if they arrive in school during years 5,6,10 or 11. This should stop some schools wrongly refusing to admit children from overseas in case this reduces their position in school league tables.

FREE SCHOOL MILK, MEALS AND THE 1999 IMMIGRATION AND ASYLUM ACT

Income support is a window to certain free educational services. Asylum-seekers and others subject to control are ineligible for income support (see Chapter 12).

Under the 1996 Education Act a local education authority must provide at maintained schools free milk, meals and other refreshment to pupils whose parents receive income support. Under the 1998 School Standards and Framework Act the Education Minister can transfer these duties to the school's governing body.

Under the 1999 Immigration and Asylum Act children whose parents are receiving support under the Act become re-entitled to free school meals and milk. This is inadequate. It excludes children from non-asylum-seeking families whose immigration status denies them income support.

FREE SCHOOL CLOTHING AND TRAVEL

Under the Education (Provision of Clothing) Regulations 1980 and the 1996 Education Act an authority can provide school clothing free or at a reduced rate for a pupil 'unable by reason of the inadequacy or unsuitability of his clothing to take full advantage of the education provided at the school'. Most authorities expect parents to be on income support.

Section 509 of the 1996 Education Act empowers local authorities to pay for travel to school. This is not necessarily income related. Manchester council's policy is based on length of journey of three miles or more.

ELIGIBILITY FOR ASSISTED PLACES

The Education (Assisted Places) Regulations 1995 allowed authorities to pay for attendance at a fee-paying school. The child must have been ordinarily resident for two years, or have been an EEA national resident in the EEA for two years, or have been granted, or have a parent who had been granted, refugee status or exceptional leave to remain by the UK government. Children of asylum-seekers were ineligible. The assisted places scheme is being phased out and no new children can go on it.

SCHOOL TRIPS ABROAD

Problems arise with school trips abroad. In many cases children with British citizenship may not require visas or, in travel to EEA countries, passports whereas non-British children may require both. There are reported incidents of non-British pupils without appropriate documents being refused leave to enter a country or of schools realising the problem at the last moment and leaving non-British children in the UK.

FEES IN FURTHER AND HIGHER EDUCATION

Under the immigration rules overseas post-school students can choose between a 'bona fide private education institution' or a 'publicly funded institution of further or higher education'. Sixth form colleges are treated as further education colleges. The latest Education (Fees and Awards) Regulations were issued in 1997 and amended in 1998. They link 'home student' fees to immigration and residency status. Staff are being asked to investigate immigration status. The Department for Education and Employment issues a *Guidance on Fees* for college staff. Annex 2 contains four pages of immigration passport stamps. The regulations exempt education institutions from race relations prosecution for charging higher fees.

CONSEQUENCES OF NON-PAYMENT OF FEES

The academic year 1998 saw the introduction of tuition fees payable by home students of up to £1025 in higher education. Overseas student fees range between £3500 and £17,000. These figures will increase with inflation. Non-payment of fees could result in expulsion from both college and country. The *Guardian* of 22 February 1982 reported the University of Hull's Registrar as writing to overseas students threatening that non-payment would be 'reported to the immigration authorities in response to any queries they may make'.

DETAILS OF THE FEES REGULATIONS

To be classified as a 'home student' the following must be met:

- Three years' 'ordinary residence' in the UK preceding the relevant date (1 January, 1 April or 1 September) closest to the course's commencement. In 1983 the courts defined 'ordinary residence' in the case of *Shah* v. *Barnet LBC* as the place where someone is normally living for the time being.[2] Most students legally in the UK will be able to fulfil this requirement.

- Following *Shah*, the Regulations were altered. Residency now must not be 'wholly or mainly for the purpose of receiving full-time education'. This excludes from 'home student' status young people who have been in the UK as school pupils.

- The 1997 regulations established a new criterion – settlement. This slashes the numbers eligible for reduced fees. Even someone settled will not be entitled to reduced fees until in the UK for three years. This discriminates against adult children who have recently achieved family unity in the UK.

EXCEPTIONS

The Regulations contain the following exceptions to the need for settlement and three years' residence:

- People granted refugee status by the UK government or exceptional leave to remain following an asylum claim. This exemption extends to spouses and children including adopted and stepchildren. A student qualifies immediately for home student fees on the granting of refugee or exceptional leave status.

- The above exception does not apply to asylum-seekers with undetermined applications. The situation differs for students attending a further, as opposed to a higher, education course. According to its *Guidance: Tariff 2000–2001* the Further Education Funding Council (FEFC) treats as 'home' students, and funds colleges accordingly, asylum-seekers or dependants in receipt of support given under the 1999 legislation either by NASS under the full support scheme or by a local authority under the interim scheme (see Chapter 12). Unaccompanied asylum-seekers under 18 financially supported through the 1989 Children Act or in social services care are also treated as home students. All the above are treated as receiving the equivalent of a means-tested benefit.

- According to its *Guidance* the FEFC will treat as home students for further education those students settled in the UK but for less than three years and students lawfully in the UK for three years but not settled. Students without settled status and here for less than three years can be treated as home students where 'evidence demonstrates membership of the home population'. This is not explained. Presumably it includes spouses and children from overseas who are applying or waiting to apply for settled status after having been granted an initial twelve months leave.

- European Union nationals ordinarily resident, not wholly or mainly for study purposes, in an EEA country for three years prior to the course starting. Children of EU nationals are exempt if they fulfil the three years' ordinary residence requirements.

- EEA nationals resident in the UK as migrant workers. There is the need for three years' ordinary residence within an EEA country not for study purposes. Spouses as well as children are exempt if they fulfil the three years' ordinary residence requirements.

- Returning UK nationals who have lived in the EEA as migrant workers.

- People who would have been ordinarily resident for the three-year period either in the UK or the EEA except where they or their parents or their spouse have been temporarily working in another country.

- Students on a reciprocal exchange scheme where there will normally be no fees.

NEW SYSTEM OF LOANS AND OTHER FINANCIAL SUPPORT

Financial support for higher education students is determined by the Education (Student Support) Regulations, the most recent being issued in 1999. Support is available only for

- a first degree course
- a Higher National Diploma
- a Diploma in Higher Education
- a Postgraduate Certificate in Education
- some part-time courses of initial teacher training.

The Department for Education and Employment has issued an explanatory brochure: *Financial Support for Students: A Guide*.

Prior to academic years 1998 and 1999 authorities were obliged to provide higher education students with means-tested grants covering tuition fees and living costs. This has been replaced by loans for living expenses alongside grants for tuition fees paid by local authorities based on a means test.

There also exist supplementary grants for which the authority is responsible. There are for disabled students, accommodation costs in the long vacation for students who have been in care, grants for dependants and travel grants for medical courses away from college.

Colleges can in case of financial hardship provide hardship loans or access funds for small amounts. The maximum hardship loan is £250.

CRITERIA FOR LOANS AND OTHER FINANCIAL SUPPORT

The general criteria for eligibility for financial support are identical to entitlement to reduced fees. The student must be ordinarily resident for three years not as a student and with settled status.

There are exceptions, similar to the fees exceptions but with these differences. Persons refused asylum but granted exceptional leave have no entitlement to support until there has been three years' ordinary residence not as a student. European Union nationals are, simply as EU nationals, entitled to support only with tuition fees and not with other support. However, EEA migrant workers, their spouses and children are entitled to the full range of support. There is no support for exchange students.

Good practice

SCHOOL MEALS AND MILK

Children whose parents are not asylum-seekers but whose immigration status denies them income support are ineligible for free school meals or milk. Following the 1996 Asylum and Immigration Act some education authorities asked schools to waive the costs of school meals where parents were destitute and ineligible for income support. In June 1997 the council-operated Manchester Advice Service produced a leaflet 'Asylum seekers and persons from abroad: what help is available in Manchester?' confirming that Manchester schools were being asked to waive charges.

According to a letter of 17 August 1999 from Manchester's Education Department schools have been criticised by auditors where they have made free meals available when parents are not receiving income support. Good practice requires schools to ignore these criticisms. Where LEAs retain responsibility for meals they should formally advise schools to waive charges.

DISCOVERING IMMIGRATION STATUS

There remains the problem as to how a school knows which children have parents not receiving benefit because of immigration status. Good anti-discriminatory practice dictates that either all children in the school are given free meals and milk or all parents are asked about status with an explanation as to why they are asked.

SCHOOL CLOTHING

Local education authorities should provide free school clothing for all pupils who are denied income support because of immigration status. Availability of these provisions should be publicised in all appropriate languages. Travel grants should be available to all pupils irrespective of status.

SCHOOLS: CONTACTING THE HOME OFFICE

The immigration status of a child is irrelevant for school admission. Schools should never contact the Home Office. The only responsibilities that schools have are educational and pastoral ones. If a school suspects that immigration status is irregular then it should suggest that the pupil's parent(s) or guardian(s) contact a reputable immigration advisor.

APPEALING REFUSALS

If a child is refused admission to a school then the parent(s) or guardian(s) can appeal to a panel convened by the local education authority. If this is not successful a complaint can be made to the Minister for Education. In a letter of 25 April 1979 to the United Kingdom Council for Overseas Student Affairs (UKCOSA) from the then Department of Education and Science it was acknowledged that it could be unreasonable for a school to refuse to admit a child merely because he or she was in the UK on a visit of six months or less.

EXPULSION, REPORT WRITING, CAMPAIGNS AND ASYLUM

Schools can challenge expulsion from the UK. They can provide professional reports emphasising the detrimental affect of removal (see Chapter 9) and campaign as a community on behalf of the threatened pupil (see Chapter 19). Advisors should inform the school as soon as possible of the situation to ensure a proper working relationship in contesting the expulsion (see Chapter 9). There are particular good practice issues for schools in relation to unaccompanied child asylum-seekers (see Chapter 8).

EXAMPLE OF MANCHESTER GOOD PRACTICE

In June 1987 Manchester's Education Policy Sub-Committee adopted 'Guidance for schools and educational support services on the admission into maintained schools of children from abroad'(23 June 1987). The essential points are quoted here:

- 'None of the statutory duties to admit children to schools is in any way altered by a child's immigration status.

- 'When children from abroad are presented for admission, they should be dealt with through the normal admissions procedure.

- 'AT NO STAGE SHOULD PASSPORTS BE REQUESTED. Such a request would be discriminatory and does not recognise that such families will have already been subjected to a number of checks and controls as a prerequisite of entry to the country.

- 'Length of stay in this country is frequently a matter which is determined by factors outside the control of parents, i.e. whether work permits, student grants, visas, etc. are renewed. Schools should not, therefore, press this issue.

- 'As procedures for admission into the country can be subject to considerable delays, schools should advise parents that no arrangements can be made for admission to school until the child arrives in the country.

- 'Should schools receive requests from the Home Office or Immigration Authorities for information about children from abroad these should be referred in writing to the Senior Assistant Education Officer.

- 'On admission to school, children from abroad should have access to all educational services and benefits.

- 'Children from abroad should not be subjected to any medical examination other than those which are part of the normal medical routine of the school.

- 'Schools should be aware that serious problems can arise with school trips and exchange visits abroad.

- 'Schools will need to ensure that parents are aware of passport and visa requirements for their children. They should be advised to consult a Law Centre…for advice on this matter. A letter to this effect should be made available in different languages to the parents of children from abroad.

- 'It is essential that parents are made aware of these events as early as possible as it can take some months to obtain visas.'

CRITIQUE OF THE MANCHESTER GUIDANCE

These guidelines are welcome but inadequate.

Preparatory arrangements for admission can be made before a child physically arrives. Schools should recommend that parents or sponsors consult an advisor to determine the possible date of arrival.

Requests from the Home Office for information should never be passed on to anyone except the family concerned.

The costs of passports or visas for non-British children should be shared equally between all the party, British and non-British. It is possible to obtain a collective passport for British children but this is divisive where there are non-British children. Schools should reconsider the educational value of trips where controls discriminate against non-British children.

NO DUTY TO CHARGE HIGHER FEES

There is no duty on colleges to charge higher fees. The regulations state that lesser fees can be charged in cases of 'financial hardship or otherwise'. Good practice requires no differential fees.

The DfEE guidelines state: 'given that the institution's discretion is whether or not to forgo income, overseas students should not expect institutions to readily waive or reduce their fees'. Examples given of acceptable fee reduction are in collaboration with scholarship schemes and where overseas support is withdrawn.

FEES, FINANCIAL SUPPORT AND PASSPORTS

The guidance on fees invites colleges to look at passports to determine if a student has settled status. This is bad practice. Colleges charging differential fees should accept a student's self-certification (see Chapter 20).

Self-certification should also be used by bodies responsible for student financial support. The Education (Student Support) Regulations 1999 try to prevent this. They oblige a student to produce a passport in claiming financial support. The regulations allow an exception where a student 'is a refugee or does not hold' a passport. In these cases students are expected to provide 'a letter or other document issued by a responsible person which contains particulars of his date, place and country of birth and his full name on birth'. The document need not show immigration status. This leaves scope for bodies responsible for student support to accept self-certification.

CONTACTING THE HOME OFFICE: BAD PRACTICE; CONTACTING UKCOSA: GOOD PRACTICE

The guidance on fees invites students to contact the Home Office to see whether they are eligible for settlement. This is bad practice. A student requiring advice should be recommended to see an expert immigration advisor. Overseas student fees and support can be complicated. UKCOSA is able to provide expert advice. It produces a yearly guide for overseas students, the latest being *Guidance Notes for Students 2000–2001.*

OTHER SOURCES OF HELP

GMIAU has produced two leaflets for students. One is 'Information and advice on immigration status for students'. The other is 'Advice and information on grants, loans and fees for overseas students'.

Comments on casework problem at start of chapter

Schools can admit pupils even though they may have entered the UK unlawfully. The headteacher commits no criminal offence. The headteacher should recommend to X and his mother that they see an expert advisor as X's immigration status may be in jeopardy if the anonymous letter is correct. Also X's mother may be settled in the UK and X may qualify for settlement as her child if his mother has sole or main responsibility for him (see Chapter 6).

Notes

1   *R v. Chief Immigration Officer, Gatwick Airport, ex parte Kharrazi,* 1980 3 AE p.373 at p.375
2   1983 All ER p.226

CHAPTER 15

Social services, community care and immigration status

A CASEWORK PROBLEM

You are a care manager. You have a frail client, X, aged 80. She has no income of her own but is dependent on monies from a relative. She tells you she came to the UK on a visit ten years ago and has overstayed her leave. She has been previously advised that this disentitled her to benefits. You recommend that because of her frailty X be provided under Section 45 of the 1968 Health Services and Public Health Act with meals on wheels, home help and some adaptations to the home. Your line manager says that X is not entitled to community care help because of her lack of immigration status. X asks what she should do. What do you suggest?

A REAL CASE STORY

The case of the Rahman family has been described in Chapter 9. The social worker in that case worked extremely hard in both preparing a report and referring in that to the numerous other professional reports in the case. Initially the social services department declined to be involved on the grounds that the family were not settled in the UK. It required a decision by councillors to overrule this refusal. Subsequently the local authority provided much political and material support.

SCOPE OF THIS CHAPTER

This chapter has two aims. First, it shows that the link between entitlement to services and immigration status is being continually expanded and can arise unexpectedly in what can be viewed as relatively 'peripheral' services – such as the criminal compensation and former manpower services schemes. Second, it shows that since the 1999 Immigration and Asylum Act one of the most 'core' of welfare providers, local authority social services, has had much of its professional role defined and limited in terms of the immigration status of its clients.

CRIMINAL COMPENSATION

The link between eligibility and status arises unexpectedly. The *Guardian* of 1 February 1981 reported Ibrahim Khan being thrown from a building. He had lived in the UK for ten years without regularising his stay. The *Guardian* reported: 'The Criminal Injuries Board…was not prepared to make an ex gratia payment to an illegal immigrant.' A letter from St Mary's Hospital in London to his lawyers stated:

> No one here is prepared to write a report for you about this patient…There is absolutely no reason why this patient should receive preferential treatment or become a burden on the taxpayers here. I find it immoral to use public money allowing Mr Khan to become a burden on their dwindling resources.

The letter was signed 'orthopaedic secretary and overburdened taxpayer'.

MANPOWER SERVICES TRAINING

In the 1980s the Manpower Services Commission of the Department of Employment established a 'Training Opportunities Scheme'. A Commission letter of 16 April 1981 to Frank Allaun MP stated:

> Applications from non-EC nationals are not normally accepted unless the applicants are resident in Great Britain and their stay in this country is not subject to any time limit and/or employment restrictions.

THE 1999 IMMIGRATION AND ASYLUM ACT

The Asylum Support Regulations 2000 (Chapters 11 and 12) reveal a profoundly patronising attitude towards the rights of asylum-seekers to receive community services. They say that asylum-seekers receiving support under the 1999 Act may be provided with '(a) education, including English language lessons, (b) sporting and other developmental activities'. However, these services 'may be so provided only for the purposes of maintaining good order among such persons'.

COMMUNITY CARE LEGISLATION AND THE 1999 ACT

The 1999 Act gives a repressive role to local authority social services through making significant care in the community functions dependent upon status. No one 'subject to immigration control' (see Chapter 12) is eligible for care services detailed in the Act. The present government is acutely conscious of the ability of radical advisors to have used alternative legislation to replace benefit and housing rights taken away by the 1996 Asylum and Immigration Act (see Chapters 11 and 12). This prompted the government to search out and make dependent on immigration status all possible community care legislation that it was thought might compensate for the total withdrawal of benefits and housing entitlements in the 1999 Immigration and Asylum Act.

RELEVANT COMMUNITY CARE LEGISLATION

Adult residential care is provided by Section 21 of the 1948 National Assistance Act, which the 1999 Act limits (see Chapter 11 and 12). Domiciliary and community based services are designed to prevent vulnerable groups requiring residential care. Social service responsibilities and powers for domiciliary and community based services for disabled adults are contained in Section 29 of the National Assistance Act and for disabled adults and children in Section 2 of the 1970 Chronically Sick and Disabled Persons Act.

This legislation leaves some groups excluded from day care. Two new provisions, now limited by the 1999 Act, filled the gaps. Section 45 of the 1968 Health Services and Public Health Act provides for services for frail elderly people – where need arises through frailty caused by age not illness. Day care services for the ill or those recovering from illness (as opposed to the 'chronically sick') are provided by Schedule 8, paragraph 2, of the 1977 National Health Service Act.

THE 1999 ACT LIMITING COMMUNITY CARE LEGISLATION

The 1999 Act excludes those 'subject to immigration control' from Section 45 of the 1968 Act and Schedule 8 of the 1977 legislation where the applicant's needs arose:

> solely – (a) because he is destitute; or (b) because of the physical effects, or antici-
> pated physical effects, of his being destitute.

This limitation is the same as Section 21 of the 1948 National Assistance Act. The removal of services is potentially injurious. This is clear from circulars amplifying community care legislation. The legislation imposes no duties on authorities but gives the secretary of state (for health) the power to impose duties or approve the use of local authority discretionary powers.

DHSS Circular 19/71 gives social services discretion to provide the following to promote old people's welfare under Section 45 of the 1968 Act: meals and recreation in the home or elsewhere, information on services for elderly people, travel assistance to participate in Section 45 services, assistance in finding boarding accommodation, social work support and advice, home help and home adaptations, subsidy of warden costs, warden services.

Appendix 3 of the Department of Health's local authority circular LAC (93)10 directs authorities to provide the following under Schedule 8 of the 1977 Act for those having a mental disorder: training centres, day centres, sufficient social workers to help in the identification, diagnosis, assessment and social treatment of mental disorder and to provide social work and other domiciliary and care services. The circular approves social services providing the following to physically and mentally ill people: meals at day centres, meals on wheels, advice and support, night-sitter services, recuperative holidays, facilities for social and recreational activities, services for alcoholic or drug-dependent persons.

THE 1999 ACT, SCOTTISH AND IRISH LEGISLATION

The Act also excludes persons subject to controls from the following legislation:

- general social welfare services under Section 12 of the 1968 Social Work (Scotland) Act

- provision of residential nursing accommodation under Section 13A of the 1968 Act

- provision of care and after-care under Section 13B of the 1968 Act

- provision of mental health services under Section 7 of the 1984 Mental Health (Scotland) Act

- provision of after-care services under Section 8 of the 1984 Act

- provisions preventing illness or after-care under Article 7 of the Health and Personal Social Services (Northern Ireland) Order 1972

- provision of general social welfare under Article 15 of the Order.

Good practice

CARE IN THE COMMUNITY: LOOPHOLES IN THE 1999 IMMIGRATION AND ASYLUM ACT

The restrictions on the 1968 Health Services and Public Health Act, the 1977 National Health Service Act and the Scottish and Irish legislation require care managers to investigate the immigration status of elderly people, physically or mentally ill people and those recovering from illness.

Good practice requires care managers, local authority legal departments and advisors to search for loopholes in the 1999 legislation and for alternative statutory authority for service provision. The potential loopholes are the same as those in respect of Section 21 of the National Assistance Act (see Chapters 12 and 13). In particular it is important to stress where possible that any need for services is not as a result of destitution and that deprivation of services will have adverse mental, and not just physical, health consequences.

ALTERNATIVE NON-RESIDENTIAL CARE LEGISLATION

Community care law is confusing irrespective of immigration status. Luke Clements in his book *Community Care and the Law* (Legal Action Group 1996) has said: 'contradictions and inconsistencies run like fault lines through the community care legislation, which has been well described as a set of often incomprehensible and frequently incompatible principles' (p.94). This renders the assessment of alternative legislation difficult. However, community care laws untouched by the 1999 Act are parts of the 1948 National Assistance Act and the 1970 Chronically Sick and Disabled Persons Act.

The following are relevant in determining whether the 1948 and 1970 Acts can perhaps be used by asylum-seekers and others subject to controls:

- Section 29 of the 1948 Act providing for non-residential care remains untouched. The section helps those

who suffer from mental disorder of any description and other persons aged eighteen or over who are substantially and permanently handicapped by illness, injury or congenital deformity or such other disabilities as may be prescribed by the Minister.

The juridical problem is whether this encompasses frail elderly people where frailty is not caused by illness.

- Where Section 29 is available then the services that local authorities must or may provide are contained in the Department of Health's local authority circular LAC (93)10, Appendix 2. This is similar, though not identical, to the services in Appendix 3 described above.

- Section 29(6)(b) of the National Assistance Act states: 'nothing in the foregoing provisions of this section shall authorise or require...the provision of any accommodation or services required under the National Health Service Act 1977.' This was inserted into the 1948 legislation because both Acts contain similar provisions. However, for people subject to immigration control there is now no overlap between the 1948 Act and Schedule 8 of the 1977 Act, as people subject to controls are excluded from Schedule 8. This suggests that irrespective of immigration status Section 29 can be invoked for accessing the equivalent non-residential support that would otherwise be obtainable under the 1977 Act.

- Section 29 of the 1948 Act is confined to persons over 18. However, Section 2 ('Provision of welfare services') of the 1970 Chronically Sick and Disabled Persons Act has no age limitations.

FURTHER POTENTIALLY USEFUL LEGISLATION

- Section 21 of the 1948 National Assistance Act has, irrespective of issues of asylum, been used by local authorities to provide *residential* nursing accommodation for which charges can be made. Use of Section 21 is now restricted for asylum-seekers and others subject to controls. However, there is alternative legislation for residential nursing *care*. The Court of Appeal held in the case of *Coughlan* that residential nursing care is usually an NHS, not local authority, responsibility and is free. This responsibility flows from Section 3 of the 1977 National Health Service Act which places duties on the NHS to provide nursing services for those who are or have been ill. Local authority responsibility for nursing care exists only where this is incidental to the provision of accommodation. This case is discussed by Gordon and Ward in the *Legal Action Group Bulletin* of September 1999. Section 3 is not limited by the 1999 legislation in respect of immigration status. Where accommodation is provided by an area health authority then people not 'ordinarily resident' here cannot be charged under the NHS (Charges to Overseas Visitors) Regulations as the staff are not employed to work under the direction of a hospital (see Chapter 16).

- Under Section 47 of the 1990 National Health Service and Community Care Act, social services are obliged to assess potential service users for their needs under community care legislation. This does not guarantee that needs will be met. Each local authority is able to draw up its own eligibility criteria. Case-law suggests that there is normally no obligation to meet needs where financial resources are unavailable.

- Local authorities and health authorities have a duty under Section 117 of the 1983 Mental Health Act for the after-care of certain patients. These are patients detained under the Act, remand prisoners and people detained under the 1971 Immigration Act and transferred to hospital under the Mental Health Act. Section 117 services are potentially unlimited and cannot be charged for.

- The 1996 Community Care (Direct Payments) Act empowers local authorities to make payments for community care direct to individuals in need of such care to allow them to buy in their own services. Many authorities have not implemented this scheme. However, it appears to be a possible avenue to help those excluded from benefits and community care legislation by the 1999 Act.

- Some exclusions from community care of those subject to controls may be challengeable under the European Convention on Human Rights. For instance there may be breach of Article 8 where someone is kept in hospital because lack of domiciliary services renders living at home unviable.

THE SCOTTISH LEGISLATION

The 1999 Immigration and Asylum Act was enacted at the point where a Scottish parliament came into existence. However, the Act put severe limitations on Scottish community care legislation without the government even consulting the new parliament. It is not certain that the UK government has reserved powers to unilaterally to alter Scottish community care legislation. It may therefore be possible to mount legal challenges on this basis.

REPORT WRITING

Social services and individual social workers have a positive and proactive role in many immigration cases. This is through the provision of welfare reports as a crucial element in the contesting of expulsions. These reports require a particular expertise which should be the subject of social work training (see chapter 9).

Comments on casework problem at start of chapter

The 1999 Immigration and Asylum Act excludes from support under Section 45 of the 1968 Health Services and Public Health Act people subject to immigration control where the need for support arises through destitution or adverse physical consequences as a result of destitution. However, in this case X is not destitute as she receives money from a relative and her frailty does not arise through destitution. Depending on how much money X receives from her relative and irrespective of her immigration status, she may be asked by her local authority to make a contribution for services provided under Section 45 of the 1968 Act. This is a discretionary power and can be waived (Section 17 of the 1983 Health and Social Services and Social Security Adjudications Act). Moreover, it should be possible to regularise X's immigration status and for her to obtain settlement. The Home Office operates a concession against the expulsion of someone in the UK unlawfully for fourteen years (see Chapter 12). X does not fit within this policy. However, there is another concession against the expulsion of those over 65 (see Chapter 6). One of your roles as a worker within a local authority social services department is to arrange for an expert immigration advisor to see X. Once X obtains lawful settlement she will then become definitely eligible not only for services under community care legislation limited by the 1999 Immigration and Asylum Act but also for benefits. She will not need to be financially reliant on her relative.

CHAPTER 16

Medical services and immigration status

A CASEWORK PROBLEM

You are a general practitioner (GP). Y is visiting his children and was given entry for six months. He is in pain and consults you. You have to decide whether to register Y as an NHS patient. Is this in any way dependent on his immigration status or residence in the UK? Assume that you have registered him. You advise that he should see an arthritis specialist at the local hospital. Is Y entitled to free NHS hospital diagnosis and treatment? He has four weeks left of his visit and the consultant's waiting list is six months for NHS and three months for private patients. Y asks you to write to the Home Office requesting an extension of stay to see the consultant. Is this a legitimate part of your work under the NHS? Y wants to stay permanently if he cannot care for himself and wants your support in this. He asks you about any possible state benefits to which he may be entitled as a result of his medical condition. You give a prescription to Y. He asks if he is entitled to prescribed drugs from a chemist without payment. What is your role, if any, in this case?

A REAL CASE STORY

The Assadis, an asylum-seeking family, sought treatment from a Manchester GP. Treatment was refused as they were not British. Action under the 1976 Race Relations Act was commenced. The GP's practice made an out of court settlement.

SCOPE OF THIS CHAPTER

This chapter examines an aspect of the welfare state of which even many of those working within it are ignorant, namely the abolition of free hospital treatment based on immigration status. There is a particular ideological significance to this link between entitlement and status. The significance is that the statute first enabling this limitation to be included in secondary legislation was enacted in 1949. This was virtually at the very inception of the welfare state of which the NHS was core, with its promise of free treatment at the point of delivery. This echoed the coinciding in the early twentieth century of Liberal welfare reforms and the linking of welfare to immigration status.

FURTHER READING RESOURCES

From Ill-Treatment to No Treatment (South Manchester Law Centre 1981) by Steve Cohen examines the introduction of regulations denying free health treatment. Their implementation is detailed in 'Immigration and Health: A Survey of NHS Trusts and General Practices' (a research paper produced by GMIAU and Manchester Metropolitan University 1997) by S. Cohen, D. Hayes, B. Humphries and C. Sime. The Mental Health Foundation has produced *Mental Health Care for Refugees and Asylum-Seekers: A Guide for Advisory Workers*.

CAMPAIGN TO DENY NHS TREATMENT

The 1946 National Health Service Act established the NHS. Since then there have been accusations of 'abuse' by people from abroad. W. Smithers MP on 17 February 1949 asked:

> how many foreign visitors have received medical attention under the National Health Service in Britain during the last six months; and how [the Minister] proposes to compensate State doctors for the services they have rendered to these foreigners who contribute nothing to the National Health Service.

Aneurin Bevan, Minister of Health and architect of the NHS, initially took a principled position. In a parliamentary debate of 19 October 1949 he stated:

> It amazes me that we should assume there is something wrong in treating a foreign visitor if he or she falls ill. The assumption is one of the curses of modern nationalism.

SUCCESS OF THE CAMPAIGN

The campaign against free treatment based on immigration status was successful. Bevan capitulated. This is clear from the debate where Bevan denounced restrictions on access to the NHS. Lieutenant-Colonel Elliot MP said Bevan had

> stated at a press conference, and his words were subsequently broadcast, that he had arranged for immigration officers to turn back aliens who were coming to this country to secure benefits of the health service.

So as long ago as 1949 immigration controls were (unlawfully) used by a Labour government to prevent access to the NHS.

Bevan announced that he was proposing to introduce legislation allowing regulations to be made charging those not ordinarily resident in the UK. This was included in the 1949 National Health Services Amendment Act and re-enacted in the 1977 NHS Act.

UNLAWFUL DENIAL OF TREATMENT

No regulations were made until 1982. However, by the 1960s denial of treatment to patients perceived as not resident was routine (if illegal) for some hospitals. In June 1963 the Ministry of Health issued a circular to this effect: 'Memorandum of guidance to hospital authorities, hospital treatment for visitors from overseas.'[1] In 1974 the Department of Health and Social Security issued a circular 'Use of the National Health Service by people from abroad'.[2] This did not progress beyond a draft but was cynical. It stated:

> Where maternity treatment is concerned... it is feared that if [patients] obtain this treatment without difficulty it might encourage others to come over and try their luck. It is suggested, in any case, that they should as far as possible be directed away from such centres of excellence as the London Teaching Hospitals and distributed evenly where their presence will cause the least irritation to hospital staff.

In October 1979 the DHSS issued similar guidelines to inner London hospitals, under the title 'Gatecrashers'.

HOW TREATMENT WAS DENIED: INTERNAL CONTROLS

These guidelines were followed by some hospitals. The *Guardian* of 23 May 1981 reported the denial of treatment to some black patients by St Stephen's Hospital in London.

As significant as denial of treatment was the fact that all patients, in practice black patients, became vulnerable to questioning about immigration status. Lord Avebury in the House of Lords (6 April 1976) revealed: 185 Asian women attending the Leicester General Hospital's ante-natal clinics have been asked to produce their passports, and that one woman who refused to do so having previously had a confinement at the hospital was refused ante-natal care.

HOSPITALS AS AGENTS FOR THE HOME OFFICE

The flip-side of treatment denial was the role that hospitals assumed in reporting patients to the Home Office. A *Guardian* article of 5 December 1979 was headed 'Ministry tells doctors to spy on migrants'. A young Turkish-Cypriot girl required emergency treatment at St Bartholomew's Hospital in London. She had lived in the UK since 1974 but overstayed leave. A hospital clerk contacted the DHSS about her status. The DHSS contacted the Home Office. Her surgeon complained to the British Medical Association and said: 'This was a fundamental breach of medical ethics and could have led to the patient's arrest in his hospital had he not warned her not to attend.'

NATIONAL HEALTH SERVICE (CHARGES TO OVERSEAS VISITORS) REGULATIONS 1982–2000

Regulations enacted in 1982 allowed charging for hospital services to patients not ordinarily resident in the UK. These were replaced by the National Health Service (Charges to Overseas Visitors) Regulations in 1989 and amendments were made in 1991, 1994 and 2000. Some of these amendments reflect the establishment of NHS trusts and primary care trusts. In 1988 the DHSS published a *Manual of Guidance: NHS Treatment of Overseas Visitors* for NHS staff which is still operative though outdated.

FEATURES OF THE CHARGING REGULATIONS

Although the regulations refer to 'overseas visitors' this is confusing. They do not simply affect tourists. They make black people who are settled in the UK susceptible to questioning about immigration status. Many of those liable to charges are not simply holiday-makers. They include relatives of those settled in the UK denied family unity and able to see their family only in their capacity as short-term visitors.

The regulations define an overseas visitor as anyone not 'ordinarily resident' in the UK. Ordinary residence is not defined. A definition was given by the House of Lords in the case of *Shah* v. *Barnet Council* (see Chapter 14). This was not concerned with health issues but with the interpretation of ordinary residence for obtaining a student grant. It was held that ordinary residence referred to the place where someone is lawfully living for the time being for a settled purpose as part of the regular order of their life. Most overseas students are ordinarily resident. According to the guidelines someone 'intending to stay in the UK for less than six months should not usually be regarded as ordinarily resident'. It would seem that someone who does intend to stay longer than six months should be exempt from their first day in the UK. The six months' period is arbitrary and should be challenged where people studying in the UK for a shorter period are charged for treatment.

The regulations cover only services provided by hospitals but such services are wide-ranging. They include treatment at all hospitals, including community hospitals, and services provided under the direction of hospitals. These include in-patient and out-patient treatment, day cases, routine home dialysis, continuous ambulatory dialysis and supply of artificial limbs and appliances.

Hospital maternity services, including termination, are not exempt from payment. The guidelines state:

> Where a baby is born in hospital, mother and child count as a single patient so long as both are in hospital following the birth. If one is discharged and the other remains, bills will continue for the one remaining.

CHARGES

Charging under the regulations differs from private treatment as patients are liable irrespective of whether they agree to be charged. Patients are sometimes asked to sign an undertaking to pay for treatment but this is unnecessary. The guidelines suggest that deposits 'equivalent to the full estimated cost of the hospital charges' should be taken in advance of treatment. If the patient were to return abroad the hospital could pursue payment there. It is unlikely that this would happen. Sometimes friends or relatives are asked to sign as guarantors but this should be resisted as the debt can be enforced in the UK.

SERVICES EXEMPT FROM CHARGES

There are a number of exemptions:

- Treatment in a casualty or accident and emergency department but not including a dental or ophthalmic emergency department. Liability begins if someone becomes an in-patient or is referred to an out-patient clinic.

- Services provided by staff who are not employed by, or who do not work under the direction of, a hospital. This would encompass emergency ambulance services, midwifery and health visiting.

- Family planning services.

- Treatment for certain diseases whether or not the diagnosis is confirmed. There are over thirty diseases listed under three headings. They include notifiable diseases such as cholera, diseases to which the public health legislation is applied, such as tuberculosis, and food poisoning infections such as salmonella.

- Treatment of sexually transmitted diseases. In the case of HIV/AIDS this includes only diagnostic testing and subsequent counselling but not treatment and drugs.

- Compulsory psychiatric treatment under the Mental Health Act or treatment conditional on a probation order.

CATEGORIES OF PEOPLE EXEMPT FROM CHARGES

There are exemptions for a broad range of people. The exemptions extend to spouses or children under 16, or 19 if still in full-time education. The main categories are:

- Anyone in the UK for at least twelve months immediately prior to treatment. This is irrespective of immigration status, so someone who has overstayed leave is entitled to free treatment after twelve months. The guidelines say that absences abroad of up to three months are disregarded.

- Anyone taking up permanent residence by coming for settlement or subsequently applying for settlement. According to the guidelines, 'If an application for settlement is pending, the patient should be deemed exempt'. This is important. It means that a visitor who, for example, requires settlement on compassionate grounds becomes exempt from charges once an application is made. The guidelines state: 'If an application [for settlement] has been refused, the patient is liable [for charges].'

- Anyone accepted as a refugee or who has applied for asylum status. The guidelines make no mention of failed applications. Advisors should argue that during all periods contesting a refusal a person remains an asylum-seeker.

- Anyone in prison or detained by the immigration authorities.

- Anyone in the UK for work purposes, including students on a sandwich course. According to the guidelines this exemption does not include au-pairs.

- Seafarers on UK registered ships and offshore workers on the UK sector of the Continental Shelf.

- War disablement pensioners and war widows.

- Certain UK state pensioners living overseas.

- Anyone working overseas with ten years' residence in the UK who has been working overseas for not more than five years or has been taking leave in the UK at least every two years, or has a contractual right to do so or a contractual right to a passage to the UK on completion of employment.

- Members of the UK armed forces.

- Diplomatic staff.

- EEA nationals. This exemption applies only to treatment the need for which arose during the visit. European Community Regulation 1408/71 grants an exemption for all treatment for whatever condition where the EEA patient's own social security institution gives prior authorisation.

The UK has reciprocal health agreements with various EU and other countries. A list is included in the guidelines. The terms of the agreements differ. Most are restricted to exempting treatment where the need arose during the visit. Under the guidelines this exemption applies to maternity care only where 'the woman became pregnant or aware of her pregnancy after her departure for the UK or the treatment required is other than a planned delivery'.

HOW REGULATIONS WORK IN PRACTICE

The charging regulations are intrusive. All NHS patients should be asked about their residency status to determine liability. Even in hospitals where all patients are questioned, however, it is black or non-British patients who will feel the most vulnerable irrespective of their actual immigration status.

The guidelines state that there should be a two-tier system of questioning. Questioning should normally be at registration or pre-registration. Stage 2 should be carried out by an officer of supervisory grade. Stage 1 consists of three questions. The first is, 'Have you (or your husband or wife or mother or father) been living in the UK for the last twelve months?' If the answer is yes then no further questions are to be asked. The second question is, 'Are you (or your husband or wife or mother or father) going to live in the UK permanently?' If the answer is yes then no further questions are to be asked. The third question is, 'On what date did you (your husband, wife or parent) arrive in the UK?' If it is thought that an answer is untruthful or a patient has not clearly established that they are not liable to charges then there is a Stage 2 interview. The guidelines provide complicated flow-charts for the purpose of this interview.

CHECKS ON PASSPORTS AND OTHER DOCUMENTS

The guidelines state:

> Passports should not be requested, in view of the difficulty of correctly interpreting the information contained in them, except to verify that a person belongs to a European Community or reciprocal agreement country.

In practice many patients will often consider it less of a burden voluntarily to produce a passport to prove exemption from payment. This is how passports become the common currency of welfare entitlement.

In 1995 the Department of Health drew up a new draft *Manual of Guidance*.[3] This was never formalised. However it revealed, at Appendix H, the degree of intrusion considered permissible. It lists 'acceptable evidence of identity and residence in the UK'. The list is headed by 'passport' and includes flight tickets to the UK showing single and not return journey, bill of lading for shipping of personal belongings, letters referring to transfer of funds from previous country to the UK and copies of correspondence between the patient and the authorities in previous country of residence showing that the patient will be moving to the UK on a certain date.

CONTACT BETWEEN HOSPITALS AND THE HOME OFFICE

The guidelines state: 'there may be doubt about the facts of a patient's stay in this country. If the patient consents, the DHSS may be asked to resolve such a doubt by reference to the Home Office.' In practice patients who do not have access to legal advice will usually consent to the Home Office being contacted if the alternative is to go untreated.

The guidelines say:

> the patient should be reassured that the only information passed to the DHSS about the patient will be his or her name and date of birth since these are the only identifying particulars required.

It is difficult to know why this is reassuring as this is sufficient information to alert the Home Office as to immigration status and the fact that the patient probably lives near the inquiring hospital.

EFFICIENCY SCRUTINY

The relationship between the present Department of Health and the Home Office can be understood only in the context of the governmental Efficiency Scrutiny. This 'study of inter-agency co-operation on illegal immigration' transforms welfare agencies into immigration detectives (see Chapter 1). The Health Service was mentioned as one such agency. In other words the charging regulations are no longer just about saving money for the NHS – if ever they were just about that. They have become a mechanism for immigration control.

GENERAL PRACTITIONERS, DENTISTS, OPTICIANS AND CHEMISTS

The charging regulations extend only to hospitals. In February 1984 the Department of Health and Social Security issued a circular 'National Health Service family practitioner services for overseas visitors'.[4] This emphasised:

> The new charges apply only to hospital services and there is no change in the statutory position of family practitioner services (FPS). It therefore continues to be a matter for the discretion of the individual doctor, dentist or optician, whether to accept a particular person as an NHS patient.

The circular then advises:

> there is no objection to offering private treatment…to patients from other countries. Ministers would consider it particularly appropriate to offer private treatment if it appears that the patient has come to the UK specifically to obtain treatment.

GPs, dentists, opticians and chemists should be careful about refusing to register or treat patients from overseas. As seen at the start of this chapter, there has been one case where such a refusal was followed by payment for discrimination under the 1976 Race Relations Act.

In 1997 the British Medical Association (BMA) produced a circular 'Access to health care for asylum seekers following the implementation of the Asylum and Immigration Act 1996' confirming that asylum-seekers have the right to register with an NHS doctor.

EXTRA MONIES FOR GPS

GPs are entitled to enhanced fees under Section 36 of the 1997 NHS (Primary Care) Act to take account of resource implications of asylum-seekers and others moving into a health authority area. Also, following the twenty-seventh report of the Independent Doctors' and Dentists' Review Body into doctors' pay, an extra £5 million has been allocated annually to support various local development schemes. One of these targets asylum-seekers and refugees.

PRESCRIPTION, WIG, DENTAL, OPTICAL AND HOSPITAL TRAVEL CHARGES

Pharmaceutical medicines, dental treatment, sight tests, glasses, contact lenses, wigs and travel to hospital for NHS treatment are free for those on income support, job seeker's allowance, working families' tax credit or disabled persons' tax credit. Asylum-seekers and others subject to controls are normally disqualified from receipt of these benefits (Chapter 12). However, those on low or nil income are entitled to the above NHS services for free or at reduced costs. It is necessary to complete form HC1 issued by the Department of Health. Refunds can be claimed by filling in form HC5. The notes to the application form for support under the 1999 legislation say that the National Asylum Support Services will, where support is being given, provide asylum-seekers with a certificate (HC2) entitling them to the above NHS services for free. Vouchers will also be available for the cost of glasses or contact lenses.

Good practice

GOOD PRACTICE FOR LEGAL ADVISORS

There are points in the 1988 Manual of Guidence which can be used positively.

The guidelines state: 'In view of the difficulty of proof it will be right to give the patient the benefit of the doubt.' This should be quoted in any case where liability is disputed.

It has been seen that a settlement application leads to exemption from charges. However, a client should be warned that a tactical settlement application which fails will almost definitely mean any future application to return to the UK will be refused.

The guidelines state: 'Medical attention must take priority over ensuring payment.' In any dispute about the commencement of treatment prior to payment of a deposit then payment should be resisted and this paragraph quoted.

FREE TREATMENT AND REMAINING ON COMPASSIONATE GROUNDS

There will be situations where a client requiring treatment may positively want settlement. Clients are often anxious as to whether a settlement application will be prejudiced if it leads to free hospital treatment. Normally an application will not be prejudiced – particularly if the whole basis of the compassionate grounds is that treatment is not obtainable in the country of origin. If the client entered the UK in the capacity of a private patient (see Chapter 17) then the advisor will have to provide a cogent explanation as to why settlement is now being requested or what has happened to the monies previously available for private treatment.

CHARGING REGULATIONS AND ETHICAL ISSUES FOR MEDICAL WORKERS

The charging of 'overseas' patients and the checking of migrants, immigrants and refugees for residency status poses ethical issues for NHS workers. The fundamental issue is whether the NHS exists to provide treatment or to be an agent of government immigration policy. Concomitant with this is the issue of whether treatment should be withheld because of residency status.

DOCTORS AND NURSES

These ethical questions are posed at their sharpest for front-line workers such as doctors and nurses. The guidelines attempt to involve these workers in the charging regulations. The guidelines state: 'The government's policy of charging overseas visitors for NHS hospital treatment has been supported by the medical profession.' No proof is given of this. Elsewhere it is said: 'Doctors and Dentists should be encouraged to read this Manual.'

Exemptions to the regulations based on specified medical conditions cannot be implemented without doctors providing the hospital administration with a diagnosis of a patient's condition. The guidelines say that there 'should be well understood arrangements by which doctors can draw the attention (of administrators) to patients suffering from any of these diseases' – that is, infectious diseases the treatment of which is exempt from payment. The guidelines provide a standard form, to be used for EEA and reciprocal agreement countries. Hospital doctors and dentists have to specify whether treatment is 'treatment the need for which arose during the visit'. Arguably this represents a breach of doctor–patient confidentiality.

Hospital nurses are sometimes obliged to take on the administrative role of registering patients and may become implicated in immigration status investigation. Prior to the first charging regulations in 1982, the DHSS set up a Working Party on the Treatment of Overseas Visitors. Its report was announced in parliament on 22 February 1982 by Norman Fowler, the Minister for Health. The Working Party disclosed (Appendix 4):

At one hospital, for example, patients attending the largest clinics were registered by nursing staff in the clinic in order to relieve congestion at the normal registration point while at others nurses were involved in registering patients who had been admitted direct to a ward... Not all hospitals had administrative staff on duty at night and it would be necessary therefore for nursing staff to confirm eligibility at the time of treatment.

MENTAL HEALTH PATIENTS

There is no exemption for voluntary treatment under the Mental Health Act. The consequences were articulated in a letter to the *Guardian* of 2 February 1982 from Dr Anthony Clare on behalf of MIND, the National Association for Mental Health:

> The decision to charge overseas patients seeking informal admission to mental illness hospitals poses a number of ethical issues... Such charges will no doubt act as a disincentive for people suffering stress or other psychiatric problems from seeking care... It is not difficult to envisage that the new rules, which favour those who are compulsorily detained, may prove a self-fulfilling prophecy. This may occur because individuals will delay treatment until their condition requires the use of compulsion. Alternatively, psychiatrists and patients will, either covertly or overtly, decide that it is preferable to use compulsory powers where the patient cannot afford the service... One can imagine, for example, the impact of a series of (residence) questions on a severely depressed patient or the potential for alienation where there is persistent questioning of a patient with black or brown skin who is perfectly entitled to treatment.

TRAINING FOR HOSPITAL ADMINISTRATORS

The research paper on 'Immigration and health: a survey of NHS trusts and general practices' revealed an alarming ignorance of the operation of the regulations. The research found:

> there was a very varied understanding of categories of people who would be exempt from charges. The findings suggested that 'common sense' understandings were being used to identify those who were ineligible, and figuring largely here were 'immigrants', 'refugees' and 'overseas students'. Not only can this lead to inappropriate questioning of certain people seeking settlement in the UK but it can make all black people settled here susceptible to interrogation about their immigration status.

The guidelines recommend staff training. The research also identified the need for staff training on the regulations. However, it posed the question 'What kind of training?' and concluded:

> the need is not for detailed instruction in the identification of overseas visitors and ensuring payment is extracted when required. Understanding of the rules and the 1988 Manual of Guidance is important, but the main purpose of such

training should be towards raising questions about the withholding of NHS medical treatment from those who need it, and about appropriateness and ethical integrity of NHS staff implementing what is effectively immigration controls.

NON-COOPERATION BY HOSPITALS

Though under a duty to enforce the charging regulations, hospitals still retain the option of simply refusing to cooperate in this enforcement. This option has been chosen by some hospitals without apparent consequences and is considered further in Chapter 20.

GOOD PRACTICE FOR GPS

GPs should never refuse treatment on grounds of residency or immigration status. GPs who refer overseas patients to hospital for NHS treatment should warn them that they may be charged. It is important that GPs understand the exemptions to the overseas charging regulations and should inform patients accordingly. For GPs to be able to fulfil this practice it is necessary that they become aware of the residency status of patients referred to hospitals. This requires asking all referred patients their status with an explanation as to why the question is being asked.

BAD PRACTICE FOR GPS

The circular considered above on 'National Health Service: family practitioner services for overseas visitors' says that GPs referring overseas patients for NHS hospital treatment should advise them 'to enquire at the hospital as to their detailed entitlements and liabilities'. This is bad advice. Patients who are concerned about liability for charges should be advised to consult a reputable immigration advisor.

Comments on casework problem at start of chapter

You can register Y as an NHS patient. Under the charging regulations Y would not be entitled to free hospital diagnosis and treatment. As a visitor he is not 'ordinarily resident'. He would become exempt from hospital charges by applying for settlement.

There are tactical issues. If Y wishes to return overseas but make future visits then a refused settlement application will result in future visitor refusals. Otherwise the best advice is to make a settlement application. Another issue is the timing of a settlement application. It may initially be best to request an extension of leave to see a consultant. It is the consultant's report which may provide the basis for a settlement application (see Chapter 9). To obtain an extension it may be worth offering to speed up matters by seeing the consultant privately.

Y, while having only temporary permission to remain in the UK, would not be entitled to benefits (see Chapter 12). Prescription medicines are obtainable free if on income support. Y is not entitled to income support. Those with little or no income can obtain prescription medicines at a reduced price or free by completing form HC1.

As a GP it is legitimate to help Y. The basic advice is that Y needs an expert representative. All communications to the Home Office should go through and be agreed by the representative. Within this context you should be prepared to write to the Home Office in support of an application to remain to see a consultant. To preserve possible appeal rights the application must be made during the period of existing leave. Subsequent reports should be prepared by the consultant.

Notes

1   HSIB/94150/20/70
2   NHSC/IS/74
3   ELG **/1995
4   FPN 353

CHAPTER 17

Further health issues for medical workers and others

A CASEWORK PROBLEM

You work at a gay and lesbian centre. X is not British but has settled status and is worried that he can be expelled for having AIDS. He has a partner, Y, a visitor from Iran, who met X in the UK. They have lived together for three months. Y wants to stay permanently as his partner and carer. Y's leave expires in two weeks. They ask your advice.

A REAL CASE STORY

It took three years for Mohammed Butt to obtain entry clearance to join his fiancée. However, he was refused entry on arrival in 1982 as a tuberculosis (TB) suspect. He was given 'temporary admission' on condition he paid for tests. A consultant confirmed that he had no infectious TB. He remained following a campaign and an appeal.

SCOPE OF THIS CHAPTER

Issues of health, detailed throughout this book, are fundamental to the ideology and implementation of controls. This chapter ties together health issues by raising further matters not previously examined, namely medical controls on entry, HIV/AIDS, carers, torture and asylum, and some historical background to eugenicist discourse.

FURTHER READING RESOURCES

GMIAU and Manchester Metropolitan University have produced *They Make You Sick: Issues of health and immigration control* by Steve Cohen and Debra Heyes (1997) and a pack of annotated medical and legal documentation on *Health and Immigration Control* (updated 1996). *Critical Social Policy* (1984) published Paul Gordon's 'Medicine, racism and immigration control'. *Migrants Against HIV/AIDS* is an international journal opposed to controls and supporting those with HIV/AIDS.

HISTORY OF HEALTH AND IMMIGRATION CONTROL

The alien is demonised as diseased within eugenicist arguments for controls (see Chapter 21). The depiction of Jews as a health hazard was core to the Aliens Act campaign. Robert Sherard in the *Standard* newspaper of 1 January 1905 described Jews as 'filthy, rickety jetsam of humanity, bearing on their face the evil stigmata of every physical and moral degradation'.

Trachoma, an eye disease, was used to justify exclusion. Jew and trachoma became synonymous. The *Jewish Chronicle* reported cases, for instance:

> Schloime Wismewski, nineteen, a wood turner from Warsaw, afflicted with trachoma said he left Russia to join his uncle Abram Stone, a tailor living at 27 Bury New Road, Manchester… Mr Stone said the youth was his nephew and if the Committee would admit him he would see that the best medical attention available should be obtained until the afflicted eyes were cured… The case being one of ordinary trachoma the alien was rejected. (16 August 1907)

BRITISH MEDICAL ASSOCIATION

Myths equating black people with disease were spread by the British Medical Association in the agitation for post–1945 controls. From 1956 the BMA passed resolutions virtually every year demanding control. Venereal disease and tuberculosis played the demonising role. In 1965 the BMA published *The Medical Examination of Immigrants*. This stated that the BMA 'has for some time been concerned about the possible risk to health to the people of this country of the increasing flow of immigrants from overseas'. The pamphlet rejected the 'view held by some that Commonwealth citizens should have completely free access to this country'.

DOCTORS AGITATE

Many individual doctors supported exclusion. The *Lancet* of 9 October 1965 published an article on 'Immigration in the Midlands'. This spoke of immigration causing a 'burden' on health services. It advocated social engineering. Black communities would be broken up and 'more evenly distributed' – analogous to refugee dispersal under the 1999 Immigration and Asylum Act (see Chapter 13). The article contained crude stereotypes. Maternity services were over-burdened 'due…largely to the increasing proportion of pregnancies that occur in immigrants'. Health visitors were over-burdened as

> difficulty is experienced in discussing diets because some sects are vegetarians and others eat only certain types of meat… The high incidence of illegitimate births among West Indians…causes additional work.

School health services were over-burdened as 'teachers report that Asian children frequently soil toilet seats'.

CONTRADICTIONS

Supporters of controls faced a contradiction. The Ministry of Health in the 1950s advertised in the Caribbean and the Indian subcontinent for labour for the NHS. The Home Secretary acknowledged in parliament: 'Our hospitals…would be in difficulties were it not for the services of immigrant workers' (16 November 1961). Alongside recruitment of black labour was propaganda about black consumers somehow abusing the NHS (see Chapter 16). However, the labour dependency continued after the first Commonwealth Immigrants Act of 1962. Anwar Ditta struggled to gain entry for her children (see Chapter 6). The *New Statesman* of 22 February 1980 reported Anwar sewing pillow cases for an NHS subcontractor at just one penny a pillow case. She helped maintain the welfare state – the same state that denied her children entry.

REFUSAL OF ENTRY ON HEALTH GROUNDS

The 1962 Commonwealth Immigrants Act denied entry to anyone 'undesirable for medical reasons'. The present rules provide for medical examination overseas and on entry to the UK.

Examinations overseas are conducted by locally contracted doctors supervised by a medical referee. Examinations in the UK are conducted by medical inspectors. Medical inspectors are appointed by the Minister for Health but usually paid by district health authorities. The applicant pays the costs of medical examination overseas. The final decision is made by entry clearance or immigration officers on medical advice.

Refusal to submit to examination can lead to entry refusal. Anyone coming to the UK for more than six months should 'normally' be referred for examination. Under the rules:

Any person seeking entry who mentions health or medical treatment as a reason for his visit, or who appears not to be in good mental or physical health, should also be referred [for examination].

Where medical advice is that 'a person seeking entry is suffering from a specified disease or condition which may interfere with his ability to support himself or his dependants' then the entry clearance or immigration officer 'should take account of this, in conjunction with other factors'. There is provision for entry on 'compassionate grounds'. A condition can be imposed to report to the local medical officer for environmental health for further examination. Failure to report is a criminal offence.

EXEMPTIONS

Those with a right of abode or returning residents cannot be denied entry on medical grounds. European Council Directive 64/221 denies EEA nationals entry on public policy, security or health grounds. It lists diseases and disabilities leading to exclusion:

A. Diseases which might endanger public health

1. Diseases subject to quarantine listed in International Health Regulation No. 2 of the World Health Organisation of 25 May 1951;

2. Tuberculosis of the respiratory system in an active state or showing a tendency to develop;

3. Syphilis;

4. Other infectious diseases or contagious parasitic diseases if they are the subject of provisions for the protection of nationals of the host country.

B. Diseases and disabilities which might threaten public policy or public security

1. Drug addiction;

2. Profound mental disturbance, manifest conditions of psychotic disturbance with agitation, delirium, hallucinations or confusion.

REFUSAL ON MEDICAL GROUNDS IN PRACTICE

Guidance to medical inspectors in the UK and medical referees overseas are contained in internal instructions. These were leaked by the *Guardian* of 21 September 1979 under the headline 'Abnormal sexuality used to ban immigrants'. This revealed the wide categories used to exclude medically:

> Immigrants who are not EEC nationals may be certified as undesirable entrants for other reasons. These include mental disorder, senility, conduct disorder – 'e.g. alcoholism, drug addiction, abnormal sexuality' – tuberculosis, venereal disease, leprosy, or any other disease, bodily deformity or 'fits' which would prevent the immigrant supporting himself or his dependants. Immigration officers will normally refer to medical inspectors anyone who appears to be mentally or physically abnormal, anyone who appears not to be in good health and 'any person appearing to be bodily dirty'.

COMING TO THE UK FOR PRIVATE MEDICAL TREATMENT

NHS treatment is not 'public funds'. There is provision under the rules to come to the UK for private treatment or consultation. This is effectively no recourse to public funds through the back door. The rules impose the following:

- There must be compliance with the usual visitors' rules (see Chapter 3).

- In cases of a communicable disease the medical inspector must be satisfied there is no risk to public health.

- The course of treatment must be finite.

- Evidence must be available of:

a) the medical condition requiring consultation or treatment; and b) satisfactory arrangements for the necessary consultation or treatment at his own expense; and c) the estimated costs of such consultation or treatment; and d) the likely duration of his visit; and e) sufficient funds are available.

- Entry is given for six months but can be extended. Extensions will be granted where medical bills are being paid with evidence from a registered medical practitioner who holds an NHS consultant post or who appears in the Specialist Register of the General Medical Council of satisfactory arrangements for private medical consultation or treatment and its likely duration; and where treatment has already begun, evidence as to its progress.

SWITCHING TO PRIVATE MEDICAL TREATMENT

The rules permit someone in the UK in another temporary category to apply to remain longer for private treatment. Best practice is often to apply to remain permanently on compassionate grounds as this could avoid hefty medical bills (see Chapter 16). The risk is that if the settlement application is refused then the applicant will be refused an extension for private treatment or future re-entry.

HIV/AIDS

There exist two Home Office internal instructions 'AIDS and HIV positive cases'[1] and 'Enforcement Action in AIDS and HIV Positive Cases'.[2] These make the following points:

[The] fact that a person is suffering from AIDS or is HIV positive is not grounds for refusing entry clearance or leave to remain. [However] the fact that an applicant has AIDS or is HIV positive is not in itself sufficient grounds to justify the exercise of discretion [to remain].

Although entry should not be refused simply because a person has HIV/AIDS yet if someone discloses the illness 'he should provide evidence of his ability to meet the costs of such medication or treatment during his stay'. The legality of this is arguable. The rules are silent on costs of treatment – except for those coming for treatment.

In considering compassionate grounds the instructions state:

persons certified as having AIDS should be distinguished from those where the person concerned has been diagnosed as HIV positive. A person who has been diagnosed as HIV positive may still be well and a serious case for exceptional treatment is unlikely to arise. [Where a person] has only a few months to live...cases will be referred back...to reconsider the merits of allowing the person to remain for a limited period on compassionate grounds.

The Home Office is reluctant to allow an applicant with AIDS convicted of an offence to remain for any period. The *Guardian* of 3 May 1997 reported the case of D, convicted of importing cocaine. The Home Secretary wanted to expel him to St Kitts in spite of his having AIDS and of there being no family, means of support or medical treatment in St Kitts. The European Court of Human Rights found against the UK. The Associated Press of 23 July 1999 reported the case of M who was threatened with deportation to Uganda after a conviction for indecent assault. M had AIDS with a short life expectancy. The High Court overruled the Home Secretary.

An applicant wanting to remain on compassionate grounds must provide a consultant's letter detailing:

a) he has AIDS or is HIV-positive, b) his life expectancy, c) the nature and location of the treatment he is receiving, d) his fitness to travel if required to leave the country.

The enforcement instructions say that availability of treatment overseas must be assessed:

In many cases the medical facilities and treatment in the person's country of origin will be substantially less advanced than those available in the United Kingdom. This is likely to be true as regards any serious illness and does not in itself constitute grounds for allowing someone with AIDS/HIV to remain. However there may be cases where it is apparent that there are no facilities for treatment in the applicant's own country. Where evidence suggests that this absence of treatment would significantly shorten the life expectancy of the applicant it will normally be appropriate to grant leave to remain.

None of this means it is impossible to contest cases where facilities, however inadequate, exist overseas or where the applicant is HIV-positive but has not got AIDS. It does mean that it is essential to explain why stay in the UK is imperative.

CARERS

Home Office instructions exist on applications from a person in the UK in a temporary capacity to remain as a carer for someone 'suffering from a terminal illness such as cancer or AIDS, or is mentally or physically disabled'. The document, called *Carers*, was updated in 1998 and states that applications should be considered to care for a relative but 'applications…to care for a sick or disabled friend should normally be refused'. This seems based on homophobia. Exceptions are made for emergency cases 'or where there is nobody else in the United Kingdom to whom the patient can turn'. In the case of same-sex and other unmarried couples, advisors should stress that the relationship is akin to that of relatives.

Applications for settlement should normally be refused: 'once alternative arrangements are made or if the patient should die then the carer will be expected to return home'. Extensions of stay should initially be for three months. Subsequent leave may be granted for twelve months. This does not mean that settlement is always refused. It means that any application has to justify why settlement is required. It might be possible to argue that life-expectancy is inde-terminate and it would cause uncertainty if the carer had continually to apply for renewal.

An application for an initial period of leave to remain should be supported by a letter from a doctor giving details of the illness/condition, the type of care required, details of care currently provided and a long term prognosis.

The instructions detail required information if further leave is requested. Best practice is to provide this information on any initial application. The information consists of

> a letter from a registered medical practitioner who holds an NHS consultant post with full details of condition/illness and long term prognosis [along with] a letter from the local authority Social Services Department, where they are known to be involved, advising of their level of involvement and the perceived benefits of the presence here of the applicant.

Best practice is for social services to support the application under its care in the community programme. The instructions require

> full details of the patient's family in the United Kingdom and, if applicable, details of how the patient was previously cared for and why these arrangements are no longer considered suitable and/or are no longer available.

Details should be provided about the carer, proof of maintenance and accommo-dation, the carer's employment in the country of origin and whether the carer is married because

> as a general rule a person seeking to remain in the UK on a long term basis as a carer should normally be unmarried and have no dependants.

The problem in remaining as a carer is illustrated by the case of Atia Idrees, who wanted to care for her grandmother Alam Bibi (aged 77) who was half-blind and semi-crippled. Atia met the criterion in the carer instructions. However, it took a major campaign to stop the Home Office expelling her. The case is described in the *Observer* of 13 April 1997.

The instructions allow for *either* friends or relatives overseas to come to the UK as a carer. Applications are considered under the visitors' rules (see Chapter 3) which require proof of intent to return overseas within six months.

TORTURE AND ASYLUM

Medical issues appear in asylum cases with allegations of physical or mental torture. Evidence of torture can prove 'persecution' under the UN Convention relating to the Status of Refugees. The 1999 Immigration and Asylum Act makes provision for certain asylum appeals to be fast-tracked without rights of appeal from an adjudicator to the Immigration Appeal Tribunal. This does not apply where evidence 'establishes a reasonable likelihood that the appellant had been tortured'. Article 3 of the European Convention on Human Rights forbids torture or inhuman or degrading treatment. It is unnecessary here to prove the asylum grounds in the UN Convention, namely political opinion, race, religion, nationality, membership of a social group (see Chapter 8). Article 3 of the UN Convention Against Torture forbids removal of people to a country where they may be tortured. In a report of January 1995 to the Torture Committee of the United Nations the UK government pledged not to so remove anyone

MENTAL HEALTH AND IMMIGRATION CONTROL

The 1983 Mental Health Act enables the deportation of patients detained under that Act. In a parliamentary written answer of 21 June 1999, George Howarth MP announced that there had been twenty-five deportations up to 1996 and one since.

Severe mental health problems may provide 'compassionate grounds' to contest expulsion. The Home Office served a notice of deportation on Santokh Singh, a diagnosed schizophrenic, after conviction for manslaughter. The Immigration Appeal Tribunal overturned the notice 'in the light of the appellant's mental condition and the need for on-going in-patient care'.[3]

Mental health can be adversely affected by an expulsion threat and become an argument within compassionate grounds (see Chapter 9).

Mental health issues arise in asylum matters. Psychological disorder can provide proof of persecution. The detention of asylum-seekers in the UK can lead to mental ill-health. This has been documented by Dr C.K. Pourgourides and published by the North Birmingham Mental Health NHS Trust as *A Second Exile*.

Policy, ethical and practice issues

In the late 1970s publicity was given to medical intervention in administering controls. This intervention was X-ray testing to 'prove' the age of applicants and virginity testing to 'prove' the unmarried status of female fiancées (see Chapter 5). Some doctors supported these practices. Dr R. Woodland, a medical inspector at Heathrow Airport, writing to the *Lancet* of 21 April 1979, said:

> The abuse of immigration laws is also common and the assumption of false identity an ever present problem…an inspection of the introitus or a vaginal examination may be indicated to help clarify matters.

YELLOWLEES REPORT

'Virginity testing' was stopped following protests, especially from the Asian women's group AWAZ. X-raying for age was stopped after protests by particular individuals such as Lord Avebury and his assistant Ted White (who wrote a widely circulated report on X-raying which was used in campaigning), along with lawyers such as Sarah Leigh and Graham Smith. The government commissioned a report on *The Medical Examination of Immigrants* by its Chief Medical

Officer, Sir Henry Yellowlees. The report was published in 1980 by the Department of Health and Social Security with a supplementary report on bone X-rays produced in 1982. It colluded with questionable ethical assumptions and contained crude stereotypes. It justified controls on people with 'mental disease or instability or psychopathy with a propensity to violence'. It advocated exclusion where entry poses 'a significant burden on the health or social services of the United Kingdom'.

ARE CONTROLS ON GROUNDS OF HEALTH BENEVOLENT OR MALEVOLENT?

Excluding someone with a contagious or infectious disease may appear reasonable. Doctors attached to the Port Medical Inspectorate and local environmental health departments may see their role as benevolent. The Consultant for Communicable Disease Control employed by Manchester City Council wrote an internal document on 'The medical role with regards to immigrants' in 1995. He justified medical examination for immigration purposes to 'protect the public health'.

This misses the point. It is the responsibility of doctors to try to cure the sick, not to ban them. Neither public nor private health has been the real political issue in the demand for controls. The actual agenda was and is the stigmatisation of the alien. This is clear from the Instructions to Medical Inspectors which list 'conduct disorders', as opposed to medical disorders, used to exclude on medical grounds. The BMA report (published in 1965 and described above) advocated excluding those suffering from 'another category of disease...mental disorders (including subnormality, schizophrenia and psychopathic disorders)...drug addiction and alcoholism'. It is odd classifying these conditions as 'diseases'. The pamphlet acknowledges:

> They are not infectious diseases but have in common that sufferers from them may be unable to support themselves or their dependants and may then become a drain on the resources of the state.

It is here that 'burden on the state' becomes synonymous with 'diseased'. The authors of the pamphlet acknowledge: 'We are also aware that it is on social rather than medical grounds that [exclusion] can be justified.'

PRESENT POSITION OF THE BRITISH MEDICAL ASSOCIATION

The BMA has softened its anti-alienism. Its 1979 annual representative meeting condemned as unethical virginity tests and radiological examinations carried out 'solely for administrative and political purposes'. It has produced guidelines in respect to asylum-seekers. Its 1993 handbook *Medical Ethics Today* has a section on 'Doctors examining asylum seekers'. There is a 1995 briefing paper on 'Doctors with dual obligations' discussing the examination of asylum-seekers by port medical officers. It produced a 1997 briefing paper on 'Access to health care for asylum seekers following the implementation of the Asylum and Immigration

Act 1996'. Though welcome, these publications are inadequate. They are confined to asylum-seekers and ignore other issues. Zed Press is shortly publishing a new BMA publication, *The Medical Profession and Human Rights: Handbook for a Changed Agenda*. Advance publicity suggests that medical issues of immigration control are again confined to asylum, though these will be treated broadly and will address issues of report writing in support of asylum applications, medical involvement in deportations and treatment in detention centres.

GOOD PRACTICE AND HIV/AIDS

The Terrence Higgins Trust provides specialist help and representation in conducting these cases.

The golden rule as in all health cases is normally to argue for the maximum, settlement, and contest any decision giving less (see Chapter 9). There needs to be a proper explanation as to why less is insufficient. In weaker cases, that is in cases of less serious illness, this maximum approach will not always be appropriate.

It may be possible to claim asylum as a member of a persecuted social group having HIV/AIDS (see Chapter 8). The 1998 IND instructions on failed asylum applications state that exceptional leave to remain should be given 'Where...return would result in substantial damage in the physical/psychological health of the appellant or his dependants'. Arguably interruption or termination of combination drug therapy fits these criteria.

Because of the instructions requiring proof of finances for medication and treatment, the best advice for those with HIV/AIDS wishing entry to the UK is that they should neither voluntarily mention the illness nor carry documentation or medication showing its existence. Immigration officers can examine luggage though this is rare.

GOOD PRACTICE AND CARERS: LENGTH OF STAY REQUESTED

Any request for three or twelve months' leave should, to make it coherent, be accompanied by some explanation as to how the patient will be subsequently cared for. However, this renders a future settlement application more difficult. The best advice, particularly in a strong case, is to request settlement and to put the burden on the Home Office to give less.

Any overseas application is more difficult. All else being equal, best practice is probably for a carer's application to be limited to six months as required by the visitors' rules with an explanation why it is limited. If later it becomes obvious that longer stay or settlement is required then the appropriate application can be made.

CARE IN THE COMMUNITY

The instructions on carers refer to Care in the Community arrangements and confirm that attendance allowance 'is paid to the patient rather than the carer and therefore the carer would not be considered to be in receipt of public funds'.

The 1989 government White Paper *Caring for People* emphasises: 'Helping carers to maintain their valuable contribution to the spectrum of care is both right and a sound investment'.[4] This should be quoted in carer applications.

There is a High Court decision which helps carers from overseas.[5] This concerned the Polish sister and brother-in-law of an incapacitated British citizen. The Home Office refused them permission to remain as carers in spite of no other family members being available. The local authority, Hackney, supported the application and regarded residential care as inappropriate. The court over-ruled the Home Office. The judge quoted guidance under the 1990 National Health Service and Community Care Act which explained the scheme's objective is 'to enable people to live in their own homes wherever feasible and sensible'.

The 1995 Carers (Recognition and Services) Act gives carers the right to demand local authority assessment of their ability to provide care. An assessment cannot in law prevent expulsion. It could be a tactical factor in gaining local authority backing against expulsion.

CARERS OF CHILDREN

There is one repeating issue of the extended family: relative applications to come to the UK as a visitor to meet and care for a new-born child. Entry clearance officers are liable to refuse such applications as being disguised work with no end date. Best advice is to say that the purpose of the visit is to see, as opposed to care for, the baby. It would help gain entry if it can be shown that the parents had made definite arrangements for the care of the child by someone other than the visitor on the completion of any maternity and/or paternity leave. Proof of definite commitments to return to the country of origin would also help the visitor application.

GOOD PRACTICE IN ASYLUM REPORT WRITING

Good practice in report writing and medical report writing was discussed previously and is relevant here (see Chapter 9).

There are particular matters relating to asylum where the claimed persecution is physical or psychological harm. Practice issues are detailed in two publications. One is the *Best Practice Guide to Asylum Appeals* by Mark Henderson published by ILPA. Second is *Guidelines for the Examination of Survivors of Torture* produced by the Medical Foundation for the Care and Victims of Torture. The foundation's guidelines contain a section in lay language on the methods and physical side-effects of torture. It explains which scars can result from torture or assault and which can arise from 'innocent' causes. The section is also in a 1993 joint BMA/Medical Foundation circular on 'Asylum Applicants: medical report guidelines for examining doctors'.

COMPILING ASYLUM REPORTS

A history of the mistreatment should be taken. A medical report should not repeat the client's entire experiences leading to the asylum claim. This is the advisor's task. However, the report should address matters stated by the client which explain his or her physical state and/or mental distress. It will be relevant to ask the client about details of detention (for example withholding of food or drink, confinement in total darkness), details of psychological torture (for example mock executions, solitary confinement) and details of physical torture (for example number of assailants, whether a doctor was involved, types of weapons used). The record of torture should include the client's account of the immediate effects (for example whether it resulted in partial or total unconsciousness) and the after-effects (for example the length of time for scars to heal).

More than one consultation may be necessary. The client may have been disorientated by the mistreatment and reliving the mistreatment may be highly distressing. The Medical Foundation Guidelines suggest:

> it may be wise not to stick too rigidly to the convention of taking the history before the examination but to elicit some aspects of the history while the physical examination is taking place.

Applicants need to be questioned about their present physical and psychological condition. It is important to elucidate symptoms suggestive of psychological disorder. The Medical Foundation guidelines list symptoms such as sleep disorder, nightmares, loss of concentration, hypervigilance, mood changes, panic attacks, asthma, hyperventilation, indigestion and susceptibility to external stimuli such as sudden noises or the sight of uniforms.

There is the need for a physical and psychological examination. Every scar and other lesion should be measured and recorded. Scars should be illustrated on an outline diagram. There should be noted psychological abnormalities such as hyperalertness, lack of concentration or heightened response to sudden movement, touching, noise or bright light.

The report should contain a separate section on 'interpretation'. The applicant may attribute some scars to previous accidents and not torture. It will show that the applicant is not prone to exaggeration and will enhance her or his credibility where scars caused by torture are distinguished from others.

If the report does not support or contradicts allegations of torture then the doctor should discuss this with the client and advisor. If evidence is inconclusive then the report should state that it is compatible with an allegation of torture and not in conflict with it.

GOOD PRACTICE FOR LEGAL ADVISORS IN ASYLUM REPORT WRITING

Finding a medical expert in asylum cases presents difficulties. The Medical Foundation can be contacted about their doctors. However, there are waiting lists and these doctors are London based. There are alternative sources of expertise.

Solicitors specialising in personal injury cases can recommend experts. The Law Society's *Directory of Experts* lists medical experts. Doctors involved in specialisms can provide expert opinions. Plastic surgeons can provide reports on injuries inflicted by torture.

Where there is a gap between seeing the applicant and the applicant seeing a medical expert then it is important to arrange photographic evidence of scars or bruising. Otherwise evidence may fade.

It is wrong to assume that because there are no external physical marks then a physical examination is unnecessary. For instance, bomb shrapnel may be lodged inside a person unknown to them.

Comments on casework problem at start of chapter

X has settlement and is in no danger of expulsion. Y must make an application before leave to remain expires. This will allow an appeal on any refusal. Y cannot remain with X under the immigration rules. There are no rules for same-sex partners, people with HIV/AIDS nor carers. There is Home Office policy for these. The policy on HIV/AIDS addresses issues only where the overseas partner has the illness. Home Office policy on gay relationships requires cohabitation for two years (see Chapter 7). X and Y have cohabited for three months. One option is for the advisor to prolong the case to extend the cohabitation period. The policy on carers is confined to 'relatives' and states that carers will not normally be granted settlement. However, it is best practice normally to argue for settlement. Y's advisor must deal explicitly with these issues with respect to carers and provide the information required by the instructions. It should be emphasised that settlement is wanted because life-expectancy with AIDS is indeterminate. The policy of not granting leave to friends should be met by proof that there is no one else to care for X, the couple are more than friends and local social services support the application.

Notes

1   BDI 3/95
2   DP 3/95
3   TH/2738/93
4   Cm 849
5   Zakrocki, *Times Law Reports* 3 April 1996

CHAPTER 18

Probation and immigration status

Double punishment

A CASEWORK PROBLEM

You are a court probation officer. A and B have been convicted of dealing in heroin. They were born abroad of non-British parents. A has lived in the UK since 1974 and B since 1970. You have to prepare a pre-sentence report. Is deportation an issue? Should you address it? A colleague, a prison probation officer, asks your advice about C and D, who are in prison after conviction for fraud. C came to the UK on a visit four years ago and D became British through naturalisation in 1979. The matter of deportation has never been raised by anyone in authority. C and D want to know if they are safe from deportation. Your colleague asks if she has any role in their immigration case.

A REAL CASE STORY

Andy Anderson was born in Jamaica. He joined his family in the UK in 1976 and was given permanent residence in 1978. In 1987 he was convicted of supplying cannabis. He had a long-standing relationship with a British citizen, which eventually resulted in marriage and children. Andy was sentenced to four years' prison. In the course of sentence he was without warning served by the Home Office with a notice to deport. His partner contacted an immigration advisor at GMIAU. An appeal was lodged. A large number of reports plus oral evidence from many of the report writers was presented on Andy's behalf. His own through-care probation officer submitted a report, helped to co-ordinate other reports and gave oral evidence. Further reports came from a prison governor, a prison chaplain and two prison education officers. A report on the family and children was made by an assistant director of social services in Manchester. In addition Andy's partner, also his co-defendant, formed the Partners of Prisoners Support Group (POPs) as a result of her experiences. This is a self-help organisation designed to help maintain family life while a partner is in prison. At the appeal, evidence of the work of POPs was given by several of its members along with the deputy chief probation officer for Greater Manchester, the director of the Prison Reform Trust and an official from the National Association for the Care and Resettlement of Offenders (NACRO).

In spite of the above, Andy lost his appeal. After further representations along with a campaign, he was allowed to remain. Andy's case, the positive role of the probation service and an analysis of the professional reports are documented in the campaign's pamphlet, 'A long, sharp shock', available through GMIAU.

SCOPE OF THIS CHAPTER

The political effect of immigration law is to criminalise *all* subject to it whether they have committed any criminal offence or not. The immigration legislation authorises detention, for instance of asylum-seekers, where there has been no offence, no charges, no prosecution, no court intervention.

The criminalisation of those who have committed no criminal offence places the situation of those who *have* been found guilty of an offence right at the ideological centre of immigration control. They are used to justify controls as necessary to exclude the so-called 'deviant'.

This is not just an ideological question. Non-British people subject to controls who commit a criminal offence can pay a real material price. In addition to other punishment they can be deported. This is their double punishment.

The aim of this chapter is to look at double punishment from the perspective of those threatened by it and to examine good practice issues for probation officers and lawyers.

FURTHER READING RESOURCES

A range of literature has been produced by the Campaign Against Double Punishment. This consists of *A Resource Pack on Double Punishment*, a major, annotated pack of relevant documents, *No Immigration Laws, No Double Punishment*, papers from the Campaign's 1992 national conference, *No Deportation of Black Prisoners*, the manifesto of the Campaign, and *Information and Advice for Convicted Prisoners under Threat of Deportation*.

DOUBLE PUNISHMENT: THE HISTORY

The centrality of criminalisation and double punishment is a constant within controls. Under the first legislation, the 1905 Aliens Act, the *only* deportation grounds were a court certifying that an alien was claiming 'parochial relief' or the court recommending deportation following conviction.

Most of those deported were Jewish. On 22 October 1920 the *Jewish Chronicle* reported a meeting of the Aliens Committee of the Board of Deputies of British Jewry which condemned 'aliens being punished twice for the same offence'. Many were deported for offences relating to prostitution. The *Jewish Chronicle* of 4 April 1909 reported a meeting in Cardiff organised against prostitute women where it was stated:

Owing to the leniency of the Cardiff stipendiary magistrate a few years ago, two Jewesses out of thirty-seven who had been before him were allowed to remain in

Cardiff, the other thirty-five having been deported. These two Jewesses had been the means of bringing sixty other Jewesses to Cardiff who were on the streets of the city today and alien men were living on the shame of these poor creatures.

At the time of the agitation leading up to the 1962 Commonwealth Immigrants Act there was a similar characterisation of the alien as prostitute or pimp within the context of a general condemnation of alien sexuality (see Chapter 2). During the attacks on black people in Notting Hill in 1958 the *Manchester Guardian* reinforced this stereotype. It reported on 3 September 'The most sordid case' of an English woman with a 'brown skinned son' being allegedly forced into prostitution by her partner.

THE FORGOTTEN HISTORY OF TRANSPORTATION

There is nothing inevitable about a law allowing the deportation of convicted non-British prisoners. Its enactment was a political decision. Alternatively there is nothing inevitable about a law protecting British prisoners from expulsion. Indeed historically the transportation overseas of British convicts predates immigration control by several centuries. A. Ekirch in the introduction to his book *Bound for America: The Transportation of British Convicts to the Colonies 1718–1775* (Clarendon 1987) describes the historic process:

> As early as 1597, Parliament gave magistrates the power to exile rogues and vagabonds 'beyond the seas', and in 1615 James I authorised pardons for condemned felons on condition of banishment to the New World. But not until Parliament's passage a century later of the 1718 Transportation Act did Britain systematically adopt foreign exile as a punishment for serious crime.

According to Ekirch (p.23) over 30,000 men and women were transported to America from the beginning of the trade in 1718 to its end in 1775. George Rudé, in the introduction to his book *Protest and Punishment: The Story of the Social and Political Protesters Transported to Australia 1788–1868* (Clarendon 1978) calculates that nearly 162,000 people were transported to Australia.

DOUBLE PUNISHMENT TODAY

There are two routes today by which people can be deported following conviction. First, as part of a sentence a court can make a recommendation to the Home Office. This is only a recommendation. The Home Office has to decide whether to act on it. A recommendation can be made only where the defendant is over the age of 17 at the time of conviction. The offence must be punishable with imprisonment.

The second route is through the Home Office invoking its administrative powers to deport on 'conducive to public good' grounds. A notice to deport can be served without warning. Appeal cases have held that a deportation notice can be served even where a court has declined to make a recommendation.

There is an appeal right against a notice to deport. The appeal was previously heard before the Immigration Appeal Tribunal but since the 1999 Immigration and Asylum Act is heard before an adjudicator. There is no right of appeal within the immigration appeal system against a court recommendation though it can be appealed as part of the court's sentence.

PRELIMINARY ISSUES OF DOUBLE PUNISHMENT FOR PROBATION OFFICERS

Probation officers can help defendants and prisoners under threat of deportation. This is by virtue of having a close professional relationship with those caught within the criminal justice and penal system. To help defendants and prisoners it is necessary to appreciate four points.

First, there is an exemption to double punishment. No Commonwealth or Irish citizen can be deported who was ordinarily resident in the UK on 1 January 1973 and also was ordinarily resident for five years before a court recommendation or service of notice of deportation on public good grounds.

Second, EEA nationals are subject to double punishment. However, these nationals are privileged in that deportation can be only on grounds of public policy, public security or public health. Only particularly serious offences can lead to deportation and only where the person's continued presence is detrimental to the UK.

Third, it has been held by the European Commission of Human Rights and the European Court of Human Rights that one group may be protected from double punishment by Article 8 of the Convention which guarantees respect for family life. These are foreign-born children subject to deportation after a criminal conviction but who have lived most of their lives in the country to which their parents emigrated. In *Lamguindaz* v. *UK*, a 23-year-old Moroccan who had been in the UK for sixteen years was deported after convictions for drugs supplying. The Commission held that this breached Article 8 and the Home Secretary allowed Lamguindaz to return. Mr Schermers, one of the judges, stated:

> Even independent of human rights considerations, I doubt whether modern international law permits a state which has educated children of admitted aliens to expel these children when they become a burden. Shifting this burden to the state of origin of the parents is no longer so clearly acceptable under modern international law.

Fourth, a person given refugee status can be subject to double punishment. The United Nations Convention on the Status of Refugees allows the deportation of a refugee 'who, having been convicted by a final judgment of a particularly serious crime, constitutes a danger to the community'.

TYPES OF CONVICTIONS LEADING TO DOUBLE PUNISHMENT

Not all convictions result in deportation. Each case must be considered separately. Sometimes it is difficult to advise on the likelihood or otherwise of the threat of deportation. Drugs offences, certainly drugs offences involving supply or importation, are regarded as serious. Drugs have replaced prostitution and pimping in the demonisation of the alien. Minor offences, for instance driving offences, will not attract deportation unless there are extraordinary circumstances.

Even in the case of serious offences other circumstances need to be taken into account. In the leading case examining the criteria for a court recommendation, the Court of Appeal in R v. Nazari[1] made the following observations:

- it must be considered whether the continued presence of the accused in the UK is to the country's detriment

- the nature of the political system operating in the accused's country of origin is a matter for the Home Secretary and not for the court in making a recommendation

- the court must look at 'the effect that an order recommending deportation will have upon others who are not before the court and who are innocent persons. This court and all other courts would have no wish to break up families or impose hardship on innocent people'.

Various criminal offences exist under the 1971 Immigration Act and subsequent legislation. For example entering the UK without permission, overstaying the time limit of a leave to enter and breaching other conditions of entry are offences which can lead to a recommendation. Prosecutions are rare. It is easier for the Home Office to effect expulsion through its own administrative powers.

CHRONOLOGY AND PERSONNEL OF DOUBLE PUNISHMENT

Double punishment can be triggered by a series of state officials – immigration officers, police, crown prosecutors, judges and prison governors. Police and prosecution involvement in initiating the process of court recommendations is noteworthy. It is a principle of criminal law that both should be neutral on matters of sentence.

There is a chronology of double punishment from arrest to possible deportation. Much of this is found in internal circulars and circular instructions from the Immigration and Nationality Directorate of the Home Office or the Prison Service.

A defendant must be given seven days' written notice before a court can make a recommendation. There is a standard Home Office form (IM3) containing this notice. IM3 is a three-page purported explanation of who is liable to deportation. It is available only in English and is barely comprehensible. There is nothing in the legislation giving responsibility for serving the IM3. The Home Office gives responsibility to the police. Home Office circular 13/98 is titled 'Liaison with the Immigration and Nationality Directorate of the Home Office and Reporting the convictions of persons subject to immigration control to the Home Office'. It states that the 'service of a notice of liability to deportation will usually be the duty of the police'.

The IND is anxious to ensure that the police do serve the IM3. Circular 13/98 says:

> Experience has shown that a court recommendation provides the most efficient and effective means of securing the deportation of those subject to immigration control who commit criminal offences and forces should bear this firmly in mind when dealing with offenders subject to immigration control.

Recommendation is the usual preferred option because it does not carry any immigration appeal rights.

This leaves the question as to how the police know whether someone is subject to control. The police have an open invitation to investigate the immigration status of black people in their hands. They have a justification to stop and question black people solely about immigration status. It is another form of the old 'sus' laws.

THE POLICE AND THE IMMIGRATION SERVICE

The link between the police and the immigration service is another example of internal controls. Circular 13/98 reveals the extent of co-operation. This is mediated through the Evidence and Enquiry Unit of the IND (formerly known as the Immigration Status Enquiry Unit). This Unit is able:

- to provide a central point of contact through which the police can ascertain the immigration status of a foreign national;

- to provide witness statements confirming the immigration status of a foreign national for use in court proceedings. Staff…are also available to attend court to provide an 'expert witness' in support of the statement or to clarify other immigration related issues;

- to provide police with access to the personal files relating to individual foreign nationals.

FURTHER CHRONOLOGY

If the police fail to serve the IM3 this will not necessarily stop the court proceeding to a recommendation. The court can adjourn a case for seven days even after conviction to allow service of the IM3. A letter from the Solicitor-General to Keith Bradley MP of 9 July 1992 says that prosecutors have been instructed by the Solicitor-General to seek adjournments to allow service of the IM3.

The Home Office has itself wrongly sought to intervene in the sentencing process. It was revealed in 1969 in the case of *Khan* v. *Shea* that the Home Office had published a circular to the courts urging that a recommendation for deportation be made in cases following a conviction for offences under immigration legislation.[2]

Circular 13/98 gives police the responsibility of reporting all recommendations to the Home Office. This circular urges continued pursuit even where there has been no recommendation. It tells police to report certain convictions so deportation on conducive grounds may be considered. Police are asked to report where:

(a) the conviction was for an offence under the Immigration Act 1971

(b) the conviction was for a drugs offence

(c) the conviction was for a crime against the person

(d) any conviction where a custodial sentence of 12 months or more was imposed or where a shorter period was imposed but a person had within the last five years been sentenced to a term of imprisonment of at least 12 months.

The circular states that police 'have discretion to report cases falling outside these criteria where exceptional circumstances are considered to merit it'.

The IND has expressed concern that reliance on police reporting is not always effective in spotting prisoners liable to deportation. Therefore the Prison Service issued circular instruction 23/1986 ('Notification of inmates who may be subject to deportation') to prison governors 'with the aim of identifying potential candidates' for deportation on conducive grounds.

PRISON ALLOCATION AND HOME LEAVE.

Double punishment has further consequences. First, it affects prison allocation. A Prison Service letter of 2 April 1991 to governors states:

> The Home Secretary regards it as unacceptable that a convicted prisoner (of any type) who is subject to enforcement action under the Immigration Act 1971...should be given the opportunity to evade removal from the United Kingdom by walking away from an open establishment...in future the norm should be that prisoners who are subject to removal action should not be allocated to open conditions...there may be circumstances justifying departure from the norm in certain circumstances. A clear example would be where there was a priority need to keep a mother and baby together and the only suitable unit was an open establishment.

Second, the deportation issue affects home leave. Previous Prison Service instructions have made it clear that governors have power to grant home leave only where someone liable to removal is still in prison by order of the court. If detention is authorised by the Home Office under Immigration Act powers, for instance after completion of sentence, then only the Immigration Service have power to release. Home leave is dealt with in Prison Service circular instruction 36/1995 'Release on Temporary Licence'. The circular emphasises:

> Governors should give careful consideration to the risk of absconding in cases where a deportation order has been signed and the prisoner is nearing the end of

his sentence... It does not follow that a non-UK national prisoner subject to deportation proceedings or removal as an illegal entrant will abscond and should therefore be automatically discounted from the scheme.

RELEASE ON LICENCE

Double punishment impacts on parole. Section 46 of the 1991 Criminal Justice Act affects 'prisoners liable to removal'. The Act defines four groups of prisoners as liable to removal:

- prisoners against whom a deportation notice has been served. Since the 1999 Immigration and Asylum Act deportation is limited to conducive to public good grounds and cases of court recommendation;
- prisoners who have had a court recommendation;
- prisoners refused leave to enter the UK (the main example being drug couriers not settled in the UK);
- alleged illegal entrants.

Following the 1991 Criminal Justice Act, release on licence for prisoners liable to removal is rarely about release into the community. It is a mechanism for speeding up expulsion. The position of prisoners liable to removal is as follows.

All prisoners, whatever their immigration position, sentenced to less than twelve months, are automatically and unconditionally released after the half-way point of sentence without probation supervision.

For all other short-term prisoners, those serving a sentence of less than four years, release also occurs at the half-way point. This is on licence and is subject to supervision by a probation officer. However, for prisoners liable to removal there is no supervision requirement. Probation therefore no longer has any role in post-release supervision and pre-release plans become largely irrelevant.

For long-term prisoners, those serving a sentence of more than four years, release is at the two-thirds stage. It is on licence and subject to supervision. Again for prisoners liable to removal there is no supervision requirement. Long-term prisoners can be released at half-way point on the recommendation of the Parole Board. However, the Home Secretary can release a prisoner liable to removal at half-way point without the case going before the Board. This speeds up expulsions.

Occasionally a prisoner liable to removal may be released on the appropriate parole date without immediate expulsion. According to circular instruction 34/1992 deportees in this situation

may look to the probation service for general support and help with accommodation. In such cases the seconded probation officer should take on the work.

The 1997 Crime (Sentences) Act changes the law about early release. There is no commencement date and it may never become operational.

Policy and good practice issues

LEGITIMACY OF PROBATION INTERVENTION

The probation service has seemingly hard choices to make in deciding whether helping prisoners threatened with expulsion is a legitimate part of its practice. This is because the service has a responsibility towards its clients but its ultimate paymaster is the Home Office.

In practice this choice should not be difficult. Client welfare is paramount. It is not a question whether it is legitimate to help clients under threat of the immigration laws. It would be transparently illegitimate to refuse such help. It would offend all notions of anti-discriminatory and anti-racist practice. Section 95 of the 1991 Criminal Justice Act refers to 'Persons engaged in the administration of criminal justice' and gives to the Home Secretary responsibility for 'facilitating the performance by such persons of their duty to avoid discriminating against any person on the ground of race or sex or any other improper ground'.

There is growing recognition within the service of the legitimacy of supporting defendants and prisoners threatened with expulsion. Greater Manchester Probation Service, with GMIAU, produced a pamphlet for its officers, 'Immigration Act prisoners', though this is now out of date. Nottingham Probation Service has produced its own resource pack. Support for prisoners at risk of expulsion has also come from the National Association of Probation Officers (NAPO). At its 1991 conference NAPO passed a resolution to 'campaign for the abolition of all immigration controls' and to 'press for the more active intervention of probation staff on behalf of clients at the risk of deportation and the training necessary to do this'. The Greater Manchester branch of NAPO has combined with the Immigration Aid Unit and Partners of Prisoners to establish the Campaign Against Double Punishment.

VIEW OF THE ASSOCIATION OF CHIEF OFFICERS OF PROBATION

The Campaign Against Double Punishment has been influential within the probation service. This is evidenced by an important policy change within the Association of Chief Officers of Probation (ACOP). Previously ACOP assumed that non-British prisoners have no desire to remain in the UK and wish to return as quickly as possible to their country of origin. In June 1993 the Association produced a paper, 'Foreign nationals and the criminal justice system: a strategy for probation services'. This failed to address the issue of those prisoners who wished to fight expulsion.

However, in April 1997 the ACOP Anti-Racism Action Group produced a new paper on 'Criminal conviction and deportation'. This legitimised the probation role in helping prisoners threatened by expulsion. It stressed:

It is important that staff and managers recognise the importance of high quality specialised advice for offenders who are faced with the prospect of deportation.

> Identification of such sources and access routes to them should be seen as essential in developing services for offenders in this category.

This document recognised that probation could have a constructive role on immigration issues:

> At the present moment the most likely contribution will be the submission of reports at the request of the prisoner or his/her representative.

SUPPORT FOR WHICH PRISONERS AND WHICH CLIENTS?

There are many people in detention who have never been and never will be charged with an offence. These are prisoners being held solely under Immigration Act powers. Some are in privately run detention centres, such as Campsfield House in Oxford, where probation has no presence. Others are kept in prison establishments.

There is a policy issue here for the probation service and particularly prison probation. This is whether its professional help should be extended to those in prison who have not been through the criminal justice system.

The ACOP document 'Criminal conviction and deportation' does not address this issue. However, it would be wrong to refuse probation support in these circumstances. The fact that Immigration Act prisoners have never had their case heard within the criminal justice system is a positive reason why probation and welfare help should be offered. Section 14 of the 1993 Probation Service Act, which defines the functions of probation officers, does not preclude this. Indeed it imposes a 'duty' to 'supervise the probationers and other persons placed under their supervision and to advise, assist and befriend them'.

WORKING WITH PRISONERS

Prisoners vulnerable to removal have support needs over and above that of the norm. There is a need to reassure prisoners where there is no likelihood of deportation. This can be a matter of law as some people are exempt from expulsion. However, it can be a matter of assessment that should involve the legal representative. There is the need for regular information about the processes of expulsion where these have been initiated.

The need by prisoners for information is recognised within the Prison Service. Circular instruction 23/1986 states:

> The Governor should ensure that inmates are informed that a notice of intention to deport has been issued, are aware of their appeal rights and are kept informed of subsequent progress of their case.

Prisoners liable to removal have another specific support need. This is deciding whether to resist expulsion from within detention. Legal intervention or campaigning can prolong detention beyond the release date (see Chapter 9). Freedom or deportation is a terrible choice to make. Only the prisoner can make it. Proper advice on the anticipated case outcome needs to be offered before a relatively realistic decision is made.

WORKING WITH ADVISORS

Probation officers need to work closely with a client's advisor to ensure that there is no contradiction between the professionals. Sometimes the probation officer needs to educate the advisor. Many criminal lawyers are inexperienced in matters of immigration law (conversely immigration lawyers may be inexperienced in criminal matters).

Some lawyers see a court recommendation as a relatively soft option. Instead it needs to be vigorously contested as part of mitigation of sentence.

A recommendation, irrespective of any other sentence, carries automatic detention under the immigration legislation unless the court otherwise directs. Defence lawyers need to resist detention. In the late 1970s the JCWI highlighted the scandal of these detentions going uncontested. The Home Office immigration department issued circular 113/1978, 'Detention pending deportation' stating:

> Although the provisions of the Bail Act 1976 do not apply...it may be thought that detention would not be appropriate unless there were good reasons to suppose that the person would abscond or commit further offences if released on bail.

This circular is still operational. Under the 1982 Criminal Justice Act release can be made subject to residency and reporting restrictions.

Criminal lawyers are sometimes ignorant that a recommendation can be appealed as part of sentence.

Criminal lawyers may be inexperienced in dissuading the Home Office not to act on a recommendation. This should involve the preparation of new material. It is important to show that there has been a positive change in circumstances, or a consolidation of the previous family and domestic circumstances, since the recommendation was made. The Home Office does not consider whether or not to act on a recommendation immediately after sentence. This may occur well into sentence. The representative needs to stress that this period should be spent in strengthening family relationships and in other ways building a case. The advisor needs to be in contact with the Home Office to see when the recommendation is to be considered.

Criminal lawyers often fail to alert clients to the possibility of deportation becoming an issue even without a court recommendation.

Criminal lawyers are sometimes ignorant of tactics. One way of resisting a recommendation is to argue that the Home Office has the option of deportation on conducive grounds– and then subsequently to resist such deportation on the grounds that the court declined to make a recommendation. Court cases have held that deportation is not absolutely precluded in such cases but none the less it is a point worth arguing.

Criminal lawyers often fail to understand other best practice issues involved in resisting a notice of intention to deport on conducive to public good grounds. Best practice is to try to discover as early as possible the Home Office's own intentions. This could involve the representative initiating contact with the Home Office. Though such contact could prompt the Home Office into action yet there are already procedures in place for the police and prison governors to report potential deportation cases to the Home Office. Home Office practice is now to give a prisoner formal notice if deportation is being considered and invite the prisoner to provide reasons within twenty-eight days why deportation should not be enforced. This is little time to respond. Any response should come through the prisoner's representative who can send a 'holding letter' promising a substantive response later.

Criminal lawyers often do not realise that to try to pre-empt a notice of deportation it is necessary to start to build up positive evidence from the date of conviction, if not before. Again the need, however difficult, for a prisoner to maintain consistent contact with any partner and children is pivotal.

Criminal lawyers often cease contact with the client after sentence. One reason is financial and difficulties with legal aid. This breaking of contact can be disastrous for a client who, perhaps several years into sentence, is confronted by a notice to deport on conducive grounds.

Whether or not a prisoner has retained contact with the original criminal lawyer, he or she may prefer a specialist immigration advisor. This leaves open another question. A prisoner may be separated by a great distance from his or her family. The question is whether it is better to have an advisor who works near the prisoner or one who works near the family. Experience has shown that it may be preferable that the advisor is in the vicinity of the family. Prisoners move around the system, which makes any constant rapport difficult. A local advisor and the family can see each other regularly over a long period and can work together as a team.

The central argument against expulsion will often be the consequences on family members rather than on the prisoner. An advisor local to the family may be better placed to commission reports dealing with family members. Where there are children of the family it is important for a local social services report and for a local school report to show that a relationship has been maintained and has developed with the parent in custody.

REPORT WRITING

A critical part of a probation officer's role in helping prisoners liable to removal is the provision of professional reports. General issues in report writing have been examined in Chapter 9. The following issues are matters specific to probation workers:

- Issues of pre-sentence reports. If an IM3 has been or will be served on a defendant prior to the hearing then the possibility of a recommendation is a live issue which needs to be addressed and contested in the report.

- Arguments about family unity and particularly the need to preserve proper contact with children go to the heart of all reports. As seen above, the Court of Appeal stressed that this is one of the criteria in assessing whether a recommendation should be made. Chapter 9 examined the Home Office internal instructions on expulsion of families and children. The scope of these policy instructions are restrictive in cases of criminal convictions. Instruction DP 3/96 on marriage policy states:

   > the severity of the offence should be balanced against the strength of family ties. Serious crimes which are punishable with imprisonment or a series of lesser crimes which show a propensity to re-offend would normally outweigh family ties.

- Reports required to contest deportation after conviction are not normally the appropriate place to challenge the correctness of that conviction. The Home Office will regard this as a closed matter.

- However, it will be appropriate to place the criminal activity in context. For instance it may be a first offence.

- Reports contesting deportation must address the likelihood or otherwise of reoffending. They must deal with matters of rehabilitation. It is important to show, if possible, that a prison sentence has so helped to rehabilitate a prisoner that the risk of reoffending is remote. Internal prison reports could prove helpful, for instance reports from chaplains or tutors or even governors.

- Probation reports for convicted prisoners could be prepared by a prison probation officer or a home through-care officer or both.

BAD PRACTICE

There is no point in someone threatened with expulsion following a serious criminal conviction applying for British citizenship. Such a person will not be granted citizenship. One of the criteria for naturalisation is that the applicant be of 'good character'. Timothy Raison, the minister responsible for immigration control, stated in the committee stage of the British Nationality Bill: 'A person with a serious criminal record cannot be regarded as a person of good character' (19 March 1981).

ISSUES OF GENDER AND SEXUALITY

There is one other practice issue – whether support against expulsion should be given to prisoners convicted of violence to or abuse of women or children. The politics of this are discussed in Chapter 21.

REPATRIATION

Some prisoners ask whether it is possible to be repatriated to a prison in the country of origin. This is usually asked by prisoners arrested on entry, for instance for drug importation, with no intention of remaining in the UK. It particularly concerns mothers with children overseas. The Repatriation of Prisoners Act 1984 allows for such prison transfer. Information to governors is contained in Prison Service circular instruction 101/1995 and there is a multilingual prison service leaflet to prisoners. The scheme is confined to nationals of certain countries, mainly those signatory to the 1985 European Convention on the Transfer of Sentenced Persons, of which the only non-European signatories are Canada, Cyprus, Turkey, USA and Zimbabwe. There exists the 1993 Commonwealth Scheme for the Transfer of Convicted Prisoners, which only Malawi, Nigeria, Trinidad and Tobago and the UK have signed. Finally there is a bilateral agreement with Thailand. With the above exceptions the scheme is not available to people from Africa, Asia, the Caribbean, the Indian subcontinent, Latin America and the Middle East. Any transfer requires the agreement of both governments concerned. This can take so long that a sentence may be complete before a decision is made. Middlesex Area Probation Service has produced a pamphlet, 'Drug couriers: a role for the probation service', which essentially concentrates on support for those prisoners wishing to return as soon as possible to their country of origin.

Comments on casework problem at start of chapter

D cannot be deported. He is British. B is immune from deportation if he is a Commonwealth or Irish citizen ordinarily resident in the UK on 1 January 1973 and for the last five years. A may be at risk of a court recommendation because dealing in heroin is considered an extremely serious offence. You need to ask him or his representative whether an IM3 has been served. Alternatively the court may grant an adjournment before sentence for the IM3 to be served. You need to discuss this possibility with A's representative, who should enquire from the Crown Prosecution Service whether it is intended to seek an adjournment. If deportation is an issue then you need to address and argue against it in a pre-sentence report. C is under risk of the Home Office seeking to deport him on conducive to public good grounds, for which he will have an appeal to an adjudicator. However, the Home Office could remove him as overstaying his permitted leave, for which there are no longer appeal rights (see Chapter 3). Your colleague has a role in offering professional help, including preparation of reports requested by C's representative.

Notes

1   1980, 3 ALL ER p.880
2   1969 Cr. LR p.84

PART FOUR

Resolving the Political and Practice Issues

CHAPTER 19

Professional practice and campaigning

A CASEWORK PROBLEM

You have been X's social worker for several years. X now tells you that she is under threat of removal. She came to the UK as a visitor and overstayed her leave. She asks your advice about having a campaign and your help in establishing one. Another client is Y, who has also overstayed. You met Y only when her advisor, through your line manager, asked you to prepare a report for the Home Office on the adverse effect of removal on her children. There is already a defence campaign. Y asks that the campaign be allowed to reproduce some of your report in campaign material. What do you do?

A REAL CASE STORY

> Sometimes it was overwhelming. Sometimes it seemed impossible to beat the government and the faceless Home Office officials who were fighting to protect their interests and those of powerful friends in the Nigerian regime. Sometimes it was so hard to pull ourselves together and comfort one another. What gave us strength to go on was the thousands of people we had never met who flooded us with letters of support.

This is a statement by the Onibiyo family, who claimed asylum from Nigeria. After the Home Office refused there was a successful campaign initiated by the Lambeth branch of UNISON trade union to which a family member belonged. The branch published 'Reunited: how we won' which contains information about the politics and organisation of campaigns.

SCOPE OF THIS CHAPTER

In many ways if it were not for campaigns this book would not have been written. It is campaigns which have alerted many people, including welfare professionals, to the reality of controls. Campaigns have transformed the private, namely expulsions and family divisions, into the public.

Campaigns are no longer unusual. The Home Office in correspondence will refer to 'campaign cases'. Campaigns are part of the whole jigsaw of controls and opposition to them. They are as legitimate a form of contesting expulsion as are court actions. The two often go together. The aim of this chapter is to show that family workers and managers need not have anxieties about appropriate professional involvement in campaigns. The important question to be addressed is the level of involvement that is appropriate.

FURTHER READING RESOURCES

UNISON nationally has produced a *Campaigning Guide to Asylum and Immigration*. This is important because many welfare professionals are UNISON members. The National Coalition of Anti-Deportation Campaigns publishes its own regular newsletter. GMIAU has produced a leaflet in several languages on 'Law, tactics and campaigning if you are threatened with deportation or removal' (though the legal section is now out of date). It has also published *Still Struggling After All These Years* – the history of campaigns by Steve Cohen.

There are two books for 9–12-year-old children which explain the effect on school life of the deportation of pupils. Both have accompanying teacher's packs. The first is *Zeynep* – how William Patten Infants School in London unsuccessfully campaigned against the expulsion of the Hasbudak family. The book and pack are out of print but may be available from the school or libraries. The second is *A Fight to Belong* by Alan Gibbons, a novel based on the successful campaign by St Philips Primary School in Manchester stopping the deportation of Florence Okolo and her children (see Chapter 10). The novel recounts imaginative activities by pupils, such as the letter that one wrote to the adjudicator at the family's appeal: 'How would you feel if you were deported to Nigeria? I bet there's no jobs for Adjudicators out there!' The book and pack are available commercially or from any of its publishers – GMIAU, St Philips School or Save the Children. The Institute of Race Relations has a website on 'Schools Against Deportation'. The Ahmed Iqbal Ullah Anti-Racist Archives in Manchester is compiling an archive of immigration campaign material including several videos made by campaigns.

HISTORY OF CAMPAIGNS

Campaigns should not be romanticised. Some are huge, many are small. What they have in common is that they are rooted in communities and are irrepressible – they can appear anywhere and are the flying pickets of opposition to controls. They are unique to post-war controls. Most campaigns have been about preventing expulsions. Some have been about the right to come to the UK.

The first anti-deportation campaign was in 1974 in defence of Franco Caprino, an Italian worker who was essentially being deported because of his trade union activity within the catering industry. Campaigns became a regular occurrence when they spread to the black community. Saeed Rahman in 1977 and Abdul Azad in 1978 had anti-deportation campaigns in Bradford. After the Tories came to power in 1979 campaigns developed nationally. This was partially a response to Margaret Thatcher's election speech claiming that the country was being 'swamped by an alien culture'. It also indicated the growing political confidence of the black community. In 1979 there was widespread media coverage of the campaigns against the deportation of Nasira Begum from Manchester and that of Anwar Ditta, from Rochdale, to gain entry for her children. Their victories led to a rapid growth in campaigns. It has been noted (see Chapter 1) that within Greater Manchester there were thirty-six campaigns between 1978 and 1987. Most were successful. The most dramatic defeat was that of Viraj Mendis, a Sri Lankan asylum-seeker, who accepted sanctuary in a local church which was broken into after a major police operation.

Good practice

It may seem odd to refer to 'good practice' in the context of campaigning which is a political activity that does not appear to lend itself to the norms of professional conduct. On a personal level everyone can choose whether they wish to be involved in a campaign. This is not the issue. The issue is the level of involvement that is professionally justifiable.

ROLE OF LOCAL AUTHORITIES IN A CAMPAIGN

Manchester City Council has much good practice in relation to financing and supporting campaigns (see Chapter 1). It is possible for Manchester residents to obtain a grant of £500 to establish a campaign. There also exists a Manchester Immigration Needs Trust offering individual financial support (see Chapter 12). Manchester, however, shows bad practice as no publicity is given to the availability of these monies.

ROLE OF WELFARE PROFESSIONALS IN A CAMPAIGN

Welfare professionals are not political commissars. Their main role in a case will not be through their involvement in a campaign. It will be through the provision of their expertise and reports. These reports are not public property. They are confidential to the client and the advisor. Whoever else sees them, including campaign members, is the client's decision.

It is important that welfare practitioners are aware of a campaign's existence and recognise its legitimacy, so that everyone is working in the same direction. Family professionals need to be aware of the good practice points contained within this chapter. This knowledge will improve the quality of reports by situating them in a context where the client is demanding rights rather than pleading for mercy.

It will always be professionally constructive for a practitioner to attend at least one campaign meeting to become better acquainted with all the issues. On other occasions a deeper participation could be professionally appropriate. A common example is that of school children under threat of removal. There have been cases where the campaign has been based within the school and where teachers, including the head teacher, governors, parents and trade union representatives of the school's teaching and non-teaching staff have been actively involved.

JUDICIAL RECOGNITION OF CAMPAIGNS

The courts have recognised that sectors of the public may oppose expulsion and the Home Office must take this into account. Law and politics here coincide in favour of applicants. Bakhtaur Singh was an Indian musician under threat of deportation. He attracted thousands of people to music festivals. The House of Lords held that this was a critical factor and overruled the Home Office decision to deport.[1] This case went as far as the Law Lords discussing whether the threat of industrial action to prevent a deportation could be evidence in support of a deportee. They rejected this proposition. None the less this case provides authority for the proposition that the Home Office must take into account the strength of public, community and professional disquiet as expressed in an anti-deportation campaign.

ROLE OF THE LEGAL ADVISOR IN A CAMPAIGN

Immigration advisors should not act as a loyal opposition to the Home Office. There is no point going through legal formalities without having a perspective, however remote, on winning a case. Campaigns may provide that perspective. Advisors have to be honest about the chances, or otherwise, of a successful outcome. On the other hand legal representation should be about efforts to win cases. It is therefore the responsibility of the representative to initiate discussion about campaigns.

Advisors have a responsibility to liaise with campaigns. Campaign members need to know constantly about the legal processes, the different stages and the predicted time-scale of a case. Campaigns require this information in order to plan activities. None of this should be seen as burdensome by advisors. It should be recognised as a valid way of helping to win cases. The existence of a campaign can help advisors and relieve some of their burdens. It is seen below how campaigns can make accessible professional reports that might otherwise be unobtainable. Campaigns can, by strengthening the resolve of clients, transform them into stronger participants in their own case.

ROLE OF THE CLIENT IN A CAMPAIGN

Ultimate ownership of a campaign should rest with the person or people under threat. It is their life. It is their campaign. They have the right of veto over campaign activities. A campaign cannot work without the active involvement of those under threat. No campaign can be built *for* someone. It has to be built *with* them. Central to the campaign has to be the continued participation of those under threat, their family and friends. A campaign without this participation will at best be high-powered charity.

BASIC GOOD PRACTICE POINTS ABOUT CAMPAIGNS

Understandably not every client wants a campaign. Campaigns transform the personal into the political and the private into the public. There cannot be an anonymous or secret campaign. For most people the very idea of a campaign is initially embarrassing. No one comes to the UK expecting to engage in a public battle to remain. However, there is a professional obligation, especially on advisors, to suggest the option. Clients threatened by expulsion need to appreciate that they cannot rely on the law, legal mechanisms or lawyers to remain when it is precisely the immigration law that is sanctioning their removal.

The prospect of a campaign may be intimidating yet for most people the alternative of being forcibly removed is more intimidating. Although a client's initial reaction may be negative, the issue needs to be constantly on the agenda. Clients need to be reassured that the solidarity of a campaign and its supporters can help develop psychological as well as political strength to contest the Home Office.

Not every client needs a campaign. Campaigns are usually necessary when settlement is wanted on compassionate grounds outside the immigration rules.

WHEN SHOULD A CAMPAIGN BEGIN? THE 1999 IMMIGRATION AND ASYLUM ACT

The decision to campaign is that of the person or family under threat. In making a decision certain questions are regularly raised. In particular, when should a campaign begin? It is no use waiting to start a campaign until after the legal processes have been completed. This is usually too late to achieve victory. It misunderstands what is the real issue here – namely that the legal processes are themselves usually inadequate when the law itself does not allow for settlement. It also underestimates the huge power of the Home Office. Campaigns need to start as soon as possible, to have sufficient time to organise a challenge to this power. There is no point in continually postponing the decision. Delay is harmful.

The need to organise immediately has become vital since the 1999 Act. This abolishes any independent right of appeal against deportation. This will considerably speed up the process of removal (see Chapter 3). The 1999 legislation has three particular consequences for building campaigns:

- One of the future responsibilities of advisors will be to devise creative methods of slowing down the legal process (see Chapter 9).

- Where it is anticipated that the Home Office may refuse an application then the best advice is to start the campaign even before the Home Office makes a decision.

- Where a person has overstayed, there exists a danger of being apprehended, detained and removed without the possibility of legal challenge under the immigration appeals system. There will still remain some possible legal processes – an appeal on human rights grounds, an appeal under the proposed Race Relations (Amendment) Act, an

asylum application and judicial review. These are avenues to be
explored by the legal advisor. The decision to regularise immigration
status, the decision as to when to inform the Home Office and the
decision as to when to start a campaign are tactical issues to be
discussed with an advisor. If a decision is made to regularise status then
the best advice is to start a campaign immediately.

OTHER QUESTIONS ASKED BY CLIENTS

Can a campaign harm a case by annoying the Home Office? Being under threat
of expulsion is itself the worst situation. Nothing can aggravate it. A campaign
can only make it better.

How big should the campaign be? The answer to this is the bigger the better.
Size matters. GMIAU in its pamphlet on deportation and removal advises:

> there is no use in only having a small campaign. There is no use in limiting the
> campaign to small-scale activities. The real, visible, strength of a campaign can be
> measured by the number of people it attracts to its public activities. The golden
> advice is to think big in building the campaign and its events. The Home Office is
> very powerful so the campaign needs to be powerful in order to stop the deporta-
> tion or removal. The campaign needs to get national and not just local support.
> So successful campaigns often require a lot of travel in order to build support.

The converse of this is also true. A weak, disorganised campaign can be harmful.
It causes demoralisation to those under threat. It allows the Home Office or an
adjudicator to make an adverse assessment of community support.

ROLE OF A CHILD CLIENT

Where children are under threat, it is essential to take their wishes into account. In
the case of very young children this may not be feasible. For children of school
age it becomes more appropriate the older they become. A child may feel embar-
rassed, uncomfortable and guilty about other children knowing of their personal
situation. A positive resolution to these fears is to explain that by involving the
school centrally in the campaign a child can actually make friends. Any school
that does actively campaign must take this issue on board.

NO GUARANTEES

There is no guarantee that a campaign will ensure success – no more than good
legal representation can ensure success. No promise of success should ever be
made to a client. Some cases can be won without campaigns. Others can be lost
with campaigns. Everything about immigration control is a risk.

Statistically most campaigns do win. However, campaigns are not like
trumpets outside the walls of Jericho. The walls of the Home Office do not
collapse at the first sound of a campaign. Just the reverse. There are often many

set-backs. Appeals may be lost. There may be several Home Office refusals. The Home Office may back down only at the last moment.

AVOID TRIUMPHALISM

Community-based activists should avoid a naive triumphalism. People under threat of controls should keep away from immigration advisors who guarantee victory and they should be sceptical of campaigners who guarantee victory. Even in those campaign cases that have been victorious, it is often impossible to assess scientifically the positive effect of a campaign as compared with the positive effect of the legal representations. All that is possible is to try to make some reasoned assessment. However, the aim and sole purpose of any campaign must be to force the Home Office to give in. A campaign is a stick. Compassionate grounds contained within legal representations are the carrot.

CAMPAIGNS AS A WAY OF OBTAINING PROFESSIONAL REPORTS

Campaigns can strengthen legal representation by opening otherwise unavailable welfare avenues. The campaign in defence of the Okolo family illustrates this relationship between legal representation, professional practice and campaigning. Florence Okolo and her two children were under threat of deportation after being deserted by the father/husband. Because of the strength of the campaign, and in particular the active involvement of the Okolo children's school, political support was obtained from Manchester City Council. This in turn made it possible to access written reports and oral evidence from the local director of education, the chair of education and the director of social services. This in its turn further legitimised the involvement of the school's teachers in the campaign. At the time Florence, who obtained a degree in Nigeria, worked as a cleaner at Manchester Metropolitan University. The Senate of the University passed a resolution supporting her and sent a representative to speak at her appeal. The substance of all this evidence was not particularly unique in comparison with other similar cases. It showed that deportation would have a detrimental effect on the children's education and general welfare and that Florence had the support of her employer. However, the prestigious and elevated form this evidence took would not have been remotely accessible without the campaign legitimising the case.

A 'HUMANITARIAN' OR A 'POLITICAL' CAMPAIGN?

Often there is discussion within a campaign about whether the campaign should be 'political' or 'humanitarian'. There is anxiety that an openly political campaign may alienate potential supporters whereas it is suggested that an emphasis on the humanitarian, that is, compassionate, aspects of a case would widen support. This suggestion is sometimes reflected in campaign literature. The slogan of the Okolo Family Defence Campaign was 'Join us in the fight to stop this inhuman deportation', which presupposes there could be a 'humane' deportation. The slogan in another successful campaign, the Marion Gaima Defence Campaign, was 'Compassion not deportation', which avoids confronting the central issue, namely that everyone should have the *right* to be here.

Both the Okolo Family Defence Campaign and the Marion Gaima Defence Campaign were militant, well-publicised campaigns. Florence Okolo and Marion Gaima were members of the UK's largest trade union, UNISON, and the union supported them both. Within this context it may seem carping to criticise a couple of slogans. However, there is a battle for ideas going on here. What these slogans do is to reproduce within the campaigning context the distinction between the 'worthy' and 'unworthy' – a distinction that campaigns should be overcoming, not emphasising. The polarisation between the political and the humanitarian is misconceived. What often passes for humanitarianism is its direct opposite. It is the reduction in public of the individual to a set of welfare, health and educational standards by which they ought to be allowed to remain here. It is victimology.

DEMANDING SUPPORT – NOT BEGGING FOR IT

By their very existence campaigns make a powerful statement. They demand rights not contained in the written law.

This is the reality almost irrespective of what is written in campaign literature. However, the literature should reflect this reality. A campaign need not beg for support. It should demand it. Clients are not to blame for their situation. This is the product of immigration controls. They need not feel ashamed about demanding support. Campaigns are about solidarity not charity. There is no need for a campaign to publicise every aspect of the 'compassionate' details of a person's case. Details should be kept publicly to a minimum otherwise the person under threat will be stereotyped as vulnerable (see Chapter 10).

This is why the campaign in defence of Shabana Rahman (see Chapter 9) raised the slogan of 'Solidarity not pity'. Such a slogan poses an alternative way of contesting cases. It suggests a way forward based on demanding rather than pleading. It counterposes collective solidarity to individual sympathy. Of course a slogan in itself does not resolve all the difficult issues. Neither the campaign in defence of Shabana nor her advisor were publicly silent about her disability. However, this was presented in a context of shared struggle rather than an individual pleading lenience.

COLLECTIVISING CAMPAIGNS

Each campaign must acquire its own support and strength. However, working with other people under threat and with other campaigns can lead to a collective strength. The GMIAU leaflet advises:

- You should meet and discuss with other people who have had campaigns and won. You can learn from their experiences.

- You should also meet with other people who are presently having campaigns against deportation or removal. There is strength in unity and in joining in with each other's activities.

- You should invite all other anti-deportation campaigns, both locally and nationally, to your events. You and your campaign should also join in events organised by other campaigns. If you give other people support then they will support you back.

Sometimes 'umbrella' groups have been established locally or nationally to co-ordinate similar campaigns. In the 1980s there existed the United Families Campaign fighting for the right of Bangladeshi children to join families in the UK. Also in the 1980s was the Immigration Wives and Fiancées Campaign. This was composed of women fighting for the autonomy of women. It was based on a woman's right to be joined by a husband or, if she had come from overseas, her right to leave a husband without losing immigration status. There now exists the National Coalition of Anti-deportation Campaigns which facilitates contacts and joint events and with offices in Birmingham, London and Manchester. In addition there exist campaigns in solidarity with detainees at Campsfield, Oakington and Harmondsworth detention centres.

ORGANISING A CAMPAIGN

The GMIAU leaflet contains advice on organising a campaign. There is one basic piece of advice – campaigns should not be timid. As it says in the Onibiyo pamphlet, 'Reunited: how we won' – 'Above all, be bold!'

The campaign should meet weekly at the same place, on the same day and at the same time. If meetings are not held weekly then people will not remember the dates and will not come regularly. Any organisation that supports the campaign should be asked to send one of its members to the campaign committee. The place, date and time of committee meetings should be given in the campaign leaflet.

Campaigns are expensive. Well-organised campaigns can cost tens of thousands of pounds. Because of the restriction on benefits (see Chapter 12) some campaigns may have to raise essential living expenses. A bank account needs to be opened. The campaign leaflet must contain an appeal for money. Every campaign event should be used to collect money. There are some charities which may help fund leaflets or other activities. One is the Council of Churches for Britain and Ireland.

CAMPAIGN LEAFLET

- A campaign should quickly after its inception produce a standard leaflet which explains the case and asks for support. The explanation should be short and contain the minimum of personal detail.

- The leaflet needs to be translated into appropriate language(s). The translation should appear on the same leaflet as the English. This makes distribution easier. The translation should be professionally undertaken and not inferior to the English version.

- The leaflet should be written so it can be used throughout the campaign and not become outdated with each development. Campaigns can last a long time. An initial print run of 75,000 leaflets is not unusual.

- The leaflet should ask people to write protest letters to the Home Office. Personally written letters are treated more seriously than standard printed letters. Supporters should be asked to send copies to the campaign. They can then be produced at any appeal and a database of support established.

- The leaflet should contain the Home Office case reference number and supporters told to quote it in all letters. The address to send letters to is 'The Home Secretary, Queen Anne's Gate, London SW1 9HT'.

- The campaign needs its own address and preferably telephone number to put on the leaflet. Deciding on a postal address is urgent.

OTHER CAMPAIGN MATERIAL

The campaign needs a petition distributed locally and nationally with the campaign's address to which it can be posted back. Well-organised campaigns have attracted over one hundred thousand signatures. Petitions can be submitted at appeals and, as part of a publicity event, to the Home Office.

Large-size multilingual posters should be produced for display.

Campaigns have produced videos, often made by students on video production courses. It is worth contacting local colleges to see if they run such courses.

INTERNET TECHNOLOGY – INTERNATIONAL SUPPORT

Publicity can be given by the National Coalition of Anti-Deportation Campaigns on its Internet page. This is also a way of gaining international support as protest letters can be sent to British embassies overseas.

GETTING THE SUPPORT OF OTHER ORGANISATIONS

A campaign needs support from organisations. The campaign leaflet should ask organisations to invite a speaker to one of their meetings. The more meetings addressed by campaign members and particularly by the person(s) under threat, then the more chance of gaining support. Personal visibility builds a campaign.

If the client under threat is a union member, the union should be asked for political and financial support at local, regional and national level.

Comments on casework problem at start of chapter

As X's long-term social worker there is an issue as to why you did not know about her immigration problem earlier. X may not have appreciated the danger she was in. This raises the question as to whether you should have asked X about her immigration status at the start of your professional relationship. Is this bad or good anti-racist practice (see Chapter 4)? You should now be able to advise X on the matters explained in this chapter and that any campaign would require her active involvement. You need also to tell X that before deciding on a campaign she needs to discuss law and tactics with an immigration advisor. You should discuss with your line manager X's request that you help to establish a campaign. Usually, though not always, it would appear more professionally appropriate for X's advisor or members of the community to establish the campaign with yourself attending campaign meetings where necessary.

Y has an advisor and a campaign. There is an issue as to the confidentiality of your report. As the report has been commissioned by Y's advisor on her behalf then she should have the right to say whether it can be reproduced. You could question with Y the wisdom of the campaign quoting passages of a private or intimate nature and whether Y should make her family's life so public. You could emphasise that this sort of publicity would only portray Y and the children as a bundle of weaknesses and vulnerabilities (see Chapter 10).

Notes

1   1986 Imm AR p.352

CHAPTER 20

Good practice, welfare agencies and non-compliance

A CASEWORK PROBLEM

> You are a care manager. You have an elderly client, X, receiving domiciliary services under Section 45 of the 1968 Health Services and Public Health Act. You receive an anonymous letter saying that X entered the UK without permission. Your line manager says that you must inform the Home Office. He says that X's immigration status disentitles her to support under the 1968 Act.

A REAL CASE STORY

> In Wandsworth in 1983, Dora Amoako, a local hospital worker...was threatened with deportation as an overstayer, after approaching the Housing Department's Homeless Persons Unit for assistance. It emerged that the Unit had contacted the Home Office; a council spokesman, confirming this, commented: 'She could not prove her right to permanent residence here, so we warned her we would be making investigations – which normally include approaching the Home Office' (*Balham and Tooting News*). After a local campaign, supported by Wandsworth Council, the Home Office relented and allowed Dora to remain. (This story is from the JCWI pamphlet *No Passports to Services*)

SCOPE OF THIS CHAPTER

One issue constantly emerges in training. This is whether agencies or workers providing welfare can comply with laws which, if they had not had statutory approval, would breach race relations legislation.

These matters have been considered by reputable bodies. In November 1984 the Commission for Racial Equality submitted a document to a governmental review of housing benefit. It stated:

> Local authorities are thus being put in an invidious position. On the one hand they have a statutory duty under the 1976 Race Relations Act to carry out their various functions with due regard to the need to eliminate discrimination and to promote good opportunities. On the other hand, under DHSS Regulations and

Circular Guidance they have to implement Regulations which are fundamentally racist.

This quotation is found in *No Passports to Services*, which comments on denial of housing benefit to overseas students:

There appears to be no legal discretion for local authorities to eliminate the racism of the new regulation itself. Nevertheless, given their obligations under the 1976 Race Relations Act, local authorities might like to consider whether, as part of an overall strategy for their response to Britain's racist and sexist immigration controls, they should refuse to implement the regulation.

This chapter looks at what non-compliance would mean in practice and its legal and political implications.

NATURAL LAW

There are judicial comments that could provide juridical support to some degree of non-compliance. These comments have invoked concepts of the 'higher good'. In the first case, *R* v. *London Borough of Hammersmith* in 1996, holding that local authorities had obligations to asylum-seekers under the National Assistance Act, Mr Justice Collins referred to the 'law of humanity'. In the case of an overstayer too ill with AIDS to travel, another judge held 'humanity stood above the law' and the local authority was obliged to offer support under the same Act (see Chapter 12).

Concepts such as the 'law of humanity' echo old notions of the supremacy of 'natural law' over 'man-made law'. Such constructs hid what were essentially political decisions challenging state law. The incorporation of the European Convention and amendments to the Race Relations Act bring closer the possibility of some law being held unlawful or non-compliance being held lawful.

MEANING OF NON-COMPLIANCE

Non-compliance is arguably an appropriate reaction by professional staff developing good anti-racist practice. There are important issues to be considered.

Non-compliance is not always easy to conceptualise. It clearly includes a refusal to report someone to the Home Office. It becomes more difficult for benefit and service providers where benefit is linked to immigration status. Refusal to determine status could result in *all* claimants having benefits refused irrespective of status. This is because it would be impossible to know which claimants were not subject to immigration controls.

NHS HOSPITALS

It would be unrealistic to expect government controlled departments, such as the Benefits Agency, to adopt policies of non-compliance. Some local authorities, through distaste of internal controls, might be willing to engage in the debate.

There is one group of statutory agencies which sometimes refuse to comply with internal controls. These are hospitals. Hospitals have a duty to obtain payment from overseas patients under the National Health Service (Charges to Overseas Visitors) Regulations. The research paper 'Immigration controls and health' (see Chapter 16) reported some hospitals declining to impose charges and not suffering legal consequences.

EMPLOYERS' LIABILITY: PERSONNEL DEPARTMENTS

Employers can be criminally liable for hiring labour not authorised to work (see Chapter 3). The Immigration (Restrictions on Employment) Order 1996 establishes a defence to criminal charges if the employer checks and keeps a copy of one of thirteen listed documents such as a P45 or a passport. The Home Office has produced a pamphlet 'Prevention of illegal working: guidance for employers'. This contains an appendix on understanding UK passport stamps. Employers are being asked to make judgements on matters on which they have no competence. One major refugee organisation informs job applicants that it requires proof of eligibility to work as it 'must follow the law'. The Commission for Racial Equality has issued its own guidelines for employers, 'Racial equality and the Asylum and Immigration Act 1996'. This also assumes an obligation on employers to demand documents showing eligibility to work. The 1999 Immigration and Asylum Act compels the Home Secretary to issue a code of practice ensuring employers avoid unlawful discrimination. However, there is no legal obligation to ask for documentary proof. All that this evidence does is provide a defence in event of prosecution. Organisations have a choice as to whether to ask for such proof. This is not even an issue of non-compliance. It is a matter of good anti-racist practice in not investigating status versus the possible risk of future prosecution. Personnel departments and personnel officers should, with union support, argue that it is not their role to investigate immigration status.

THE 1999 IMMIGRATION AND ASYLUM ACT

The issue becomes difficult when the lack of immigration status itself becomes the pathway to benefits and services, albeit second-rate benefits and services. This is the problem posed by the 1999 legislation. Should local authorities refuse to engage with the Home Office in the provision of accommodation for asylum-seekers?

The refursal to enter into voluntary agreements with the Home Office through NASS is quite lawful. The issue is one of non-cooperation rather than non-compliance. There is an arguable case that immigration controls are now so regressive that the provision of immigration control defined welfare services compromises the provider and is incompatible with anti-racist practice and opposition to social exclusion.

THE 1999 ACT AND CONSTRAINTS ON LOCAL AUTHORITIES

There is concern within government that local authorities will refuse to engage with the new legislation. There is anxiety that authorities will not voluntarily enter into contracts to provide accommodation. Consequently the legislation compels authorities to give the Home Secretary 'such information about their housing accommodation (whether or not occupied) as he may from time to time request'. The Home Secretary has the power to designate any area as a 'reception zone' where 'he may direct the local authority to make...accommodation available'.

The Memorandum from the Local Government Association to the Special Standing Committee on the Immigration and Asylum Bill is clear (see Chapter 1). Local authorities prefer voluntary agreements and oppose an imposed scheme. However, in future authorities may consider an imposed scheme is preferable to voluntary collusion.

SHOULD LOCAL AUTHORITIES CO-OPERATE WITH THE SCHEME?

Doubtless many councillors and council workers consider they are assisting asylum-seekers through the provision of accommodation. What in fact they are doing is legitimising a system of forced dispersal. In a letter of 27 June 2000 from the North West Consortium to the Manchester branch of the National Coalition of Anti-Deportation Campaign it is said '...local authorities across the North West remain firmly committed to playing their full part in the dispersal programme'. However it is the compulsory nature of this dispersal scheme, the absence of security of tenure for dispersed asylum-seekers, the surveillance role undertaken by local authorities as landlords, linked to a level of financial assistance below that of income support, that is precisely the problem. Moreover, local authorities have to accept major political responsibility for initiating this scenario. It is local authorities which headed the campaign against their own obligation to provide support under the 1948 National Assistance Act and the 1989 Children Act. It was this self-serving agitation which resulted in the so-called support provisions of the 1999 Act. The way forward is not co-operation with the new scheme. The way forward is to demand that asylum-seekers and others subject to immigration controls be given full rights under homelessness legislation and benefit regulations – and indeed that these rights be improved for everyone irrespective of immigration status. Non co-operation is one way of forcing this onto the political agenda.

LIVERPOOL CITY COUNCIL AND REGIONAL CONSORTIA – PRINCIPLE OR PRAGMATISM?

One significant local authority, a lead member of the North West consortium, has withdrawn from the scheme. The *Guardian* of 21 September 2000 reported the withdrawal of Liverpool. This pullout seems to have been partially motivated by principle, namely the rehousing by NASS of 1000 dispersed asylum seekers in sub-standard private property within Liverpool. However the council was primarily guided by financial self-interest. The utilisation of private accommodation and the decrease in the overall number of asylum-seekers requiring accommodation meant that some of its own property set aside for asylum seekers remained empty, leading to a large debt.

Moreover the *Manchester Evening News* of 14, 22 and 29 September 2000 reported that Manchester and the rest of the North West Consortium had still to sign a contract with NASS for the provision of public sector accommodation. The South West Consortium is a relatively open body which produces a regular newsletter. Its newsletter of 3 October 2000 condemned 'the emphasis from the Home Office...on minimum cost rather than suitability of location and the sensible planning of services'. It predicts that the South West Consortium will wind itself up and doubts whether contracts will be signed with NASS by the North West, Wales, South Central and East of England consortia. What all this shows is:

- Many asylum-seekers are themselves engaged in active resistance to the new scheme. They are voting with their feet by refusing to be dispersed outside of London and the South East (see Chapter 13). This means NASS is under less pressure to do deals with all the consortia. It is quite content to negotiate with a reduced number.

- Local authorities can exit or not co-operate with the scheme without any immediate Home Office reprisals requisitioning council accommodation – which is one of the fears leading to local authority voluntary collusion.

- The dispersal scheme is still in force though involving only some consortia. It remains on the statute book and can be reactivated nationally whenever the Home Office considers that necessary and viable.

- Any sympathy with consortia or local authorities which have lost monies through accommodation being under-used by asylum-seekers would be misplaced. The main support local authorities can give to asylum seekers is political support. Political support means withdrawing en block from colluding with the new legislation. It means withdrawing on a statement of principle against involuntary dispersal and not because the financial rewards are inadequate.

THE 1999 ACT AND THE VOLUNTARY SECTOR

Voluntary sector agencies can refuse to enter into contracts with the Home Office without fear of compulsion. These contracts may have the appearance of being enabling and helpful. Examples are the new 'one-stop' agencies that the Home Office has established through funding voluntary sector organisations. These organisations have been given a two-fold role. First, to act as 'reception assistants' advising on support available under the 1999 legislation. Second, to offer advice as to local welfare facilities and the availability of legal representatives. The role of these agencies is described in a draft *Process Manual for the Asylum Support System* issued by the Home Office in February 1999 and also in the April 2000 pamphlet *The New Asylum Support Scheme*. Their functions as reception assistants include helping complete application forms for support. They are also expected to, offer options and information on welfare and accommodation to asylum-seekers and to advise asylum-seekers so as 'to enable them to identify alternatives' to the Act's statutory support scheme. This contradicts the essential role of the voluntary sector which is to act as an advocate against state authority and not as a vehicle to direct those in need away from state support, however meagre that support.

Most of the larger voluntary sector organisations dealing with refugees have succumbed to entering into contracts as assistance agencies and providers of one-stop services on a regional basis under the 1999 legislation. According to a circular of 6 December 1999 from Refugee Action, this body along with its partners (the Refugee Council, Scottish Refugee Council, Welsh Refugee Council, Refugee Arrivals Project, Migrants Helpline) have formed the Asylum Support Programme Steering Group and been promised £8 million annually by the Home Office. As well as having an advice function these agencies will be expected to organise emergency accommodation for new applicants not yet accepted into the full support scheme (see Chapter 13).

SHOULD VOLUNTARY SECTOR AGENCIES CO-OPERATE WITH THE SCHEME?

This co-operation is usually justified on the basis that it is better that benevolent welfare-orientated agencies provide services rather than these being offered by more repressive Home Office or commercially orientated organisations. This simply reproduces the problem which is that of the repressive nature of controls themselves.

These voluntary sector organisations have not complied with everything demanded by the Home Office and this non-compliance represents hope for future good practice. They have refused to administer the Dickensian 'hard cases' fund supposedly supporting some asylum-seekers after a refusal of their asylum claims.

The *Guardian* of 3 and 15 April 2000 reported one positive example within the retail trade of voluntary sector non-cooperation. The charities Oxfam, Barnardo's, Shelter, Marie Curie and Save the Children have refused to accept the new vouchers in their shops – at least in their present form where change cannot be given (see Chapter 12). Oxfam, which has 840 charity shops, has called upon major retailers to follow its example.[1]

REGISTERED SOCIAL LANDLORDS

Registered social landlords can be viewed as part of the voluntary sector. As voluntary sector agencies they are unique in that the 1999 legislation, Section

100, allows the Home Secretary to compel them to offer support. They are in any event being encouraged by the Housing Corporation to voluntarily act as housing providers under the new scheme. This is made clear in the Corporation's November 1999 Guidelines for registered social landlords on the provision of housing and support services for asylum. It has been seen previously that many of these guidelines appear positive (see Chapter 13). However they do not even start to raise the question as to whether such co-operation in an essentially reactionary scheme should be encouraged. The Guidelines themselves reveal some irresolvable contradictions. For instance they are introduced by the Home Office in the person of the Director of NASS, who is hardly neutral on the dispersal scheme. The Director uses the opportunity to again emphasise that the point of the scheme is to 'discourage those who apply for asylum on economic grounds'. Colluding with NASS in this way challenges the independence of the Housing Corporation. RSLs need to consider whether they want to engage in a scheme which is premised on defining and excluding many asylum-seekers as 'bogus'.

FURTHER READING MATERIAL ON THE VOLUNTARY SECTOR

There are two contrasting publications, one explicitly supporting voluntary sector involvement with the new legislation and the other opposing it. The pamphlet in support is *The Role and Funding of the Voluntary Sector in Relation to the Proposed Asylum Process*. This was produced in February 1999 in the name of the Asylum Support Voluntary Sector Action Group. It is uncritical of the legislation and its support scheme. This is not surprising as the Action Group was established by the Home Office and had representatives from the IND along with the three major refugee advice organisations – the Refugee Arrivals Project, Refugee Action and the Refugee Council. On the other hand a detailed and highly critical account of the role of the voluntary sector in the new poor law scheme is contained in 'Supping with the Devil' by Steve Cohen in a collection of essays, *From Immigration Control to Welfare Control*, edited by Beth Humphries and Ed Mynott and to be published late 2001 by Routledge.

TRADE UNIONS

Non-compliance makes sense only if backed by the union and/or employer at the highest level. Unions regularly pass resolutions against linking entitlements to immigration status. These unions have been ambiguous in supporting a position of non-compliance. UNISON, the local authority workers' union, is an example. *Focus*, the union's journal, reported the debate on a resolution urging non-compliance at its 1996 annual conference (28 June 1996). One delegate said: 'Our members are being asked to act as immigration officers. It's not a job they applied to do!' The resolution was narrowly defeated yet somewhat contradictorily *Focus* reported the conference supporting 'a major publicity campaign in support of non-cooperation'. Another issue of *Focus* stated: 'Branches have been issued with advice on how to resist any attempts to force members to carry out immigration checks' (19 July 1996). This advice referred to employers' liability and stated: 'branches should ask employers to refuse to implement checks on the immigration status of employees.' It also referred to service users, stating: 'Branches should demand a full risk assessment where staff are asked to carry out checks on the immigration status of service users.'

There is a form of non-engagement that USDAW, the shopworkers' union, could consider. Shopworkers could take Oxfam's lead and refuse to accept vouchers under the scheme introduced in the 1999 legislation – pressurising the government to reintroduce full, monetary based, benefits for asylum-seekers and others subject to controls.

MORE ON LOCAL AUTHORITIES

Good anti-racist practice requires that local authorities and other statutory agencies should never contact the Home Office to enquire about immigration status. Otherwise that status could be jeopardised.

Unfortunately some publications urge local authorities to contact the Home Office. In 1996 the Refugee Council and the Association of London Government published *No Place to Call Home* – a report and recommendations for London local authorities on the implementation of new legislation affecting refugees and asylum-seekers. This says:

> The London boroughs are recommended to use the IND…the IND should be contacted only when boroughs reasonably believe a person may have entered or remained in the UK in breach of immigration laws or where immigration status is relevant to their eligibility.

Agencies should never report a claimant for allegedly being in breach of controls. Wherever status is unknown or unclear or there is a suspicion of irregularity then the only action to take is to refer the claimant to a competent and independent agency that can assist in the claim and in clarifying or regularising status.

DISCIPLINARY POLICIES

Paper policies against liaising with the Home Office are insufficient. Employers should have disciplinary procedures which can be invoked against workers who breach confidentiality by reporting service users (or colleagues) to the Home Office for allegedly breaching controls. It should be a disciplinary offence of a lesser nature for staff to contact the Home Office to verify or discover a service user's status.

Trade unions need to consider whether union membership is compatible with reporting colleagues or service users to the Home Office with a view to them being dismissed and/or deported.

SELF-CERTIFICATION

In the absence of non-compliance by workers then self-certification by claimants is the minimum demanded by good anti-racist practice.

Claimants should be able to sign a simple 'self-certification' form confirming entitlement. The burden should be on the agency dispensing welfare to disprove this. Unless there are exceptionally strong counter-indications then there is no need to verify the claimant's statement. Benefit of the doubt should be given to the claimant. There should be a presumption in favour of eligibility. In practice such a presumption does exist – but only for white people. The pamphlet *No Passports to Services* correctly argued that 'further enquiries' and 'verification' proposed by various circulars are impracticable and unacceptable:

> They are impracticable because they require...staff to make decisions about complicated questions of immigration and nationality that are beyond many lawyers. They are unacceptable because they open the way to a 'pass-law' situation, whereby any black or 'foreign-looking' [person] may have to provide detailed proof of nationality or immigration status in order to gain access to ordinary benefits.

Self-certification of ordinary residence for free hospital treatment should not be problematic (see Chapter 16). The DHSS guidelines state that at Stage 2 interviews 'officers may, but need not, seek corroboration for patients' statements'. Best practice would be to accept statements by a patient which show exemption from charges. Self-validation should be the norm. This would avoid the need for the production of documentary evidence, the significance of which requires proper training in immigration law to understand. The guidelines state that a patient should be given the benefit of any doubt about status.

Passports should never be demanded to prove identity. Passports are unique documents containing personal details as well as information about immigration status. The pamphlet *No Passport to Services* reports that in November 1983 Camden Council agreed:

> all Committees of the Council be requested to instruct Council departments not to request passports for identification purposes from members of the public.

The Home Office in its October 1996 circular to local authorities on exchange of information (see Chapter 1) states in Annex 2:

> The relevant department or division of the authority should specify a contact point through which all inquiries or responses will be channelled. The contact point may be a named individual or, if more convenient, a particular post.

As a matter of best practice no authority should designate such a post. If an authority declines to follow best practice then it should produce a yearly inventory on the operational nature of such a post. Where there is a designated post then it is reasonable for employers to invoke disciplinary procedures against other staff contacting the Home Office.

MANCHESTER GUIDELINES: A CRITIQUE

Manchester Council has produced staff guidelines. These are contained in the director of social services's report to the Policy and Resources Committee of 20 January 1997. Though relatively progressive they fail to meet acceptable anti-racist standards. For instance:

- 'The city council will only enquire as to immigration status where this is legally required.' This is useless in those situations where benefits are tied to immigration status.

- 'Where the issue of immigration status arises, staff will ask to see documentation from the Home Office where this is available.' This echoes the problem as to why only some claimants are required to produce Home Office documentation. An anti-racist policy would be to ask all claimants. However, most white people will not have Home Office documents as their status will never have been an issue.

- 'Staff will not ask to see passports unless this is volunteered by the person concerned.' This restates the problem as many black people and refugees will volunteer production of passports if this quickly accesses welfare.

- 'Where verification of a person's status is needed, supporting statements from the person's solicitor will usually be accepted.' Advisors should not be drawn into internal control. An advisor may have a different assessment of a person's immigration status from the Home Office. Self-assessment should suffice. As a last resort it is preferable that the advisor is contacted rather than the Home Office.

- 'Where it is not possible to satisfactorily verify a person's status in any other way, contact with the Home Office will only be made with the written consent of the person concerned.' This emphasis on consent is important but inadequate. Contact with the Home Office should never be made. The person should be recommended to see an independent advisor.

- 'Each department will control contact with the Home Office by restricting contact to a senior nominated officer or a nominated deputy.' This fails to mention disciplinary sanctions to be imposed on non-nominated staff contacting the Home Office.

- 'Where the person is uncertain whether to give their consent, the senior nominated officer will advise the person to seek independent advice from their solicitor or legal representative.' This is good practice. The authority should keep a list of free and expert advisors.

- 'Where no consent is given and verification is required, the service will cease to be provided until verification can be provided.' This is unsatisfactory. Service provision should continue until entitlement is disproved.

- Policies are inadequate without staff being regularly informed, trained, updated and monitored. The guidelines are silent on this.

Comments on casework problem at start of chapter

There is no obligation on you to report X to the Home Office. You should see what policies, if any, your employer has. The authority may have a designated officer within your department whose role it is to liaise with the Home Office. You should contact your union to ensure that this officer does not contact the Home Office on the basis of an anonymous letter. Section 45 of the 1968 Health Services and Public Health Act is now linked to immigration status (see Chapter 15). It is doubtful whether an anonymous letter obliges an authority to reassess eligibility for services. X may be eligible for support under other community care legislation irrespective of status (see Chapter 15). You have a responsibility to warn X about the letter and suggest that she gets proper advice if it is true.

Notes

1   Press release of 3 April 2000; also see *Guardian* letters 17 March 2000

CHAPTER 21

Conclusion

Fair controls or no controls?

A CASEWORK PROBLEM

> You are an immigration advisor. X consults you. Her husband arrived sixteen months ago. The relationship deteriorated. She left him. She says that he married to gain entry and wants him removed. What do you advise?

A REAL CASE STORY

> In January 2000 Mike Tyson, the boxer and convicted rapist, was allowed entry into the UK. There were protests and a failed judicial review of the Home Secretary's decision allowing entry.[1]

SCOPE OF THIS CHAPTER

The problem in understanding controls is not their racism. Controls are manifestly racist. The accumulation of real life examples in this book is proof of this. The problem is whether controls can be divested of racism.

Many people support controls precisely because they are racist. Pemberton Billing MP supported the 1919 Alien Restriction Bill against Jewish immigration suggesting in parliament: 'Why not badge these aliens' (15 April 1919). Such remarks are today rarely expressed openly. The debate has shifted.

One oversimplistic and over-personalised way of looking at immigration controls is to concentrate on the racism of some individual immigration officials and to argue that all problems will be resolved by tackling the issue at this personal level. It is true that some officials are racist. The *Daily Mail* of 3 January 1979 reported that immigration officers at Heathrow wanted to stage a pantomime *Whittington Singh* about a young Punjabi who got into the UK and rose to great heights in the Heathrow immigration department. An IND internal report published in 1994, *A Review of Race Awareness Training*, quotes IND case-workers:

> It's another Nigerian wedding…all Somalis are liars…Poles are white Nigerians…Turks just have a different moral code when it comes to telling the truth.

However, not every IND worker is racist and the issue is not whether individual officials are racist. Not one of the numerous case histories given in this book necessarily reveals personal prejudice by officials. Controls are racist independent of the motives of those operating them. The racism is institutionalised.

In the Preface to this book it is emphasised that there is need for a debate. This is a debate between those who are in agreement in criticising the present laws as being racist but who disagree as to the way forward. The disagreement is both profound and simple. On the one hand it is argued that controls can be restructured, stripped of their racism and rendered 'fair'. On the other hand it is argued that controls are in themselves unfair and racist and their very existence is incompatible with justice.

Though this split exists yet it is often hidden and rarely explicitly articulated. A debate is necessary to bring it out into the open. This is because one view is so dominant that its alternative is virtually silenced or hardly heard. The dominant view is the one advocating 'fair' controls. This now represents the majority, 'common sense' position on controls. It manifests itself in many different arenas. Perhaps its strongest base is within the trade union movement. For instance *Focus*, the journal of UNISON, reported that the 1995 TUC Black Workers' Conference demanded a 'campaign for fair, non-racist immigration and asylum laws' (10 May 1995). However, as seen below, a similar perspective is shared by civil liberty organisations such as the Cobden Trust and exists within academia.

There are two reasons why this represents the dominant position. First, the ideology of controls is so powerful that any position rejecting the totality of this ideology is immediately seen as extreme and unrealisable. Second, the emphasis on the need for 'fair' controls is itself a response to the culture of resistance against deportations and removals (see Chapter 19). Prior to this culture emerging in the 1970s there was no discourse in favour of fair controls. Campaigns against expulsion essentially deny state authority to impose controls. The call for 'fair' controls reasserts this authority in language making controls appear acceptable.

There is also an insidious process here which makes a debate important. The voice of opposition to the concept of controls appears at times to have been deliberately stifled. It is seen below that the two most important books advocating fair controls explicitly decline to enter into a debate about 'no' controls.

Similarly at the 1990 Trades Union Congress there was a resolution opposing all controls. The General Council simply asked that this be withdrawn, which it was.

The aim of this chapter therefore is primarily to make this polemic explicit. It does this by examining contradictions within the position of 'fair' controls and seeing how these contradictions can lead to support for some quite reactionary propositions. At the same time there is a discussion as to why the ideology of controls is so powerful and dominant. Finally, there is tackled a question that is fundamental to this book and which is as important as the debate itself. This is: What actual difference can result in the practice of welfare professionals and community activists through the adoption of a theoretical position of opposition to all controls?

FURTHER READING RESOURCES

As is clear from the above there is very little literature that explicitly argues for no controls. A recent publication is *Open Borders: The Case Against Immigration Controls* by Teresa Hayter (2000, published by Pluto). *Imagine There's No Countries* charts the historic and international material. *Workers Control Not Immigration Controls* examines the position taken by trade unions. Both are published by GMIAU. *A Hard Act to Follow*, published jointly in 1988 by South Manchester Law Centre and the Viraj Mendis Defence Campaign, examines the relationship between state and controls and this is developed in 'The mighty state of immigration controls' by Steve Cohen (Social Policy Review, vol. 7, 1995).

CRITIQUE OF 'FAIR' CONTROLS

'Fair' controls is a contradiction. This is seen in a 1994 collection of essays, *Strangers and Citizens*, produced by the Institute of Public Policy Research, published by Rivers Oram Press and edited by Sarah Spencer. These essays attempt to justify the concept of 'fair' controls.[2]

There cannot be fair controls. Their existence ensures that some people will be excluded and exclusion would be unfair to them. The editor of *Strangers and Citizens* promotes entry of 'legitimate' asylum-seekers and 'genuine' visitors (pp.345–6). This implicit attack on the 'illegitimate' and the 'non-genuine' is identical to the present 'unfair' system. In discussing family unity she asserts: 'The validity of marriage should be questioned if there is evidence of abuse'(p.343). The language of 'abuse' mirrors the present 'unjust' system. If some marriages circumvent controls then the only way of stopping these is to have no controls. This option remains undiscussed. Instead the book argues for the retention of one of the most notorious and damaging immigration rules, namely that 'marriages in which one partner is an immigrant may be subject to a one year probationary period'(p.343). Any schema of controls will retain tests to determine whether applicants fit the criteria. Once this is seen as acceptable then the repressive machinery of control must also be accepted. None of this can be fair.

'FAIR' CONTROLS AND THE FAMILY

Normally the argument for 'fair' controls is based on family unity. However, what is fair about limiting rights to those within the monogamous heterosexual nuclear or extended family or even within same-sex relationships? Why should sexuality and/or romance and/or being in a relationship be the criteria for settlement? What is fair about excluding the single, celibate or promiscuous (see Chapter 7)?

LACK OF JUSTIFICATION FOR CONTROLS

The ideologues of 'fair' controls assume without argument that controls are necessary. Sarah Spencer asserts: 'In immigration policy, government has the right to put the interests of its existing residents, including members of ethnic

minorities, before those of individuals who want to settle here' (p.319). No justification is provided.

The ideological dominance of controls cannot be overemphasised.
Campaigns against a particular expulsion can involve thousands of people. It is a
different matter convincing these thousands to oppose controls in principle. The
vast majority see controls as reasonable and natural not as ideological and
political.

This unquestioning acceptance extends into academia. One professorial con-
tributor to *Strangers and Citizens* writes: 'There is no realistic hope of giving up
[controls]. It would therefore be best to begin by accepting [controls] as an ines-
capable fact'(p.91).

There is a block on conceptualising the absence of controls. In 1986 the
Cobden Trust published *Towards a Just Immigration Policy*. The Introduction states
that no controls 'is thought by some people to be the only just policy, by others to
be...absurd... It is not examined in any of the chapters that follow'.

HOW CONTROLS AND OTHER IDEOLOGIES WERE LEGITIMISED

The strength of popular acceptance of controls is remarkable given their
modernity (see Chapter 2). Prior to the 1905 Aliens Act the dominant ideology
was free movement of people and goods within an extremely powerful doctrine
of free trade. It took twenty years of agitation for controls to be implemented. The
struggle for controls legitimised a host of related and reactionary ideologies –
welfarism, labourism, Malthusianism, eugenicism. These were mostly
half-formed or of only theoretical relevance until the debate over controls.
Advocates of 'fair' controls ignore this history.

EUGENICISM

A constant in the demand for control has been discredited theories of population
and eugenics. The reactionary nature of these ideas renders nonsense the
sanitisation of controls.

Eugenicism is a pseudo-science. It substitutes rational analysis of society with
a mystical one based on conflict between 'races', itself a pseudo-biological
construct, with only the fittest surviving.

The 1905 Aliens Act agitation transformed eugenics into popular ideology.
Dr Robert Rentoul in 1906 wrote *Race Culture or Race Suicide?* with one chapter
headed 'Some causes of national degeneration and degeneracy. Undesirable alien
immigrants and emigration of our fit'. The campaign for controls against black
Commonwealth citizens reintroduced eugenicist argument with doctors again
being partially responsible (see Chapter 17).

MALTHUSIAN POPULATION THEORIES

For over a century advocates of control have argued that the UK is overpopulated.
In a 1902 rally for controls, a letter was read from the author Marie Corelli saying

that the 'evils of overcrowding in London...the size of the British Islands on the map...is out of all proportion to the influx of alien population' (*East London Observer* 18 January 1902). This argument was used to exclude Jewish refugees from Nazism. The Home Secretary, Sir Samuel Hoare, imposed visa controls on Germans and Austrians by stating in parliament 'indiscriminate admission... would have grave economic results in aggravating the employment problem, the housing problem and other social problems' (22 March 1938). Theories of overpopulation reappeared against black people. The Labour government's 1965 White Paper, *Immigration from the Commonwealth*, spoke of 'the need to control the entry of immigrants to our small and overcrowded country'.[2]

Overpopulation theories predate the modern immigrant. Thomas Malthus devoted his career to attacking the urban poor for causing overpopulation. His *Essay on the Principle of Population* went through six editions from 1798 to 1826. Malthus was anti-working class. He considered there were too many workers. His views became a matter of popular discourse when switched by other agitators to immigrant workers. These views persist today. The *Guardian* in a feature of 9 September 1999 headed 'Population explosion' stated uncritically: 'Thomas Malthus warned more than 200 years ago that population could, and one day would, outstrip food supplies' and that overpopulation in the UK was due to 'baby booms and immigration'.

CONFUSIONS IN THE MEANING OF 'OVERPOPULATION'

Those who justify present controls and argue for more controls on the basis of 'overpopulation' are rarely clear about what they mean by this. The fundamental argument appears to be literally one of space and that there is physically insufficient space within the UK to permit immigration. For instance the Labour government White paper quoted above describes the UK as 'small and overcrowded'. This argument was used throughout the entire twentieth century. If the UK really was overcrowded in this spatial sense a century ago, then by now either the country would have sunk or else Britons would be living on each other's shoulders. This emphasis on the concept of space, or the lack of it, is redolent of the Nazi concept of *Lebensraum* used to justify the invasion of the USSR in order to provide land for the pure, German *Volk*.

On other occasions 'overpopulation' appears to refer to lack of sufficient material resources to ensure employment, housing and welfare entitlements. For instance the *Manchester Evening News* in 1903 ran a five-part series called 'The aliens of Manchester' in which it listed eleven arguments in favour of controls (26–30 January). These emphasised employment and housing issues. Yet only four decades later there was constructed a welfare state which purported to be based precisely on the promise of universal welfare, full employment and housing for all. The truth is that the construct of overpopulation cannot be looked at abstractly. It relates directly to the forces and relations of production. No one knows what level of production could be achieved in a rational, planned economy.

All these theories of overpopulation rest on an assumption which is sometimes hidden and other times made explicit but which is always racist. This is that the population is not too large in the abstract but what is too large is the 'alien' population. The eleventh and final justification given for controls in the *Manchester Evening News* series of 1903 is simply 'That the foreign population of this country is already unduly large!' This is also a justification offered for internal controls and the denial of welfare provision based on immigration status.

THEORIES OF UNDERPOPULATION

A variant of the above is not so much that there is an overpopulation of 'foreigners' but that there is an underpopulation of the supposedly indigenous white British inhabitants. This is overtly racist.

The erection of the post–1945 welfare state was justified by theories of underpopulation which were themselves then linked to eugenicist arguments. These theories and not any universalist concept of welfare inspired William Beveridge whose report provided the ideological basis for the welfare state. Beveridge justified family allowances as replenishing the nation following wartime slaughter. He wrote: 'A civilised community should be concerned with its own breed... Pride of race is a reality for the British.'[4] Richard Titmuss, the famous ideologue of welfare, was inspired by similar eugenicist, underpopulationist theories. He wrote: 'The future of the white peoples now depends in the main not upon further reductions in mortality but upon their birth rate.'[5]

LABOURISM AND WELFARISM

These ideologies gained acceptance because they were spread by mass organisations. The two sources spearheading agitation for controls were rooted among the urban masses. This explains why controls today have widespread support. Ideology does not disappear with time. Unless resisted it grows through reproduction.

One source of agitation was the trade union and early socialist movement. In 1892 the Trades Union Congress (TUC) passed a resolution 'to prevent the landing of foreign pauper aliens to our shores'.[6] Ben Tillett, a rank-and-file dockers' leader and member of the Independent Labour Party (ILP), argued for controls at the London Trades Council. He denounced Jews in *Labour Leader*, the ILP's paper, as 'the most consistent and determined money grubber we know' (19 December 1894). This image of Jew as capitalist contrasts with the TUC's image of Jew as pauper.

The labour movement legitimised the nexus between controls and welfare. Industrial unionism, socialist organisation, the demand for immigration controls and the movement for national welfare reform arose at this time and converged, with honourable exceptions, at their birth. In 1895 the TUC held a conference devising questions for parliamentary candidates. These linked progressive demands for reform of the Poor Law, health and safety legislation, abolition of the House of Lords and the nationalisation of the means of production with the reactionary demand for immigration control (*Manchester Evening News* 11 July 1895). Demands for welfare reform combined with a virulent nationalism, expressed through state control of foreign workers, provided the ingredients for what is now described as *labourism*. The conceptualisation of welfare as limited to British nationals and designed to improve the British 'stock' defined *welfarism* as a narrow, jingoistic construct.

BRITISH BROTHERS LEAGUE

Much of the above is hidden history but not hidden from fascistic movements. In March 1980 *Spearhead*, the then magazine of the National Front, praised 'the obvious patriotism and candid racialism of these early socialists'. Ironically modern fascists seem unaware that the other source of agitation for the 1905 Act was a proto-fascist group – the British Brothers League. This existed between 1901 and 1905. Its base was London's East End. By 1902 it claimed 12,000 members, eight branches and had presented a petition to parliament of 45,000 signatures (*Jewish Chronicle* 31 October 1902). It mounted spectacular rallies. The *Jewish Chronicle* of 17 January and the *East London Observer* of 18 January 1902 reported an indoor rally attracting 4000 supporters at which Marie Corelli's letter was read. It was preceded by demonstrations from Stepney, Hackney, Shoreditch and Bethnal Green.

The rally passed resolutions linking controls and welfare, namely:

> That this meeting is of the opinion that the housing problem in London is insoluble until the immigration of the foreign houseless poor is prevented [and] That this meeting declares that the continued influx of destitute aliens tends to lower the standard of life desirable for English citizens.

POST-WAR CONTROLS

The pattern was repeated post–1945. The 1955 General Council Report to the TUC conference reported a delegation visiting the Minister of Labour, telling him: 'The Government must have a policy which could ensure that the rate of immigration could be controlled.'[7] The 1962 Commonwealth Immigrants Act was a victory for so-called 'race-riots' in Notting Hill and Nottingham in 1958. These uprisings against black people linked controls to welfare. The *Manchester Guardian* of 2 September 1958 reported Oswald Moseley's fascistic Union Movement circulating a leaflet stating 'Protect your jobs. Stop coloured immigration. Houses for white people – not coloured immigrants!'

CONTROLS AND DEFINITION OF STATE

The argument for 'fair' controls ignores the issue of national identity and state definition. In the nineteenth century imperialist glory gave Britain its national identity. With the decline of imperialism it is twentieth-century immigration control, defining who can come and who can remain, providing this identity.

A parliamentary debate of 15 February 1983 tightening the marriage rules illustrates this. It is not coincidental that the question of national identity was posed in respect of the construct of family acceptable within immigration control. The nexus between controls, the family and welfare state is critical.

Harvey Proctor MP said: 'The main battlefield in defence of national identity has been located in the debates over the immigration rules.'

John Stokes MP stated:

> Control of immigration into this country is absolutely vital for our national identity and cohesion…after defending the nation and keeping the Queen's peace, the government's responsibility for control of immigration is of the next importance. It is no use being mealy-mouthed on this subject. It is not sufficient to say that control of immigration is in the interests of good race relations. It is necessary in the interests of something even more important than that. The control is necessary for our very survival as a nation – so that England, which has survived for 1000 years with its incomparable history and contribution to civilisation, can remain recognisably and unmistakably English.

These views represent mainstream political opinion. In the *Mail on Sunday* of 19 February 1995 Kenneth Baker, a former Home Secretary, wrote: 'the autonomy of a country in policing its borders is just as vital in preserving national sovereignty as currency or any other matter.'

KINDER, KIRCHE, KÜCHE

The case of Viraj Mendis in the 1980s received international publicity after he was given church sanctuary (see Chapter 19). The *Daily Star* of 4 April 1987 denounced him as an 'atheist and a revolutionary communist and therefore an enemy of Church and State'.

Justifications for controls are saturated with the themes of 'race', family and church. These are the pillars of nation which controls are designed to protect – pillars reminiscent of the Nazi trinity of 'Kinder, Kirche und Küche'. The ideological nexus between controls and Christianity has been seen in the case of the marriage rules (see Chapter 5). A *Daily Star* editorial of 9 May 1988 invoked the language of the Crusades, condemning a suggested 'network of sanctuaries for illegal immigrants… It is not as if these wretches are Christians; they despise our faith and are fighting holy wars to destroy us'. Ideology going back one thousand years cannot simply be ignored and replaced by an ideologically 'fair' theory for controls.

BODIES OF ARMED MEN AND THE 1999 IMMIGRATION AND ASYLUM ACT

A feature of controls is state power compared to individual powerlessness. This transcends issues of fairness. Frederick Engels in his 1884 book *Origin of the Family, Private Property and the State* coined his phrase about the state being a body of armed men.[8] Engels never had immigration controls in contemplation.

However, controls are central to the state's repressive mechanisms. Violence is the ultimate sanction in control enforcement. This is illustrated by the notorious death on 28 July 1993 of Joy Gardner while being arrested by the police and immigration service. It is confirmed by the 1999 legislation which raises immigration officers' powers to those of the police without even any independent body to investigate abuse. Immigration officers are trained both to resist and inflict violence in enforcing arrests. The *Independent* of 19 May 1999 reported: 'Immigration officers are to be taught how to use CS spray and batons, shown how to handle and restrain prisoners and be instructed in unarmed combat.' This duress is not surprising. Rather it is inevitable once the need for controls is accepted. However, it is hardly 'fair'.

IMMIGRATION SERVICE UNION

Immigration officers have organised themselves politically through their own union, the Immigration Service Union (ISU), which has been refused TUC affiliation. The ISU broke away from the Society of Civil and Public Servants in 1981. It has taken on the role of agitator for harsher controls. For instance in September and October 1986 it ran a massive press campaign forcing the government to impose visa controls on Indian subcontinent nationals. By 15 October the *Independent* was describing the ISU and not the Home Office as virtually running Heathrow through instructing its members as to whom to refuse entry. This is described in *For a World Without Borders* (published 1992 by GMIAU). The ISU is clear that controls are never about fairness but are politically driven.

CONTROLS AS ANTI-WORKING CLASS

The poor are the main victims of controls. They cannot meet the 'public fund' requirements. Proposals in *Strangers and Citizens* would increase this class bias. It argues for 'entrepreneurial immigration'(p.200) and a 'system of positive selection of those migrants with most to contribute' (p.344).

Controls weaken working-class organisation. This is ironic given union support for their imposition. Section 3 of the 1919 Alien Restriction (Amendment) Act stated:

> If an alien promotes or attempts to promote industrial unrest in any industry in which he has not been bona fide engaged for at least two years immediately preceding in the United Kingdom he shall be liable on summary conviction to imprisonment for a term not exceeding three months.

A court sentence could carry a recommendation for deportation. This section, not used for many years, has never been repealed. Throughout the 1920s it was regularly used to deport Jewish members of the Communist Party.[9] In a parliamentary debate of 22 October 1919 Colonel Wedgewood, opposing the law, said:

I understand that there are numerous officials of Jewish trade unions in the East End, most of which unions are affiliated with the local trade and labour council, and the officials are already resigning from their posts as secretaries and from the trade and labour councils because they are afraid that, by being on the trades and labour councils, they may involve themselves on a charge of promoting or attempting to promote industrial unrest.

INTERNATIONAL LEGITIMISATION OF CONTROL OF FREE MOVEMENT

The UK is not unique in its controls and in linking status to entitlements. Every industrial and imperial metropolis has similar restrictions. For black people and refugees it is not Fortress Europe. It is Fortress World. It is not only imperialist countries exercising controls. The elites in countries devastated by imperialism resort to controls to sustain economies perpetually on the verge of collapse. None of this can have anything to do with 'fairness'. It is driven by global economic forces underpinned by a global racism. Examples are:

- In 1996 the USA enacted the Personal Responsibility and Work Opportunity Reconciliation Act excluding lawfully settled residents without USA citizenship from accessing many means-tested benefits.

- Japanese controls and the use of cheap Pakistani labour has resulted in increased racism. The *International Herald Tribune* of 4 January 1990 reported:

  > A month ago, for example, the National Police Agency acknowledged that it had circulated an internal memo to police stations that Pakistanis working in Japan have a unique body odour, carry infectious diseases and tell lies 'under the name of Allah'.

- The Dominican Republic has an economy exploited by the world sugar market. In its turn it superexploits Haitian migrant labour during the harvest season only to subsequently expel this labour. The *Guardian* of 4 September 1998 reported on 'the near-slavery endured by Haitian labourers in the Dominican Republic and the abuse of their rights by a government that refuses to grant them legal status'.

- The Baltic states (Lithuania, Latvia and Estonia) are, following the break-up of the USSR, in transition to capitalism. Since independence in 1991 they have erected controls. These controls have little to do with their own economies. They have everything to do with the economies of the EU, which the Baltic states are anxious to join. The EU sees these countries as a buffer zone excluding refugees and migrants from mainland Europe. The Nordic states (Sweden, Denmark, Norway) help to finance this zone.[10]

CONTROLS AS A PRODUCT OF ECONOMIC FORCES

The economic forces behind immigration restrictions are far more powerful than considerations of 'fairness'. This is a world where freedom of movement is not so much prevented as controlled to ensure that sufficient, but no more than sufficient, numbers of dispossessed workers and peasantry of the Third World become transformed into the undocumented and superexploited underclass of the metropolitan ghettos. It is a world where immigration controls can be turned on or off like a tap depending on perceived economic need. At the time when the UK government is implementing its 1999 legislation and the fast-track deportation of unskilled refugees it has announced plans for 'fast track entry for skilled foreigners' from Asia and Eastern Europe 'to ease shortages of key workers in booming industries such as IT management and engineering'. This was reported in the *Guardian* of 3 May 2000. The following day the *Guardian* ran an article about the UK, the USA and Japan headed 'We need more immigrants – the young and skilled are in desperately short supply'. On the other hand and at the other extreme, many economies tolerate the presence of untrained alleged unlawful entrants precisely because their status allows for super exploitation. A *Guardian* article of 22 March 2000 headed 'Immigrants needed to keep West working' describes how a ship carrying 825 Kurdish asylum-seekers was washed ashore in Calabria, Italy. The Italian government positively welcomed the Kurds as providers of cheap, unskilled labour.

In the face of these global economic forces the issue is not at all one of 'fair' controls. Rather it is one of no immigration controls combined with adequate labour laws to protect the wages and conditions of migrants, immigrants and asylum-seekers.

WHAT IS UTOPIC? WHAT IS REASONABLE?

Advocates of the retention of UK immigration laws but on the basis of 'fairness' emphasise that all other states have immigration controls and that there exists no model of a country comparable to the UK without controls. Therefore it is suggested that abolition of control is utopic and unattainable but reform is reasonable and achievable. The reverse is the case.

Abolishing controls would require a huge political movement. It might even require a revolution. However, attempts to reformulate controls as 'fair' would require a miracle. It is futile. It is as futile as King Canute's attempt to turn back the sea. Immigration restrictions borne out of anti-Semitism and anti-black racism cannot simply have their history rolled back leaving controls but jettisoning the racist theories sustaining them. Advocates of 'fair' controls ignore issues of welfare. Any system of 'non-discriminatory' law would require rewriting the welfare system. Controls represent a victory for fascistic organisations pre–1914 and post–1945. No legislative regime created out of such activity can be rendered 'non-racist'.

The fact that other countries have controls is not an argument to retain controls in the UK. Just the opposite. The fact that controls exist elsewhere simply shows that the ideology of control is international, which is a paradox given the nationalism used to justify controls. It is this paradox, this contradiction, which is a weak link in the chain of controls now stretching round the world.

These arguments have been played out historically once before. In the early years of the twentieth century supporters of protectionism, that is support for import controls and against free trade, pointed to the fact that other newly industrialised states did not practise free trade. Ironically the movement in favour of import controls was called 'fair trade' and its leading advocate, Joseph Chamberlain, also agitated for immigration controls against the free movement of labour. However, in the debate over import controls it was the 'free traders' who won out (though ironically in the debate over control on the free movement of people it was the restrictionists who won out).[11]

Finally, it is also incorrect to argue that in the modern world there exists no model of a regime without controls. There does exist such a model, albeit an imperfect one. This is the European Economic Area. This is imperfect in that to the outside world the EEA constitutes 'Fortress Europe' and to those within the EEA who do not have a nationality of a member state there is no freedom of movement (see Chapter 3). However, for those with an EEA nationality, or who are part of the family of an EEA national, there is freedom of movement. This is a freedom entitling millions of, mainly white, people to come to the UK. It is also a freedom which is simply ignored by those who campaign for controls on the basis that the UK is overpopulated.

Good practice

The alternative to the present law is not 'fair' controls but no controls. This argument is relevant for welfare professionals, legal advisors and community activists. It has consequences for anti-racist workplace practice.

CONTESTING ALL CASES

A position predicated on the inherent racism of controls means that no distinction can be made between 'worthy' and 'unworthy' cases. Likewise it is wrong for advisors to contest only apparently 'winnable' cases. Honesty is essential about the chances, or lack of them, of winning cases. However, given tactical acumen, there are sometimes surprising victories. Dividing cases into the 'winnable' and 'unwinnable' reproduces the issue of meritorious and non-meritorious cases which itself presupposes a distinction between fair and unfair controls.

TACTICS NOT FAIRNESS

Controls can present themselves as non-discriminatory. The immigration rules state that officials 'will carry out their duties without regard to the race, colour or religion of persons seeking to enter or remain in the United Kingdom'. Most people equate law with justice and therefore many welfare professionals assume that 'fairness' will in the last resort be shown by immigration officials. Because controls can never be fair, issues of tactics become central to good practice.

COLLECTIVISING CASES AND CAMPAIGNS

A position of opposition to all controls means adopting critical positions towards 'compassionate' grounds and not stereotyping clients as victims (see Chapter 10). It requires challenging the legitimacy of controls through supporting campaigns (see Chapter 19). It means collectivising cases and campaigns.

The conventional approach to casework is to prepare cases individually. The political nature of immigration cases means exploring and offering clients a different approach – which can of course be rejected. This is to move away from the atomisation of cases towards collectivising them. It is the atomisation of casework which leaves clients vulnerable to be picked off one by one by the Home Office. Collectivising cases helps to prevent this.

- Clients should be encouraged to meet others who have or have had the same predicament. This allows for shared learning, reassuring clients that their situation is not unique.

- Advisors should organise surgeries so that clients facing the same problem have the opportunity to meet.

- Campaigns can be collectivised on various levels by bringing together those in similar circumstances (see Chapter 19).

MALE VIOLENCE

A policy question in the Introduction to this book is 'Should support be given to someone under threat of expulsion following violence or other abuse to women or children?' One example sometimes met by probation officers is that of a non-British client subject to deportation following a rape or paedophilia conviction. Another example is that of marriage breakdown within the probationary period following domestic violence leading to the male partner's removal.

These scenarios appear to give controls the power to punish unacceptable behaviour. This is false. Controls are never about enforcing codes of behaviour. They are about enforcing status. They are about controlling black people and refugees. The deportation of a criminal offender has nothing to do with the offence. It has everything to do with the immigration status of the offender. Otherwise a British prisoner would not be immune and transportation overseas would remain a punishment as it was in the eighteenth century (see Chapter 18). Nor is it about public protection. Deportation removes the danger overseas, which itself can be viewed as racist. The same applies to expulsion of the male partner following domestic violence and marriage break-up. If removing a woman following the disintegration of marriage is racist then it is equally racist to remove a man irrespective of the reasons for disintegration.

This is an area where the 'personal' and the 'political' not so much meet as collide. There is a conflict between the racism of controls and the sexism of male behaviour. The conflict may be irresolvable in a society where both are prevalent and where there exist no mass movements challenging either. The existence of such movements might allow for some political resolution to the issue rather than it presenting itself as an individual choice by welfare practitioners or advisors as to whether and how to act for the client. It would be wrong to posit one side of the conflict, the racism or the sexism, as being more important than the other.

An analogous question raised in this book's Introduction is 'Can controls ever be used for progressive purposes – such as denying entry to rapists?' This question assumed national prominence with the entry of Mike Tyson described above. The case raises many questions, not least the Home Secretary's hypocrisy in allowing entry for Tyson on 'compassionate' grounds, but denying entry to thousands of members of globally divided families. However, it is extremely problematic to call for racist laws to be used against misogynous men. It strengthens the law, leaving untouched the misogyny.

UNIONISING THE UNDOCUMENTED

Another example of the repressive nature of controls preventing their use for progressive or 'fair' purposes is sanctions against employers for hiring undocumented labour (see Chapters 3 and 20). The 1978 report of the Labour-majority House of Commons Select Committee on Race Relations recommended sanctions and showed the TUC supporting sanctions, though both Labour and the TUC opposed their introduction in 1996 by the Tories. Historically the labour movement has used two arguments justifying sanctions as progressive. First, unauthorised, undocumented labour undermines wages and conditions. Second, such labour is itself superexploited. However, transforming employers into Home Office agents cannot defend wages or conditions nor prevent exploitation. This was the position of Manchester's Policy Committee of 20 January 1997. A chief executive report welcomed sanctions as preventing sweated labour. The committee correctly rejected this, arguing that encouraging employers to check immigration status would increase their powers of exploitation. None the less this Council now checks the status of its new workers. Politically what is required against sweated labour is unionisation of the undocumented and a campaign for regularisation of status.

REGULATION OF IMMIGRATION ADVISORS

The 1999 legislation introduced the regulation of advisors (see Chapter 4). This again shows how controls cannot be used for progressive purposes, including regulating themselves. The banning of racketeering advisors will drive the industry underground. It is a major step towards rendering ineffective or outlawing agencies which offer dedicated professional help alongside a political position of opposition to controls. The Act states that the Immigration Services Commissioner should ensure advisors 'do not seek to abuse any procedure...in connection with immigration or asylum including any appellate or other judicial procedure'. The legislation also allows for the future possibility of advisors being fined by the Immigration Appeal Tribunal for contesting appeals without 'merit'. What distinguishes law centres, immigration aid units and committed private solicitors is their determination to use any legal and tactical procedure for the client's advantage. This can be contrasted with racketeers who prolong cases to hike up fees. Politically committed advisors are now open to allegations of 'abuse' and to be penalised because of their commitment.

In the 1930s there developed a similar phenomenon of crooked advisors. The *Jewish Chronicle* of June 1940 advertised the services of Eli Fox 'Insurance Broker and Naturalisation Agent' in Manchester. The only way to abolish crooked immigration advisors is to abolish immigration controls.

THE REGULATORY SCHEME AND LOCAL OR VOLUNTARY SECTOR WORKERS

It is also unclear who falls within prescribed exemptions to the scheme. This leaves open other forms of restraint on those helping immigrants, migrants and asylum-seekers. Immigration practitioners will be within the scheme though barristers, solicitors and legal executives will be regulated through their own professional bodies. Members of Parliament and government employees will be exempt. A letter of 4 May 2000 from the Immigration Advisors Unit of the IND states: 'advising someone to seek immigration advice would not be caught [within the regulatory scheme] providing that no initial immigration advice was given'. A letter from the Policy Directorate of the IND of 7 March 2000 suggests that social workers, benefit advisors and women's refuge workers providing immigration advice 'in the course of their business' will not be exempt unless employed by a government department.[12] Any attempt to control local and voluntary sector workers will be regressive and should be met by legal challenge.

NON-COMPLIANCE

Internal controls demand guidance in workplace practice for welfare workers. Another question raised in the Introduction was 'Can there be good anti-racist practice in the face of inherently racist laws?' Such practice is viable, hence the practice guides in this book, but only within a context where issues of non-compliance and non-cooperation are viewed as professional issues based on non-discriminatory practice (see Chapter 20).

BATTLE FOR IDEAS

The essential racism of controls makes it impossible to reformulate restrictions rendering them 'fair'. There is a battle for ideas taking place and no concession should be made to the reactionary ideas underpinning controls. This can be seen in single-issue campaigns where the issue has often been posed as one of sexual or gender 'equality' while ignoring the nationalism and racism within controls (see Chapter 2).

The argument here is not against campaigns for the repeal of particular aspects of controls. What is being argued is that the politically incorrect basis of some campaigns has encouraged the Home Office to level down the rights of others to effect a spurious equality based on the lowest common denominator.

JUST ANOTHER BRICK IN THE WALL

Sometimes the demand for 'fair' controls is posed in terms of the repeal of the latest piece of legislation, which today means the 1999 Act. This is inadequate. It leaves a century of legislation intact. Each new law is just another brick in the wall of controls. Removing one brick is insufficient and it is utopic to consider that bricks can be removed one at a time going back to 1905. The whole wall has to go.

AN ALTERNATIVE TRADITION

This is a tradition opposing all controls. It is found in communities directly under threat and is based on the self-organisation of those threatened. It can be seen in the struggle over the 1905 Aliens Act. The imposition of the Act met with opposition from Jewish workers. The *Jewish Chronicle* of 21 August 1894 reported a demonstration being held in Whitechapel against TUC support for controls. It passed the following resolution:

> This mass meeting of Jewish trade unionists is of the opinion that the vast amount of poverty and misery which exist is in no way due to the influx of foreign workmen, but is the result of the private ownership of the means of production; and this meeting calls upon the government to pass a universal compulsory eight hours a day with a minimum wage as an instalment of future reform.

Jewish opposition, though insufficient to defeat the legislation, neutralised English trade union support for controls and persuaded some trade unionists to oppose controls. The *Eastern Post* of 20 September 1902 reported Jewish workers organising a rally against controls in Whitechapel. On the platform were W.P. Reeves of the Women's Union League, Margaret Bondfield, Secretary to the National Union of Shop Assistants, Frank Brian of the Dockers' Union and Alderman Hayday of the Gasworkers' Union.

The pattern repeated itself in the second half of the century. Black people took the initiative in organising against controls. A demonstration against the proposed 1971 Immigration Act was described by the *Times* of 5 April 1971:

> Indian, Pakistan and West Indian immigrant organisations from all over Britain marched through London...protesting against the Immigration Bill... A dozen organisations including the Supreme Council of Sikhs, the Indian Workers Association and the West Indian Standing Conference took part.

This tradition of opposition to all controls has not disappeared. It re-emerges in miniature each time someone demands to come or remain irrespective of the rules. It is a tradition which has made trade unions rethink their position on controls to the extent that they will support individual campaigns against expulsion.

NO ONE IS ILLEGAL

The language of controls shows that issues of fairness are irrelevant. In all other areas of law it is the activity that is unlawful not the person. Under immigration law human beings are reduced to being non-persons, to being 'illegal'. This is a status redolent of the medieval outlaw where whole groups of people are literally outside the protection of the law. As the law changes so yesterday's lawful entrant becomes tomorrow's illegal immigrant. All good immigration practice is based on an awareness that 'No one is illegal'.

Comments on casework problem at start of chapter

If the husband has been given permanent settlement, it is highly unlikely that the Home Office would reopen the case. It normally does this only where it suspects there exists a financial marriage racket. If the husband has not yet been given settlement, your role as an immigration advisor is not to advise on how to effect expulsion; in fact the husband may ask for your help. However, for the husband to obtain settlement he will need a letter from his wife, which obviously will not be forthcoming.

Notes

1   It is intended to introduce new rules denying entry to people sentenced to a prison sentence of ten years or more or for a crime involving violence, sexual violence or guns. A discretion to allow entry will remain in exceptional circumstances (Guardian 25 October 2000)
2   See extended book review by Steve Cohen in *INLP*, vol. 8, no. 4, 1994.
3   Cmnd 2739, para. 12
4   'Child allowances and the race', in *The Pillars of Security* (Unwin Brothers 1943)
5   Problems of Population (English Universities Press 1944)
6   Trades Union Congress Report 1892, pp.53 and 69
7   *Workers' Control not Immigration Controls*, p.16
8   On pp.206–7 of 1978 edition by Foreign Languages Press, Peking
9   Steve Cohen, 'Anti-communism in the construction of immigration controls', *INLP*, January 1990
10   Steve Cohen, 'Lithuania here I come', *INLP*, vol. 13, no. 3, 1999
11   See Gainer, *The Alien Invasion* (Heinemann 1972) ch. 6 and Cohen, *It's the Same Old Story* (Manchester City Council 1987) p.12, on the relationship between the movements for control on goods and on labour
12   IMG/99 20/93/1

Appendix: Useful addresses

These addresses are for organisations referred to in this book.

They are included primarily to locate the publications, including government publications, mentioned in the study. Some of the literature referred to in the text is no longer in print but may be available from the Ahmed Iqbal Ullah Anti-Racist Archives, which have been established in Manchester. Home Office letters to which reference is made and which were sent to the author are also deposited in these archives. Many of the other letters quoted were circulated in the regular mailings of the Immigration and Legal Practitioners' Association.

Most of the (non-governmental) organisations listed have other functions, such as campaigning, training or giving advice. GMIAU and JCWI are the lead organisations in providing immigration advice and representation and training. They also produce publications and will advise on campaigns. ILPA provides training as well as producing its own publications.

AGENCIES OFFERING ADVICE AND REPRESENTATION

Greater Manchester Immigration Aid Unit
400 Cheetham Hill Rd
Manchester M8 9LE
Tel: 0161 740 7722
Email: gmiau@ein.org.uk

Joint Council for the Welfare of Immigrants
115 Old St
London EC1V 9RT
Tel: 020 7251 8708
Email: jcwi@jcwi.org.uk
Website: www.jcwi.org.uk

Children's Legal Centre
University of Essex
Wivenhoe Park
Colchester Essex C04 3SQ
Tel: 01206 873820

Human Rights and Public Law Telephone Line
c/o Public Law Project
Birkbeck College
Malet St
London WC1E 7HX
Tel: 0808 808 4546
or c/o Liberty
21 Tabard St
London SE1 4LA

Immigration Advisory Service

County House
190 Great Dover St
London SE1 4YB
Tel: 020 7357 6917
24 hour helpline: 020 8814 1559

Law Centres Federation

Duchess House
18–19 Warren St
London W1P 5DB
Tel: 020 7387 8570

London Advice Services Alliance

2nd Floor
Universal House
88–94 Wentworth St
London E1 7SA
Tel: 020 7377 2748
Email: info@lasa.org.uk
Website: www.lasa.org.uk

Refugee Council

Bondway House
3–6 Bondway
London SW8 1SJ
Tel: 020 7582 6922/020 7582 4947
(Unaccompanied child asylum-seekers panel)
Website: www.gn.apc.org/refugeecounciluk/

Refugee Legal Centre

Sussex House
39–45 Bermondsey St
London SE1 3XF
Tel: 020 7827 9090
Email: ric@refugee-legal-centre.org.uk/
Website: www.refugee-legal-centre.org.uk/

reunite: International Child Abduction Centre

PO Box 24875
London E1 6FR
Tel: 020 7375 3441(admin)
020 7375 3440 (advice line)
Email: reunite@dircon.co.uk
Website: www.reunite.org

South Manchester Law Centre

584 Stockport Rd
Longsight
Manchester M13 0RQ
Tel: 0161 225 5111
Email: s-mcr-lawcentre@dial.pipex.co

Terrence Higgins Trust
52–54 Gray's Inn Rd
London WC1X 8JU
Tel: 020 7831 0330

UKCOSA Council for International Education
9–17 St Albans Place
London N1 ONX
Tel: 020 7226 3762
Email: enquiries@ukcosa.org.uk
Website: www.ukcosa.org.uk

CAMPAIGN ORGANISATIONS

Cambridgeshire Against Refugee Detention c/o CUSU
11–12 Trumpington St
Cambridge CB2 1QA
Email: card@zensearch.net
Website: ban.joh.cam.ac.uk/-maicl/CARD.html

Campaign Against Double Punishment c/o POPs
Suite 4b Building 1
Wilson Park
Monsal Rd
Manchester M40 8WN
Tel: 0161 277 9066
Email: families@surfaid.org

Campaign to Close Campsfield
111 Magdalen Rd
East Oxford OX4 IRQ
Tel: 01865 558 145/01865 557 282
Email: BMackeith@aol.com
Website: users.ox.ac.uk/-asylu

Close Harmondsworth Campaign
10 Endsleigh St
Southall
Middlesex UB2 5QL
Tel: 020 8571 5019

Migrants Against HIV/AIDS
70 rue de la Fraternité
93170 Bagnolet
France
Tel: + 33 06 80 87 48 60
Email: migrants@hivnet.ch
Website: www.aegis.com/maha/home.html

National Coalition of Anti-Deportation Campaigns
110 Hamstead Road
Birmingham B20 2QS
Tel: 0121 554 6947
Email: ncadc@ncadc.org.uk
Website: www.ncadc.org.uk/

Refugee Women's Legal Group c/o Immigration Law Practitioners' Association (see below)

Schools Against Deportation c/o Institute of Race Relations
2–6 Leeke St
King's Cross Rd
London WC1X 9HS
Tel: 020 7837 0041
Website: www.homebeats.co.uk/sad/index.htm

Southall Black Sisters
52 Norwood Rd
Southall
Middlesex UB2 4DW
Tel: 020 8571 9595

Stonewall Immigration Group
c/o Central Station
37 Wharfdale Rd
Islington
London N1 9SE
Tel: 020 7713 0620
Email: info@stonewall-immigration.org.uk
Website: www.stonewall-immigration.org.uk

TRADE UNIONS

UNISON
1 Mabledon Place
London WC1H 9AJ
Tel: 020 7388 2366

UNISON (Lambeth branch)
6A Acre Lane
London SW2 5SG
Tel: 020 7737 2134

SPECIALISED SOURCES FOR REPORTS

Amnesty International
99–119 Rosebery Avenue
London EC1R 4RE
Website for country reports: www.amnesty/alibi/index.html

International Gay and Lesbian Human Rights Commission
Asylum Project
1360 Mission St
Suite 200
San Francisco CA 94103
USA
Tel: + 1 415 255 8680
Email: iglhrc@iglhrc.org
Website: www.iglhrc.org/

International Social Service
Cranmer House
39 Brixton Rd
London SW9 6DD
Tel: 020 7735 8941

Medical Foundation for the Care of Victims of Torture
96–98 Grafton Rd
London NW5 3EJ
Tel: 020 7284 4321

Refugee Studies Programme Documentation Centre
Queen Elizabeth House
University of Oxford
21 St Giles
Oxford OX1 3LA
Tel: 01865 270722
Email: rsc@qeh.ox.ac.uk
Website: www.qeh.ox.ac.uk/

UN Commission on Human Rights Reports
UNHCR
Millbank Tower
21–24 Millbank
London SW1P 4QP
Tel: 020 7828 9191
Website: www.unhcr.ch.refworld/un/un.htm

US Department of State Country Reports
US Department of State
Washington DC 20520
USA
Tel: + 1 202 647 4000
Website: www.state.gov/www/issues/human_rights

OTHER ORGANISATIONS

Ahmed Iqbal Ullah Archives
Ground Floor
Devonshire House Precinct Centre
Oxford Rd
Manchester M13 9PL
Tel: 0161 275 2920
Email: rrarchive@man.ac.uk
Website: http: //les.man.ac.uk/ rrarchive/

Association of Chief Officers of Probation
4th Floor
8–9 Grosvenor Place
London SW1X 9SH
Tel: 020 7823 2551

Barnardos
Tanners Lane
Barkingside
Ilford
Essex IG6 IQG
Tel: 020 8550 8822
Email: pdubarnardos@compuserve.com

British Agencies for Adoption and Fostering
Skyline House
200 Union St
London SE1 0LY
Tel: 020 7593 2000

British Medical Association
Archives Dept
BMA House
Tavistock Square
London WC1H 9JP
Tel: 020 7387 4499
Website: www.bma.org.uk

Chartered Institute of Environmental Health
Chadwick Court
15 Hatfields
London SE1 8DJ
Tel: 020 7928 6006
Email: cieh@cieh.org
Website: www.cieh.org.uk

Churches Together in Britain and Ireland (formerly) Council of Churches for Britain and Ireland
Inter-Church House
35–41 Lower Marsh
London SE1 7RL
Tel: 020 7620 4444
Email: trudy.thorose@ctbi.org.uk

Commission for Racial Equality
Elliott House
10–12 Allington St
London SW1E 5EH
Tel: 020 7828 7022

CRE publications are now sold through:
Central Books
99 Wallis Rd
Hackney
London E9 5LN
Tel: 020 8986 4854

Electronic Immigration Network
Progress Centre
Charlton Place
Ardwick Green
Manchester M12 6HS
Tel: 0161 273 7515
Email: admin@ein.org.uk
Website: www.ein.org.uk

Immigration Law Practitioners' Association (ILPA)
Lindsey House
40–42 Charterhouse St
London EC1M 6JN
Tel: 020 7251 8383
Email: info@ilpa.org.uk
Website: www.ilpa.org.uk

Local Government Association
Local Government House
Smith Square
London SW1P 3HZ
Tel: 020 7664 3000
Website: www.lga.gov.uk/lga/asylum/index.htm.
Sue Lukes
Email: suelukes@compuserve.com
Website: ourworld.compuserve.com/homepages/suelukes

Manchester Metropolitan University
Dept of Applied Community Studies
799 Wilmslow Rd
Didsbury
Manchester M20 2RR
Tel: 0161 247 2000

Mental Health Foundation
20–21 Cornwall Terrace
London NW1 4QL
Tel: 0207 535 7400
Email: mhf@mhf.org.uk
Website: www.mentalhealth.org.uk

Middlesex Area Probation Service
4th Floor Glen House
200 Tottenham Court Rd
London W1P 9LA
Tel: 020 7436 7121

National Association of Citizens' Advice Bureaux
Myddleton House
115–123 Pentonville Rd
London N1 9LZ
Tel: 020 7833 2181

North Birmingham Mental Health Trust
Academic Unit
Trust Headquarters
71 Fentham Rd
Erdington
Birmingham B23 6AL
Tel: 0121 6235 5000

North West Consortium for Asylum Seekers (East Region)
Minehead Resource Centre
Minehead Avenue
Withington
Manchester M20 IFM
Tel: 0161 448 9915

Nottingham Probation Service
Marina Rd
Nottingham NG7 1TP
Tel: 0115 935 1011

Post-Adoption Centre
5 Torriano Mews
Torriano Avenue
London NW5 2RZ
Tel: 020 7284 0555

Runnymede Trust
133 Aldersgate St
London ECIA 4JA
Tel: 020 7600 9666

St Philips Primary School
Loxford St
Hulme
Manchester M15 6BT
Tel: 0161 226 2050
Email: dalby@stphilips.manchester.sch.uk

Save the Children
17 Grove Lane
London SE5 8RD
Tel: 0207 703 5400
Website: www.savethechildren.org.uk

Shelter
88 Old St
London EC1V 9HU
Tel: 020 7505 2135
Website: www.shelter.org.uk

Workers' Educational Association
North West District
Crawford House
Precinct Centre
Oxford Rd
Manchester M13 9GM
Tel: 0161 273 7652

GOVERNMENT DEPARTMENTS/AGENCIES

Audit Commission Publications
Bookpoint Ltd
39 Milton Park
Abingdon
Oxon OX14 4TD
Tel: 0800 502030
Website (for full text of 'Another Country'):
www.audit-commission.gov.uk/ac2/NR/LocalA/prasylum.htm

Department for Education and Employment (*For the Guidance on Fees*)
International Students Team
Sanctuary Buildings
Great Smith St
Westminster
London SW1P 3BT
Tel: 020 7925 5324/5339

DfEE (*For Financial Support for Students: A Guide*)
Mowden Hall
Staindrop Rd
Darlington
Co. Durham DL3 9BG
Tel: 0800 731 9133
Website: www.dfee.gov.uk

DFEE (*For Code of Practice on School Admissions*)
DFEE Publications
PO Box 5050
Annesley
Nottingham NG15 ODJ
Tel: 0845 602 2260
Email: dfee@prologistics.co.uk

Department of Environment

Transport and Regions Zone 1/H5
Eland House
Bressenden Place
London SW1E 5DU
Tel: 020 7890 3665

Department of Health

Wellington House 133–155
Waterloo Rd
London SE1 8UG
Tel: 020 7972 2000
Website: www.open.gov.uk/doh/dhhome.htm

Department of Social Security

The Adelphi
1–11 John Adam St
London WC2N 6HT
Tel: 0207 712 2171

Further Education Funding Council

Cheylesmore House
Quinton Rd
Coventry CV1 2WT
Tel: 024 7686 3000
Website: www.fefc.ac.uk

Home Secretary (Minister's private office)

Home Office
Queen Anne's Gate
London SW1H 9AT
Tel: 020 7273 4604

The Housing Corporation

149 Tottenham Court Rd
London
WIP OBN
Email: enquiries@housingcorp.gov.uk
Website: www.housingcorp.gov.uk

Immigration and Nationality Directorate
Policy Directorate
Apollo House
36 Wellesley Rd
Croydon CR9 3RR
Tel: 0870 606 7766
Fax: 020 8760 8777
Website: www.homeoffice.gov.uk/ind/hpg: hpm

Immigration and Nationality Directorate
National Asylum Support Service
Quest House
11 Cross Rd
Croydon CR9 6EL
Tel: 020 8633 0572
Website: www.homeoffice.gov.uk/ind/assd/assd.htm

Immigration and Nationality Directorate
Application Form Unit
Block C Whitgift Centre
Wellesley Rd
Croydon CR9 1AT
Tel: 0870 241 0645 (for ordering forms)
0870 606 7766 (for inquiring as to the appropriate form)

The Joint Entry Clearance Unit (JECU)
89 Albert Embankment
London SE1 7TP
Tel: 020 7238 3858
Website: www.fco.gov.uk/travel/dynpage.asp

Social Services Inspectorate
Department of Health
Richmond House
79 Whitehall
London SW1A 2NS
Tel: 020 7972 4300

EXTRA-NATIONAL ORGANISATIONS

Council of Europe
Documentation
Centre Point 1
67075 Strasbourg Cedex
France
Tel: + 33 3 88 41 20 00
Email: point_i@coe.fr
Websites: www.coe.fr./. (home page)
www.coe.fr/tablconv/35t.htm (European Social Charter ratifications)

European Convention on Social and Medical Assistance Ratifications
Website: www.coe.fr/tablconv/14t.htm

United Nations High Commission for Refugees (UNHCR) (address given above)

Subject Index

access to children 169
accommodation, definition of 49
adoption 90
  coming to the UK as an adopted child
    91
  coming to the UK for adoption 90, 93
  demanding payment 99–100
  good practice
    and Judge Bracewell 100–1
    in local authority reports 100
  Hague Convention 1993 92
  informal (de facto) adoptions 91–2
  in the UK 172
  non-family and inter-family adoptions
    90
  problematic of 'full' adoptions 99
  procedures 93–4
  reports required for entry clearance 100
  seeking settlement as an adopted child
    91
  useful non-governmental guides 98–9
Adoption Act 1976 172
Adoption (Designation of Overseas
  Adoptions) Order 1973 91
Adoption (Intercountry Aspects) Act 1999
  92, 99
adoption orders 168
Adoption Panel 93
Adoption: The Future 99, 100
advisors *see* immigration advisors
advocacy 146
after-entry control 47
Africa 288
age, gender and sexuality 116–34
Ahmed Iqbal Ullah Anti-Racist Archives,
  Manchester 292, 334
Algeria 189, 204
Aliens Act 1905 18, 33, 36, 38, 117, 137,
  182, 263, 276, 316, 328
alien sexuality 41
Aliens Order 1920 137
Aliens Restriction Act 1914 33

Aliens Restriction (Amendment) Act 1919
  33, 35, 137, 313, 321
Allocation of Housing (England)
  Regulations 2000 209
America 277
Amnesty International 125, 130, 333
Another Country 223
anti-black racism 323
anti-semitism 323
appeals
  against refusal of family visits to the UK
    48–9
  preparing for 68
applications
  overseas forms 65
  importance to be given to forms 65–6
  and same-sex or unmarried heterosexual
    relationships 111
  in UK or overseas? 62
  from within UK 64–5
  where and when a settlement application
    should be made 102
Asia(ns) 33, 40, 73, 74, 183, 231, 251,
  263, 269, 288, 323
Association of Chief Officers of Probation
  (ACOP) 283, 284, 335
  Anti-Racism Action Group 283
Association of Chief Police Officers 213
Association of London Government (ALG)
  25, 309
asylum 116–34
  basic legal issues 118
  cases 116, 134
  falsification of history 117
  general good practice 126
  international framework of modern
    asylum law 118
  persecution of gay men and lesbians *see*
    under same-sex relationships
  persecution of women *see* gender issues:
    persecution of women
  politics of 117–18
  stereotyping non-Western countries
    118–19
  unaccompanied children 119–22
    fingerprinting and detection 121–2
    good practice 126–31

adjudicator guidelines in appeals
127–8
'Children First and Foremost'
128–9
draft guidelines on examination
and determination of asylum
claims by unaccompanied
refugee children 130–1
legal representation, local
authorities and asylum
determination process 129
legal representatives: ethics 126–7
other practice issues for legal
representatives 127
particular social work practice
issues in asylum determination
process 129–30
practice issues for schools 131
welfare issues, local authorities
and Children's Act 128
Home Office *Guidance Notes* and local
authority social services 121
Immigration Rules 119–20
Panel of Advisors for Refugee
Children 120–1
UN Convention on the Rights of the
Child 1989 120
UNHCR *Guidelines* 120
UNHCR *Handbook* 120
Asylum and Immigration Act 1996 21, 33,
50, 118, 186, 200, 206, 216, 237,
243, 256, 270
Asylum and Immigration Appeals Act
1993 33, 48, 118, 122
Asylum Processes Stakeholder Group 193
Asylum Screening Unit 24
'Asylum Seekers and Persons from Abroad:
New arrangements from April 2000'
193
Asylum-Seekers Service, Islington 187
Asylum Seekers Support 26, 196
Asylum Seekers Vouchers System – April
2000' 195
Asylum Support Appeals (Procedure) Rules
2000 193
Asylum Support (Interim Provisions)
Regulations 1999 193, 196–7, 216

Asylum Support Programme Steering
Group 307
Asylum Support Regulations 2000 190–1,
210–11, 218, 222, 227, 243
Asylum Support Voluntary Sector Action
Group 308
Australia 277
Audit Commission 213, 338
Austria(ns) 45, 91, 317
AWAZ 269

bad timing 142
Baltic states (Lithuania, Latvia, Estonia)
322
Bangladesh(is) 40, 46, 47, 86, 87, 91,
103, 104, 138, 184, 207, 299
Barnardos 119, 224, 335
Barnet, borough of 205
Belgium 45
Benefits Agency 185, 202, 303
benefits and immigration status 181–203
appealing against support refusal 192–3
Asylum and Immigration Act 1996 186
attendance allowance 188
cases 181, 203
child benefit 184, 188
child tax allowance 184
cost of travel to interviews and appeals
193
council tax benefit (CTB) 187, 193
critique of support scheme 195–6
disability living allowance 188
disabled person's tax credit 188
exemptions under the Social Security
(Immigration and Asylum)
Consequential Amendments
Regulations 2000 188–90
family and disability benefits 189–90
means-tested benefits 188–9
family allowances 184, 188
good practice 198–203
challenging new support scheme 200
charity support and the 1999 Act
201
claiming public funds 201–2
habitual residence 202–3
local authority charity initiatives 201

loopholes: challenging local authority refusals under National Assistance and Children Acts 199–200
national insurance numbers 202
searching for alternative legislation 200–1
state benefits 198
what is left of National Assistance Act 1948 and Children Act 1989 198–9
government forced to agree vouchers review 196
habitual residency 184–5
hard cases fund 192
application form and notes 192
history
pre–1914 182
1919–45 183
post–1945 183
housing benefit (HB) 183, 187, 193
Immigration and Asylum Act 1999: exclusion from state benefit 187–8
income-based jobseeker's allowance 187, 194
income support 187, 193, 194
Inland Revenue 184
interim provision 196–7
invalid care allowance 188
liaison with Home Office 185
modern law and practice 185
living with friends/relatives on benefits 193–4
national Assistance Act 1948 and Children Act 1989 186–7
national insurance (NI) numbers 185
new proposals 197–8
new 'support' scheme: Asylum Support Regulations 2000 190
details 191
phasing in of full support scheme 197
pre-history 182
restrictions on National Assistance Act 1948 and Children Act 1989 190
severe disablement allowance 188
social fund payment 187
social services 187
liaison with Home Office 187

surveillance of supported asylum-seekers 194–5
working families' tax credit 188
Zimbabwean farmers and the Income-Related Benefits and Jobseeker's Allowance (Amendment) Regulations 2000 198
bereavement of a partner 142
Best Practice Guide to Asylum Appeals 126
Birmingham 184, 206, 299
Birmingham Community Development Project 184
black people 183
bottomless pit theory 40
intrusiveness applied to 75
Board of Deputies of British Jews 205, 276
Bolton Council's Environmental Department 220
Bolton Education Authority 167
Bradford 292
British Agencies for Adoption and Fostering (BAAF) 90, 98
British Airways 120
British Brothers League 319
British citizenship 46–7
naturalisation forms for 66–7
British Dependent Territories 46
British Medical Association 251, 256, 263, 270, 335
present position of 270–1
British Nationality Act 1948 41
British Nationality Act 1981 33, 46, 47, 51, 53, 168, 176, 287
Bury Metropolitan Borough Council 212, 217

Cambridgeshire Against Refugee Detention 332
Camden Council 310
Campaign Against Double Punishment 276, 283, 332
campaigns
cases
hypothetical 17, 44, 53, 70, 73, 85, 86, 103, 105, 114–15, 116, 134, 135, 152, 153, 164, 165, 176, 181, 203, 204, 227, 229, 241,

242, 247–8, 249, 260, 262, 274,
    275, 288, 291, 301, 302, 312,
    313, 329
real
    A and B (gay relationship) 153
    Algerian asylum-seeker 204
    Andy Anderson 275–6
    Anwar Haq 136
    Anwar Ditta's family 86, 264,
        293
    Assadi family 249
    Atia Idrees 268
    destitute asylum-seeker in
        Kensington and Chelsea 181
    Dhanniah Hahiru Alghali 167
    Dora Amoako 302
    Fleur 171
    Florence Okolo 154, 160, 162,
        297–8
    Hanif's son 170
    Khalid Khan 167, 169, 173
    Manda Kunda 135, 142
    Marion Gaima 298
    Michelle Ricablanca 165, 174
    Mike Tyson 313
    Mohammed Butt 262
    Ms J (Pakistani woman) 116
    Najat Chaffee 157
    Nasira Begum 293
    Nasreen Achtar 141
    Onibiyo family 291, 299
    Paul Ho 229
    Rahman family 54, 135, 140,
        146, 167, 242, 298
    Siddique family 73
    Sorin Mihai 105
    Viraj Mendis 293
    Yaqoob (Pakistani heart patient)
        44
general 163
good practice 293–300
    avoid triumphalism 297
    basic good practice points about
        campaigns 295
    campaign leaflet 299–300
    campaigns as a way of obtaining
        professional reports 297
    collectivising campaigns 298–9

demanding support, not begging for
        it 298
    getting support of other organisations
        300
    'humanitarian' or 'political'
        campaign? 297
    Internet technology – international
        support 300
    judicial recognition of campaigns 294
    no guarantees 296–7
    organising campaign 299
    other campaign material 300
    role of child client 296
    role of client in campaign 294
    role of legal advisor in campaign 294
    role of local authorities in campaign
        23, 293
    role of welfare professionals in
        campaign 293–4
    when should campaign begin?
        Immigration and Asylum Act
        1999 295
        other questions asked by clients
            296
history 292–3
professional practice and 291–301
Campaign to Close Campsfield 332
Campsfield House Detention Centre,
    Kidlington, Oxfordshire 284, 299
Canada 40, 119, 288
Cardiff 276–7
carers 267–8
    of children 272
Carers (1968) 267
Carers (Recognition and Service) Act
    (1995) 272
Caring for People (1989) 272
Caribbean(s) 89, 288
carriers' liability and employer sanctions
    50
Central Point of Contact Unit (CPC) 24
Channel Islands 208
charity
    local authority charity initiatives 201
    support and the 1999 Act 201, 307
Chartered Institute of Environment Health
    220, 335
Child Abduction Act 1984 176

Child Abduction and Custody Act 1985 176
Child Benefit Act 1975 184
child orders
  contact orders 169
  in local authority care 174–6
  residence orders 169, 170
  wardship 169, 170
Child Poverty Action Group 20, 182
child protection law *see* immigration law vs child protection law 165–77
children
  basic immigration rules 88
  cases 86, 103
  and dividing families 86–94
  DNA tests 88–9, 103
  exclusion undesirable 89–90
  and expulsion 138–9, 140
  good practice 96–101, 161–2
    children as autonomous beings 96–7
    immigration issues and social service corporate planning 98
    interviewing children, by immigration officials 97–8
    listening to children 97
    see also asylum: unaccompanied children: good practice
  and intrusiveness 87
  and lone parents 89
  'non-genuine' child: critique of DNA testing 88–9
  unaccompanied *see* unaccompanied children *under* asylum
  see also adoption; parents
Children Act 1989 17, 22, 24, 101, 128, 146, 147, 165, 166, 168–75, 186, 190, 191, 198–200, 217, 224, 236, 305
  welfare checklist 173
'Children First and Foremost' 128–9, 224
Children (Leaving Care) Bill 2000 224
Children's Legal Centre 127, 130, 330
Children's Rights Development Unit 96
Child Welfare Implications of UK Immigration and Asylum Policy (1998) 28, 83, 154
China 46
Christianity 320

Chronically Sick and Disabled Persons Act 1970 244–6
Churches Together in Britain and Ireland (formerly Council of Churches for Britain and Ireland) 335
claiming public funds 62–3
clients
  asking their immigration status 56
  changing advisors 57–8
  helping to get proper advice 57
  helping to retain dignity 57
  who do not know their status 56
Close Harmondsworth Campaign 332
'cluster' areas, government guidelines on 218–19
Cobden Trust 314, 316
Code of Guidance on the 1985 Housing Act 207
Code of Guidance on Parts VI and VII of the Housing Act 1996 (Allocation of Housing Accommodation and Homelessness) 226
Code of Practice: School Admissions 231
Commission for Racial Equality (CRE) 26, 27, 205, 231, 302, 304, 335
Committee for Non-Racist Benefits 20
Common Travel Area (UK, Ireland, Channel Islands and Isle of Man) 208–10
Commonwealth citizens 46
Commonwealth Immigrants Act 1962 12, 18, 33, 34, 35, 264, 277, 319
Commonwealth Immigrants Act 1968 33, 46
Commonwealth Scheme for the Transfer of Convicted Prisoners 268
Communist Party 321
Community Care (Direct Payments) Act 1996 247
Community Legal Services Commission 58, 193
Conservative Party/governments 23, 33, 292, 326
consortia, local authority 212
  politics 212–13
'Consultation document on the min regulations under Part VI of the Immigration and Asylum Act 1999' 195

Consultation Paper on Review of Appeals
    (1988) 143
contact (access) order 169
'Contacting the IND' 21–2
Contributions Agency 202
control issues
    bodies of armed men and Immigration
        and Asylum Act 1999 320–1
    British Brothers League 319
    cases 313, 329
    confusions in meaning of
        'overpopulation' 317–18
    controls and definition of state 319–20
    controls as anti-working class 321–2
    controls as product of economic forces
        322–3
    critique of 'fair' controls 315
    eugenicism 316
    fair controls or no controls? 313–29
    'fair' controls and the family 315
    good practice 324–9
        alternative tradition 328
        battle for ideas 327
        collectivising cases and campaigns
            325
        contesting all cases 324
        just another brick in the wall 328
        male violence 325–6
        non-compliance 327
        no one is illegal 329
        regulations of immigration advisors
            326–7
        regulatory scheme and local or
            voluntary sector workers 327
        tactics not fairness 324
        unionising the undocumented 326
    how controls and other ideologies were
        legitimised 316
    Immigration Service Union (ISU) 321
    internal controls 19–20
    international legitimisation of control of
        free movement 322
    Kinder, Kirche, Küche 320
    labourism and welfarism 318–19
    lack of justification for controls 315–16
    Malthusian population theories 316–17
    modernity of controls 32–3
    post-war controls 319

    theories of underpopulation 318
    what is utopic? what is reasonable?
        323–4
cost of travel to interviews and appeals
    193
council housing
    allocation from the register
    homelessness accommodation
Council of Churches for Britain and
    Ireland 299
Council of Europe 34
    Social Charter (CESC) 189, 203, 208,
        209
Court of Appeal 167, 171, 199, 206, 207,
    246, 279, 287
Crawley Council 206
Crime (Sentences) Act (1997) 282
Criminal Injuries Board 243
Criminal Justice Act 1991 166, 282, 283
Criminal Law Bill amendment 1885
Crown Prosecution Service 288
Croydon 192–3
custodianship 169
Cyprus 107, 189, 288
Czech Republic 189

Defective Premises Act 1972 222
Denmark 45, 114, 322
Department for Education and
    Employment (DfEE) 231, 233, 234,
    236, 338
Department of Education 21
Department of Education and Science 238
Department of Employment 243
Department of Environment 207, 338
Department of Environment, Transport
    and the Regions (DETR) 208, 216
Department of Health 90, 93, 94, 101,
    129, 187, 199, 224, 244, 246, 256,
    257, 339
Department of Health and Environment
    21
Department of Health and Social Security
    (DHSS) 51, 251, 255, 258
Department of Social Security 21, 185,
    189, 193, 339
deportation and removal *see* expulsion
deskilling 28–9

Directory of Experts on Conditions in Countries of Origin and Transit 151
Disability Rights Commission 200
Divide and Deprive 184
division of families
  spouses 73–85
DNA testing, critique of 88–9
domestic violence
  and expulsion 141, 159
  reports dealing with 147–8
Dominican Republic 322
Dudley Council 206

Earlham Primary School 231
Earl William 215
East African Asians 33, 46, 210
Eastern Europe 32, 323
East Europeans 27, 118
East Midlands Consortium 212
East of England Consortium 212, 306
Education Act 1944 230
Education Act 1996 233, 234
Education (Assisted Places) Regulations 1995 234
Education (Fees and Awards) Regulations 1997 234
Education (Miscellaneous Provisions) Act 1948 233
Education (Provision of Clothing) Regulations 1980 234
education services and immigration status 229–48
  admission to schools 230–1
  cases 229, 241
  consequences of non-payment of fees 234–5
  criteria for loans and other financial support 237
  details of the fees regulations 235
  duties to attend school and obligations to admit to school 233
  eligibility for assisted places 234
  entitlement to state school education
  European nationals 233
  exceptions 235–6
  fees in further and higher education 234
  free school clothing and travel 234

free school milk, meals and 1999 Immigration and Asylum Act 233
  good practice 237–41
    appealing refusals 238
    contacting Home Office: bad practice; contacting UKCOSA: good practice 240
    critique of the Manchester Guidance 239–40
    discovering immigration status 238
    example of Manchester good practice 238–9
    expulsion, report writing, campaigns and asylum 238
    fees, financial support and passports 240
    no duty to charge higher fees 240
    other sources of help 241
    school clothing 238
    school meals and milk 237
    schools: contacting Home Office 238
  grants/loans 236–7
  history 230
    post–1945 230–1
  liaison with Home Office 231
  new system of loans and other financial support 236–7
  previous circulars 231
  public funds and private education 232
  school league tables 233
  school trips abroad 234
Education Act 1993 167
Education (Student Support) Regulations 1999 240
Efficiency Scrutiny 20–1, 23, 231, 256
elderly parents and grandparents 95–6
  autonomy of elderly people 101
  basic immigration rules 95
  collecting proper evidence 101–2
  emotional dependency 95
  financial dependency 95
  good practice 101–3
  over 65 concession 103
  parents under 65 and other relatives 96
  remembering what was said at visitor's interview 102–3
  problems: proof of age 95

where and when a settlement application
    should be made 102
Electronic Immigration Network (EIN) 28,
    62, 336
employer sanctions and carriers' liability
    50
England 197, 203, 208, 210, 219
Environmental Health Act 227
Environmental Health Authority 221
Environmental Protection Act 1990 222
Essay on the Principle of Population (Malthus)
    317
Estonia 322
Ethiopians 206
eugenicism 316
European Commission on Human Rights
    51, 278
European Community 51, 206, 233
European Convention on Human Rights
    42, 50–1, 80, 131, 139, 144, 147,
    167, 190, 200, 227, 247, 268, 303
and same-sex relationships 113–14
European Convention on the Recognition
    and Enforcement of Decisions
    concerning Custody of Children 176
European Convention on the Transfer of
    Sentenced Persons 288
European Convention on Social and
    Medical Assistance (ECSMA) 189,
    203, 208, 209, 340
European Council 233, 264
European Court of Human Rights (ECHR)
    42, 51, 267, 278
European Court of Justice 45, 51, 184,
    189
European Economic Area (EEA) 45, 46,
    48, 114, 184, 188, 189, 206, 209,
    210, 234, 236, 254, 258, 264, 278,
    324
EEA nationals and marriage 78, 79
European Economic Area Act 1993 45
European Union (EU) 11, 45, 46, 51, 64,
    78, 91, 93, 185, 236, 237, 322
law and same-sex relationships 114
Eviction Act 1997 211, 217
'exceptional leave to remain' (ELR) 118
exclusion, undesirability of 89–90
expulsion (deportation and removal)

critique of concept of compassionate
    grounds 153–64
battle of ideas 159–60
cases 153–4, 157, 160, 162, 164
compassionate grounds as tactical
    device 155–6
domestic violence 159
exceptionalism and competition of
    the oppressed 158–9
dehumanisation 156–7
good practice 160–3
    avoiding pathologisation in report
        writing 161
    balance of forces 160–1
    basic good practice points 161
    campaigns 163
    and children 161–2
    countries of origin 163
    good anti-racist professional
        practice 160
    as strengthening a case 162–3
    and women 162
idealisation of family 156
living in the Western world 158
New Labour – old problematic 159
stereotyping of black people 157
stereotyping of countries of origin
    157–8
strange world of compassionate
    grounds 154
those left outside the game 156
report writing *see* report writing
tactics 135–52
bereavement concession and rule 142
cases 135–6, 140, 141, 152
children born in UK 140
of children in UK without parents
    138
compassionate grounds and
    immigration rules 137–8
constructive 138
critique of 1999 concession 142
of entire families and of family
    members of someone being
    expelled 140
of family members of people settled
    here 138
following domestic violence 141

good practice 142–52
    bad timing 142
    client contact with Home Office
        143–4
    giving up the fight? 145
    good timing 143
    how much time to context
        expulsion? 144
    informing other professionals in
        good time 145
    making time 142
    playing for time: long stay
        concessions 143
    regaining appeal rights 144
    staying while contesting a case
        144
    tactics, time and 1999
        Immigration and Asylum Act
        143
    timing of fresh representations
        143
government policy changes 141
history and politics of 137
ill health and 142
parent with access rights 139
of partners 141
presence of children 138–9
routes to 136–7

Fairer, Faster and Firmer (1998) 12, 35, 117,
    122, 151 159, 210
family 37
    dividing
        children, parents and other relatives
            86–104
        spouses 73–85
    expulsion of entire families and of family
        members of someone being expelled
        140
    'fair' controls and 315
    social policy research on 74
    visits to the UK, appeals against refusal
        of 48–9
    see also children; family
Family Court 168
Family Immigration Rights (FAIR) 41
Filipinos 89
Finance (No. 2) Act 1980 184

financial dependency 95
Financial Support for Students: A Guide 236
fingerprinting and detection 121–2
Finland 45
First Report of the House of Commons
    Select Committee on Race Relations
    and Immigration (1978) 40
Focus 308, 314
Foreign and Commonwealth Office
    (JECU) 65, 94
Fortress Europe 45–6, 322, 324
Framework for the Assessment of Children in
    Need and Their Families (2000) 129
France 41, 45, 124, 197
Further Education Funding Council
    (FEFC) 235, 236, 339

Gas Safety (Installation and Use)
    Regulations 1998 220
gays and lesbians see same-sex relationships
Gender Guidelines for the Determination of
    Asylum Claims in the UK (1998) 122–3,
    124, 125, 132
gender issues 38–9, 42, 287
    good practice 131–3
        adjudicator hearings 133
        asking the right questions 132–3
        documentary evidence 133
        engendering the asylum process
            131–2
        gender and procedural issues 132
        other gender-sensitive techniques 133
    persecution of women 122–5
        commentary 124–5
        Convention ground 124
        definitions and clarifications 122–3
        failure of state protection 124
        gender blindness 122
        persecution and serious harm 123
        UK case-law and 'serious harm' 123
Geneva Convention on Refugees Coming
    from Germany 230
Germany/Germans 27, 45, 117, 317
good professional practice and tactics
    61–2
good timing 143
Greater London Council 205
    Anti-Deportation Working Group 136

Greater Manchester Immigration Aid Unit (GMIAU) 11, 22, 27, 28, 58, 62, 68, 77, 84, 89, 92, 97, 98, 99, 111, 120, 164, 166, 174, 226, 241, 262, 275, 276, 283, 292, 296, 298, 299, 321, 330
Greater Manchester Probation Service 283
Greece 45
Guidance Notes for Students 2000–2001 240
Guidance Notes for Those Working with Unaccompanied Children Claiming Asylum 121
'Guidance of the Clergy with Reference to the Marriage and Registration Acts' (1982) 84
Guidance on Fees 234
Guidance: Tariff 2000–2001 235, 236
Guidelines for registered social landlords on the provision of housing and support services for asylum seekers (1999) 223
Guidelines on Policies and Procedures in Dealing with Unaccompanied Children Seeking Asylum (UNHCR) 119, 120, 123, 134
Guidelines on the Protection of Refugee Women 133
Guide to Intercountry Adoption Practice and Procedures, A (1997) 90
Guide to Persons from Abroad, A 185
Gulbenkian Foundation 216

Hackney Council 26
Hague Convention on Civil Aspects of International Child Abduction 176
Hague Convention on Jurisdiction, Applicable Law and Recognition of Decrees relating to Adoptions (1965) 91
Hague Convention on the Protection of Children and Co-operation in Respect of Inter-Country Adoptions (1993) 91, 92
Haitians 322
Handbook on Procedures and Criteria for Determining Refugee Status (UNHCR) 118, 120, 127
Haringey Council 206
Harmondsworth Detention Centre 299

Hawley Report 40
Health and Personal Social Services (Northern Ireland) Order 1972 245
Health and Social Services and Social Security Adjudications Act 1983 248
health issues for medical workers and others 262–74
 agitation of doctors 263
 British Medical Association 263
 carers 267–8
 cases 262, 264, 268, 274
 coming to UK for private medical treatment 265–6
 contradictions 264
 exemptions 264–5
 history of health and immigration control 263
 HIV/AIDS 266–7
 mental health and immigration control 269
 policy, ethical and practice issues 269–74
  care in the community 271–2
  carers of children 272
  compiling asylum reports 273
  are controls on grounds of health benevolent or malevolent? 270
  good practice and carers: length of stay requested 271
  good practice and HIV/AIDS 271
  good practice in asylum report writing 272
  good practice for legal advisors in asylum report writing 273–4
  present position of BMA 270–1
  Yellowlees Report 269–70
 refusal of entry on health grounds 264
 refusal on medical grounds in practice 265
 switching to private medical treatment 266
 torture and asylum 268–9
 see also medical services and immigration status
Health Services and Public Health Act 1968 242, 244, 245, 247, 302, 312
High Court 101, 107, 122, 123, 147, 186, 267, 272

Practice Direction 176
Hillingdon Council 206
history of controls 32–43
  alien sexuality 41
  bottomless pit theory of black family 40
  consequences for welfare workers 33–4
  destruction of the Jewish family 38
  dividing of black families and gender
    issues 38–9
  employment justification 34–5
  English nuclear family 37
  family 37
  gender: problematic of equal
    opportunities 42
  lesbian and gay sexuality 43
  modernity of controls 32–3
  policy issues 41–3
  population and eugenicist justification
    35
  primary purpose role 39–40
  problematic of the family 41–2
  racism 35
  regulation of labour
  role of Labour movement in agitating for
    controls 36
  role of local authorities in agitating for
    controls 36
  welfare justifications 34
  welfare legislation 36
history of entitlement and immigration
    status
  benefits 182–3
  education 230
  general 32–41
  housing 205–6
  medical services 250–2
  probation 276–7
  social services 242–3
HIV/AIDS 19, 113, 153, 154, 186, 253,
    262, 266–7, 271, 303
HM Customs and Excise 52
Homelessness (Asylum-Seekers) (Interim
    Period) (England) Order 1999 216
Homelessness (England) Regulations 2000
    209–10
Home Office 12, 13, 18, 20, 21, 24–6,
    28, 30, 38, 41, 48–51, 57, 62–6, 69,
    75, 76, 78–80, 83, 84, 89, 102, 108,
    111, 112, 114, 118, 120–3, 127,
    130, 132, 135–44, 147–52, 155,
    158, 160, 164, 165, 168–70, 172–6,
    185, 187, 190–4, 196, 200, 202,
    211–15, 217–19, 225–7, 229, 231,
    232, 238–40, 251, 255, 256, 260,
    266–9, 271, 272, 275, 277, 279–81,
    283, 285–8, 294–7, 300, 302–4,
    306–12, 325–7, 329, 339
  approaching through advisor 55
  Asylum Division 97
  be careful with 64
  circular to local authorities 23–4
  client contact with 143–4
  correspondence to and from 63
  Guidance Notes and local authority social
    services 121
  guidelines on child deportation 168–9
  Home Secretary 339
  immigration guidelines 21
  Immigration and Nationality Division 21
  intervention in adoption case 172–3
  intervention to stop a court order being
    made 169–70
  liaison with 185
  not a benevolent institution 55
  rejection of medical reports 150
  representations and professional reports
    to 63
  social services liaison with 187
  Unaccompanied Children's Module 121
homophobia
  modern judicial 107
  and sexism and racism 107
Hong Kong 46, 229
hospitals as agents for the Home Office
    251
House of Commons
  Select Committee on Race Relations 326
  Social Policy Section of HoC Library 92
  Special Standing Committee on the
    Immigration and Asylum Bill 25
House of Lords 27, 123, 124, 173, 251,
    252, 294, 318
Housing Accommodation (Amendment)
    (England) Order 1999 216
Housing Act 1985 222
Housing Act 1996 205, 207–9, 223, 225

Housing Benefit (Amendment) No. 3
    Regulations 1984 183
Housing Benefit and Council Tax Benefit
    (Amendment) Regulations 1994
Housing Benefit General Regulations 193
Housing Committee of the Association of
    Metropolitan Authorities (now Local
    Government Association) 207
Housing Corporation 308, 339
Housing (Homeless Persons) Act 1977
housing services and immigration status
    204–28
cases 204, 227
chaos of dispersal scheme and resistance
    of asylum-seekers 217
criticism by local authorities 216
critique of the new scheme 213–14
details of the new scheme: Asylum
    Support Regulations 2000 210–11
good practice 217–27
    adequate accommodation and entry
        clearance 225
    agreement between asylum-seeker and
        local authority 221–2
    agreement between asylum-seeker and
        NASS 222
    agreement between local authority
        housing providers 221
    asylum seekers with positive Home
        Office decisions – moving home
        225
    Audit Commission report 223
    Chartered Institute of Environment
        Health 220
    free and well-publicised local
        authority support 226
    further environmental health good
        practice 220
    government guidelines on 'cluster'
        areas 218–19
    Housing Corporation report 222–3
    housing of unaccompanied
        asylum-seeking children 224
    housing for unaccompanied
        asylum-seeking children after
        18th birthday 224–5
    Immigration and Asylum Act 1999

limiting the Tower Hamlets decision
    226–7
local consortia: secretive or
    accountable? 218
Local Government Association
    guidelines 219
London Consortium and meeting
    disability needs 219–20
by Manchester 222
need to monitor content of
    certificates of accommodation
    226
positive government statements 218
repairs and other contractual
    responsibilities on housing
    providers and NASS 220–1
statutory obligations of housing
    providers 222
Immigration Acts 1993 and 1996 and
    Housing Act 1996 207
Immigration and Asylum Act 1999
    207–8
interim scheme 216
judiciary and homelessness legislation
    206
    illustrative cases 206
    Tower Hamlets case (1993): housing
        officers as Home Office agents
        207
local authority consortia 212
    politics 212–13
local government history 205–6
1999 Act's support scheme: dispersal
    210
private landlordism and the 1999 Act
    214–16
regulations 208–10
    Allocation of Housing (England)
        Regulations 2000 209
    Homelessness (England) Regulations
        2000 209–10
    Persons Subject to Immigration
        Control (Housing Authority
        Accommodation and
        Homelessness Order 2000 208
surveillance of accommodated
    asylum-seekers 214
Human Rights Act 1998 51, 144

Human Rights and Public Law Telephone
    Line 320
Hungary 189

Iceland 45
Immigration Act 1971 33, 44, 45, 46,
    140, 167, 279, 281, 328
Immigration Act 1988 33, 47, 77
Immigration Act 1993 51, 207
Immigration Act 1996 51, 207
immigration advisors
  and applications 62
  basic good practice for 62–70
  case preparation and evidence 67
  good practice and form filling 64
  good professional practice and tactics
    61–2
  immigration issues as legitimate area of
    professional work 60
  keeping up to date with the law 62
  making use of MPs 69–70
  outlawing crooked 58
  preparing for appeals 68
  preparing for interviews 68–9
  proceed with caution 64
  and refused immigration applications: a
    warning 64
  regulation of 326–7
  role of 55–6
  training 61
Immigration Advisory Service (IAS) 58,
    83, 331
Immigration Aid Unit 283
Immigration and Asylum Act 1999 11, 14,
    23, 24, 30, 36, 47–9, 51–2, 58, 62,
    103, 110, 118, 136, 140, 152, 164,
    182, 195, 196, 198, 201, 207–8,
    210, 217, 222, 233, 242–5, 247,
    248, 263, 268, 278, 295, 304–7,
    320–1, 326, 328
  advising on undertakings 67
  and Anglican Church 80
  appeal rights against deportation and
    removal 51–2
  'bogus asylum-seeker?' 52
  exclusion from state benefit 187–8
  housing dispersal scheme
  and marriage registrars 78–9

  one-stop appeal statements 66
  tactics, time and 143
  voucher scheme
  welfare and voluntary sector 25–6,
    304–8
Immigration and Asylum Appeals
    (One-Stop Procedure) Regulations
    2000 52
Immigration and Housing (1995) 207
Immigration and Nationality Directorate
    (IND) 21, 23, 24, 47, 50, 66, 77, 78,
    83, 89, 91, 92, 97, 98, 109, 120,
    121, 125, 185, 190, 231, 271
    279–81, 308, 309, 313–14, 327,
    339, 340
  Asylum and Appeals Policy Directorate
    132
  Evidence and Enquiry Unit 280
  Immigration Advisors Unit 327
Immigration and Nationality Enquiry
    Bureau (INEB) 24
Immigration and Refugee Board of
    Canada 119
Immigration Appeals (Family Visitor)
    (No.2) Regulations 2000 48
Immigration Appeals (Procedure) Rules
    133
Immigration Appeal Tribunal 49, 74, 101,
    113, 124, 125, 268, 269, 278, 326
Immigration (Carriers' Liability) Act 1987
    33, 50
Immigration Control Procedures (1985) 26
Immigration controls are out of control (1993)
    27
Immigration from the Commonwealth (1965)
    317
immigration law vs. child protection law
    165–77
  adoption proceedings 172–3
    Home Office intervention 172–3
  can a child protection order prevent
    removal? Home Office guidelines
    168–9
    adoption orders 168
    contact (access) order 169
    custodianship 169
    wardship and residence (custody)
      orders 169

cases 165, 167, 169, 170–3, 176
good practice 173–6
   Children Act welfare checklist 173
   local authority orders 174
   making early applications for court
      order 173
   regularising stay of child in care or
      under supervision 175–6
   should local authority apply for
      order? 175
   value of court order 174
Home Office intervention to stop court
   order being made 169–70
legal and political power of immigration
   control 166
political and legal supremacy of
   immigration controls 166–7
residence proceedings 171–2
   a glimmer of hope 171–2
undermining child protection legislation
   167–8
wardship proceedings 170–1
   leading case 170
   other cases 170–1
Immigration Law Practitioners' Association
   (ILPA) 62, 78, 126, 132, 151, 232,
   336
Immigration (Leave to Enter and Remain)
   Order 2000 47
Immigration Needs Trust 201
Immigration (Restrictions on Employment)
   Order 1996 304
Immigration Rules 119–20
Immigration Service 121, 132, 166, 174,
   186
Immigration Service Enforcement
   Directorate 194
Immigration Services Commissioner 58,
   326
Immigration Services Tribunal 58
Immigration Service Union (ISU) 321
Immigration Status Enquiry Unit 24
Immigration Widows Campaign, London
   39
Immigration Wives and Fiancées
   Campaign, Manchester 39, 299
In and Against the State 27

Income-Related Benefits and Jobseeker's
   Allowance (Amendment) Regulations
   2000 198
Independent Doctors' and Dentists'
   Review Body 257
Independent Labour Party 318
India(ns) 46, 85, 90, 91, 142, 158, 171,
   288, 328
'Information for Members of Parliament
   about immigration and nationality
   enquiries' (2000) 69
Inland Revenue 184
Institute of Public Policy Research 315
Institute of Race Relations 117, 292, 333
Instructions to Medical Inspectors 270
Intercountry Adoption 98
*Intercountry Adoption: Pre and Post-adoption
   Practice and Procedures* 98–9
internal controls 19–20
International Gay and Lesbian Human
   Rights Commission 334
   Asylum Project 134
International Social Service 102, 138,
   151, 334
interpreters 59–60
   at Home Office interviews and appeals
      60
interviews
   with children by immigration officials
      97–8
   preparing for 68–9
   remembering what was said at 82,
      102–3
intrusiveness
   and black families 75
   and children 87
   and marriage registrars 79
Iran(ians) 124, 214, 262
Ireland 45, 208, 278
Islamabad 39
Italians 206
Italy 45, 323

Jamaica 47, 275
Japan 322, 323
Jewish Chronicle 38, 87, 117, 182, 183,
   205, 230, 263, 276, 319, 327, 328

Jewish refugees/immigrants 27, 32, 33, 34, 35, 36, 38, 117, 263, 276, 313, 317, 318, 321, 328
job offers, no recourse to 76
Joint Council for the Welfare of Immigrants (JCWI) 20, 58, 62, 90, 164, 182, 184, 185, 285, 302, 330
Joint Entry Clearance Unit (JECU) 65, 340

Kensington and Chelsea, borough of 205
Kent 218
  County Council 217
  police force 213
Kenya 33
Kosovan asylum-seekers 23, 213
Kurds 323

Labour councils 22
Labour Exchanges Act 1909 37
Labour Party/governments 23, 33, 35, 36, 110, 117, 151, 159, 196, 210, 317, 326
Lambeth, borough of 205
Latin America 288
Latvia 322
law, keeping up to date with 62
Law Centres Federation 58, 321
Law Society 126, 274
  Children's Panel 127
League of Nations 230
Leena Corporation 215
Legal Aid Board (now Community Legal Services) 58
legal advisors
  and legal aid 58
  and marriage ceremonies 84–5
legal aid
  and legal advisors 58
  for same-sex partners under advice and assistance scheme 111
Leicester General Hospital 251
lesbian and gay sexuality 43
  see also same-sex relationships
Liechtenstein 45
Lithuania 322
Liverpool 212–13, 216
  City Council 215, 305–6
  and regional consortia 305–6

local authorities
  and adoption 99
    good practice in reports 100
  agreement between asylum-seeker and 221–2
  campaigns 23
  charity initiatives 201
  consortia 212, 305–6
    politics 212–13
    secretive or accountable? 218
  constraints on 305
  contact with Home Office 23–4, 121, 309
  co-operation with Immigration and Asylum Act 1999 304–6
  general 22, 36
  Home Office Guidance Notes and local authority social services 121
  investigating immigration status
  legal representation and the asylum determination process 129
  link workers 59
  Liverpool 212–13, 215, 216, 305–6
  Manchester 22, 99, 146, 185, 201, 212–13, 216, 221, 222, 226, 237, 306
  orders 174–5
  support from 193, 197
  welfare issues and Children's Act 128
Local Government Association 25, 200, 205, 207, 212, 213, 220, 305, 336
  guidelines 219
Local Government Finance Act 1988 187
local government history 205–6
local state and national state 22
London Advice Services Alliance 182, 331
London and the South East 210, 214, 219, 299, 306, 319
London Consortium 212
  and meeting disability needs 219–20
London County Council 205, 230
London Trades Council 318
lone parents 89
loyalty tests 53
Luxembourg 45

maintenance, definition of 49
Malawi 288

Malaysia 113
male violence 325–6
Malta 189
Man, Isle of 208
management responsibilities 61
Manchester 22, 23, 39, 185, 212–13,
    216, 221, 226, 263, 275, 299, 305,
    327
  good practice by 222, 238–9
  guidelines for social work reports 146
    critique 311–12
  see also Greater Manchester Immigration
    Aid Unit (GMIAU)
Manchester Advice Service 201, 237
Manchester City Council 270, 293, 297,
    326
Manchester Education Department 237
Manchester Education Policy
    Sub-Committee 238
Manchester Housing Department 223
Manchester Immigration Needs Trust 293
Manchester Metropolitan University 297,
    336
Manchester Policy Committee 326
Manchester Social Services Department
    223
Manchester Social Services Immigration
    Liaison Officer 146
Manpower Services Commission 243
Manual of Guidance (1995) 255
Manual of Guidance: NHS Treatment of
    Overseas Visitors (1988) 252, 259
Marie Curie (charity) 307
Marion Gaima Defence Campaign 298
marriage
  issues of breakdown without violence or
    children 148–9
  polygamous 77
  registrars 83–4
    draft guidance to 80–1
    and intrusiveness 79
    and Immigration and Asylum Act
      1999 79–80
Marriage Act 1836 80
Medical Ethics Today 270
Medical Examination of Immigrants, The
    (1965) 263

Medical Examination of Immigrants, The
    (1980) 269
Medical Foundation for the Care of
    Victims of Torture 219, 225, 272,
    273, 334
Medical Profession and Human Rights:
    Handbook for a Changed Agenda 271
medical services and immigration status
    149–50, 249–74
  campaign to deny NHS treatment 250
    success of campaign 250
  cases 249, 260
  categories of people exempt from
    charges 253–4
  charges 253
  checks on passports and other
    documents 255
  contact between hospitals and the Home
    Office 255–6
  Efficiency Scrutiny 256
  extra monies for GPs 257
  features of the charging regulations 252
  good practice 257–60
    bad practice for GPs 260
    charging regulations and ethical
      issues for medical workers 258
    doctors and nurses 258–9
    free treatment and remaining on
      compassionate grounds 258
    good practice for GPs 260
    for legal advisors 257
    mental health patients 259
    training for hospital administrators
      259–60
  GPOs, dentists, opticians and chemists
    256-
  hospitals as agents for the Home Office
    251
  how regulations work in practice 255
  how treatment was denied: internal
    controls 251
  National Health Service (Charges to
    Overseas Visitors) Regulations
    1982–2000 252
  prescription, wig, dental, optical and
    hospital travel charges 257
  services exempt from charges 253
  unlawful denial of treatment 251

see also health issues for medical workers and others
Members of Parliament 327
  making use of 69–70
mental health and immigration control 269
Mental Health Act 1983 167, 247, 253, 259, 269
Mental Health Foundation 336
Mental Health (Scotland) Act 1984 245
Middle East 288
Middlesex Area Probation Service 288, 336
Middlesex County Council 230
Migrant Helpline 307
Migrants Against HIV/AIDS 332
MIND, National Association for Mental Health 259
Ministry of Health 264
Ministry of Labour 183, 319
Modernising Social Services 129
Montserrat 189, 208–10
Morocco/Moroccans 189, 278
Mosscare 223
Muslims 91, 124

National Assistance Act 1948 22, 24, 186, 190, 194, 198–200, 209, 217, 243–6, 303, 305
National Association for the Care and Resettlement of Offenders (NACRO) 275
National Association of Citizens' Advice Bureaux 20, 337
National Association of Probation Officers 283
National Asylum Support Service (NASS) 25, 190–7, 201, 203, 210–14, 217–19, 224–5, 227, 235, 257, 304–6, 308
  agreement between asylum-seeker and 222
  Refugees Integration section 192
  and repairs and other contractual responsibilities on housing providers 220–1
National Coalition of Anti-Deportation Campaigns 292, 299, 300, 305, 333

National Crime Squad 52
National Criminal Intelligence Service 52
National Front 210, 319
National Health Service (Charges to Overseas Visitors) Regulations 1982–2000 246–7, 252, 304
National Health Service (NHS) 246, 249, 255, 258–60, 264–6, 268
  NHS hospitals 303–4
National Health Services Act 1946 250
National Health Services Act 1977 244–6, 250
National Health Services Amendment Act 1949 250
National Health Service and Community Care Act 1990 201, 247, 272
National Health Service (Primary Care) Act 1997 257
National Institute for Social Work 121
National Insurance Act 1911 18, 182
National Insurance Act 1946 183
national insurance numbers 185, 202
nationality
  EU nationals 45
  types of British nationality 46–7
'Nationality Law' (1980) 53
National Police Agency 322
naturalisation forms for British citizenship 66–7
Nazism 33, 117, 317, 320
Netherlands, the 45, 114
New Asylum Support Scheme, The 307
Newcastle 214
Newham Council 206, 231
New Zealand 113
Nigeria 153, 164, 288, 291, 292, 297
non-family and inter-family adoptions 90
'non-genuine' child: critique of DNA testing 88–9
No Passport to Services (1985) 55, 303, 310
No Place to Call Home (1996) 309
Nordic states 322
North Birmingham Mental Health Trust 337
Northern Ireland 190, 191, 197, 208, 210, 245
Northern Ireland Housing Executive 210
North East Consortium 212

North West Consortium for Asylum
     Seekers 212–13, 217, 221, 305–6,
     337
Norway 45, 114, 322
Nottingham
  Probation Service 283, 337
  racist attacks 1958 41, 319
Notting Hill racist attacks 1958 41, 277,
     319

Oakington Detention Centre 299
Office for National Statistics 80, 81, 84
Okolo Family Defence Campaign 297–8
Old Age Pensions Act 1908 18, 182
Oldham local authority 226
on-entry control 47
one-stop appeal statements: Immigration
     and Asylum Act 1999 66
Organisation of African Unity Convention
     Relating to the Specific Aspects of
     Refugee Problems in Africa 118
*Origin of the Family, Private Property and the
     State* (Engels) 320
outlawing crooked advisors 58
'overpopulation', confusions in meaning of
     317–18
overseas marriage interviews 81–2
Oxfam 307, 309

Pakistan(is) 39, 40, 46, 76, 85, 86, 89,
     91, 124, 141, 165, 170, 184, 322,
     328
Panel of Advisors for Refugee Children
     120–1, 127, 129
parent(s)
  lone 89
  with access rights 139
  see also children; elderly parents and
     grandparents; family
Parliamentary Group on the Feasibility and
     Usefulness of a Register of
     Dependants 40
Parole Board 282
Partners of Prisoners Support Group
     (POPs) 275, 283
People in Paper Chains 184
Performance and Innovation Unit 90
persecution

of gay men and lesbians 125–6
and serious harm 123
of women 122–5
Personal Responsibility and Work
     Opportunity Reconciliation Act (US,
     1996) 322
Persons Subject to Immigration Control
     (Housing Authority Accommodation
     and Homelessness Order 2000 208
Philippines 165
Poland 189
Poles 27
Police and Criminal Evidence Act 1984
     60
police station interviews 60
Political Asylum Questionnaire 130
politics of immigration control 26
Poor Laws 181, 182, 195–6, 318
Port Alert System 176
Portugal 45
Post-Adoption Centre 99, 100, 337
practice issues
  asylum and children 126–31
  asylum and gender 131–3
  and basic policy 29–30
  benefits 198–203
  campaigns 293–300
  children 96–101
  controls 324–9
  deskilling 28–9
  education 237–41
  expulsion 142–52, 160–3
  general 54–70, 96–104, 302–12
  health issues 269–74
  housing services 217–27
  lesbians, gay men, same sex and
     non-marital relationships 110–15,
     134
  medical services 257–60
  parents 101–3
  probation 283–8
  relatives 101–3
  schools 131
  sexuality 134
  social services 245–7
  spouses 81–5
  welfare agencies and non-compliance
     302–12

pre-entry control 47
'Prevention of illegal working: guidance for employers' 304
primary purpose rule, repeal of, and intention to live together 77–8
Prisoners Act 1984 288
Prison Reform Trust 275
Prison Service 166, 279, 281, 284, 288
probation and immigration status 275–88
  cases 275–6, 288
  chronology and personnel of double punishment 279–80
  double punishment
    history 276–7
    today 277–8
  forgotten history of transportation 277
  further chronology 280–1
  police and immigration service 280
  policy and good practice issues 283–8
    bad practice 287
    issues of gender and sexuality 287
    legitimacy of probation intervention 283
    repatriation 288
    report writing 286–7
    support for which prisoners and which clients? 284
    view of Association of Chief Officers of Probation 283–4
    working with advisors 285–6
    working with prisoners 284–5
  preliminary issues of double punishment for probation officers 278
  prison allocation and home leave 281–2
  release on licence 282
  types of convictions leading to double punishment 278–9
  'Proposed interim support arrangements' 213
Probation Service Act 1993 284
Process Manual for the Asylum Support System (1999) 307
public funds
  claiming 62–3
  consequences of claiming 49–50
  and constructs of welfare 49
  and disability issues 82–3
  and private education 232
  no recourse to 76–7

Quality Protects Programme 129

Race Relations Act 1976 51, 249, 256, 302, 303
Race Relations (Amendment) Bill 1999 26, 51, 144, 167, 295
'Racial equality and the Asylum and Immigration Act 1996' 304
racism 35, 323
  and homophobia and sexism 107
Refugee Action 307, 308
Refugee Arrivals Project 192, 307, 308
Refugee Children: Guidelines on Protection and Care (1994) 128
Refugee Council 121, 127, 182, 204, 224, 233, 307–9, 331
Refugee Housing Association (RHA) 223
Refugee Legal Centre 58, 331
Refugee Legal Group 126
Refugee Studies Programme Documentation Centre 334
Refugee Women's Legal Group (RWLG) 122, 132, 333
registered social landlords (RSLs) 222–3, 307–8
removal and deportation see expulsion
repatriation 288
Repatriation of Prisoners Act 1984 288
report writing 96
  advocacy 146
  asylum reports 272
    compiling 273
    good practice for legal advisors 273–4
  avoiding pathologisation in 161
  Children Act 1989 147
  community worker 151
  on domestic violence 147–8
  educational 151
  general issues 145–6
  Manchester guidelines 146
  medical 149
    content of 149
    gravity of illness 150
    Home Office rejection of medical reports 150

length of stay requested 150
multiple reports 146
other issues of marriage breakdown
    148–9
probation and asylum 152, 286–7
social services 247
social work reports 146, 151
specialist country of origin reports 151
violence to women in UK in temporary
    capacity 148
reunite: International Child Abduction
    Centre 176, 331
right of abode 46
*Right to Be Here: A Campaigning Guide to the
    Immigration Laws* 136, 163
Roma 27
Romania(ns) 90, 91, 105, 125, 189
children for adoption 92
Royal Commission on Alien Immigration
    36, 210
rules, immigration 47
Runnymede Trust 20, 337
Russia 32, 263

St Kitts 267
St Philips Primary School 337
same-sex relationships 105–15
    case 105, 114–15
    critique of concession rule 109
    current policy and immigration rules
        108–9
    good practice 110–15, 134
        accumulating evidence 134
        accumulating two years' prior
            cohabitation 112
        compassionate grounds
            and family approval 113
        HIV/AIDS 113
        European Convention on Human
            Rights 113–14
        European Union law 114
        evidence of cohabitation 111–12
        helping clients to 'come out' 111
        legal aid under advice and assistance
            scheme 111
        political asylum and sexual identity
            114

should application be made in any
    event? 112
support for same-sex couples 111
history of non-marital heterosexual
    relationships 107–8
homophobia, sexism and racism 107
making the application 111
persecution of gay men and lesbians 125
    commentary 126
problematic of equality under
    immigration controls 110
two-year cohabitation requirement prior
    to application 109
Save the Children 119, 131, 307, 337
Schools Against Deportation 333
Schools Standards and Framework Act
    1998 231, 233
Scotland 190, 191, 197, 208, 210, 245,
    247
Scotland Consortium 212
Scottish Refugee Council 307
Securicor 214–15
*Separated Children in Europe Programme –
    Statement of Good Practice* (1999) 129
serious harm
    and persecution 123
    and UK case-law 123
Sex Discrimination Act 1975 167
sexism, homophobia and racism 107
sexual identity and political asylum 114
sexuality
    alien 41, 106
    good practice 110–15, 134, 287
Sexual Offences Act 1967 107
Sharia law 124
Sheffield 230
Shelter 215, 216, 307, 337
Sierra Leone 189
Slovakia 189
Slovenia 189
Social Fund Guidance Manual 225
social policy research on division of
    families 74
Social Security Act 1980 67
Social Security Administration (Fraud) Act
    1997 185, 186
Social Security Contributions and Benefits
    Act 1992 67

Social Security (Immigration and Asylum)
  Consequential Amendments
  Regulations 2000
  exemptions under 188–90
  means-tested benefits 188–9
Social Security (Persons from Abroad)
  Miscellaneous Amendments
  Regulations 1996 186
social services
  cases 242, 247–8
  community care and immigration status
    242–8
  community care legislation and 1999
    Act 243
  corporate planning and immigration
    issues 98
  criminal compensation 242–3
  department (SSD)
    and adoption 93–4
  good practice 245–7
    alternative non-residential care
      legislation 245
    care in the community: loopholes in
      1999 Immigration and Asylum
      Act 245
    further potentially useful legislation
      246–7
    report writing 247
    Scottish legislation 247
  Home Office *Guidance Notes* and local
    authority social services 121
  and housing 220
  Immigration and Asylum Act 1999 243
  Manpower Services Training 243
  1999 Act
    limiting community care legislation
      244
    Scottish and Irish legislation 244–5
  relevant community care legislation
    243–4
Social Services Inspectorate (SSI) 61, 119,
  128, 129, 340
Social Work (Scotland) Act 245
social work reports 146
Society of Civil and Public Servants 321
Sodexho Pass International 195
Somali community 223
Southall Black Sisters 141, 333

South Central Consortium 212, 306
South Manchester Law Centre 11, 20,
  185, 331
South West Consortium 212, 306
Soviet Union 317
  collapse of Soviet bloc 27, 322
Spain 45, 114
Spearhead 319
Special Standing Committee on the
  Immigration and Asylum Bill 305
sponsorships and undertakings
  advising on 67
spouses
  Anglican Church and 1999 legislation
    80
  cases 73–4, 85
  discriminatory nature in practice 76
  EEA nationals 78, 79
  immigration rules 75–6
  intention to live together and repeal of
    primary purpose rule 77–8
  intruding into marital home 78–9
  no recourse to public funds and job
    offers 76–7
  practice issues 81–5
    better safe than sorry 81
    legal advisors and marriage
      ceremonies 84–5
    marriage registrars 83–4
    overseas marriage interviews 81–2
    public funds and disability issues
      82–3
    remembering what was said at any
      previous interview 82 twelve
      months' probationary rule 78
  see also marriage
Sri Lankans 293
Statement of Special Educational Needs
  167
Stonewall Immigration Group 111, 114,
  333
Strangers and Citizens (1994) 315, 316, 321
Supplementary Benefit Act 1966 183
Supplementary Benefit (Aggregation,
  Requirements and Resources)
  Amendment Regulations 1980 183
Supplementary Benefits Commission
  (SBC) 185

Support arrangements – 16 to 17 year old unaccompanied asylum seeking children 224

Surviving the Asylum Process in the UK 200

Sweden 45, 114, 322

Switzerland 91, 189

Sylhet Tax Pattern, The 184

Tamil asylum-seekers 215

Terrence Higgins Trust 332

Thailand 288

timing
  bad 142
  of fresh representations 143
  good 143

Tobago 288

Tool Kit 212

Tories *see* Conservative Party/governments

Towards a Just Immigration Policy (1986) 316

Tower Hamlets, borough of 206, 207
  limiting the decision 226–7

trade unions 308–9
  Dockers' Union 328
  Gas Workers' Union (GWU) 50, 328
  Immigration Service Union (ISU) 321
  National Union of Shop Assistants 328
  Shopworkers' Union USDAW 309
  Transport and General Workers' Union (TGWU) 50, 196
  Trades Union Congress (TUC) 196, 314, 318, 319, 321, 326, 328
    Black Workers' Conference 1995 314
    General Council 314, 319
  UNISON 83, 291, 292, 298, 308, 314, 333
  Women's Union League 328

training 61

Training Opportunities Scheme 243

translation of documents 60

Treatment Possibilities in Kosovo (2000) 152

Treaty of Rome 45

Trinidad 288

Tunisia 189

Turkey 189, 288

twelve months' probationary rule 78

Uganda 33, 267

UK Agenda for Children 96, 97

Unaccompanied Asylum-Seeking Children 61

underpopulation, theories of 318

Unemployment Insurance No. 2 Act 1921 183

Union Movement 319

United Families Campaign 299

United Kingdom Council for Overseas Student Affairs (UKCOSA) 238, 240, 332

United Nations (UN)
  Commission on Human Rights Reports 334
  Convention Against Torture 269
  Convention on the Elimination of All Forms of Discrimination Against Women 1979 123, 124
  Convention on the Rights of the Child 1989 96, 97, 120, 128, 147, 167, 200
  Convention on the Status of Refugees 1967 118, 268, 278
  Declaration on the Elimination of Violence Against Women 1993 123
  High Commission for Refugees (UNHCR) 118, 120, 122, 132, 340
  Interim Administration (Department of Health and Social Welfare) 152
  Platform for Action 1995 123

United States 40, 288, 322, 323
  Department of State Country Reports 334

University College London Hospital Trust 26

University of Hull 235

unmarried partners

violence
  domestic
    and expulsion 141, 159
    reports dealing with 147–8
  male 325–6
  to women in UK in temporary capacity 148

voluntary sector 25–6, 306–8

Wales 197, 203, 208, 210, 219

Wales Consortium 212, 306

Wandsworth, borough of 302

wardship and residence (custody) orders
169
welfare agencies, good practice and
non-compliance 302–12
cases 302,
disciplinary policies 309
employers' liability: personnel
departments 304
Immigration and Asylum Act 1999 304
and constraints on local authorities
305
and voluntary sector 306–7
Liverpool City Council and regional
consortia – principle or pragmatism?
305–6
local authorities 309
meaning of non-compliance 303
natural law 303
Manchester guidelines: critique 311–12
NHS hospitals 303–4
registered social landlords 307–8
self-certification 309–10
should local authorities co-operate with
the scheme? 305
should voluntary sector agencies
co-operate with the scheme? 307
trade unions 308–9
welfare, immigration control and the
family 18–19
welfare practitioners 19
case preparation and evidence 67
cases 54, 70
and politics 29
role of 55–6, 293–4
training 61
vulnerability of 26
see also clients
welfare state and Home Office 20
Welsh Refugee Council 307
West Africans 89
West Indians 205, 263, 328
West Midlands Consortium 212
Westminster Council 200
Widows, Orphans and Old Age
Contributory Pensions Act 1925 183
Wolverhampton Council 206
Woodcote Property Management 214
women and good practice 162

Women's Movement 157
Workers' Education Association 59, 338
Working Party on the Treatment of
Overseas Visitors 258
World Health Organisation 265

Yellowlees Report 269–70
Yorkshire and Humberside Consortium
212

Zaire (Democratic Republic of Congo) 189
Zimbabwe 198, 288

Author Index

Abdulaziz, N. 42
Achtar, N. 141
Ahmady, M. 124
Akram, M. 87
Alexander II 32
Alghali, D.H. 167
Allaun, F. 243
Amin, A. 39
Amoako, D. 302
Anderson, A. 10, 275, 276
Anderson, F. 10
Arfeen, I.U. 39
Assadi family 249
Avebury, Lord 251, 269
Ayotte, W. 119
Azad, A. 292

Baker, K. 320
Balkandali, S. 42
Barlow, A. 106
Basovski, M. 87
Bassam, Lord 26, 51, 80
Beale, J. 230
Begum, N. 10, 293
Belcher, W. 36
Bevan, A. 250
Beveridge, W. 318
Bhabna, J. 38, 74, 152, 164
Bhatia, V. 74
Bibi, A. 268
Billing, P. 313
Blake, N. 45
Blatch, Baroness 123
Bondfield, M. 37, 328
Bracewell, Judge 171
Bradley, K. 280
Brian, F. 328
Brown, Lord Justice S. 199
Butt, M. 262

Cabales, A. 42
Callaghan, J. 34
Ceauçescu, N. 90

Chaffee, N. 157
Chamberlain, J. 324
Clare, A. 259
Clements, L. 10
Coffey, A. 90
Cohen, S. 20, 32, 39, 134, 182, 250, 262, 292, 315, 329
Collins, Justice 303
Collins, W. 20
Corelli, M. 316, 319
Crausby, D. 191, 213
Crawley, H. 116, 122, 123
Cronin, K. 166

Denning, Lord 170, 206, 229
Din, S.U. 86
Ditta, A. 10, 86, 264, 293
Doebbler, C. 181
Dominelli, L. 28
Dyson, Judge 123

Eagle, A. 184
Ekirch, A. 277
Ellenborough, Lord 182
Elliot, Lt.-Col. 250
Ellmann, R. 107, 115
Engels, F. 320
Evans-Gordon, Major 34

Fell, A. 35
Feria-Tinta, M. 181
Finch, N. 182, 219
Fitzpatrick, P. 10
Fowler, N. 258
Fox, E. 327

Gaima, M. 298
Gainer, B. 32, 329
Gandhi, M. 230
Gardner, J. 321
Gata-Aura, T. 105
Gerrard, N. 108, 110
Gibbons, A. 292
Gordon, P. 20, 262
Guedalla, V. 119
Gurden, H. 35

Hampson, K. 38
Hanif 170

Haq, A. 136
Haq, R. 136
Haq, S. 136
Hayes, D. 250, 262
Henderson, M. 126, 272
Ho, P. 229
Hoare, S. 317
Hoffman, Lord Justice 171
Hollis, Judge 170, 171
Howard, M. 21
Howarth, G. 269
Humphries, B. 250, 308
Hurd, D. 77, 89

Idrees, A. 268

Jackson, D. 101
Jackson, Prof. 74
Jacobs, S. 205
Jones, A. 28, 83, 154, 161, 164
Jordan, C. 41
Joseph, K. 185

Kapp, Y. 230
Keetch, D. 10
Khan, I. 242, 243
Khan, K. 167, 169, 173
Khan, S. 167
Kirkhope, T. 108
Knight, A. 79
Kunda, M. 10, 135, 136, 142, 154

Labouchere, H. 107
Lal, S. 87
Lamguindaz 278
Leigh, S. 87, 269
Leighton, J. 104
Lewis, I. 24, 80, 166
Loane, J. 36
London, L. 32
Lowther, J. 107
Lukes, S. 10, 205

Macdonald, I.A. 45
McLean, N. 166
Macnamara, T. 183
Maher, M. 51
Malthus, T. 35, 317
Matondo, F. 171

Mendis, V. 293, 320
Miah, S. 138
Mihai, S. 105, 114
Millore, A.H. 117
Moore, R. 32
Morris, L. 205
Mortimore, C. 87
Mosley, O. 319
Mynett, M. 230
Mynott, E. 182, 308

Nehru, J. 230
Newnham, A. 20
Nield, H. 35

O'Brien, M. 79, 103, 108, 109, 141, 218
Okolo, Awele 10, 154, 292
Okolo, Anwule 10, 154, 292
Okolo, F. 10, 154, 162, 292, 297, 298
Osborne, C. 34

Parker, A. 230
Patel, M. 142
Pearl, M. 223
Penzance, Lord 77
Pourgourides, C.K. 269
Powell, E. 40
Proctor, H. 320
Pyke, Judge 105

Rahily, S. 205
Rahman, A. 10, 135, 242
Rahman, M. 10, 242
Rahman, R. 10, 135, 242
Rahman, S. 10, 135, 167, 242, 292, 298
Raison, T. 38, 287
Reeves, W.P. 328
Rentoul, R. 316
Ricablanca, J. 165
Ricablanca, M. 165, 174
Roche, B. 24, 191, 213
Rosenblatt, J. 166
Roucou, G. 10
Rowe, A. 218, 227
Russell, Lord 170
Russell, S. 119

Samuel, S. 230
Schermers, Judge 278

Sherard, R. 263
Short, R. 34
Shutter, S. 10, 38, 74, 152, 164
Siddiqui, K. 73
Siddiqui, N. 39
Siddiqui, R. 10, 73
Silver, J. 36
Sime, C. 250
Singh, B. 294
Sivanandan, A. 117
Smith, G. 269
Smith, Lord Justice S. 207
Smithers, W. 250
Spencer, I. 32
Spencer, S. 315
SSI 61
Stanbrook, I. 38
Steyn, Lord 125
Stokes, J. 320
Stone, a. 263
Storey, H. 20
Straw, J. 80, 84
Symons, A.L. 41

Tabed, A. 134
Taylor, D. 182
Thatcher, M. 37, 292
Tillett, B. 318
Titmuss, R. 318
Tyson, M. 313, 326

Vraciu, I. 125, 126

Wallace, T. 32
Wardle, C. 113
Webb, J. 113
Wedgewood, Col. 321
White, A. 37
White, T. 269
Whitelaw, W. 40
Widdecombe, A. 21
Wilde, O. 107
Wilkins, G. 20
Wilkins, W.H. 41
Williams, A.T. 36
Wilson, A. 87
Wismewski, S. 263
Woodland, R. 269

Yaqoob, M. 44
Yellowlees, H. 269

Zetter, R. 223